D1713526

WORK OF LOVE

WORK OF LOVE

*A Theological Reconstruction of
the Communion of Saints*

LEONARD J. DeLORENZO

University of Notre Dame Press
Notre Dame, Indiana

University of Notre Dame Press
Notre Dame, Indiana 46556
undpress.nd.edu

Library of Congress Cataloging-in-Publication Data

Names: DeLorenzo, Leonard J., author.
Title: Work of love : a theological reconstruction of the communion of saints /
    Leonard J. DeLorenzo.
Description: Notre Dame, Indiana : University of Notre Dame Press, [2017] |
    Includes bibliographical references and index.
Identifiers: LCCN 2016049589 (print) | LCCN 2017000765 (ebook) |
    ISBN 9780268100933 (hardcover : alk. paper) | ISBN 0268100934 (hardcover :
    alk. paper) | ISBN 9780268100957 (pdf) | ISBN 9780268100964 (epub)
Subjects: LCSH: Communion of saints—History of doctrines.
Classification: LCC BT972 .D45 2017 (print) | LCC BT972 (ebook) |
    DDC 262/.73—dc23
LC record available at https://lccn.loc.gov/2016049589

To Lisa

"Forever Amen"

CONTENTS

ACKNOWLEDGMENTS

Writing is often an experience of solitariness and yet all throughout writing this book I was aware of my dependence on those whose company I neither could nor ever would want to do without. Who I am, what I believe, how I think, and why I "do" theology are all tied up in my relationships with those who love me, inspire me, teach me, and hold me accountable to the gifts I have received. Truly, I am not myself by myself. Any good that I may have achieved in this work redounds to those who have shared and who continue to share their goodness with me. The greatest good I have received is the gift of faith, without which I would be incapable of doing theology at all. My first word of thanks must therefore go to my catechists and all those who formed me in faith.

My debt of gratitude to Cyril O'Regan is immense. Through countless discussions over the span of many years, my interest in researching this topic took shape while both the range of my considerations widened and the seriousness of my thought deepened. I have grown to admire Cyril for a great many things both within and outside academia, but above all I have come to admire his capacity for admiring others. Both his example and his interest in my work have encouraged me to become more generous and committed in kind. I am likewise grateful to Larry Cunningham, who opened his vast reservoirs of wisdom to me on all things related to the communion of saints. Larry read drafts of this work throughout my writing period and never failed to respond with constructive criticism that was in equal measures substantive and encouraging. I also had the good fortune to work with John Betz, whose very first topical conversation with me yielded one of the most important insights for what would later become the second and fourth chapters of this work. Along with Cyril and Larry, John provided helpful guidance as I explored this topic theologically and otherwise. The unnamed scholarly reviewers who read and commented on my manuscript as it was being considered for publication offered remarkably helpful feedback that prompted me to improve this work in important respects. I am grateful for their thoughtful consideration of this work as well as for the work of all on the editorial team at the University of Notre Dame Press.

This work would not have been possible without the support of John Cavadini, for whom I have worked for more than a decade in the McGrath Institute for Church Life at Notre Dame. In addition to teaching me how to read Augustine, I am grateful to John for his confidence in me and for caring so deeply for my personal, professional, and scholarly development. This work is in many ways a fruit of the connection between the Church and the academy that I have learned to cherish from my work in the McGrath Institute for Church Life, where intelligent, generous, and innovative colleagues surround me on a daily basis. I do not take them or our work together for granted. I am uniquely indebted to the undergraduate students, high school students, and professional ministers with whom I have had the pleasure of exploring faith for more than a decade in the Notre Dame Vision program. Just about every facet of this theological work grew out of what I first learned and experienced in that community.

I am likewise grateful to the members of Notre Dame's Department of Theology, where I studied and now have the privilege of teaching courses. My special thanks go to Mary Catherine Hilkert, Brian Daley, Matt Ashley, Bob Krieg, Jan Poorman, David Fagerberg, and Vittorio Montemaggi, among others, from whom I received a theological education of unsurpassed quality. I would be remiss if I failed to mention the inestimable influence of my colleague and closest friend Tim O'Malley, who, among other things, was a constant conversation partner at every phase of this writing project and whose own scholarship inspires admiration.

My final words of thanks go to those to whom I owe the most. I extend my deepest gratitude to my parents, who gave me life and whose confidence in me I have never doubted a day in my life. I offer my thanks to my brother Stefan, who always will be my "best man" and who teaches me how to be a better man. And to the Pendarvis family into which I entered through marriage—to my mother- and father-in-law Betsie and John, my brother-in-law Justin, and my sisters-in-law Christi and Mary (along with spouses and those who will be)—I give thanks for the joy and privilege of sharing in the richness of their familial life, which has been, at times, without a ceiling . . . literally.

My final word of thanks goes to my wife Lisa, to whom I dedicate this work. If I have learned anything in contemplating the communion of saints it is that the life of the saints is a life of charity, wherein the good of another becomes one's very own good. If this is true, then I am blessed to share my life with someone who witnesses to the validity of sanctity every day. In addition to contributing to the life of the Church in her own way through her gifts of leadership in liturgical music and catechesis, Lisa was the one who, during all the many days that I researched and wrote, took the lead in caring for the more important things, namely our five beautiful children: Caleb Elijah, Felicity Thérèse, Josiah Xavier, Isaac James, and Gianna Magdalene. Life in our family is indeed a foretaste of the Heavenly City. For this and much more, thank you, Lisa.

+Advent 2016+

INTRODUCTION

The saints are good company. They are the heroes of the faith who blazed new and creative paths to holiness; they are the witnesses whose testimonies echo throughout the ages in the memory of the Church. Most Christians—at least most Catholics—are likely to have their own favorite saints: those individuals who inspire and console believers as they pray and struggle in the particular setting of their own lives. Much has been written about many of these saints and even, in fact, about sainthood itself; however, this work is not concerned with individual saints per se. What I seek to examine in the pages that follow is the *communion* of the saints, with the conviction that what makes the saints holy and what forms them into a communion is one and the same. Moreover, this communion is vital to the life of the faithful as well as to the meaning and destiny of all creation.

The saints testify to God's work of love as it draws to completion. They are the ones who desire, know, and will along with the content and style of God's own way of loving. This story of sanctity is enshrined in the creed Christians profess—specifically, the Apostles' Creed. In this symbol, the movement from who God is to what God has done gives way to the sanctification of life into which redeemed creatures are drawn. In this space, the saints stand as pedagogues who witness to the fullness of humanity in the culmination of God's action in the world. Put another way, the saint is God's address: in the saint, God speaks to creation, creation speaks to God, God finds his creation present, and one finds the presence of God. In their fullness, then, the saints offer what they represent: the communion of human persons in union with the love of God. The saints, therefore, may only be apprehended in truth to the degree that they are known as partakers of communion. They embody an objective reality that demands a conversion to a distinctive mode of subjective apprehension. Those who wish to know and understand this holy communion must strain forward toward the way in which the blessed saints abide in love (see Phil. 3:13).

As persons defined by the movement of divine love, the saints share in the personhood of Christ. They are, as it were, the embodiment of the love of Christ, and the communion they share comes forth as a gift and requires a response. The gift is a unity that is not self-produced and the response is the desire for this union to be complete. The exchange in this giving and receiving communicates life as a being-with and a being-for, with the expression and constitution of the communion of saints as the accompaniment of one with and for another—unto all others. In this communication of life, the communion of saints emerges from a desire stronger than death.

Claiming that communion is stronger than death is no small thing. Surely this challenge can be ameliorated by either attenuating the meaning of communion or softening the closure of death; however, neither move is compatible with the Christian faith. Christianity is concerned with the proclamation of an unbreakable bond of communion that pierces through the soundless darkness of death. To *think* rightly about the communion of saints requires an unreserved confrontation with the meaning (or meaninglessness) of death; to *live* fully toward the communion stronger than death demands a disposition to hoping in what does not and cannot come from one's own power alone. Taking death seriously leads to reimagining the validity of acts of communication and the bonds of communion, and this renewal of the imagination is only possible according to the form and content of revelation. This is knowledge born in the valley of humility and it is the only path by which we can know the saints as they are, in communion.

The belief in the communion of saints belongs to the eschatological dimension of the Christian faith. It is, in other words, a matter of hope. The dimensions of Christian hope are provided by and conform to the dimensions of Jesus Christ, who stretches the communication of the Word of Life to the limits of creaturely existence and indeed to the extreme distance of creaturely nonexistence in sin. In this work, I aim to present the *communio sanctorum* as an article of faith that is, as I state in chapter 3, "properly Christological in that it concerns the complete action of the Incarnation, pneumatological in that it pertains to the Spirit's work of forming community in the bonds of charity, and ultimately Trinitarian in that it fundamentally entails graced participation in the divine life of persons-in-communion." As appropriate to a theological inquiry, this treatment of the *communio sanctorum* begins with its incorporation as an article of faith in the Apostles' Creed, proceeds to elucidate the meaning of what this article expresses with eschatological studies in theological anthropology and ecclesiology, and at last arrives at (or rather returns to) a more substantive understanding of sacramental and liturgical practice before explicating the communion of saints as a work of love. In what amounts to a distinctly Catholic construction, one may measure the ecumenical and perhaps even interreligious value of this book according to the degree to which I successfully show the coherence of the Catholic emphasis on communion, both in terms of the Church in via and in its eschatological fullness.

Chapter 1 is primarily dedicated to measuring the parameters of my project. To begin, I trace the path by which the *communio sanctorum* traveled from the practice of faith to a declared article of faith that was incorporated into the baptismal creed. In the name of the Triune God, the faithful ultimately profess belief in what the sanctification of life in union with God begins to look like, specifically in the third part of the creed under the belief in the Holy Spirit. The incorporation of the *communio sanctorum* into the creed results from the Church's growing recognition that exercising communion with the saints is intrinsic to the one faith it professes. In diagnosing the contemporary situation, though, I contend that while there is certainly something like a notional assent to the doctrine's claim to the uninterrupted union among the saints, what remains obscured or, more poignantly, under-considered, are the twin questions of why and how the modern person is to believe in the communion of saints in deed as well as in word. In short, I argue that the Christian imagination in the modern period is ailing from the reduction of faith to the boundaries of reason and the exiling of God from the workings of the world into a remote realm of impenetrable mystery into which the dead disappear. The twofold challenge to fully professing belief in the communion of saints is therefore epistemological and theological—that is, it concerns our ways of knowing and the manner of believing in who God is. I contend that the (un)reality of death shows the urgency and baldness of both dimensions of this challenge.

In chapter 2, I interrogate the modern notions of death. I begin with a socio-historical analysis of the development of customs relating to the phenomenon of death and the correlative ways in which the surviving community treats the dying (and the dead). I observe how these modern approaches to death both promote and derive from an impetus to isolate individuals from one another. I then take up a poetic proposal to something like a secular analogue to the communion of saints in the work of Rainer Maria Rilke. What the Bohemian-Austrian poet shows is the promise of a fertile imagination that nonetheless fails because of the content of what informs his imagination. The treatment of Rilke helps us to see that both the energy and the content of an imagination are crucial to properly forming the eschatological imagination. In the latter part of the chapter, I examine modern secular philosophical approaches to death, most notably Martin Heidegger's but also with an eye toward Friedrich Nietzsche. On the one hand, my task in this chapter is to critique the prevalent inclination to ignore death and the concerted refusal to say anything about it. On the other hand, my task is also to critique the tendency to say too much about death in the wrong way. This treatment of the distinctively modern approaches to death thus leaves us in search of an account of death that depends on neither ignorance nor mythology.

In due course, I present the death of Jesus Christ as the key to the true meaning (or meaninglessness) of death. His death is the unadorned foundation upon which communion is built. In chapter 3, I thus begin to recast death in Christian terms, leading ultimately toward the goal of asking the question of the human person in a theological register. To do so, I pursue a Christological keynote by following the Incarnate Word to the extreme creaturely distance from God in the state of being dead; only thus may we more adequately apprehend the gift of life that is given in his Resurrection. In the course of this pursuit, I consider the human person according to such questions as the relationship between freedom and subjectivity, time and eternity, and individuality and sociality. I also seek to locate my inquiry within the biblical narrative and especially ancient Israel's developing belief in the resurrection of the dead. As the beginning of the constructive portion of my work, this chapter commences the exploration of communication and communion in three interrelated spheres: communion among the dead (chapter 3), communication from the blessed dead to the living (chapter 4), and communication of the living among themselves and to the blessed dead (chapters 5 and 6).

Chapter 4 subsequently focuses on the desire to show how communion extends from the dead to include the living (i.e., those still on pilgrimage) across the chasm of death. I begin with a theological exegesis of the Resurrection appearances as recorded primarily in the Gospel of Luke and the Gospel of John. My aim is to elucidate how the unfathomable act of God in the Resurrection of Jesus Christ first critiques and then transforms the desires of those to whom the risen Christ comes. I then proceed, in the chapter's second section, to move in the opposite direction to study how the quest to discover the truth of one's own existence is oriented to the discovery of the unsolicited gift of God's mercy. Augustine's *Confessions* is my primary text for this purpose. I carry forward what I gain in the early sections of the chapter to build toward a theological anthropology in which the natural desire of the human person is transformed by and according to how God freely fulfills this desire. Henri de Lubac's modern retrieval of Augustinian theology provides much of the impetus for this task, which leads me, in the chapter's end, toward a substantive description of the saint as the one whose desire is fulfilled in willful conformity to God's own way of giving in Christ. I contend that on this eschatological horizon the truth of human persons is revealed in full.

In chapter 5 I situate the communion among created persons within the communion of God in the body of the Church. To do so, I first turn to Dante's *Commedia* as part of a larger attempt to respond to the prevalent suspicion of hierarchically ordered relations, most especially in the work of other contemporary Catholic theologians who are likewise interested in recovering a more robust eschatological imagination. I argue that Dante presents a compelling image of eschatological relations that redounds to the original social order of humanity according to God's act of creation. I examine the eschatological dimensions of the theologies of creation from Augustine and Karl Rahner, respectively, in order to advance my thesis. From there, I explore three journeys "from freedom to freedom" in an attempt to connect the issue of creaturely dignity to the future to which God calls his beloved. In the chapter's concluding pages I draw out the pneumatological and Christological dimensions of the communion of saints in the sacramental and liturgical life of the Church, which is itself dependent on the gift of God's own communion.

Throughout these chapters I seek to develop and defend the thesis upon which this theological reconstruction of the communion of saints builds: love works in community, for communion, or not at all. In the sixth and final chapter, I seek to observe this dynamism as the logic of Scripture itself, which is incarnate in Christ and becomes the very movement by which his saints are transformed in building communion. Beginning with the prologue to John's Gospel and connecting to the narratives of Jesus's transfiguration, I eventually examine how Moses prefigures Christ in the role he assumes and prefigures the saints in the work he inspires. What we see in anticipatory fashion in Moses approaches fulfillment in particular saints, who witness to the efficacy of divine mercy that redeems and sanctifies creation. We will study four such figures in this line of sanctity: Thérèse of Lisieux, Teresa of Avila, Teresa of Calcutta, and Dorothy Day. Based on the logic of Scripture that becomes the grammar of communion in the saints, I then make a statement about the theological question of the intermediate state before concluding with a reflection on the prayers concerning the dead in the Church's liturgy and, subsequently, the concrete devotions of the faithful that testify to the unrelenting particularity of God's love for particular persons. In learning to perceive how the saints embody the work of love, we draw closer to apprehending how the communion that the saints build becomes the eschatological fulfillment of Christ, who is *the realization of what is hoped for and the evidence of things not seen* (Heb. 11:1, NAB).

CHAPTER 1

INDEFINITE ARTICLE

Looking Backward

The "communion of saints" is a definitive mark of the Christian imagination conformed to the mystery of salvation: the communion of holy persons invites and demands an act of faith for Christian belief to build toward completion. In fact, it is the exercise of fidelity to the promises of Christ in the face of death that gave this expression its primary meaning for Western Christianity. This meaning was carried into and is now borne by the Apostles' Creed, "the most universally accepted creed in Western Christendom."[1] Every saint has a history and so does the article of faith that attests to the communion in which they share. The lives of saints arise from the work of God in the world while the article symbolizing their communion arises from the Church's reflection on the life of faith in the Spirit.

Why this article of the "communion of saints" does not appear either in the Niceno-Constantinopolitan Creed or the Old Roman Creed is a question whose answer at once signifies the hope that springs from the merits of Christ and the deficiency of this hope, by and large, in the modern world. Put another way: as certain communities in the Early Church confronted death through the practice of faith, the belief in the communion of saints was espoused, and as death is avoided, ignored, or parodied in more contemporary times, the essential meaning of the communion of saints slips away. The sober confrontation with the meaning (or meaninglessness) of death forces the issue of the validity of the communion of saints. Death provides the occasion for asking the question of the saints' communion in the proper terms; therefore, the primary issue in the communion of saints is not actually death, but rather divine freedom. In the silence of death, the Word of God speaks anew. Accordingly, the axial conviction around which this present work turns is that the communion of saints is intrinsically and inextricably connected to the love of Christ: the Incarnate Word.

While the two following chapters deal with death more directly in preparation for hearing this Word aright, this chapter begins by tracing the development of the doctrine concerning the communion of saints from the experience of the faithful into the baptismal creed. From there, I attend to the ecclesial pronouncements from the Second Vatican Council that confirm the perennial validity of the belief in sharing of communion among members of the Church who abide on both sides of death, so to speak. In the final sections of the chapter I diagnose the current state of notional and real assent to belief in this unbroken communion of saints in the modern milieu in order to ultimately identify the precise problematic with which the remainder of this work is concerned. Through the turns of this chapter, I seek to elucidate how the communion of saints—both as a reality and as a stated article of faith—grows from and shapes a Catholic ethos, as well as how the flagging vitality of belief in this communion in the practice of the faithful signals the diminishment of the faith itself.

The Development of a Doctrine

The term "communion of saints" most likely came from the East, where the meaning of the expression was clear. In Greek, *koinonia ton agion*—the equivalent to Latin's *communio sanctorum*—unmistakably indicates "participation in the Eucharistic elements."[2] To this day priests in the Byzantine liturgy lift up the consecrated gifts and exclaim, "Holy things for the holy people,"[3] further locating the central meaning of the communion for the Eastern Church in the sharing of the Sacraments.

In the West, however, there was much greater fluctuation in the meaning of *communio sanctorum*. Upon close inspection of the historical evidence as to what primary meaning the phrase carried as it was incorporated into the Apostles' Creed, "the inescapable conclusion," as one prominent scholar puts it, is that, "so far as the creed is concerned, the dominant conception, at any rate between the fifth and eighth centuries, was 'fellowship with holy persons.'"[4] It is during these very centuries that certain Christian communities first enacted the meaning of the *communio sanctorum* as they practiced their faith and reflected on the death of the martyrs.

The Apostles' Creed is itself an elaborate form of the Old Roman Creed, from which all variant baptismal creeds derive. Evidence of the final form of the Apostles' Creed dates to the first half of the eighth century, while its adoption into the Roman baptismal rite likely did not occur until at least the middle of the ninth century.[5] Prior to these dates, the first surviving creed to attest to the presence of *communio sanctorum* is the formulary on which Nicetas of Remesiana commented in the fourth century.[6] Extant documents from this period point to the Gallic regions of Western Europe as the place of origin for the meaning of *communio sanctorum* as it was eventually carried into the Apostles' Creed. As distinct from most of the other statements of faith that were incorporated into the creeds in the Early Church—and particularly those creedal statements that developed in ecumenical councils—the development and the incorporation of *communio sanctorum* seem to have taken place without a polemical situation or crisis of heterodoxy to spur its definition. Instead, this article developed through devotional faith practices of Christian communities in Gaul.

As J. N. D. Kelly argues, the intensity of faith of particular Christians, in a particular era, in this particular region, helped the article of *communio sanctorum* to gain recognition as intrinsic to the faith:

> The fourth century witnessed an enormous expansion of the devotion which the Church had paid to its saints and illustrious dead from the earliest times. Even at the beginning of the third century the author of the *Passion of Perpetua and Felicitas* assured his readers that his purpose in writing out what had happened was to enable them to enjoy communion with

the holy martyrs and through them with Jesus Christ. . . . It is evident that in the fourth century the consciousness of communion with the redeemed in heaven, who had already tasted of the fullness of the glory of Christ, was as real and as rich in hope to the theologians as to circles of ordinary Christians. Thus, although it involved no polemical *arrière pensée,* "communion of saints" gave expression to conceptions which were very vividly present to the minds of fourth and fifth century churchmen, particularly in those regions of Western Europe where . . . the Apostles' Creed was molded into its final shape.[7]

What we hear from Kelly is that the occasion for the articulation of this article as part of the creed arose from the devotions to the blessed dead that were abundant and thriving in the regions where the Apostles' Creed developed. In other words, as the faithful exercised the faith into which they were immersed at Baptism, they applied this faith to the veneration of first the martyrs and then other holy witnesses. Only after this application of the faith was exercised did it come to be recognized as normative for the faith. Devotion drew out orthodoxy.

If Kelly's argument is indeed well founded, then we may readily conclude that "the fellowship with holy persons" that these Gallic Christians practiced was a fellowship with martyrs they had known in their time, or the memory and testimony of whom were offered to them on behalf of their own or other Christian communities (as in the case of Perpetua and Felicitas). In these martyrs they saw the power of the Christian faith spoken unto death, and their reverence for these martyrs was their own affirmation of the validity of the promises of Christ, a promise that redounds throughout the Gospels, that *whoever believes in me, even if he dies, will live, and everyone who lives and believes in me will never die* (John 11:25–26, NAB). They saw the martyrs as living testaments to belief in Christ: these were the ones who allowed their deaths to become the capstone of their witness. So when the Gallic Christians began to venerate other holy witnesses—those whom presumably they had known or whose stories of faith were, again, handed on through the Christian communities—they exercised their imaginations to recognize that a life lived in faith was itself a witness to the validity of the promises of Christ, even when that life of faith did not end in martyrdom per se.

In either case, these Christians practiced the Christian faith in life and especially in the confrontation with death, and they allowed the dimensions of the faith they practiced to expand into a veneration of the blessed dead in virtue of those promises of Christ to which they remained steadfast. In doing so, they did not invent a new aspect of the one faith; rather, they allowed the meaning of the one faith to unfold in their lives. As one commentator suggests, "Perhaps the communion of saints could not be properly and fully understood from the beginning, because the impact of Christian martyrdom in the church was yet to be experienced fully."[8]

The Orthodoxy of the Body of the Faithful

While it is likely common for one to interpret a creed as that which sets and maintains the normative elements of faith so that adherents may assume these elements into their practice of the faith, the history of the development of *communio sanctorum* shows a different side. What this history helps to reveal is how the practice of faith contributes to the development of the doctrines themselves. Attending to this double-sided nature of doctrine, Jaroslav Pelikan observes that "It is the purpose of 'doctrine' in all the creeds and confessions of faith, and in all the periods of church history, to promote, strengthen, and regulate, but also and first of all to articulate . . . 'the orthodoxy of the body of the faithful' in the church."[9] Pelikan borrows the phrase "the orthodoxy of the body of the faithful" from John Henry Newman, who argued for the relationship between, on the one hand, the legitimate authority of the Church to codify what it believes, teaches, and confesses, and, on the other hand, the authority of the body of the faithful who are active subjects and, in the words of Paul's Letter to the Ephesians, *members of one another* (4:25, RSV).[10]

Pelikan follows Newman's lead to contend that when a teaching is set down in a creed or confession,

[it] is not replacing or even correcting or revising or amplifying what the laity have in fact been believing and teaching all along, though perhaps without really knowing it. It is simply articulating and defending this

against recent heretical adversaries, or it is making it more precise by the adoption of a more technical theological vocabulary, or it is transposing it from the implicit to the explicit and from the unconscious to the conscious. Therefore the laity are still confessing their own faith in this text.[11]

In light of what was noted above regarding the absence of heterodox opposition or polemical *arrière pensée* pertaining to the incorporation of *communio sanctorum* into the Apostles' Creed, the teaching on the communion of saints corresponds to the last instance Pelikan mentions. By including *communio sanctorum* as an article of faith in this creed, the Church took what was implicit in the application of the faith and made it an explicit element of the faith itself. This articulation came through recognizing the importance of what was first a practice of the faith, and not through the clarification of the orthodoxy of the faith against a heterodox misinterpretation.

The placement of *communio sanctorum* as one of the last articles recited in the Apostles' Creed further indicates what kind of article it is, for the creed itself internally operates according to what we might dub a narrative logic. What is proclaimed in the creed is already, and quite significantly, a development of belief from what is professed to what is lived. Though Pelikan does not directly consider how the creed testifies to the relationship between the profession of faith and the embodiment of faith on the part of believers, he does speak to the development of Christian creeds from an even more primitive creed. Observing this development can serve as preparation for exploring the narrative logic of the Apostles' Creed itself.

In his treatment of the rules of faith in the Early Church, Pelikan claims that the primal creed "behind and beneath all the primitive creeds of the apostolic and sub-apostolic era" is in fact Israel's great prayer, the *Shema*.[12] Christian faith stands in continuity with this foundational Jewish belief that *The Lord our God is one Lord* (Deut. 6:4, 5–9; 11:13–21; Num. 15:37–41, RSV). Upon the testimony of Jesus himself, this foundation remains intact. As Pelikan notes, when Jesus was asked to identify the most important commandment, he responds with the *Shema*: *Hear, O Israel: the Lord, our God, the Lord is one; and you shall love the Lord with all your heart, and with all your soul, and with all your mind, and with all your strength* (Mark 12:29–30, RSV). Pelikan thus sees the *Shema* as a primitive, even foundational creed upon which the creeds of the Christian faith build and develop. The doctrine of the Trinity, which is itself both the deepest content and the structural framework of the Niceno-Constantinopolitan Creed and the Apostles' Creed alike, remains in continuity with what the *Shema* professes even as it develops beyond the *Shema*'s eloquent terseness. The belief in the Father, the Son, and the Holy Spirit, which the Christian creeds present, "keep[s] the monotheism of *The Shema* intact and inviolate [as its] root assumption."[13]

The Christian doctrine of God as Trinity develops from Israel's monotheism: the Jewish doctrine of God's oneness. Not only is Israel's entire story predicated on this basic truth that it claims, but the Christian story also stands upon the claim to the absolute sovereignty of *the God of Abraham, Isaac, and Jacob* (Acts 3:13; cf. Matt. 22:32; Exod. 3:6, RSV). Of course, the Christian story moves beyond the Jewish story in claiming Jesus Christ as the Son of God and thus God's definitive self-revelation in history. For this reason, the second part of the Apostles' Creed—like the Niceno-Constantinopolitan Creed—rehearses what the apostles witnessed as the mystery of the life, death, and Resurrection of the One who was called the Father's beloved Son at both his Baptism (Mark 1:11; Matt. 3:17; Luke 3:22) and his Transfiguration (Mark 9:7; Matt. 17:5; Luke 9:35). Whereas the first part of the creed names the first person of the Blessed Trinity the sovereign Lord who is the origin of all things—in direct continuity with the *Shema*—this second part of the creed names the second person of the Blessed Trinity as an object of Christian belief and in so doing takes his personal history as the culmination of the salvation history of God's people. The mystery of the life and person of Jesus Christ is thus professed as the power and the mercy of the one God (cf. 1 Cor. 1:24). The story of Israel's faith is carried forward and culminates in the Incarnate Word.

In naming the third person of the Blessed Trinity as an object of Christian belief in the third part of the creed, the Church acknowledges the gift it has received. The gift comes in the person of the Holy Spirit, who falls upon the disciples at Pentecost (see Acts 2:1–13). It is the Holy Spirit who makes the disciples partakers in the mystery of the Father and the Son. As F. J. Badcock notes, "The work of salvation is stated to be accomplished in our Lord by the end of the second paragraph," and for those who see an inner logic to the structure of the creed, the third part concerns the bestowal of "the benefits won by Christ."[14] The creed's third part carries forward the belief expressed in the first part as to the unoriginate Father who is the origin of all things, as well as the belief in the second part as to the sonship and lordship of Jesus Christ, who accomplishes salvation. The third part concerns the life of the Holy Spirit, who brings creation to fulfillment and communicates salvation.

Under the belief in the Holy Spirit, we find doctrinal statements regarding the things that the Spirit brings about in the communication of divine life. At the mention of the Holy Spirit, the creed itself opens up to include the effects of God's self-giving. In articulating these things as dimensions of its one faith, the Church professes what participation in the life of the Triune God means—that is to say, the Church acknowledges what the sanctification of life in union with God begins to look like. With the creed, the faithful claim that because the Holy Spirit is given, *the holy catholic Church* comes into being, *the communion of saints* is summoned, *the forgiveness of sins* is offered, *the resurrection of the body* safeguards the validity of history and of all creation, and this share in God's life is radically open-ended as *life everlasting*. In the third part of the creed, the Church reads forward the narrative it has received regarding the sovereignty of God the Father and the salvific mysteries of Jesus Christ the Son. The belief in the Holy Spirit brings about the renewal of the imagination of "the body of the faithful" in conformity with the love of Christ. With this imagination, the faithful see and profess the graced nature of their own lives through the work of God. This profession is an elaboration—based on the witness of the life of faith—to what was already presented in the *kerygma*: that "the Holy Spirit" is the one "who inspired ancient prophets and whose breath is the life of the holy church."[15] The breath of the Spirit fills the body of the Church.

Pelikan identifies what I have here called "an elaboration" with terms Thomas Aquinas offers in the first part of the *Summa Theologica*, where the Angelic Doctor treats the doctrinal development of the Spirit's procession from the Father and the Son.[16] Aquinas argues for the continuity of orthodox teaching in the Christian creeds even as they undergo change through clarifying statements or additional phrases. The changes do not lead to the formulation of new creeds, but rather make explicit what was implicit in the faith expressed in the earlier creed. "The underlying presupposition for Thomas here is the continuity of orthodox teaching and therefore the presence already from the beginning, though only implicitly, of doctrines that subsequently become explicit."[17] In line with this Thomistic principle, we may see *communio sanctorum* as a doctrine that was recognized as always already part of orthodox teaching when it was incorporated into the Apostles' Creed at a comparatively late date. This addition, which, as we have seen, comes about through the intensity of devotional practices of Christians particularly in a certain region during a certain era, further defines the one faith that was handed down from the apostles. It so happens that this specific article required additional time for the experience of the Christian community—and especially the phenomenon of martyrdom—to illuminate this dimension of orthodox belief.

State of the Communion

Communio sanctorum was first believed implicitly and practiced devotionally—almost instinctively—before it was confessed explicitly and handed down in the creed. Upon reflection, the Church recognized the practice of exercising communion with the saints as intrinsic to the one faith it professed, and thus incorporated this dimension of life in the Spirit into the final section of its baptismal creed. Even today, when the profession of faith is made prior to the rite of Baptism in the Catholic Church, the final affirmative responses to the interrogations of faith lead to the celebrant's announcement that "This is our faith. This is the faith of the Church. We are proud to profess it, in Christ Jesus our Lord." The communion of saints is an element of that faith which the Church proudly professes.

The most recent ecumenical council confirms this truth. In the Second Vatican Council's *Dogmatic Constitution on the Church—Lumen gentium*—the Church is proclaimed to be composed of a "union of wayfarers with the brothers and sisters who sleep in the peace of Christ" and that "this union is reinforced by an exchange of spiritual goods."[18] The Church recognizes that "some of [Christ's] disciples are pilgrims on earth, others have died and are being purified, while still others are in glory."[19] Though death separates the wayfarers from those in the glory of heaven and those being purified after death, the council acknowledges that the faith it inherits and now professes entails belief in a "living communion"[20] between the living and the (blessed) dead—that is, the council espouses belief in an interchange between different spheres of existence. It teaches "that the authentic cult of the saints [consists] . . . in a more intense practice of our love."[21] The practice of love unfolds as the living communicate with the saints through giving thanks to God for them, accepting their ancestors' faith as their own, asking for their help through prayer, remembering their lives and witness, and joining them in the praise of God in the liturgy.[22]

Although it does not use the phrase "communion of saints" in this document, the council does describe and vouch for the practice of communion, which, as the council attests, has always been a part of the faith. As though it were intentionally giving a defense of the development of orthodox teaching from its implicit reality to explicit declaration, the council announces that

> The church has *always* believed that the apostles and Christ's martyrs, who gave the supreme witness of faith and charity by the shedding of their blood, are closely united with us in Christ; it has *always* venerated them, together with the Blessed Virgin Mary and the holy angels, with a special love, and has asked piously for the help of their intercession. Soon there were added to these others who had chosen to imitate more closely the virginity and poverty of Christ, and still others whom the outstanding practice of the Christian virtues and the wonderful grace of God recommended to the pious devotion and imitation of the faithful.[23]

The practice that began in the first few centuries of the Church of venerating the blessed dead and exercising communion with them—a practice that was formally recognized as proper to the faith itself in conformity with belief in the Holy Spirit who unites the living and the dead through the merits of Christ—is here proclaimed as original to the Christian faith from its inception.

Through the council, the Church speaks with authority regarding the truth and importance of this union that "is in no way interrupted"[24] between the living and the dead who share in the love of Christ. Whereas once this union existed in the practices of the faithful who clung to the promises of Christ without an explicit doctrine to define this dimension of faith, in the present age the doctrine is clearly established not only as an article recited in the baptismal creed, but also through the authoritative teaching of an ecumenical council. While now that which was once absent—the doctrine—is clearly present, the question becomes whether that which was once present—the practice—remains so. Is that which is confessed explicitly supported in the practice of faith of the modern Christian?

In an essay dealing with this very chapter of *Lumen gentium*, Karl Rahner indicates that the *Constitution* is attentive to the teaching of the Church but not to the practice of the faithful regarding this teaching:

> By these statements—this is the message of the decree whether explicitly or implicitly expressed—the situation is made clear. We can and should venerate the saints. The only thing left for us to do is to respond with the reality with which we have been presented in the appropriate manner, and in fact to venerate the saints. At this point, however, it may appear to the man of our own times that one factor of decisive importance has been overlooked, namely himself. In other words the question has not been answered as to why and how he, in view of his own special peculiarities, can achieve any kind of relationship with the world of the saints even though the objective reality of this world is not denied.[25]

According to Rahner's assessment, the "man of our own times" does not find in this teaching of the Church the means, the motivation, or the grist for the imagination that will lead him, in his unique particularity, into a lived relationship with the blessed dead. Even when this Christian joins in the Church's liturgy and, partaking in the Sacraments, shares in the "spiritual goods" or "holy things" of the Church's communion, he does not easily conceive of himself as participating in a communion with the saints per se.

Unmistakably, the council confirms the objective fact of a communion that binds together the Church's pilgrims with those in the glory of heaven and those in the state of purification. In Rahner's view, however, it does not answer the twin questions of why and how the modern person actually venerates the saints. These questions point to an even more fundamental twofold question: why and how do we believe in the communion of saints? Even though this belief has been exercised throughout the centuries within the Church and, by at least the middle of the ninth century, was explicitly articulated as an article of faith, what has yet to be satisfactorily accomplished is a systematic theological account of why and how this belief is intrinsic to the Christian faith as such. This theological account is neither the source of the practice of faith nor a necessary prerequisite for an articulation of faith; rather, the theological account helps tie together the practice and the articulation so that when the former is flagging—as Rahner suggests it is in the modern age—the theology can explicate what is professed, thereby revealing once again what has always been proclaimed.[26] Theology, in this case, assists doctrine in directing the very practice that gave rise to the doctrine in the first place.[27]

Rather than dealing with either distinct individuals or an abstract communion, veneration of the saints is concerned with relating to particular persons bonded together in communion. The communion in which the faithful profess belief as *communio sanctorum* is a communion of holy persons who, according to *Lumen gentium*, are united to both the Church's pilgrims and those undergoing purification after death. What is as-yet theologically underdetermined is how that which makes these particular persons holy is precisely that which forms them into one communion. In other words, what unites them as a communion and what makes them holy is one and the same: the love of Christ that becomes their own way of loving.[28] The unique particularities of these holy persons were, each in their own way, conformed to and transformed by the love of God in Christ. At the same time, though, this transformation that brought them into the union of one body, for holiness, which is the graced sharing of divine life, is impossible in isolation. Holiness entails communion, for holiness is given in the Spirit, who is the communion of the Father and the Son given over to the world.[29] As an article of the Christian faith, *communio sanctorum* at once indicates the unsubstitutable particularity of holy persons, their communion in Christ through the Spirit, and the bonds that unite them. As noted above, in the East it is on the bonds—especially the Sacraments—that the primary emphasis of the "communion of saints" has traditionally been placed. In the West, however, the most universal of all the Christian creeds—the Apostles' Creed—presents the article as that which arose from the veneration of holy persons. It is this practice that the Church says the faithful can and should continue today.

Communing with the saints is not an arbitrary recommendation; rather, it is essential to professing and practicing the Christian faith in its fullness. For when the Church announces its saints, it proclaims the permanent validity of the humanity of Christ and the real, historical efficacy of the Incarnation. On this point, Rahner seeks to make the connection between the pronouncement of sainthood and the mystery at the heart of the Church:

> When the Church declares someone to be a Saint, this is much more a necessary part of the Church's realization of her own being . . . she must be able to state her holiness in the concrete. She must have a "cloud of witnesses" whom she can indicate by name. She cannot merely maintain that there is a history of salvation (without it being known exactly where it takes place with real, final success), but she must *really relate* that very eschatological history of salvation which she is herself. The prize of her actual Saints belongs to her innermost being and is not merely something which she "also" achieves "on the side," something which has been inspired by a purely human need for hero worship.[30]

In Rahner's estimation, this is important because the heart of the Christian faith is the Incarnation of the Word of God, who was not merely "at one time of decisive importance for our salvation . . . he is *now* and for all eternity the *permanent openness* of our finite being to the living God of infinite, eternal life."[31] The union of divine and human natures in the one person of Jesus of Nazareth is the once for all event of salvation that, through the Spirit, is a mystery contemporaneous with all of history.

In recognizing the holiness of its own members, the Church confesses the truth of the Incarnation: that the humanity of Christ was neither temporary nor simply apparent. The humanity of Christ was and is real; it was and is the same humanity that the members of the Church possess. To see the holiness of its own members, the Church sees the merits of the life, death, and Resurrection of the Incarnate Word in human history.[32] For, as noted above, the third section of the creed contains the statements of belief that pertain to the Holy Spirit, who makes present the saving mysteries of Christ (recited in the second part of the creed) and thereby opens creation to participation in divine life. The Church's saints are both beneficiaries and heralds of this work of sanctification. Their communion with one another and eschatologically with the whole Church is guaranteed in the person of the Holy Spirit.

The status of *communio sanctorum* is at once a Christological and a pneumatological matter. It is Christological in that it concerns the full reach of the Incarnation to humanity—and indeed creation—as such, and it is a pneumatological matter since it arises from the activity of the Holy Spirit to communicate the merits of the Incarnation to the world. Veneration of the saints is an act of fidelity to the promises of Christ through the sanctifying work of the Holy Spirit.[33] The saints are icons of God's Triunity, for they receive the eternal love of God the Father in their conformity to the mysteries of Jesus Christ, the only begotten Son, as they share in the communion of the Holy Spirit.[34]

The problem of the why and how of the modern Christian's veneration of the saints—and, furthermore, the why and how of belief in *communio sanctorum*—is thus an issue that bears directly on belief in the Incarnation. The most complete account of the mystery of the Incarnation will be the one that sees also the effects of the Incarnation on real, historical human beings as part of the eternal mystery of the person of Christ. This account will not only bear upon professions of faith, but also upon practices of faith. The theologian's role is therefore to assist in the illumination of the full mystery of the Incarnation, which, in this instance, means explicating why and how the *communio sanctorum* is inextricably enfolded within Christ's person, who is identical with his salvific work.[35]

The Diagnosis

Even though the work of Karl Rahner will not provide all the resources necessary to complete this theological task, the late Jesuit theologian does much in terms of first perceiving the problem at hand and then beginning to diagnose precisely what ails the modern Christian in his approach to the saints. In his aforementioned essay on *Lumen gentium* and the veneration of the saints, Rahner makes two significant claims regarding the challenges modern persons face in practicing communion with the saints. The first problem relates to what might be called the triumph of Kantian epistemology. For Immanuel Kant, knowledge is restricted to the phenomenal realm. Whatever may or may not exist beyond or behind what appears cannot itself be an object of knowledge and therefore is not accessible to reason. Such a view disallows any kind of true eschatology, for eschatological assertions are based in faith regarding things not seen but for which one hopes (see Heb. 11:1).[36] Rahner observes that this kind of epistemological restriction is not simply an issue of philosophical perspective, but also and especially operates in the practice of the faithful—that is, it shapes their own imaginations. It is certainly the case, he contends, that the modern Christian is unable to venerate the Church's saints and thus open herself to "prayerful communication" with these persons *as persons* since the modern Christian no longer even seems "to have any sense of being actively in communication with [her] own dead."[37] All the dead—even those closest to the Christian in her own life—have passed beyond the veil of death and thus are not present in the phenomenal realm, where they can be known and called upon.[38] "It is not," Rahner continues, "that we contest the fact that they are, in principle, living on in the presence of the God of the living, but so far as we are concerned they are not alive. They have been, so to say, completely and totally removed from our sphere of existence."[39] Kant's legacy looms in the modern Christian imagination, where death serves as an absolute epistemological and experiential boundary.[40]

A second and, in Rahner's words, "more radical reason" for the decline in the veneration of the saints has to do with the way Christians in the modern age conceive of God.[41] In a world that has become vast and moves along at an increasingly frenetic pace, the modern person is inundated with sensory images and unending parcels of knowledge. God does not appear alongside these many things as something or someone to be known. As the world becomes ever more profane in the everyday experience of the everyday person—including the everyday Christian— God seems ever more distant and incomprehensible in his remote transcendence. "God is," Rahner concludes, "to a large extent, experienced as the silent mystery, infinite in his ineffability and inconceivability."[42] God does not conform to the modern person's common ways of knowing and so God is not known except as unknowable. The problem with the veneration of saints, then, is that the modern Christian imagines that it is "into this silent, unfathomable and ineffable mystery that the dead disappear. They depart. They no longer make themselves felt. They cease any further to belong to the world of experience."[43] Even if the Christian of today searches for her beloved dead, her "gaze [meets] only with the darkness of the divinity in which nothing can be distinguished any longer."[44]

Rahner bemoans this modern tendency to construe an abstract God who absorbs everything else—even the entire world—into his sheer absoluteness. This is a form of pantheism that would seek to erase the distinctions and particularities of creation itself—the very peculiar concreteness God's Word assumed in the Incarnation—and therefore the distinctions and particularities of the saints are erased along with it.[45] The alternative to this tendency cannot, however, be a kind of polytheism (or Gnosticism) in which God and the world stand in opposition, with the saints then belonging *either* to the principality of the world *or* to the power of God.[46] The problem Rahner sees is in the false choices of holiness as absorption into God or individuality without union. As it stands now, the modern Christian seems to treat the dead as if they disappear into God, who absorbs them in his all-consuming silence, while the world progresses onward as if God were absent.

Looking Forward

Between these ailments of the Christian eschatological imagination—the epistemological horizon and the theological problem relating to the notion of God—a common factor is death. What Rahner is pointing to is that, in general, Christians in the modern period do not seem to be able to both cling to the hope of new life in the Resurrection of Christ *and* confront death as the real and total end to human life. In functionally abiding by something like Kant's epistemological restrictions, Christians fail to allow the promises of Christ, which are known in faith and not strictly by reason, to shape their belief and religious practice. Rather than seeking to pull the blessed dead back within the boundaries of what we can see and know according to the strictures of the epistemology of rational empiricism, communication with the dead in Christ requires the openness of faith to receive them with the eternal love in which they now participate.[47] Only by heeding the concrete historicity and hermeneutical priority of the fullness of the Incarnation—including and especially the Paschal Mystery—can Christians approach their own death and the death of others with the correct posture. Following Christ leads one not away from death, but through it to new life; and only against the backdrop of death is the content of Christian hope fully disclosed. Consequently, the uninterrupted union in Christ between those still living and those who have died is a matter of communication that passes through death. In order to take the eschatological truth of the communion of saints seriously, the Christian must at once observe the totality of death and cling in faith to the Resurrection. This challenge sets the agenda for the remainder of this work.

The underlying purpose driving this first chapter was to begin to establish a set of relationships: the relationship between the practices and the definitions of faith; the relationship between implicit and explicit orthodoxy; the relationship between theological explication and the congruence of Christian profession and enactment; and the relationship between human death and Christian hope. It is the last of these relationships that will move us into first the sobering analysis of modern approaches to death and then on to the rigorous contemplation of the content of Christian hope from which the constructive portions of this work arise. In subsequent chapters, I hope to show that despite the individualizing, deafeningly silent thrust of the modern approaches to death, the desire for the fullness of life is a desire for communion that comes from Christ himself, in whose body the Spirit re-members all the saints.

CHAPTER 2

SOLITARY CONFINEMENT

Regarding Christian Hope

In the closing pages of the preceding chapter, I asserted that the eschato-logical truth of the communion of saints abides in the tension of cling-ing to the hope of the Resurrection and taking death seriously as the definitive end of human life. I assented to Karl Rahner's diagnosis of the modern Christian's deficient eschatological imagination as that which is, on the one hand, plagued by a lingering Kantian epistemology and, on the other, given to a generally unannounced pantheistic assumption. In the first instance, death is treated as an absolute boundary for knowl-edge, relationship, and communication, setting as it does the impenetra-ble limit to the phenomenal real. In the second instance, the dead slip away and are absorbed into the remote transcendence of an unknow-able "God" who teleologically consumes all life and melts creaturely dif-ference in the intensity of his own being. The pervasive Kantianism thus takes death seriously, but in the wrong way, while the furtive pantheism offers a view of life beyond death that is ultimately incompatible with the personalism of the Christian faith. Impoverished views of both death and God obstruct the real assent to the uninterrupted union between the liv-ing and the dead in Christ.[1]

As an article of faith, *communio sanctorum* expresses the hope that be-longs properly to Christians. This hope is truncated and in fact parodied when the seriousness of death is ignored, for Christian hope is most essentially a hope in life that arises out of death. The paradox of Christian hope is found in its source, for through his Passion, death, and Resurrection, Christ accepts rather than avoids death in order to bring life. In fidelity to Christ himself, Christian hope takes up this same pattern of trusting in a gift of life that passes through death. To ignore death is to miss the fundamental gravitas of the gift Christ embodies and confers, a gift that promises and effects the communion of saints.

The three tasks of the present chapter all relate to the challenge of taking death seriously. First, in the interest of further specifying Rahner's claim, I briefly trace the development of what becomes the modern Western approach to death beginning from the Middle Ages. With an appeal to the work of the social historian Philippe Ariès, who studies the sociological and ritualistic changes that signal this development, I argue that a carefully orchestrated denial of death defines the prevalent modern approach.

The second task is to analyze and evaluate Rainer Maria Rilke's *Duino Elegies*, in which the poet vigorously attempted to undo this modern silence concerning death. The attention I give to Rilke's work will allow me to both detect the promise of his view for the renewal of the Christian eschatological imagination and identify the ultimate unviability of his proposal. Since my treatment of Rilke is ultimately in service of a theological aim, I intentionally read Rilke alongside the commentary that the Catholic theologian Romano Guardini provides. The fruit of this analysis will become ever more apparent in light of my third task for the chapter, which is to critically compare Rilke's non-Christian poetic vision to similarly non-Christian philosophical views that seek to address modernity's forgetfulness of death. For this final task, I primarily treat Martin Heidegger's philosophical view of death.

An overarching theme of this chapter concerns the relationship between approaches to death and the understanding of the human person. Whether in a socio-historical, poetic, or philosophical register, the views of death featured herein make decisive claims about the truth and nature of the human person. Since the doctrine of *communio sanctorum* is itself an eschatological claim about the life of persons-in-communion, these analyses of the status of the human person relative to death bear

enormous preparatory value for the eventual task of articulating a robust theological account of human persons through the life, death, and
Resurrection of Jesus Christ, who is himself the key to the communion
of saints. By the time we make the turn to the third chapter, we must be
prepared to follow Christ into the utter seriousness of death.

Forgetting Death

The French medievalist and social historian Philippe Ariès argues that the
twentieth century witnessed a rapid and radical shift in the way in which
death and dying were confronted on the individual, familial, and cultural levels. In his estimation, death, which had been so "omnipresent"
and "familiar" in the past, quickly disappeared from the consciousness
of Western societies.[2] At the end of a long, slow process of developments regarding the Western attitudes toward death over the course of
a millennium or more, he observes that "the denial of death is openly
acknowledged as a significant trait of our culture"; indeed, "death has
been banished."[3] This forgetfulness of death is a hallmark of the modern
milieu. In an effort to understand this current situation, Ariès embarks
on a broad and sweeping study of the ways in which attitudes toward
death and dying both prompted and responded to sometimes subtle and
sometimes dramatic changes in social conventions, rituals, and art. According to his interpretation, the past one thousand years have seen the
gradual "untaming" of death that ultimately resulted in a social disciplining of death through silence and intentional neglect.[4]

Ariès's study begins in the Early Middle Ages where he discovers
what will become the norm for the approach to death over the following
ten centuries. He calls this approach "tamed death." This is a "household
sort of death"[5] that boasts of well-established customs that the dying
themselves chiefly perform in their own homes, in the company of their
families and members of their communities. Death was approached as a
natural yet important part of life, which did not introduce—as will later
become the norm—a rupture between the sick and the healthy, the individual and the society, or the dead and the living. In fact, life and death
were not conceived of as being that far apart, nor was the individual

easily removed from the context of his community.[6] On the whole, a person in the Middle Ages was familiar both with the dead and with his own death.

In the later medieval period—that is, the twelfth to the fifteenth centuries—three subtle but significant shifts take place that slowly, almost imperceptibly, begin to change the common attitude toward death and dying, even while the "tamed death" is still very much in place. First, the focus of death tends slightly more toward the individual and slightly less toward the collective destiny of mankind. Second and related to the first, the judgment scene in artistic renderings moves from the remote and delayed time at the end of the world to the bedchamber.[7] Together, these two shifts emphasize the individual, his own biography, and the moment of death itself, thus joining "in a single scene the security of the collective rite and the anxiety of a personal interrogation."[8] The appearance of the cadaver in art signals a third shift within the paradigm of the "tamed death." If not yet fully feared, death nevertheless presents a sense of horror in the imagination of the late medieval person for whom death threatens to detach him from the things he possessed during his own lifetime. In summary, Ariès contends that "beginning with the eleventh century a formerly unknown relationship developed between the death of each individual and his awareness of being an individual. . . . In the mirror of his own death each man would discover the secret of his individuality."[9]

These three shifts that move the focus toward one's own death inaugurate a longer process of separating individuals from their communities. This process intensifies in the eighteenth century, when the death of the "other" captures popular attention. In the Romantic era, death is often portrayed as exalted and dramatized, disquieting and greedy. With the experience or threat of the "other's" disappearance after death, a new emphasis is placed on death as rupture, as a break from the ordinary.[10] The old familiarity with death and with the dead is losing its grip: in its place comes "a new intolerance of separation"[11] on the part of survivors, who no longer approach death through the language of longstanding customs. This general unwillingness to accept the departure of loved ones gives death a negative valence, whereas for several hundred years prior it was accepted as part of the community's and the family's life. The dying person lying in bed is no longer routinely depicted artistically since the moment and the event of the person's death per se no longer comprise the important matter. What matters now is the presence of death throughout life—the sort of death that separates one person from another whether through sickness or isolation or loneliness, and ultimately definitively at the moment of death itself. As Ariès concludes, death "has become something metaphysical . . . like the separation of man and wife or two dear old friends. . . . The pain of death is seen not as the real suffering of the death agony but as something comparable to the sorrow of a broken friendship."[12]

The old customs that enabled the dying person to preside over the assembly of her community in the face of her own impending death now enter into a period of decline since the performance of these customs requires an acceptance of death, which is precisely what the accreting unwillingness to endure separation denies. As these customs break down, death is untamed. Whereas the tamed death was the norm for centuries with subtle internal shifts taking place slowly over time, the "complete reversal in customs seems to have occurred in one generation."[13] The seeds of this revolution begin to take root in the middle of the nineteenth century, and before the middle of the twentieth century they are in full bloom.

In place of the practices and protocols that opened the individual and the community to death as part of social life, new procedures are established to deal with the unfamiliarity and general undesirability of death. The purpose of these new customs is not to make death once again familiar but instead to make it invisible. The first of these new customs is to keep the dying patient ignorant of his fate and isolated from his circumstances and from his community. In this way, the dying person is saved from the unpleasantness of his demise while the community is spared the corresponding unpleasantness of directly confronting the reality of death. The acceptable style of death becomes that in which the dying person pretends he is not going to die.[14]

The second custom, which Ariès notices emerging with World War I, is "the taboo against mourning and everything in public life that reminded one of death, at least the so-called natural (i.e., nonviolent) death."[15] Ariès likens mourning to a contagious disease in the modern milieu, a malady to public wellbeing and therefore quarantined until inoculated.[16] When one is unable to quell the tempest of mourning, social ostracization procedures are typically enacted, presumably for the good of the many. Furthering this point, funeral director and essayist Thomas Lynch detects the suppression of mourning in the rising prevalence of "celebrations of life," in which the primary objective is to reroute the living away from grief and sorrow, returning them as quickly as possible to a more convenient, unperturbed state.[17]

In order to prepare for the success of the taboo against mourning and as a way to further segregate the dying from the healthy, a third novel custom has taken hold, which Ariès labels the "medicalization of death." This final move encompasses a broad array of changes in the modern approach to death, but first and foremost it involves the relocation of the sick and dying from the home to the hospital. In this contained environment where the experts and specialists of the hospital team preside over the dying process, death is "dissected, cut to bits by a series of little steps, which finally makes it impossible to know which step [is] the real death, the one in which consciousness [is] lost, or the one in which breathing [stops]."[18] The dying (and the dead) are kept out of contact with the ordinary happenings of the world outside, granting a secluded place to suffering while allowing for the security of "collective happiness."[19] Whereas the containment of the community's pain to the hospital room leads to the denial or at most the therapizing of mourning after death, the disciplined concealment of dying persons within medical procedures goads the need to have professionals make the body "disappear" after death. Lynch bemoans the now customary absence of the actual corpse in the celebratory memorial services, noting that these "bodiless obsequies" further estrange the living from the dead. As he contends, "this estrangement, this disconnect, this refusal to deal with our dead (their corpses), could be reasonably expected to handicap our ability to deal with death (the concept, the idea of it)," which also suggests a general "inability to deal authentically with life."[20]

Ariès attributes the genesis of these modern developments primarily to the United States, which then exported its approach to death and modern life to the industrialized countries of the old continent. He introduces his analysis of the relationship between American civilization and the modern attitude toward death with an excerpt from Jacques Maritain's *Reflections on America*, published in 1965: "You reach the point of thinking in a sort of dream that the act of dying amid happy smiles, amid white garments like angels' wings, would be a veritable pleasure, a moment of no consequence. Relax, take it easy, it's nothing."[21] Death, it seems, is functionally treated as an event of no real consequence.

Whereas the old customs facilitated communication between the dying and his circumstances, the individual and the community, and the living and the dead who were not considered altogether cut off from the survivors, these new customs facilitate a radically different situation. The sick and dying are isolated from their circumstances and from the ordinary movements of the outside world. The community silently endures the separation that death incurs without giving prolonged public spectacle to any interior emotions or suffering. The society as a whole progresses on as if death were not a part of its life, cordoning off from its public square certain areas where death and dying can be contained and professionally supervised.[22]

In her book about modern funerary practices, Jessica Mitford argues that this professionalization of death for profit in order to keep it hidden under a veneer of happiness became the raison d'être of the funeral industry, especially in the United States.[23] Partially in response to the imprecision of Mitford's occasionally accurate critique, Lynch sees himself situated vocationally between the dead and the living as a funeral director, thus taking up a true form of public service as he helps the dead get where they need to be—consigning the body to the elements—while helping the living begin a changed life without the deceased.[24] Lynch vouches for the direct correlation between confronting death and authentically engaging life, meaning of course that ignoring one dimension necessarily diminishes the other.

Ariès calls this modern approach to death the "forbidden death" and the "invisible death." The disciplining of death through a new set of social practices allows the individual and the culture alike to forget death. If death cannot be forgotten altogether, then it is "domesticated once and for all by the advance of technology, especially medical technology."[25] The community is thus protected from feeling too grievously the death of one of its own members. This attitude of self-preservation against suffering both derives from and contributes to a general penchant of modern society, which "no longer has a sufficient sense of solidarity; it has," according to Ariès, "actually abandoned responsibility for the organization of collective life. The community in the traditional sense of the word no longer exists. It has been replaced by an enormous mass of atomized individuals."[26]

Interlude: Transgressing the Forbidden, Seeing the Invisible

The forgetfulness of death and the separation of individuals from communities are mutually reinforcing phenomena. By denying the reality of death, modern societies fail to foster communication at the very moment when human life reaches its culmination. By undoing the fundamental communal nature of human persons, the need to meaningfully mark the end of life is radically diminished, for the connection between one life and the next is no longer assumed. As noted at the outset of this chapter, the failure to take death seriously prevents Christians from claiming the fullness of hope that the Christian faith promises. Christians, however, are not the only ones for whom this modern malaise is troubling. An array of post-Christian secular humanists—among others—reject this general modern approach to death. As they see it, this view does not allow for the authenticity of human existence because it is predicated on the fragmentation of life according to categories designed to preserve an ideal that furtively governs the machinations of the world.

For the remainder of this chapter, I concern myself with these post-Christian critiques of the modern approach to death that Ariès describes. In the latter portion of the chapter I consider Martin Heidegger's attempt to take death seriously in an intentionally *a*theological philosophical manner. Before that, however, the heart of this chapter is given to Rainer Maria Rilke, who is at least on the surface somewhat less hostile to the Christian narrative than Heidegger, though there is no mistaking his general distaste for the Christian viewpoint. Nevertheless, and almost in spite of himself, Rilke manages to open up new avenues for reflection that may, in the end, prove fruitful for the discerning Catholic theologian. One such theologian who finds Rilke's thought intriguing is Romano Guardini, whose own commentary on Rilke's apical work I have intentionally selected from among the nearly uncountable volumes of scholarship that have been devoted to analyzing Rilke. Guardini's work is unique because of his theological commitments and the sort of questions he therefore brings to reading Rilke, even though the analysis he performs is not strictly theological. With Guardini's help, we will see that Rilke attempts to portray a new vision of death and the dead, a vision that also bridges what he believes to be the too starkly separated realms of the dead and the living. In protest to the modern view of death that Ariès describes, Rilke will reach back into the Romantic period to carry forward the sensibilities of a more open, more courageous, more welcoming disposition that sees beyond the presumed distinctions that modernity has exaggerated.[27]

Uniquely, Rilke wants to reestablish a relationship between the living and the dead without, however, starting from or proceeding toward a sense of solidarity or community among human persons to do so, as the Christian narrative would seek to do. The Christian option is nonviable for him because he believes that it tenders an inauthentic view of the beyond that attenuates not only the importance of the realm of the dead but also the realm of the living by association.[28] For Rilke, the beginning of the story will be the individual who asks the question about the possibility of real relationship; the story's end will find this individual blending into the impersonal unity of being. Rilke will try to follow this process of becoming up to and beyond the moment of change at death, a moment that heralds the deeper truth about life and death.

The Rilkean Opening

In late January 1912 Rainer Maria Rilke paced pensively along the cliffs of Duino castle, pondering a response to a troubling business inquiry, when suddenly an urgent question pulsed through him: "Who, if I cried out, would hear me among the angelic orders?" (*First Elegy*).[29] In the solitude of that windy afternoon, Rilke gave voice to the deepest existential question of human life: is there a response to the cries of my heart, or am I truly alone? Rilke's ten elegies, composed in creative outbursts over the course of the following decade, give verse to the answer that he—the attentive and skillful poet—received through inspiration he later described as radically intense and even violent.[30] The *Duino Elegies*—alongside the companion poems under the title *Sonnets to Orpheus*—is not only a work of the finest poetic achievement, but also one that makes a forceful claim to the truth of life vis-à-vis death, a claim that uniquely and simultaneously captures the prevailing view of modern man and exceeds this view.[31] Rilke is the poet of openness who paints a picture of human existence that neither needs nor welcomes divine mediation.[32] In the end, he creates the highest poetry of atheist humanism that, by logical narrative extension, proposes a wholly secular analogue to the communion of saints.

Rilke's diagnosis of the modern condition is similar to the one Rahner offers and thus bears a strong resemblance to the one I have already espoused in these pages. He thinks that modern persons invariably tend to avoid death and are thus cut off from the inaccessible beyond. With the *Duino Elegies*, he understands himself to be speaking a truth that runs deeper than this modern flatness; in fact, he conceives of himself as a kind of prophet who expresses what he hears coming through his own faculties. The *Elegies* are not restricted to the level of subjective experience; rather, they make far-reaching claims about the nature of life, death, and human existence. It is therefore appropriate that Guardini subjected this poetry to analysis in order to test the veracity of the claims made therein. I intend to show that Rilke presents a pseudo-narrative that at once assumes and subverts the form of the Catholic narrative in which he was raised. What Guardini detects is that the key to Rilke's narrative is the diminishment and eventual erasure of personhood. Rilke begins his *Elegies* with an isolating focus on the individual for whom relationship to any other is at best temporary and ends with an image of a "communion" of shared loneliness.[33] Indeed, Rilke's beginning predetermines his end.

In order to cast light on the logic running from Rilke's beginning to his end, I explicate three main themes of the *Elegies*, which work together to disclose the essential shape of Rilke's thought. These themes include Rilke's primary understanding of death, his conception of the angel, and his doctrine of love. Once these themes are sufficiently interpreted, I then evaluate and critique the status Rilke affords personhood and the divine, leading me at last to my final assessment of the Rilkean opening.

Death: The Other Relation

To Rilke, death is "life's averted half."[34] Like the dark side of the moon that is forever turned away from the sightline of the earth, death is that part of the whole hidden from the gaze of the living. Moreover, it is the very mode of the living's observation that keeps death hidden, for humans set themselves against the world as observers, yet their observation is incomplete and fallacious because they keep themselves at a distance from what they see. Rilke contends that it is an engrained tendency, especially in the modern era, for individuals to theoretically analyze existence rather than accept and be transformed through the wholeness of being.

According to the *Elegies*, death is not the end of life—a loss; rather, death is the fulfillment of what life is not in itself but nevertheless is bound to become. A telling sign of this occurs in the *Fourth Elegy*, in which Rilke brings the reader to a theater stage to watch the performance of his own heart. To quote Hamlet, "the play's the thing," and yet the reader sits as a spectator watching what really matters. The position of the spectator is the metaphor for the living human who remains removed from fully participating in the drama of existence that is the process of becoming and spends his energies instead evaluating the performance based on a critic's set of criteria. When the stage goes dark, though, this mode of observation is revealed for the deep distractedness that it is. Death brings about the position of no longer being set against the world like a spectator watching a performance; now, the spectator takes up his role in the performance he thought he was watching, becoming free to sway with the movements of the play. As with a sigh of relief, Rilke announces that this is finally a real play, as those dying are stripped of the pretenses to which the living bind themselves. Now, in death, the cycle of transformation may proceed unimpeded: the dead become, according to Rilke, "open."[35]

At the moment of death, the one who was once the spectator—who evaluates and judges and conforms to conventions that keep him removed from the drama of existence—begins to become truly free of his attachments. The mystery of becoming is the deeper truth running through both life and death, both living and dying. This deeper truth is a dominant theme of Rilke's work beginning with the *First Elegy*. The dead no longer desire their own desires; they are released from the illusion of shared responsibility. As Guardini sums up for Rilke, "all the meaningful relationships which existed between things and events on earth . . . are now like bonds which no longer have anything to tie, or garments in which there is no longer a body."[36] The dead do not murmur wishes (*Fifth Elegy*), as they inhabit a soundless fate (*Tenth Elegy*). What this portrayal of death and the dead establishes is a view of life defined as a transient and futile period in which authenticity is exercised through the renunciation of attachments, wishes, perspectives, and relationships. Death is the realm of release from one's desires, when the drama of becoming enters into fulfillment. The dead have no need of the living for they are free of all ties that bind. The living may hear the silent dead calling from the averted side of life, but only to command the renunciation of all that weighs them down and keeps them from entering harmoniously into the natural movement of the world.

Through death's disclosure, life is given its true character; Rilke seeks to define life as a space of becoming. At the close of the *Second Elegy* he likens the space of the living to a "strip of fruitful land between river and rock."[37] In this space, the true task of the living is to

> imprint this provisional, perishable earth so deeply, so patiently and passionately in ourselves that its reality shall arise in us again "invisibly." *We are the bees of the invisible. Nous butinons éperdument le miel du visible, pour l'accumuler dans la grande ruche d'or de l'Invisible.*[38] The *Elegies* show us at this work, at the work of these continual conversions of the beloved visible and tangible into the invisible vibrations and excitation of our own nature, which introduces new vibration-frequencies into the vibration-spheres of the universe.[39]

This task is poetic in nature, for it requires engaging fully with what appears in the world without becoming attached to it.[40] In a poetic manner, the measure of life unfurls through uncovering the hymn of "becoming" from each and every note of existing matter, recognizing that all the many things from which these notes come forth are passing away while the hymn itself unites the two halves of existence: life and death.[41] Death, however, is the greater half, the half in which the renunciation is complete and the drama moves unimpeded toward fulfillment.[42]

In the Rilkean view, humans are not now in a natural state—their aversion to death is the clearest sign of this malady. Humans are distracted; they are attached to their own wishes, to their own will, and to objects that appear in the world beside them.[43] Rilke juxtaposes the human with the animal in the *Eighth Elegy* to make this human deficiency apparent. Unlike the human, the animal looks out "into the Open" and does not turn its gaze back upon itself. The animal is without bounds, unconcerned with its own condition, and thus disposes itself purely in its outward gaze. The animal does not mistake itself for "a 'someone'" but is rather "a point at which existence breaks through."[44]

The "hero" whom Rilke introduces in the *Sixth Elegy* offers a glimpse into what an authentic human being might look like. Resembling the animal, the hero only ever ascends in being and charges headlong, without hesitation, into a shifting maze of perpetual danger. He renounces distractions and moves out into the Open. As Guardini reads it, the hero's "prime concern" is "'to choose' and 'be able'. . . . He masters himself by his decisiveness and dominates his environment through deeds."[45] In contraposition to this supposedly paradigmatic figure, the commonplace modern human being is a pale and distorted figment. In Martin Heidegger's estimation, this "modern man . . . is called the one who wills. The more venturesome will more strongly in that they will in a different way from the purposeful self-assertion of the objectifying of the world."[46] Like the animal and reminiscent of Nietzsche's Overman, Rilke's hero accepts life as it is.[47] He ventures out into the Open toward that unity of being that fuses the realms of the living and the dead.

According to Rilke, death is not altogether different from life, let alone life's opposite. Death is the averted half of existence, the other—and greater—part of the unity of being. In protesting death, humans fail to accept *what is* as they prop themselves up as the arbiters of reality. For Rilke, though, death is the whole landscape beyond the boundaries of this "strip of fruitful land between river and rock" that the living inhabit (*Second Elegy*). Accepting death means assenting to the dimensions of the earth and participating in the transformation of the visible into the invisible. Whereas life is the time for speaking, for singing, for poeticizing, and for praising, death is the realm where the word surpasses the speaker, the song breaks free of the singer, the poem is the realized achievement of the now forgotten poet, and the praise belongs to no one and goes to no one. The turn toward death is a turn toward the whole process of becoming unto the wholeness of being itself.

Angel: The Fullness of Being

The Rilkean angel is the absolute intensity of being; upon this being the poet fixes his imagination. This is the unknowable figure to whom the first words of the *Elegies* go out but from whom no response is possible. "Above us, beyond us, the angel plays," as Rilke says in the *Fourth Elegy*. Peter Fritz calls Rilke's angel "a voyeur of an empty world."[48] It is against this remote and personally compassionless being whom Rilke considers nonetheless perfect that existence itself is measured. The hero acclaimed in the *Sixth Elegy* is but a faint echo of this being's absolute volume.[49]

Rilke is clear that the angel of the *Elegies* is not what Christians would otherwise imagine. In a letter from late 1925, he writes, "The 'angel' of the elegies has nothing to do with the angel of the Christian heaven (rather with the angel figures of Islam). . . . The angel of the *Elegies* is that creature in whom the transformation of the visible into the invisible, which we are accomplishing, appears already consummated."[50] The ultimate achievement of the very task in which human existence is authenticated—the transformation of the visible into the invisible—is identical with the being of the angel. Rather than a personal being, the angel is more an ideal in which the whole process of becoming is contained. Through his magnum opus, Rilke is attempting to show the world from the angel's point of view.[51] In this figure, the whole of life-and-death is contained.

Rilke offers an especially fecund image of angelic existence in the *Second Elegy*, where we find one of the most elegant stanzas in all of literature:

> Early successes, Creation's pampered favorites,
> mountain-ranges, peaks growing red in the dawn
> of all Beginning,—pollen of the flowering godhead,

joints of pure light, corridors, stairways, thrones,
space formed from essence, shields made of ecstasy, storms
of emotion whirled into rapture, and suddenly, alone,
mirrors: which scoop up the beauty that has streamed from their face
and gather it back, into themselves, entire.[52]

While the first section of nature-images relates to the correspondence between object and subject in the being of the angel and the later section of architecture-images relates to the angelic order in its august majesty, the final section alone bears the extra emphasis on its singular image: *mirrors*. This image captures better than any other Rilke's conception of the angel. Angelic perfection is realized in the final retrieval of all that they give out. According to Guardini, "The Angels do not lose their glory when they radiate it. . . . This is the secret of their superhuman quality. And this is why, although they are involved in a mighty flux or movement, they remain indestructible."[53] An angel does not give any gift of itself that it does not take up again. For the angel, there is no sacrifice; for humans, on the other hand, there is nothing but loss.[54] In Rilke's haunting verse: "But we, when moved by deep feeling, evaporate; we / breathe ourselves out and away; from moment to moment / our emotion grows fainter, like a perfume" (*Second Elegy*).[55] The radical impermanence of human life in and of itself is on display in this inevitable energy loss. The only remedy is to accede to the movement of the whole, which the angel embodies, so as to return to the unity of being what has come forth from it. Human life is thus bound for erasure through absorption.

When he first introduces his angel, Rilke describes him as an "overpowering existence" (*First Elegy*). This terrifying being cannot but consume the lesser being should he draw near. The human—that is, Rilke, the poet, the man crying out on the cliffs of Duino, each of us—would be swept up in the return of glory that comes in the angel's gaze, like a mirror gathering up every last image passing before it. In the face of the total intensity of being, nothing less can stand apart. If the angel ceases to remain aloof in its majesty—high above and ignorant of the lesser creature—then it will absorb that creature without ever even knowing any change to itself.

The indifference of the angel to particular creatures is due to its relationship to the universe as a whole, which is the angel's proper sphere of existence. Rilke's angels are incapable of personal, particular feelings for individual beings; the only feeling of which they are capable is cosmic.[56] They are incapable of sensing any difference between what humans know as the "here" of the living and the "beyond" of the dead. For the angels, there is only "the great unity" in which they "are at home."[57] This facet of angelic existence underscores the inauthentic nature that comes from the human neglect of death.

At the zenith of existence, then, the angel stands as the self-fulfilled and complete, abstract and idealized, remote and indifferent, uncharitable and unsympathetic being against whom all other beings are measured and found irremediably wanting. In particular, the human who gives out and loses himself is radically inadequate, for the perfection of being is found in the one who regains all that he gives out. The response to the question of the first line of the *Elegies*—"Who, if I cried out, would hear me among the angelic orders?"—is, definitively, *no one*. If an angel did turn toward this creature, the angel would absorb and therefore erase the individuality of the lesser one. In the human's approaching death, this same process is even now in motion, whether he recognizes it or not (though likely not). With the possibility of communion with the angel ruled out completely, the individual's "loneliness becomes still deeper,"[58] and the subsequent question of the *Elegies* becomes the following: "With whom can we establish a vital relationship of giving and receiving, a mutual association in which our need of companionship would be fulfilled?" The answer the poet gives is, ultimately, "with no one and nothing."[59] The inevitability of this companionless fate becomes apparent in Rilke's doctrine of love.

Love: Seeking without Finding

The heart of the Rilkean doctrine of love is the conviction that perfect love has no object. This notion of love without object will eventually do away with the lover as subject as well as the beloved as object. Rilke imagines absolute love as pure movement freed from the confines of intentionality and communication, which only fabricate the illusion of permanence in the exchange between lovers. Rilkean love moves out into the Open as it breaks away from the transient personal poles of the lover and the beloved. This love tends ineluctably toward pure being, which overwhelms divisions, distinctions, and individuality, as we have seen already with Rilke's angel. Love ceases to be love if it stops at some object, and it fails to remain love if it attempts to confirm the presumed permanence of the subject. It is movement rather than exchange: love is only love if it goes out into empty space.

The necessity of vacuity for absolute loving squares with what Guardini calls the "deep feeling of homelessness—the sense of not belonging—which underlies Rilke's view of life."[60] In a turn toward the psychological, Guardini connects the view Rilke purveys to Rilke's own personal deficiency in establishing meaningful relationships, of ever feeling at home anywhere or of providing a home to anyone else.[61] With the *Elegies*, Rilke claims that this homelessness is constitutive of human existence, yet humans habitually deceive themselves in attempting to find a home for themselves and give a home to others through their peculiar interpretations of the world. "Our interpreted world" (*First Elegy*) is that in which a sense of permanence is assumed and asserted, as if the stream of becoming stopped with particular moments or places or persons. Through his more perceptive and accepting poetic eyes, Rilke sees that this shelter-making is fictitious. The night (*First Elegy*) appears as the last possible refuge for the homeless heart, but it too disenchants even as it covers the one who seeks rest. The one seeking a home cannot find one, just as the one who wants to give shelter to another cannot actually provide any. According to Rilke's diagnosis, the problem is not with the seeking but with the ends that are sought. He wants to uncouple seeking from ends and ultimately from origins so as to portray love as a seeking without beginning or end. This—and this alone—is a pure and unobstructed loving.

In these verses, Friedrich Nietzsche's voice echoes and Martin Heidegger's lungs draw breath. For his part, Nietzsche lambastes the desire to find and give a home, to project reason and meaning and stability into existence as if there were substantial entities that resist the current of becoming. To him, what *appears* is reality, besides which there is nowhere else to go, no one else to seek, no purpose that will explain what has, is, and will become of life. Man fallaciously desires to establish himself in a sense of meaning and to orient himself toward the demands of a definite "other." Man wants to have a reason for the way he feels; he wants to have a reason for why he acts and, moreover, he wants to find that reason within himself. He believes himself to be free—that is, a fixed point in a stream of becoming: an island of responsibility and consciousness. The problem is that, empirically speaking, man has *arrived at* rather than *departed from* consciousness, while the motivations he takes to be primary are in fact the results of a process of becoming, where becoming itself is the totality of the process. Man is addicted to this presumption of cause, agency, and intentionality. This addiction is really a failure of perception, for man is unable or unwilling to stomach life and thus live authentically. Nietzsche thus commissions his prophet to call for the disavowal of desiring things, seeking security, or willing intention: "And let this be called by me *immaculate* perception of all things: that I desire nothing of things, except that I may lie down before them like a mirror with a hundred eyes."[62]

Rilke makes a muse out of this call to perception-without-willing. It seems as if stars twinkle to elicit your gaze, or waves of the sea come to meet you, or music chances upon you from somewhere else, but, according to Rilke in the *First Elegy*, this is just the illusory desire for control and stable meaning as a form of self-validation. Rilke makes what Guardini calls "an implicit reproach" against this illusory desire as if to say, "You are only thinking of yourself. You do not recognize your trust; you only make demands."[63] The lover—the one who should exercise pure perceiving and send his gaze out into the unlimited Open—is distracted by and ultimately preoccupied with the one he sees as the beloved, believing that his love goes to that one who will give him a home and whom he may reciprocally shelter: "Weren't you always / distracted by expectation, as if every event / announced a beloved? (Where can you find a place to keep her, with all the huge strange thoughts inside you / going and coming and often staying all night?)" (*First Elegy*).[64] Rilke thus indicts lovers for acquiescing to the myth of intentionality: that self-propagating delusion that loving goes out to a "someone" and that loving makes a "someone" out of the lover. The heart moves distractedly in search of rest rather than moving for the sake of movement itself.

Hence comes Heidegger's inspiration. In his project to uncover the authenticity of *Dasein* in its manner of existence, he seeks after that "moment of vision" in which *Dasein* is freed from dissipating distractions and resolutely claims, in anticipatory fashion, the entirety of his *being-toward-death*.[65] In terms analogous to Augustine's in the *Confessions*, Heidegger describes one's dissipation in the world as occurring in one of three modes: as absorption into objects, insubstantial curiosity, and the lust for praise and validation.[66] Rilke's portrayal of the lover who fixates on the beloved shows signs of each of these three modes of falling: his loving and seeking is absorbed in his object (the beloved), he looks around for a home in the world, and he desires the validation of his existence in love's reciprocity. Authentic existence is constituted in a refusal to accept any object, horizon, or desire as constitutive of one's being; rather, as a lover without a beloved, the authentic one charges ahead unbound and without distraction. Heidegger could not agree more with Rilke when the poet writes that it is time for the lover to free himself of the burden of the beloved (*First Elegy*).

In sum, the Rilkean doctrine of love dictates that there is no such thing as a love that gives one a spiritual home in another; love does not offer a definite place of rest. The true lover is not the one who is fulfilled but instead the one who remains unfulfilled yet continues loving. Perfect love requires no longer desiring fulfillment.[67] In the process of loving, the beloved serves as nothing more than a gateway to the realm of openness. Rilke's love therefore has no ultimate use for persons as any kind of substantial beings. In fact, the notion of personhood is an obstacle to loving (as we will see more clearly in the following subsection). What the lover really loves in the beloved is the "'spacial' quality"[68] he finds there. The space in the beloved's features leads into cosmic space where the beloved no longer abides (*Fourth Elegy*). The other person—the beloved—is left behind as absolute loving moves into the Open.[69] Death, then, is the final disclosure of pure loving with a remainder of zero, for death brings about the lover's adeptness for the smooth motions of loving ultimately freed from the distracting obstacle of the beloved (*Fifth Elegy*). The beloved is now well gone: this "other" has nothing to do with the lover's pure act of loving. Moreover, the lover himself is dissolved into his act as he becomes pure movement instead of what he previously assumed himself to be: an agent with intention.[70] In the land of the dead, Rilke's thesis is most fully demonstrated: absolute loving pursues "nothing but distance" (*Seventh*

Elegy).[71] Love "attains perfection when it is directed, no longer towards any 'Thou,' but out and beyond any person or thing."[72]

Personhood: The Disturbing Factor

With these three main themes now in place, we can better conceive of how the beginning Rilke assumes preordains the end he sees. His vision of the last things is thoroughly impersonal because the poet's own speaking and own listening are the final arbiters of meaning. "This most consistent of all individualists"[73] does not grant the prerogative of meaning to any other personal agents, especially such a one whose address to him would constitute his own existence; rather, he speaks to an angel who cannot hear him and who does not speak to him. This beginning devoid of listening *to* or *for* a personal being leads Rilke to a destiny that erases personhood altogether.[74]

Rilke is a spokesperson of modernity because he assumes himself first of all; he takes his own existence for granted.[75] From the very beginning, the *Duino Elegies* takes up the situation of modernity, where individuals exist in an atmosphere "of oppressed loneliness—one might also say desolation."[76] Rilke does not question why he is or how he came into being; rather, he questions what will become of him. His doctrine of love reveals the answer he accepts: the authenticity of his existence is measured in heading out beyond all objects to the Open, thus all traces of his particularity will dissolve into the great unity of being.

As Rilke begins to make clear in the *Fourth Elegy*, this unity secures the ongoing existence of the dead who, ultimately, are relieved of all personal relations.[77] According to the portrayal of the lonely wanderer in the *Tenth Elegy*, "Death does not mean loss or deprivation but essential reality. Indeed it is *more* essential and more real than our own realm only it is situated on the 'other side.' It is one of the two 'relations' which make up the 'world' in the true sense of the word."[78] This "other relation"—life's averted half—discloses this present relation (what we call life) for what it is. Though concrete personhood—what Rilke calls personality—seems to exist in the present life of the here and now, these appearances are really rooted in the one unifying substratum of being, which is even now becoming the unified reality that overwhelms the ephemeral distinctions of time and space. As Guardini notes, Rilke's play of the heart in the *Fourth Elegy* begins to show that

> By our reality as persons we disturb the play of forms! We see here how deadly serious Rilke is in repeating that same assumption which underlies his conception of love: The "self" is a disruptive agent. And not merely when it is selfish, self-asserting and self-affirming, but just the "self" as such—the human personality.[79]

The opening question of the entire work is a question about the "self," by which Rilke means the human person as such: is the self isolated, or is it relational?[80] The answer that comes quickly near the beginning of the *First Elegy* is that the self is isolated. The question posed through the rest of the poem is then: what becomes of the self? The answer Rilke's reader receives is that the self's destiny—the task of its existence—is to erase itself as it merges into the unity of being that encompasses both the living and the dead. In fact, the first seven elegies combined present a description of how ultimately non-relational an individual person is and thus how he is bound for erasure by absorption—an outcome that the final three elegies will show.[81] Indeed, neither one in the angelic order nor any other human can respond to the loneliness of the individual.

Rilke is thus making a definitive claim about the world itself—that is, about the whole world, the entirety of reality that stretches across the realms of both the living and the dead. To see and know the world as it truly is requires a purely outward gaze like that of the animal, which peers ever-forward into the Open (*Eighth Elegy*). Twisted around, humans are oriented to seeing "objects—not the Open"; the animal, by contrast, sees "God in front."[82] It is both curious and revealing that for one of only three times in the *Elegies* Rilke here invokes the name of God, who is otherwise silent in the work.[83] Within the logic of this *Eighth Elegy*—and indeed within the logic of the *Elegies* as a whole—Rilke is most certainly reinterpreting the meaning of "God." This is not a personal God, not one upon whom one could ever aspire to gaze, whom one could know or call upon. This is not the God whom one would fear, nor is this the God who would have anything to give. There is no objective quality to this God. This God is "only 'the endless road,'" which one can only embrace through an "'inner indifference of the spirit'"[84]—that is, without desire, intention, or need. If the individual gazes forward and sees some object—some person—then he is not seeing properly; rather, he is seeing what his own impoverished desire for self-affirmation projects.[85] In the end, "God is not an '*object* of love' but something which stands beyond everything that can be approached directly: God is only 'given' to the extent that the will to confront Him has been overcome."[86] A significant achievement of Guardini's commentary is the elucidation of how Rilke's doctrine of God aligns perfectly with his doctrine of love: "Perfect love is not directed towards a person, but simply passes through him into the 'Open'. . . . And when this is achieved the real God is present, for the 'Open' is God."[87] Moreover, Rilke takes his purely erotic notion of love and construes God accordingly. In the process (of becoming), the personal element of the divine and the human alike is negated.

This view stands in direct opposition to the Christian view. For the Christian, love is understood *from* God whereas Rilke develops a notion of God from his assumption about the pure eroticism of love. The Christian view thus derives the meaning of existence in fundamentally personal terms, whereas Rilke accepts an impersonal force that serves a depersonalizing process of becoming. On the individual level, Rilke moves toward an extreme sense of particularity without an accompanying notion of relational participation—he follows this through to a conception of personhood as a self-erasing phenomenon. On the cosmic level, Rilke moves toward participation without particularity all the way through to the absolute, indiscriminate unity of being. In unique fashion, Rilke does not succumb to the exclusive options of Neoplatonic absorption or of nihilistic alienation; instead, he takes the path of nihilistic alienation to arrive at a (pan)cosmic view of absorption into being. This is not a standard pantheism, for here being itself is worshiped and the world participates in that unity.[88] Whereas both Nietzsche and Heidegger end in a loneliness unto nothing, Rilke moves toward a kind of communion between the living and the dead, although it is ultimately a thoroughly secularized communion of shared loneliness. This is what comes of the Rilkean opening.

The opening itself derives from Rilke's relationship to Christianity and a fundamental decision he makes regarding Christianity. More precisely, when he self-consciously throws off the Christian narrative, he must separate himself from that narrative's fount. Guardini recognizes this and thus comments that "As [Rilke] 'withdrew from' [Christianity] he incorporated the Christian concepts into myth—a process which is continually going on in the development of Western thought. He took away their real meaning and secularized them, giving everything . . . back to the Earth."[89] He gives God to the earth—with the fullness of the earth equated with being itself—rather than referring the earth as creation to God as Creator. He therefore violates the *Shema* and the continuous Christian narrative expressed in the creed, which begins with belief in *God, the Father almighty, Creator of Heaven and Earth.*

As a consequence of severing the world from a personal God who, as Father, creates all things through his Word as an act of self-giving communication, the final meaning of the world—now no longer understood as creation—is radically altered. As mentioned above, Rilke has an analogue to the "communion of saints," but his company remains isolated individuals whose definition comes from the existential act of pure listening to "*God's* voice" (*First Elegy*). When we recall that Rilke's God is not in any way personal but rather the Open, then we understand that Rilke's saints are passing over to the accreting unity of being that death will finally disclose.

Likewise, in place of a doctrine of the forgiveness of sins, Rilke posits novel notions of purification and something like Original Sin. The murmuring dead whom Rilke hears through their tombstones are calling out for the completion of the task they imperfectly accomplished on that "strip of fruitful land between river and rock" (*Second Elegy*) where they were to toil as the "*bees of the invisible.*"[90] They died with some lingering attachment to objects and thus their capacity for the absolute openness to being—that is, love—was deficient. Something like the doctrine of purgatory and the remission of sins hereby suggests itself. Correlatively, something like the doctrine of Original Sin faintly echoes in the close of the *Eighth Elegy*, where Rilke asks who has turned us around, away from openness. That something is constitutively and, we might say, orientationally wrong with human beings is a claim that Rilke shares with the Christian faith. Unlike the Christian faith, Rilke believes that the so-lution is the ultimate dissolution of relational bonds—to both people and things—rather than the redemption of these bonds through a divine mediator.

In place of the doctrines of the "resurrection of the body" and "life everlasting," Rilke proclaims a liberation from the confines of embodi-ment and an "'inward' transforming process which decides what we can 'take across' into the 'other relation.'"[91] The body disappears in the Rilkean view since the individual passes into the pure act of loving that sets him aright in the process of becoming. The individual is transformed into pure act and is no longer remembered as an actor. The everlasting life that Rilke imagines is one that calls back to the living from the realm of the dead, where there is already that deeper fruitfulness that inspires the singular task of those still existing between the river and the rock—that is, on this side of the world. And so Rilke sings of a new creation at the end of the *Ninth Elegy*, one in which all that is visible rises invisibly within the unity of being:

Earth, isn't this what you want: to arise within us,
invisible? Isn't it your dream
to be wholly invisible someday?—O Earth: invisible!
What, if not transformation, is your urgent command? . . .
You were always right, and your holiest inspiration
is our intimate companion, Death.[92]

In sum, Rilke changes the beginning of the narrative he received from the Christian faith and so the entire narrative that follows changes accordingly. If, as I argued primarily in the first chapter, the "commu-nion of saints" is an article of faith that develops as a logical narrative conclusion to the belief in the Father and in the Son, through the power of the Holy Spirit, then it also holds that changing the base narrative would alter the whole structure. Rilke thus offers a radically different alternative to the third part of the Apostles' Creed because he rejects the first part of the creed and replaces its claim about the personal ad-dress of God as Father and almighty Creator with a distinctively modern claim about the loneliness of the individual. Guardini sees how this new narrative at first seems like a gain since one no longer has to carry around the weight of the old narrative, except that the original narrative is like the sun that gives off rays of light and heat: "For a time, the light will go on shining and the rays of warmth will still radiate; but as soon as our link with the source is finally severed the power which issues from the source disappears as well."[93]

If the sun went dark at this moment, the earth would continue to receive its light for eight minutes. Once those eight minutes passed, there would be no source to give off new light. The modernity of a secular atheism is such a span of time: it draws its energy from a source it has since forgotten and the effects of whose extinguishment will eventually be felt. And indeed, Rilke himself appears to know this, for those who are the product of the narrative he assumes are ones for whom there is no warmth, no light, and ultimately no interpersonal communication. They are the "endlessly dead" (*Tenth Elegy*), the ones "who have gone the whole way and who attain the ultimate limits of the other world. They are remote and inaccessible. They know the final meaning of existence, but there is no word to express this meaning, for their fate is 'soundless.'"[94] Rather than persons, they are disappearing wraiths.

Why Rilke

I have undertaken this extensive treatment of Rilke's *Duino Elegies* because the vision of life after death he espouses therein is actually a description of what the Christian faith—and the hope found therein— seeks to open up. The Rilkean opening is ultimately a dark corner of isolation and noncommunication. All the same, Rilke's failure is productive from a Catholic perspective. He is able to apprehend what Nietzsche before him and Heidegger after him see regarding the need to venture into the hazards of being unto the loneliest loneliness; he is also able to move toward what Neoplatonists see regarding the desire for immortality and for the superiority of being as opposed to the transience it connects to the material world. Rilke thus makes the two right moves in the wrong way: he attempts to take death seriously but fails to do so because he reduces life to an abstract process of becoming, and he attempts to move beyond death but cannot see any real life there because the being he assumes is uncharitable in its absoluteness. Treating Rilke shows us that fully apprehending the meaning of *communio sanctorum* as an unbroken communion among the living and the (blessed) dead is not just an issue of the failure of the imagination but also of how and by what the imagination is formed.

The View from Heidegger

While it might be surprising that Romano Guardini would find Rilke helpful to the Christian theological task of renewing the eschatological imagination, it is certainly not surprising that Guardini's opinion of Rilke would differ from that of the avowedly post-Christian philosopher Martin Heidegger. Even so, the precise nature of their disagreement relative to their interpretation of Rilke's value occurs on unexpected grounds. Both Guardini and Heidegger are drawn to Rilke in part because of the way the poet confronts rather than skirts the question of death. For Guardini, Rilke's double movement of facing death and searching for the renewal of life (or being) is instructive, while his individualizing paradigm ultimately dooms his project to failure. For Heidegger, it is the combination of the confrontation with death and the existential individualism that is appealing, while the residual desire to assume rather than consistently interrogate being is what disappoints. As the final task of this chapter, I examine not only Heidegger's opinion of Rilke but also the way in which Heidegger's own distinctively modern view of death directly opposes the Christian narrative. Precisely because of Heidegger's continuity and dissimilitude with respect to Rilke's view of death, the lessons of this chapter's analysis of the modern approaches to death will become clearer as we prepare to move toward the drama of the Christian doctrines of creation, death, and resurrection in the person of Christ.

Rilke as Poet in a Destitute Time

Heidegger composed the essay "What are Poets For?" in 1946 to commemorate the twentieth anniversary of Rilke's death. The essay begins with a question that Friedrich Hölderlin penned in his elegy "Bread and

Wine": "*and what are poets for in a destitute time?*"[95] Heidegger's understanding of the time about which Hölderlin speaks allows him to stipulate what role the poet plays in such a time. In regards to this criterion, Heidegger will judge both Rilke's success and failure as a poet for such a time.

The time that Heidegger will call "destitute" is the time of technology. As one of his commentators summarizes, Heidegger considers technology to be the processes for "self-assertive production, self-assertive imposition of human will on things regardless of their own essential natures," which render everything else, "including man himself," nothing other than material for this production.[96] Technology locks human beings into an inauthentic state whereby they are alienated from their own nature.[97] This state of alienation arises from and is perpetuated by the errant human desire to assume the truth of one's own being rather than subjecting one's existence to thoroughgoing scrutiny.[98]

Interestingly, Heidegger relates the dominion of technology to "Americanism," which is predicated on the separation of man from things through the objectifying production process that moves objects through the world market.[99] Even though Heidegger is wholly uninterested in sociological analysis, the association he makes is reminiscent of the one that Ariès makes—along with Maritain, Mitford, Lynch, and others—regarding the medicalization, professionalization, and compartmentalization of dying and death for the sake of safeguarding the mythos of happiness. This destitute time of technology is the time of the "world's night," a night that lacks the "unconcealedness of the nature of pain, death, and love," in which the "realm of being withdraws within which pain and death and love belong together."[100] The role of the poet in this darkness is "to stop, listen, hear, remember, and respond to the call that comes from Being . . . to open up and take true measure of the dimension of existence."[101] The poet is the one who reaches into the abyss of being where others dare not go. Rilke is a poet in a destitute time because he recognizes the destitution of mortals who are neither aware nor capable of their own mortality and who "have not yet come into ownership of their own nature."[102] Rilke perceives and responds to the negation of death that results from the self-assertion of technological objectification. The success of Rilke lies in his attempt to "'read the word death *without* negation,'"[103] as Heidegger quotes approvingly from one of Rilke's own letters.

The poet's task is to wrestle language free from its complicity in the business of the world in order to speak truthfully. For Heidegger, truth is not a transcendent and certainly not a metaphysical reality, but rather the "unconcealedness of that which is as something is."[104] Truth is not about the correct ordering of a thing to a system, as if its framing (*Gestell*) were its truth. Heidegger's method in service of his ultimate goal—to re-mind philosophy about its forgetting about the question of being—is to interrogate "that which is" within its "framing" in order to uncouple the thing from its framing.[105] As he announced in *Being and Time*, the entry point for this interrogation of being is the human being—*Dasein*—who is "ontically distinguished by the fact that in its very Being . . . Being is an *issue* for it."[106] Through the contaminating influence of metaphysical comportment transmitted through Western philosophy, Heidegger sees modern life as destitute because the question of being, which only the particular *Dasein* can decide, is habitually neglected.[107] Heidegger lauds the poetry of Rilke because the poet confronts the singular phenomenon that "touches mortals in their nature"—that is, death.[108]

Nevertheless, Heidegger believes Rilke ultimately falls short of the measure of Hölderlin as a complete poet in a destitute time because Rilke "remains in the shadow of a tempered Nietzschean metaphysics."[109] In Heidegger's view, Nietzsche summed up Western philosophy in directly asking the guiding question of all philosophy—"What is being?"—and providing a definitive answer—"will to power."[110] Since the self-assertive will is the engine of technology, Heidegger believes this too must ultimately be overcome. Rilke's poetry—and in particular the angel of the *Duino Elegies*—comes close to this achievement but does not complete the task. As Fritz comments on Heidegger's behalf, "[Rilke] accepts a metaphysical definition of Being as worldly presence."[111] His existential interrogation of *Dasein* (to use Heidegger's term) is forestalled in the positing of being in the face of death—this is a security that the angel embodies. The move toward the participation in the unity of being that Rilke sees coming with death—"life's averted half"—stops the completion of the analysis of existential life. The poet who renders invisible what is visible in the world is still not individualized enough in the world and so cannot

authentically claim his singular existence. To Heidegger, Rilke's failure lies
in his residual pondering on the permanence of being that spans life and
death, rather than fixating fully on the closure of death.[112]

The Cause and Cure of Restlessness

This is not the first time that Heidegger approved then critiqued the creative genius of one whom he saw confronting and then recoiling from
the abyss of being. The method for existential analysis that Heidegger ultimately attempts to complete beginning with *Being and Time* is one that
he drew from an unlikely source: Augustine of Hippo. As with Rilke,
Heidegger saw in Augustine an uncommon courageousness both to perceive the destitution of mortals who do not ask the question of their
being and to enact a procedure of phenomenological self-interrogation
that responds to this inauthentic state. Even so, Heidegger did not want
to assume all that Augustine proposed because at the critical moment
of Augustine's investigation, Heidegger believed that Augustine succumbed to the allure of the metaphysical bias to assume being, thus veer-
ing the theological and philosophical traditions further away from their
attentiveness to being as such. In effect, Heidegger's engagement with
Augustine is such that he first approves of and then appropriates the
structure of his unlikely ally's project before turning on him to drain
Augustine's structure of its content in order to inaugurate an entirely different ontology that Heidegger considered uniquely suited to the rigors
of the phenomenological method.[113]

When Heidegger lectured on Augustine and Neoplatonism in 1921,
he drew his students' attention to book X of the *Confessions* because he
thought that it was not only unique among the other books in the text,
but also by far the most important. In book X, Augustine's "now" is identical with plunging himself into *memoria*, to seek an understanding of his
own being in operation. Augustine wants to grapple with the manner in
which he exists and performs his being, rather than seeking to glimpse
the substance of his being. To Heidegger, this is the climax and hermeneutical key of the whole work.

In the course of this self-engagement, Augustine first experiences (in
book X) then questions (in book XI) the issue of time. This is an issue

over which Heidegger will find himself both in agreement and in profound disagreement with Augustine. What Heidegger agrees with is Augustine's rejection of what Heidegger will later condemn as the "ordinary conception of time."[114] For Augustine (like Heidegger after him), time is not an objective, purely quantifiable chronological sequence by which a series of "nows" move from the future through the present to the past. Augustine discovers as simultaneously present to him both the present of the past (*memoria*) and the present of the future (*expectatio*) in his very own present moment of perception (*contuitus*).[115] To Augustine, it seems as though he himself is distended; hence, he is confronted with the difficulty of locating himself in this condition. In a critically approving manner, Heidegger uses this insight to develop a notion of time that appeals to anticipation (as *Dasein* always runs ahead of itself), repetition (*Dasein* encounters what it has been as it runs ahead of itself), and the moment, with the last of these being the decisive opportunity for the authentication of *Dasein* as such.[116]

More than anything, Heidegger's attention is drawn to the fact that Augustine is a problem to himself. Up to this point, Augustine cannot fully fathom or conceptualize his manner of being. His *memoria* is vast, and it is in the midst of this vastness that he experiences himself as thoroughly destabilized.[117] Not only does the sheer volume of what he is able to remember strike him, he is also astounded to acknowledge that he is able to remember forgetting.[118] Augustine is stirred to the border between confusion and wonder, especially as he discovers a desire that is unaccounted for in all he has experienced or known.[119] It appears as if he has nowhere at all to stand, no assumption to take as certain, no self-presence of being that serves as the foundation of his existence. Here, his being is his existence and his existence is his being. What Heidegger hears Augustine saying is that "I am not only the *one from* whose place the search proceeds and who moves toward some place, or the one *in* whom the search takes place; but the enactment of the search itself is something of the self. What does it mean that I 'am'?"[120] Every detail of his life is thus deemed important as Augustine now experiences himself as constitutively agitated. This is precisely what Heidegger wants: Augustine's agitation.

By Augustine's own admission, he is a burden to himself and life is a trial without respite.[121] Even more troubling, Augustine is unable to claim this trial of living as his own; he continues to be pulled apart. In analyzing these ways in which he is pulled apart, Augustine identifies three modes of dissipation. These are of prime interest to Heidegger, who is himself in search of the phenomenological analysis of the crisis of being. Augustine names these forms of dissipation the *concupiscentia carnis*,[122] the *concupiscentia oculorum*,[123] and the *ambitio saeculi*,[124] all of which we detected earlier in this chapter with Rilke's critique of the lover's insecurity. Under these headings, Heidegger hears Augustine lamenting the ways in which one becomes disconnected from oneself in one's absorption in objects, as one fails to engage in the world due to insubstantial curiosity, and in one's lusts for the affirmation of the world due to one's own deep weakness and lack of being. This third form of dissipation is both the most complete and the most impoverished since it involves the whole of one's existence in the inauthentic activity of failing to claim oneself.[125] For his part, Augustine seeks to center himself somewhere so as to be released from these forms of falling while Heidegger wants to dispel them through an act of self-determination.[126] Significantly, then, Heidegger is in close agreement with Augustine about the restlessness that Augustine discovers, but Heidegger refuses to accept the cure Augustine finds for his restlessness, which is for Augustine also the cause of his restlessness.[127]

From Heidegger's perspective, Augustine loses heart at the critical moment of investigation. Augustine proves unwilling or unable to take responsibility for himself at the apex—or nadir—of his questioning of being and thus accepts the easy relief he finds in Christian Platonism (or Platonic Christianity, for Heidegger thinks they are basically indistinguishable at this point).[128] Heidegger thus accuses Augustine of reverting to a Neoplatonic "axiologization,"[129] meaning that when Augustine experiences himself in a state of absolute flux, where his entire being appears mutable and uncertain, he gives in to the craving for immutability and certainty that will secure and measure his fluctuations.[130] To ameliorate his distention across time, Augustine needs a concept of eternity to fill his relative lack of self-presence. In Heidegger's eyes, Augustine substitutes an ontic relation (an object, God) for what was previously a purely relational intention.[131] The Platonic idea of the *summum bonum* comes to save Augustine from his instability.[132] As this idea helps Augustine escape the trial of living, Heidegger sees him as covering existential living with notions of eternity, presence, and thought.[133]

Here, Heidegger sees the full force of what Nietzsche called "Christianity's stroke of genius."[134] Augustine has furtively supplied the single idea that will control existence while simultaneously hiding its manipulative institution. Under Augustine's proposal, the question of being is safely hidden—that is, "concealed." Since for Heidegger truth is unconcealedness, this state constitutes an inauthentic existence. Heidegger thinks Augustine failed to remain rigorously phenomenological as he neglected the question of being in favor of a fabricated metaphysical assurance.[135] For Heidegger, that which is being ignored in Augustine's and metaphysic's account of being is the very thing that constitutes *Dasein's* being: death.

Facing Death

It is the residual trace of this escape to the idea of being that Heidegger finds irritating in Rilke. With Augustine, the move to metaphysics is undeniable, and for this Heidegger believes Augustine is most condemnable. Like Nietzsche before him, Heidegger accuses Augustine of resorting to theoretical thought in place of a rigorous phenomenological method in order to aid and abet the philosophical tradition in its metaphysical addiction.[136] While Rilke is not guilty of anything close to the same wholesale fraud of which Heidegger believes Augustine is guilty, Heidegger does see the poet blink for the sake of claiming some permanence to being, which, again, is represented in the angel as the embodiment of the unity of being into which all is moving. To Heidegger, Rilke does not maintain the same posture of openness that the true poet for a destitute time—namely, Hölderlin—would maintain.[137] Whereas Augustine makes a massive claim of self-assertion in positing the existence of the immutable and eternal God with respect to whom he measures his own existence, Rilke's minor assertion about the unity of being as the horizon of the Open results from a deficiency of resoluteness in the face of death.

To Heidegger, "death is the possibility of the absolute impossibility of *Dasein*."[138] Death—not God—is the singular existential phenomenon that offers *Dasein* its own horizon of being. As such, death establishes *Dasein*'s being as time, for the full measure of *Dasein* is the entirety of existence it enacts unto death. Death presents *Dasein* with what is its ownmost and death alone finally individualizes *Dasein* since one's death is that which no other can experience and which one cannot avoid. As such, death is thoroughly non-relational, for each dies his own death, alone. Finally, death is that phenomenon that is distinctively impending.[139] The extinguishment of the being of *Dasein* is the constant threat *Dasein* faces.[140]

Death, for Heidegger, is both that which offers what is most urgent for *Dasein* and that which *Dasein* routinely ignores. Death's impending possibility stirs *Dasein* to anxiety precisely as a fear that has no object, for death is simultaneously impossible for *Dasein* since once it ceases to be it no longer is *Dasein*.[141] What Heidegger asserts is that courage is necessary to accept this anxiety and claim one's own death—that is, the finite entirety of one's existence—as one's own. The forms of falling that Heidegger appropriated from Augustine obstruct this courage.[142] The key to *Dasein*'s authentic existence is to lift itself out of these dissipations through resoluteness.[143] This act of resoluteness is available in the "moment of vision," whereby *Dasein* anticipatorily claims the entirety of its existence unto death.[144] In this way, Heidegger's *Dasein* is "autoteleological," to borrow a term from Sean McGrath—its existence is definitively determined as non-dialogical, non-relational, and non-communal.[145] *Dasein* is authenticated in the individualized claiming of one's own existence. When compared to Augustine, who understands himself as constituted only in dialogue with the God whom he calls upon and whose mercy he accepts as his own continence, Heidegger's result is diametrically opposed.[146] From a beginning where Heidegger appropriated the structure of Augustine's method of interrogation, this ending shows the radical nature of Heidegger's rejection of the content and basis of Augustine's structure.[147]

Disorientation and Reorientation

I concluded the first section of this chapter with Philippe Ariès's judgment regarding the consequences of the denial of death in modern life.

"The community in the traditional sense of the word no longer exists," Ariès claims; "it has been replaced by an enormous mass of atomized individuals."[148] Heidegger is concerned with the same denial of death but, ironically, he understands the *proper* orientation toward death to bring about exactly what Ariès considered so vexing. According to Heidegger, an authentic human being cannot be anything other than ultimately atomized. The very meaning of authentic existence is to resolutely and anticipatorily claim what is one's ownmost, individualizing, nonrelational, and distinctively impending. *Dasein* rises up to authentic existence in claiming the entirety of its finite existence as its own; this means resolutely facing one's own death as the orienting phenomenon of one's existence. Heidegger's philosophy calls for an uncommon autonomous resolve that in fact borders on a heteronomous relationship to death. Not only are individuals atomized in this view, but they are also deathbound. While there is some small dispute as to whether or not Heidegger entertained certain non-existential possibilities for being after death,[149] it is undeniable that on the face of it, Heidegger's philosophy closes in on death. Death is an absolute end.

This extreme form of autonomy is the distinctive logical end of modernity's general drift. The more modern man has asserted his autonomy and relied on himself alone, the less he is inclined to invest in anything or anyone outside himself, especially a deity.[150] Perhaps this is where Heidegger's critique of Rilke actually redounds to Rilke's favor. Although Guardini accurately calls the poet the most consistent of all individualists,[151] it is also true that Rilke's poetry does not allow death to foreclose on the meaning of existence the way Heidegger's philosophy does.

While Heidegger's notion of death entails an unimpeachable finality, it does not necessarily follow that Heidegger takes death most seriously of all, or even adequately seriously. Even without appealing to a Christian response to Heidegger's portrayal of death, his concept is questioned as dubious on philosophical grounds. One of the most direct and incendiary critiques of Heidegger's view of death (and his philosophy as a whole) comes from the postmodern philosopher Jacques Derrida. Whereas Ariès sees modern Western cultures disciplining a now untamed death through a combination of death-denial, death-silencing, and medicalization, Derrida discerns that philosophy itself is in the business of disciplining

death. The worst offender is Heidegger, whom Derrida condemns for ignoring the seriousness of death by conceptualizing it.

In *The Gift of Death*, Derrida critiques philosophy for keeping vigil
over death and thus disciplining it.[152] In his view, (Platonic) philosophy disciplines the orgiastic cults with the prescription for meditating
on death and the recommendation for the lifelong practice of dying.
Christianity then suppresses the Platonic mystery in its emphasis on self-
forgetting and self-denying, as the Christian program calls for the sacrifice of one's whole being in the knowledge of sin before the tremendous
mystery of the supreme being's death. This God then gives the unsym-
metrical gift of redemption to the penitent soul.[153] In the mode of critique, Derrida argues that Heidegger attempts to conceptualize death as
the possibility of the impossibility of *Dasein*, a move that entails the intentional refusal of the Christian conception of death, God, and man.
In so doing, Derrida indicts Heidegger for assuming what Christianity
suppressed (namely, the Platonic mystery), which contains that which
the Platonic mystery incorporated in its programmatic act of disciplining (namely, the orgiastic mystery). Heidegger is guilty of thematizing
death—he draws it into an economy designed to nullify responsibility in
support of his desire for a thoroughgoing existential analytic. As such, he
exerts conceptual control over death as *my* death, disallowing any lasting
significance to the death *of* any other, or *for* any other.[154]

Though Derrida can hardly be trusted to sustain friendly relations
with Christianity, there is a certain favor that Derrida renders to a truly
Christian understanding of death and the human person through his rebuttal of Heidegger. In this way, Derrida and Rilke are connected. Heidegger's view of death has a univocal meaning: the unsubstitutability of
each *Dasein* as a being-toward-death. With Heidegger, there is nothing
left to question, nothing left to wonder about in relation to death: it is
only a decisive end and it gives a definitively atomized meaning to each
individual. While neither Rilke nor Derrida is involved in proposing any
radically hopeful views of death, they both, in their own ways, resist
this absolutely singular meaning of death with the potentially totalitarian
force it could muster. Derrida critiques the move to conceptual control
in which Heidegger is engaged, and Rilke stands upon a place of isolation to ask the question about a wideness of being that is not nullified in

death.[155] Although a full analysis of Derrida's view of death is beyond the scope of this study, the Rilkean analysis helped us to see that the poet's noncommunicative beginning led to an ultimately depersonalized end. All the same, both what Heidegger liked and did not like in Rilke is, as I suggested above, part of what makes Rilke appealing: the poet attempts to look seriously at death and the existential nature of life, while also opening up the possibility that the deepest truth exceeds him.

Remembering the Forgotten Death

The "Rilkean opening" is undoubtedly part of what drew Guardini to Rilke. The metaphysical residue that Heidegger disliked in Rilke was perhaps a sign to Guardini of the poet remembering a larger truth. Rather than excluding the Christian narrative in an outright manner like Heidegger did, Rilke was involved in certain inversions. Heidegger's treatment of Augustine displayed his intention to pursue a method of questioning without end (except of course he ended up substituting death in place of God as the final end of questioning). In Rilke, Guardini found a significant figure who not only questioned, but also provided answers. This makes Rilke both more alluring and potentially more dangerous. Guardini was drawn to the peculiarly modern existential position that Rilke represented, even as he felt compelled to deny the alleged veracity of his claims.

All the same, Rilke does find support from Ariès, Heidegger, Derrida, and others when he reproaches "all modern religions for having handed to their believers consolations and glossings over of death, instead of administering to them the means of reconciling themselves to it and coming to an understanding with it."[156] The failure on the part of religions and modern cultures on the whole to confront the meaning of death has impoverished not only the hope-filled imaginations of believers, but contemporary views of everyday life as well. If Rilke and others have prompted theologians to give fresh and significant articulations to the meaning of death, then this challenge should be heeded.

Moreover, Rilke's productive failure is a reminder to Christians that Christ alone reveals the true nature of death and that Christ himself is the hermeneutic of eschatological assertions.[157] What Rilke and all atheist humanists lack is the proper method for integrating the seriousness of death and the communion that outstrips it.[158] Only Christianity has this hermeneutic in the form of he who is given: the person of Christ. Therefore, we must follow Christ into death in order to know death for what it is; only then can we theologically follow Christ into the Resurrection and begin to understand anew what the fullness of communion promises.

This communion invites and even demands imaginative power equal to and in excess of a Rainer Maria Rilke, but the imagination must also be held accountable for what directs and shapes it. In the end, Rilke's and even Heidegger's imaginations originated from a presumption of individualistic isolation, while the prevalent cultural imagination of modernity rallies around the pervasive urge to deny the presence and consequences of death, or otherwise to caricature it. Presumptions such as these generally remain hidden, especially as worldviews are built upon such poetic, philosophical, and cultural foundations. The reason why I have chosen to follow the Christian narrative as presented in the creed as I pursue the eschatological truth expressed in the *communio sanctorum* is that I am intentionally foregrounding, from the beginning, that view of reality that gives rise to and supports such an ultimate view—one that, in this case, begins with God the Father as Creator, is inaugurated and revealed in the mystery of Christ's life, and is opened to creation through the agency of the Holy Spirit. The imagination is given unbounded room for exploration within this space of belief in the Triune God, but the imagination is also always shaped to this space. In particular, the communion whose truth we seek to understand flows from and redounds to the gift of the life of the Word made flesh. As we will see, this communion enters into death *in Christ*, rises from death *in Christ*, and gives glory to God *in Christ* as the blessed share in the love of Christ.

At the opening of this chapter I stated that the renewal of the eschatological imagination requires looking seriously at death so as to see the fundamental gravitas of the gift that Christ embodies and confers. Guardini took up the challenge of trying to understand the darkness of death from the light of faith so as to re-propose the Christian hope in the modern world. At great length, he examined Rilke's distinctively modern and innovative view of death and found it radically insufficient when compared to the truth of the human person, even if this treatment of death is far preferable to the irredeemably hardened autonomous conceptualization that Heidegger constructed. Therefore, as we prepare to search for the true seriousness of death and the deep meaning of the gift of life in the Paschal Mystery, we turn again to Guardini for instruction:

> What is death as the Christian sees it? . . . He accepts death as the provision of the Living God for his redemption. Death is no longer the Dark Fear which is the final working out of sin. It has become the means by which man shares in the change wrought by God's great compassion, the change of end into beginning. Death is the entrance into new life. . . . Christ carries man's nature to God and back again from God to man. Rather not "again," but in a new and awesome manner, in the manner of the Incarnation of the Son of God. In this manner we share by faith, not by right of our own nature and being; our share in the Incarnation is owing to grace. Indeed, as Paul repeatedly says, Christian life is the life of Christ in man and of man in Christ. In Christ the arch reaches out to the side of God for each of us. Death is the darkness which the arch has to span. . . . Death guarantees the gravity of this deliverance and of this re-creation, for without death the message of the Gospel would be sheer fantasy. By His death, Christ anchored the new life in the reality of being; by our death, we legitimately enter into the new life.[159]

CHAPTER 3

WORD OF LIFE

Toward a Christian Account of Death and Communication

Death blankets the meaning of life and shrouds the prospect of communication. Every statement about death is at once, whether explicitly or implicitly, a statement about the limits, resilience, and final meaning of communication. Death is taken as certain while the status of communication is a question that death poses to onlookers. Philippe Ariès's socio-historical research presents longstanding customs that, for nearly a millennium, facilitated communication between the dying person and his circumstances, the individual and the community, and the living and the dead, who were not considered to be altogether cut off from the survivors. In place of these old customs, new customs came into vogue in the modern period with which ruptures in communication were either newly introduced or otherwise facilitated: the sick and dying are isolated from the truth of their circumstances as well as from the ordinary movements of the world; the community silently endures the separation of the sick or dying individual from the collective body; and society as a whole presses on as if the loss that death introduces were of no real consequence. With each set of customs, the prevalent approach to death makes a claim about the prospect of communication: in the first, communication somehow abides in the separations that death incurs; while in the second, communication is eclipsed in death, leaving one to wonder if there is any significance to acts of communication after all.

The legacy of Kantian epistemology aided the shift toward the prevalent modern approach to death in the West, especially given Kant's importance in German philosophy and theology, both Catholic and Protestant. In the move to restrict the boundaries of legitimate knowledge to the phenomenal realm where reason becomes the sovereign adjudicator, customs or theories intended to extend practical reality beyond the range of reason were presented as more and more fanciful, and thus less and less credible. With such a view, death itself becomes the guardian on the boundary demarcating what can and cannot be known. At minimum, this Kantian impulse led to a settled agnosticism regarding the prospect of communication in death—an agnosticism that more often than not manifests itself in practices of ignoring death. Maximally, the Kantian epistemology in philosophy hardened into forms of nihilism, where death came to rule the meaning of life as with Heidegger and, in a more consistent and disturbing sense, with Nietzsche before him. Rilke was dissatisfied with both the agnostic approach as well as the nihilistic approach, while also finding unpalatable the views of modern religions relative to death. Whereas Kantianism refused to see beyond the event of death and modern religions failed to take life seriously with their deferral of meaning to a fantastical afterlife, Rilke wanted to account for both life and death within a more complete understanding of being. For him, there was communication across the great fissure, but as Guardini has helped show, this communication was ultimately nothing more than the echoes of final loneliness.

The Christian faith contains all the notions of death mentioned above and exceeds them. It validates a certain agnosticism about death—one deriving from an apophatic impulse—but only insofar as the fullness of truth in death as well as life exceeds what the boundaries of reason alone can hold. It recognizes the certainty of death as a real end, but without objectifying death to the point that death rules life and obtains absolute power. Finally, the Christian faith also gives an account of the relationship between life and death, but it does so only in fidelity to the testimony about he who *was crucified, died, and was buried,* who *descended into hell* and on *the third day . . . rose again from the dead.*

The aim of this chapter is to allow Christ to reveal the true limits of communication; the full drama of the Incarnation sets the boundaries for creation's life with God. Indeed, it is Christ's death and Resurrection that hold the truth about the communication of God's life. Before consorting with any philosophical schools or poetic proposals, the Christian faith is first and foremost attentive to God's absolute act of communication given to creation as Jesus Christ: the Word. In his death, Jesus Christ does not just assume the meaning of death; he gives death its final meaning. The question of communication in death was given a definitive answer in this person whose burial shrouds the disciples found very early in the morning on the first day of the week (see John 20:1–10; Luke 24:1–12).

In pursuit of the full meaning of death with which the Christian faith grapples, I undertake four distinct yet related tasks in this chapter. First, I sketch out the dimensions of a "theology of death" within Christian eschatology, for which I turn again to Karl Rahner. Second, Joseph Ratzinger will lead us into a consideration of the tension between death and the communication of life in God as presented in the biblical testimony of the Old Testament and in anticipation of the coming of Jesus Christ as Lord and Savior. Third, I pursue a rigorous account of the person of Jesus Christ as the Incarnate Word and only begotten Son of the Father that requires theologically investigating the silence of Holy Saturday. Hans Urs von Balthasar's theological work takes a leading role in this section, within which we will also listen to the testimony of Primo Levi regarding the "hell" of Auschwitz. The different theologians treated in these first three sections—especially Rahner, Ratzinger, and Balthasar—all address aspects of my primary question about communication and noncommunication (or communication through noncommunication), which taken together allow me to assume a more comprehensive view of the irreducibly paradoxical nature of the communication that runs through the communion of saints. In order to sharpen this view further still, I use the fourth and final section to posit an understanding of the gift of the resurrection of the body as comparable to but not identical with God's original act of *creatio ex nihilo*. As the summative note of the chapter, this section capitalizes on both the range of communication in Christ and the primacy of God's agency for communication.

Karl Rahner: A Theology of Death within Christian Eschatology

The End of Freedom

As a Catholic theologian, Karl Rahner had no intention of denying the significance of the world.[1] At the same time, his positive reception of the world occurs in a way other than how his former teacher Martin Heidegger instructed. Whereas Heidegger's view is Nietzschean, Rahner's is Ignatian.[2] Rahner's spirituality dictates that the true value of the world is only ever grasped in detaching from the confines of the world in order to reengage the world genuinely and holistically.[3] The reason for this worldly disengagement marks the decisive difference for Rahner in contrast to Heidegger: whereas the latter orients the human being (*Dasein*) toward the nothingness of death, Rahner's human being as spirit is "situated before being in its totality which is infinitude."[4] Rahner thus strains to hold together an openness to what is beyond the limits of the world while also taking death seriously as a real end. His notion of history stands between Hegel's Idealism, to which Rilke escaped, and the quasi-ontological status Heidegger granted to death.[5] With Rahner, the proper view of history is to see it as both finite and open to infinitude.

In order to better grasp Rahner's notion of history, it is fruitful to juxtapose him with Kant on this point.[6] Kant was keenly interested in restricting the realm of knowledge to the strict boundaries of the phenomenal realm, where the procedures of rational verification operated. Although Kant admits the existence of a noumenal realm in which free decisions are made antecedently, he declares that this realm is inaccessible to reason.[7] Therefore, while the phenomenal realm depends on the noumenal realm as a consequence relies on a cause, the causal realm is impenetrable to reason since reason is restricted to the cause-and-effect relations that occur within the world of phenomena. In this sense, Kant's history is the disclosure of what has been (freely) decided elsewhere. Moreover, the "meaning" of history is found in a universal moral law, which is absolutely binding yet impersonal. Human beings are measured according to conformity to this law, though the determination of the degree of conformity is inaccessible.[8] Rational creatures are left to deduce this law, but not to probe intention and meaning. This gives a deterministic quality to history, where the actions of human agents within history may appear to be causal but are really consequential to an antecedent and inscrutable freedom that predetermines moral actions.

Rahner rejects this notion of history. For him, history *is* the arena for freedom.[9] What gives history its true bearing is the ultimate horizon toward which all moral decisions and all actions are oriented. This horizon is made present and mediated to human agents in historically conditioned ways.[10] In every discrete and seemingly independent decision, the human agent is making a decision about the entirety of his being; therefore, each action—and in fact all actions—find their true quality in relation to an absolute goodness and truth. On the basis of this relationship, what the human agent determines about himself through free decisions in history is given eternal significance since the infinite fullness of goodness and truth is involved in the finite.[11]

Death brings an end to this period of free determinations on the part of the human agent. Since death is the end of the entire time of freedom, it bears upon the entirety of the human life.[12] In marking the real end to freedom, death discloses the fact that free decisions point beyond the boundaries of the historical life itself, which now definitively ends. Unlike Kant, for whom phenomena within history at best disclose the effects of the individual's noumenal acceptance or rejection of the moral law that is itself co-extensive with freedom, Rahner presents history as the period in which individuals make free decisions that bear upon their relationship to absolute goodness and truth.[13] A real drama pertains to Rahner's theory of history.

Becoming a Subject

At the heart of Rahner's drama of history is freedom precisely as "first and foremost freedom of being."[14] Within the particular circumstances of the historically conditioned existence of each individual being, every moral decision and every action comprises a response to the question of being that the ultimate horizon of this particular life imposes on it. Like Kant's moral law, this question of being pervades all of life without arising from anywhere within the stretch of life itself. As with Heidegger's notion of death, death here sets the boundary for this stretch of life that is the arena for creaturely freedom. Unlike both Kant and Heidegger, though, the question of being to which humans are freely disposed is personal and potentially personalizing: it is a question that comes as an address from Someone and elicits a response that would constitute personhood by relation. In the Christian faith, this ultimate horizon is proclaimed as *God, the Father Almighty, Creator of Heaven and Earth.* This is Rahner's absolute, holy Mystery.[15]

The distinctiveness of Rahner's Catholic understanding of the constitution of the human person becomes more apparent when that of the German Reformed theologian Jürgen Moltmann is placed alongside it. The thematic overlap in these theologians' respective eschatologies allows for the subtle yet substantive differences between the two to highlight for us some of the most important essential commitments of Rahner's own view. Inserting Moltmann into the present inquiry also helps to show the degrees of separation between Rahner and Rilke, and thus between Rahner and Idealism since Moltmann's theological vision bears a much closer resemblance to the process of being's ultimate becoming about which Rilke mused.

There is a fundamental conviction that guides Moltmann's view of the entirety of the human person, and therefore his theological opinion about the moment of death. To Moltmann, the human being is *always* a whole person.[16] This is because God's vision determines truth. It is hardly an overstatement to claim that Moltmann's belief in what God sees is the core of his entire theological project. God's vision is definitive, and what God sees, eternally, is the fullness of truth.

To Moltmann, the death of the human person means the end of transience, but this end does not impact God in any case because God never sees transience. Even at death, God's vision is unchanging: God sees the whole of the human person—and the whole of creation, for that matter. What happens at death is that the human person's process of becoming what God sees eternally comes to an end. The human person is now what she is eternally. Released from the transience of time, the human being immediately enters into God's eternity as a whole being, fulfilled.[17] Death, for Moltmann, is due neither to sin nor nature; death is simply the end of the frailty of finite temporality, for being is incommensurably greater than becoming.[18]

Moltmann is thus highly critical of what he calls the "myth of time." Time is not the fixed and secure quantifiable sequence of successive "now" moments that pass from the future through the present into the past.[19] Time is not the determiner of what is real: God alone is. The "myth of time" implicitly puts God at the mercy of what is secured in time, whereas Moltmann wants to make sure that time is subjected to the eternality of God. God sees what is real, what is actualized; God does not see what was or is "possible" but does not come into being as realized. *He is not God of the dead but of the living* (Mark 12:27; Matt. 22:32; Luke 20:38, NAB). Unrealized possibilities are dead to God.[20] For Moltmann, then, the future holds the possibility of God's coming; the past is that which is actual and of permanent reality; while the present is the moment of actualization, where reality is separated from empty possibilities.

Ultimately, what God sees is the reunion of the whole. God sees all of creation as one, without unrealized possibilities and without any unprocessed becoming. God sees creation eternally. God therefore also sees each human person as a part of creation.[21] The fulfillment of the human person is in becoming what she is eternally: a piece of the wholeness of creation.[22] The Hegelian family resemblance between Moltmann and Rilke is most apparent here, where the reunion of the fullness of being is the *telos* of all becoming.

When we look back to Rahner from here, what stands out are subjectivity and participation in contrast to reunion and incorporation. There is a thickness to Rahner's theological anthropology that Moltmann's lacks. In contemplating eschatological fulfillment, Rahner puts an emphatic note on ever increasing subjectivity. The human person is ontologically oriented to becoming more and more relational, to an unlimited, infinite extent (as I discuss in more detail in the following subsection). This is due to the fact that the essential characteristic of the human person as spirit is the absolute openness to all being.[23] The exercise of and ultimate actualization of this openness through definite, free decisions and actions is what constitutes the human person as a *person*. Death, therefore, is not simply the end of transience and the inaugurating moment of God's eternity—as it is with Moltmann—but rather the consummation of what has been freely growing within time as the free decision of the human person about herself in relation to the absolute horizon of being.[24] The Rahnerian doctrine of eternity is one in which free actions in time and history are given permanent significance because they express the fundamental decision of the human person—as spirit in the world—in response to the question of being that is always present. Therefore, not just what the individual does but who the individual *is* gains eternal significance in relation to God in eternity.[25]

To Rahner, death is paradoxically an active and passive endeavor for the human person. It is active in the sense that the person's death is the consummation of the achievement of that particular life. The fundamental decision that the human person has made about herself is summed up in the moment of death, when the final direction and orientation of this particular person is ultimately decided. Into her death, the human person posits the entirety of her moments of existential self-determination in response to a call. The echoes of Heidegger's influence are apparent here since both of them in some way orient the activities and decisions of the temporal life *by* (Rahner) or *for* (Heidegger) death.[26]

At the same time, though, Rahner understands death to be something that happens *to* the human person, who is passive in the face of her death. Not only does the biological moment of death tend to come without the expressed agreement of the human person, but it is also true that death is typically encountered as confusing, confounding, and uncertain. The meaning of death is not at all wholly apparent to the one who is dying and who eventually dies. In Rahner's view, death hides the truth of the person from herself. Thus, the lifelong fact of being unable to decide fully about oneself is amplified in this moment of death, when the will remains at least in some way disintegrated. From moment to moment, the integrity of the human person is in question and never more than at this final and decisive moment. As Rahner contends, "Death is guilt made visible."[27] The failure of the human person to harmoniously unite her nature and her person is disclosed in frighteningly brilliant fashion in death. The human person loses herself in death; she cannot decide wholly about herself.

In contrast to Moltmann's belief in the return of the individual to the whole of creation at death, Rahner's view of death and the eschatological dimension of human life carries a great deal more drama on the anthropological level. Instead of blandly marking the end of transience, death marks the consummation of all that the human person has determined about herself in relation to God. The responsibility that this confrontation with God at death places on the human person creates a quality of urgency and importance to what occurs and what is freely chosen throughout life. Moreover, the deeper importance comes from the unavoidable demand that the human person be responsible for herself before God. The challenge of becoming a subject before the Absolute Subject is the measure of the individual human life.[28]

Unlimited Relationality

Consistent with the rest of his thought on death, Jürgen Moltmann does not hold open the possibility for the separation of the soul from the body since, for him, what God sees is the whole person within the whole creation at the end of finite temporality.[29] Rahner is not convinced that this separation is an essential view,[30] yet he still accounts for it in a way that grants deeper insight into how he understands the relationship between individual and collective eschatology. As mentioned above, Rahner defines the human person as the openness to all being. Under the rubric of this definition, the meaning of both the soul and the body is secured. The soul is the person's permanent freedom before God—her irreducible responsibility to make a decision about herself in response to God's offer of self.[31] The soul is the person's responsibility to remain open to God as ever greater. The body, then, reaches to the full extent of all embodied existence. The body is the historical "situatedness," the network of relations, the mode and manners of (self-) expression that this particular human person possesses in actuality and in potentiality. The bodiliness of the human person is the arena for his freedom, relating ultimately to all of history and stretching toward the limits of creation.[32]

What happens at the moment of death, then, is that the soul is separated from the body, but only to the extent that the eternal significance of man's decision before God is loosed from the localization or exclusivity of the separated, bounded time and space of this individual human life. The body is meant to be the instrument of communication with all of creation, tuned to man's fundamental openness to all being. The separation of the fundamental relational capacity (the soul) from the constrained historical mode of existence only occurs for the sake of a deeper integration of the soul with the body for the sake of embracing all being. The separation allows for the deeper integration of *this* body with all of creation. In Rahner's view, there is ultimately a direct proportionality between nearness to God and participation in creation. The terror of death is that it puts an end to the claim to separateness of each individual human life, while the grace that God offers in death is that the individual is freed from these confines to achieve eschatological fullness with God according to her fundamental openness to all being. The movement from the individual to all being illuminates Rahner's integral connection between the personal and the pancosmic.[33]

The tension in which human life is lived is apparent in the two movements just mentioned: the ultimate move from the person out to the cosmic and the thwarting move that is the claim to separateness within each (fallen) human life. Within this tension the true meaning of death in the Christian view is laid bare. In Rahner's account, humanity itself is created to communicate God's blessing throughout the entire body of its members. Due to Original Sin, what *should* function does not do so in fact. Therefore, there is an "absence of the holy *pneuma*"—God's gracious presence—who sanctifies man interiorly prior to any moral decision, and, because of this, each member of the fallen body of humanity experiences a resistance in the process of self-determination.[34]

God's will in creation is to graciously raise mankind into relationship with its Creator and therefore for each member to be sanctified by virtue of the fact that he is a member of the human race. That this will is frustrated through the sin of Adam is what makes the mystery of the Incarnation redemptive in addition to sanctifying since Christ must justify what his Incarnation presupposes and constitutes: the solidarity of the human race.[35] The fact that human descendants "do not possess the state of sanctification by God's self-bestowal in Christ *precisely as descendents*"[36] shows what the nature of sin truly is: the willful refusal to communicate holiness through embodied humanity. Sin is the failure to give as gift what is received as gift—namely, the self-bestowed holy presence of God.

When Rahner says that "death is guilt made visible,"[37] this is what he means. Death is the guilt coming from the claim to separation on the part of the members of the one human body. When Paul speaks of the spiritual body, Rahner takes him to mean that this is the body that

> is pure expression of the spirit become one with the *pneuma* of God and
> its bodily existence, and is no longer its restricting and abasing element
> and its emptiness. It will be a bodily nature which does not cancel again
> the freedom from the earthly here-and-now gained with death but will, on
> the contrary, bring it out in its pure form.[38]

In the view of Christian theology, the only death is sin. Sin is the self-elected separation from the source of life and blessing, the dismemberment of the communicative body, and the individualization of concern that obstructs human solidarity and thereby opposes the *pneuma* of God.[39]

The Christological Center

Death as sin is also death as strict autonomy, the absolute neglect of relationship, and the final dissolution of meaning. This view of death is only visible in contrast to the light that Christ shines upon it. Therefore, in considering human death, Rahner moves to shape it Christologically. As mentioned above, the order of treatment seems to suggest that Rahner only arrives at the point of considering Christ at the end, but in fact it is only in virtue of meditating on what Christ reveals that any comments about truly human death were possible in the first place.

Rahner argues that the deepest truth about human death is revealed and enacted in the person of Jesus Christ. This truth opens a way for Christians and provides the norm for evaluating and seeking to understand all human death. In Christ, Rahner believes that the infliction of human death has been wielded into an affirmation of trust. In and through his very own person, Christ makes even the incommunicability of human death an event of fundamental communication. Christ actively gives himself to the Father in death, thus imbuing death's power over passive human nature with the activating energy of the life of God. Against the sheer prospect of annihilation by isolation—*My God, My God, why have you forsaken me?* (Matt. 27:46; cf. Ps. 22:1, RSV)—Christ gives himself in trust to the Father, thus speaking himself as the Word of response to the Father who seeks to break open the tomb of death: *into your hands I commit my spirit* (Luke 23:46; cf. Ps. 31:5, RSV).[40] Christ's "Yes" to the Father in his death receives a response from the Father in the Resurrection, where Christ's affirmation of trust is accepted in God's acceptance of the life of the Son, a life that opens death to communication.

The Rahnerian Sketch

We have spent a good deal of time with Rahner's theology of death as a key ingredient of his eschatology because his account presents some of the most important and basic moves that a truly Catholic understanding of human death requires. First, he safeguards the importance of history as the arena for freedom, one that does not recur as the eternal return of the same nor comes to an end that closes down the possibility of meaning. His notion of death is real, yet not totalitarian. Second, Rahner secures the substantiality of human personhood, one that finds its meaning only in connection to an absolute offer of communication that pervades yet exceeds the free decisions of a life. Rahner avoids Rilke's folly of sublating personhood into the absolute unity of being, and he frees persons from the nihilistic finitude that Heidegger's ironically heteronomous relationship to death entails for the human person. Third, Rahner strikes a note of radical relationality, even unto the furthest reaches of creation as the soul is separated from the body at death only to forge a deeper integration with the redeemed body, now fully capable of instrumentalizing the fundamental openness to all being. Fourth, Rahner allows me to define death in Christian terms as, most basically, sin. By this definition, I mean that the Christian notion of death is concerned with isolation, separation, and opposing the communication of God. Fifth and finally, Rahner points to Christ's definitive role in communicating life unto death.

These lineaments are important to the overall task in this chapter of discerning what the true limits of communication are, in Christ. All the same, this sketch is not yet sufficient for my task. To this account, I must add two more, each of which will specify and clarify the distinctiveness of the Christian claim about death and the life that outstrips it. The first account will come from Joseph Ratzinger, whose narration of the story of

Israel as the struggle between life (communication) and death (sin) will not only locate our inquiry biblically, but will also reacquaint us with the operation of narrative logic that I introduced initially in chapter 1. We will then move on to the theology of the Incarnation that Hans Urs von Balthasar offers since he gives the most complete account of the Christological center that Rahner already identified, though Balthasar does so in such a way that the drama of revelation reaches its deepest possible point according to the logic God himself provides.

Joseph Ratzinger: Communication within Salvation History

Attitudes toward Life and Death

In preparation for rearticulating the Christian belief in death and eternal life in the modern age, Joseph Ratzinger performs a social analysis regarding modern attitudes toward death. What he describes is uncannily similar to the final picture that Philip Ariès paints. In Ratzinger's eyes, today's society either ignores death or renders it banal. On the one hand, "bourgeois society hides death away," putting it under taboo, and ordering it according to "technical tasks technically handled by technical people."[41] On the other hand, death is trivialized, made into a spectacle for entertainment and the alleviation of boredom. In either case, the meaning of death is neglected. Along with this neglect, the meaning of the human person herself is neglected. As Ratzinger summarizes:

> Attitudes to dying determine attitudes to living. Death becomes the key to the question: What really *is* man? The mounting callousness towards human life which we are experiencing today is intimately bound up with the refusal to confront the question of death. Repression and trivialization can only "solve" the riddle by dissolving humanity itself.[42]

The act of denying or incessantly deferring the question of death forecloses on the question about the meaning of the human person because without looking to the limits of what, who, and why the human person is, the full meaning of the human person is obscured. Ratzinger is sensitive to the ways in which selective preferences delimit the full picture of the human person, cordoning off as they do areas of human life that are deemed undesirable or inconvenient to confront. These selective limitations fragment the understanding of the human person, reducing the full meaning of the human person to the predetermined categories that technology, economics, or the lust for comfort dictate. Death is the enemy that is avoided, but in this avoidance a distinctive capacity of the human person is left unexercised: the human person's ability to ask about herself—her meaning, her origin, and her end. As we saw with Rahner, a true anthropology must attend to death because, in addition to threatening the end of the human person, it is also the proper end that gives shape and meaning to a life.[43]

The Drama of Israel

In the interest of describing how serious attention to death opens up the full meaning of life, Ratzinger recounts the ways in which Israel's understanding of its own life developed (and even transformed) through its reflection on its experiences of death. He is interested in showing that while the belief that communication is the essence of life was deeply embedded in the ethos of ancient Israel, this belief also developed into fuller form over the course of centuries of reflection on the life of faith. What Israel's history of grappling with experiences of death shows is that Israel's most foundational belief—the *Shema*—was put under the tension of obedience.

As Gary Anderson argues in *Sin: A History*, the understanding of sin that develops in Second Temple Judaism shares an important characteristic with Anselm's theory of atonement, especially when refracted through the Patristic understanding of the sin of Adam as represented by Origen. Adam's choice to follow Eve into sin bespeaks a desire to remain united to his spouse, opening his own suffering to give witness to the immeasurable love of God for the sinner.[44] Anderson thus detects what he describes as a "narrative expansion," where humanity's sin becomes the site for God's self-donating love for humanity, ultimately recapitulated and extended in Christ.[45] To bolster his point, Anderson cites Ratzinger, who contends that the cross itself expresses "the radical nature of the love that gives itself completely,"[46] rather than simply a mechanism of propitiation on behalf of an injured and offended God.[47] In Ratzinger's own biblical theology, the suffering of Israel in its various experiences of death becomes the site for the fidelity of God (Deut. 8:1–5), who is a jealous lover (Deut. 6:15), and whose own faithfulness binds the people together through the blessing of a singular love that purifies the fragmenting curse of mistaking other gods—the gods of wealth, health, and power (Deut. 8:17–20)—as rivals to the one God. The drama of Israel's story is of learning, through suffering, what it means to believe that *the Lord our God is one Lord* (Deut. 6:4, RSV).

Existing without Life

According to Ratzinger, Israel's view of death at first mostly mirrored the views of the ancient world in which it was situated. These views were tied up in the conviction that one's actions and one's destiny were connected, such that early death was the result of wrongful action, whereas long life indicated rightful living. The balance of power for destiny rested on the nation's actions. The greatest hope was to live many years and to see one's children's children, thus enabling one to participate in the future of Israel itself.[48]

Part of the ancient view of death that Israel adopted alongside the hope for posterity was the assumption that death was not simply annihilation. For Israel,

> The dead man goes down in Sheol, where he leads a kind of un-life among the shades. . . . He is essentially cut off from the land of the living, from dear life, banished into a noncommunication zone where life is destroyed precisely because relationship is impossible. The full extent of Sheol's abyss of nothingness is seen from the fact that Yahweh is not there, nor is he praised there. In relation to him too, there is a complete lack of communication in Sheol. Death is thus an unending imprisonment. It is simultaneously being and nonbeing, somehow still existence and yet no longer life.[49]

On Ratzinger's interpretation, we can see that living to old age was a blessing because it kept one in the realm of communication where not only relationship with others was possible, but also relationship with Yahweh. The realm of the dead was, conversely, the realm of noncommunication, such that that this continuation of existence was no longer considered life.

Moreover, Israel perceived the power of death—that is, the reality of a noncommunication zone—as being operative within earthly life. With the sick and incapacitated, Israel perceived ones who were similarly cut off from the community to a certain extent, and to that extent those persons were not fully living since they were not capable of being fully involved in the dynamics of communication. This lack was decisive because it is precisely communication that offers life. In this predicament, Ratzinger sees an undeveloped kernel that will eventually grow into the fuller belief in the power of life to be communicated beyond physical death:

> If on the one hand the physically still living and breathing human being can be "dead" in a state of noncommunication, must it not also be true that the power of communion, of divine communion at any rate, is something stronger than physical dying? May there not be life beyond physical perishing?[50]

Though Israel had adopted the ancient view of some kind of shadowy existence after death, it did not yet fully consider the ramifications for its conception of Yahweh. If death had the power of limiting Yahweh's capacity for relationship and if death was so strong that it could reach even into earthly life through sickness and incapacitation, then Israel was functionally admitting that death was stronger than the One whom it daily professed to be greater than all gods and all powers.[51] Yahweh himself was limited to the nonnegotiable realm of communication, which Israel considered to be the place where death was not.

The Crisis of Belief

Yahwistic faith was not yet recognized for the inner consistency of its own thought. If communication is the essence of life, if this essence could be withdrawn or hindered not just in death but also while one was physically still living, and if Israel professed Yahweh to be the unrivaled

God—that is, that power which is unrivaled—then it should have followed that Yahweh's power is stronger than any other power, including death. A deeply riven inconsistency separated Israel's profession of faith from Israel's practice of faith in the world. As Ratzinger puts it,

> There is an inner contradiction in the affirmation that he who is life itself encounters a limitation on his power. The state of affairs which such an affirmation betrays was inherently unstable. In the end, the alternatives were either to abandon faith in Yahweh altogether or to admit the unlimited scope of his power and so, in principle, the definitive character of the communion with man he inaugurated.[52]

Placing limitations on Yahweh's power was tantamount to pledging trust in another god.

Ultimately, it was Israel's religious interpretation of its historical experience that moved Israel toward a new imagination that opened this contradiction to new meaning. On the one hand, Ecclesiastes and Job radically critiqued the long-established doctrine connecting action with destiny as these books problematized the presumed consequential nature of suffering and evil. On the other hand, the interpretation of the experience of the Exile recounted in the Servant Songs of Second Isaiah portrayed sickness, death, and abandonment in terms of vicarious suffering, whereby a positive content fills the previously negative realm of death. Mercy becomes the key to this new possibility, as suffering for another puts one at the service of life and allows God to be present where otherwise there appears to be only absence. Disease and death "are no longer forms of subjection to the absolute void of Sheol."[53] Seemingly meaningless experiences become openings for praise. Something new is created out of a situation of forsakenness.

We will meditate on the relationship between this new creation of praise and the original creation of the world toward the end of this chapter; for now, making a few brief comments about this relationship will suffice. Intriguingly, Rowan Williams interprets the Jewish sense of a new creation in the midst of experiences of death in ways similar to that of Ratzinger. When comparing Israel's return from the Babylonian Exile with the Exodus from Egypt, Williams notes that

Out of a situation where there is no identity, where there are no names, only the anonymity of slavery or the powerlessness of the ghetto, God makes a human community, calls it *by name* (a recurrent motif in Is. 40–55), gives it or restores it to a territory. Nothing makes God do this except God's own free promise; from human chaos God makes human community. But this act is not a *process* by which shape is imposed on chaos: it is a summons, a call which establishes the very possibility of an answer. It is a short step to the conclusion that God's relation to the whole world is like this: not a struggle with pre-existing disorder that is then molded into shape, but a pure summons.[54]

What both Ratzinger and Williams point to is the development of the belief in a God whose will is absolute and without precedent—a God whose power of decision creates life out of nothing.[55] As Paul sums up, this God is the one *who gives life to the dead and calls into existence things that do not exist* (Rom. 4:17, RSV). The strength of God's will to establish relationship is unrivaled, even in the realm where relationship was previously deemed impossible. The Jewish religious imagination was being opened to the new, fantastic possibility that the God whom they already believed to be greater than any other god—the one true God—was more powerful than all limits to relationship, such as those which they experienced in sickness, alienation, slavery, and exile, and which they observed in physical death. The mystery of this deep truth began to show itself in the book of Daniel with its affirmation of personal resurrection (12:2) and especially in 2 Maccabees, where the actions of the martyrs testify to their belief that Yahweh's life will reach them even in death, that *his mercy [will] give life and breath back* (2 Macc. 7:23, RSV).[56]

Stronger than Death

Ultimately, at least for Ratzinger, the mystery of God's life being stronger than death is expressed best in Psalm 73, where the psalmist, after praising God with his desire for God, expresses his profound trust in the utter strength of God's life and God's will to be in relationship with him: *Though my flesh and my heart fail, God is the rock of my heart, my portion forever* (v. 26, NAB). Here we find the raw and unelaborated, yet firm and foundational belief that God's power is truly unrivaled, even by the failing of human life and the eclipse of death. "Communion with God," Ratzinger concludes, "is true reality, and by comparison with it everything, no matter how massively it asserts itself, is a phantom, a nothing."[57] The key point here is that this development did not occur through the attenuation in the belief that communication is life, nor in the slackening of the belief that Yahweh is the all-powerful God, but rather in the strengthening of both claims. The reality of communication with God is the true reality. What Israel always implicitly believed even during its periods of unbelief is that this reality has the power to break into the circle of death and open it to life in God.[58]

The preservation of the noncommunication zone of death—along with all its tributaries throughout life—signifies the scandal of sin. Maintaining in practice that there are circumstances in which God's will to communicate life would not be efficacious is an affront to God's sovereignty, the *God of gods and the Lord of lords* (Deut. 10:17, RSV) who has done *great and terrible things* in the sight of Israel for its sake (Deut. 10:20–21, RSV).[59] The failure to trust that God would reach to Israel's places of desolation is at heart a failure to remember who God has shown himself to be through past deeds. Furthermore, to segregate certain members from the whole people because of infirmity or impurity or even death is to rend asunder what God has united in his own mercy. Death is left to reign as a rival power so long as life is organized according to any law other than the one founded on the primacy of God—these are laws in which the refusal to communicate blessing throughout the entire body of the people abounds and the desire to arrogate life as a possession overcomes the will to mediate life as a blessing through mercy.[60]

What Israel awaits, then, is the definitive pledge that will not only open its closed regions of belief to the communicative life of God, but also offer the gift that will turn the wounds of its own refusal to communicate with its God into a new creation of praise. In the language Ratzinger utilizes, the definitive eschatological fulfillment of Israel's faith would be the entry of God's life into the realm of the dead—that is, the act of communicating in the noncommunication zone. This event is precisely that upon which Christian faith is built: the life, death, and finally Resurrection of Jesus Christ, the Son of God:

In the descent of Jesus, God himself descends into Sheol. At that moment, death ceases to be the God-forsaken land of darkness, a realm of unpitying distance from God. In Christ, God himself entered that realm of death, transforming the space of noncommunication into the place of his own presence.[61]

The Downward Turn

What remains unstated, however, is the manner in which God, in Christ, takes up the "unpitying distance from God." Herein lies the greatest scandal of the full reach of the Incarnation: that God is separated from God. Here, too, lies the hidden truth of the deep mystery of God's love for the world within the mystery of God's Trinitarian life. The manner of the assumption of the noncommunication zone is also the deepest logic of the communication of God's Word. Ratzinger motions toward this deep truth, especially when he treats the article of faith that Christ *descended into hell*,[62] but he does not take up the task of elucidating in systematic fashion the manner in which Christ assumes this final loneliness. For that work, we must turn to Han Urs von Balthasar, whose theology of Holy Saturday is an attempt to give nuanced articulation to the meaning of the day whose drama is shrouded in silence.[63]

Hans Urs von Balthasar: Heeding Absolute Communication

The Form of the Question

Sin is the only death. As the will to break off communication with the source of life, sin and its consequences fabricate a false reality in which solitary figures appear to exist on their own and by their own power, but nevertheless endure only on the residual openness to communication yet to be closed off.[64] This illusion is unveiled upon physical death, when all powers are stripped from the individual and he falls helplessly into a state of being dead, where he may no longer speak or be spoken to. Ratzinger traced Israel's intuition about such a condition as Sheol—a noncommunication zone—which extended its influence throughout life

in the form of infirmity, alienation, and exile. Existentially, Ratzinger relates this to the deep loneliness that all human beings fear.[65] For his part,
Rahner heard in Christ's death the active "Yes" of trust that was met in
the Resurrection with the Father's own "Yes." This dialogue of affirmation occurred in the midst of the "No" of human death that is the passive
collapse of finitude at the end of its powers. In Rahner's view, this act not
only reveals the otherwise obscured truth of the human person as the one
to whom God speaks and who realizes his being in responding to God,
but also discloses God's free decision to love humanity, which is the truth
in which the "entire reality of Christianity is contained."[66]

What Hans Urs von Balthasar wishes to do is give greater Christological depth to the coincidental dimensions of Rahner's soteriology, in
which Rahner discovers the love of God manifested simultaneously with
the fully realized enactment of the human capacity for communication.[67]
Balthasar wants to show that in fact the mission of Jesus Christ both
enacts and reveals his identity as the Father's only Son. In other words,
Balthasar's project is to give a theological account of how the drama of
salvation history is recapitulated in the person of the Son, who in his Incarnation is the translation of Trinitarian love into time and creatureliness.[68] This salvific work, which exceeds and undergirds any purely
creaturely act, takes place in the mystery of the One whom God made *to
be sin who knew no sin* (2 Cor. 5:21, RSV).[69]

The depth to which the Word of God descends in the Incarnation
before returning to the Father in the Resurrection and Ascension sets the
boundary for the field of communication in and through creation. In probing the abyss of Holy Saturday, Balthasar gives a speculative account of this
absolute range that derives from and redounds to the content of revelation.[70] Balthasar's theological work enables me to ask a tripartite theological question that is crucial to my own project of theologically explicating
the communion of saints: to what distance or depth does God's offer of
communicating life go, what are the conditions for accepting this offer,
and who are the candidates for inclusion in God's dialogue with creation?

Innovating for Orthodoxy

Balthasar wants to allow sacred revelation to serve as the form of
beauty, the inner drama of salvation history, and the guiding logic of

all thought.[71] His theological work is the performance of this search, through which he attempts to put the mystery of God first and foremost in Christian theology, with theology then able to regulate the other disciplines.[72] Both at the beginning and ultimately in the final form of his thought, Balthasar is attending not just to the fact of the revelation of God in history, but also precisely to the climactic moment of this revelation: the Paschal Mystery. In the mystery of the three days, Balthasar sees the entire mystery of God both hidden and disclosed. As the central day of the Triduum, Holy Saturday is, in a sense, the linchpin of this paschal meditation. The silent stillness of this day guards the deepest mystery of God's self-giving and thus this day plays a fundamental role in Balthasar's Trinitarian as well as Christological thought. Though not without criticism, Balthasar's proposal as to what is revealed in and through Holy Saturday constitutes a substantial attempt to develop an underexplored area of Christian theology and indeed salvation history.[73]

The path that leads Balthasar to Holy Saturday is one in which he tries to navigate between alternatives that he deems inadequate for the task of making God both the central issue for theology and the main protagonist in salvation history. On the one hand, Balthasar resists theopaschism in denying full validity to views that make God substantially dependent on the action of history or the fact of creation. On this front, Balthasar attacks G. W. F. Hegel mainly, who sees history as the movement of God's own becoming, reaching God's own fullness as *Geist*, and thus operating according to a logic that is, itself, deeper than God.[74] Jürgen Moltmann is guilty of a similar though perhaps less severe form of this same offense in espousing a view of God's perfection as established in God's love for the world, thus undermining God's transcendence.[75] Balthasar finds Martin Luther's view likewise inadequate since Luther conceives of Christ voicing the "No" to God upon the cross and thus crushed under God's judgment.[76] This Christological view betokens an unsuitable theology of God for Balthasar, such that the Son stands in opposition to the Father, without qualification. Finally, even Karl Rahner falls under suspicion because it seems as though God somehow requires creation as a condition of the possibility of having a "Thou" or a partner for the expression of God's own self.[77]

On the other hand, Balthasar wishes to critique forms of Nestorianism or monophysitism, which do not grant full equality to the

Son as the orthodoxy of the faith demands due to either ontologically subordinating the Son as a creature to the Father or keeping his humanity disjoined from his divinity on the level of the will.[78] In these various views, the action of the Son in the economy is far easier to conceptualize and reason with because the equality with the Father is not total. Whatever happens to the Son in the economy does not—according to these views—bear upon God in himself, nor are these events revelatory of the immanent Trinity. This strict form of immutability—though seemingly free of the theopaschism of the views mentioned above—is just as inadequate to the theological task. The only path for Christian theology is to protect the Father's transcendence while accounting for God's real action in history.[79]

Kenotic Equality

Revelation points the way to approaching the mystery of the Incarnation on Trinitarian, theocentric terms.[80] If there were a scriptural norm to measure the challenge Balthasar faces, it would come from Philippians 2.[81] Here, Balthasar reads both the equality of the Son with the Father and the emptying of this equality into the economy: *Christ Jesus, who, though he was in the form of God, did not regard equality with God something to be grasped. Rather, he emptied himself, taking the form of a slave, coming in human likeness; and found human in appearance, he humbled himself, becoming obedient to death, even death on the cross* (vv. 5–8, NAB). Balthasar confronts the task of taking both major themes of this hymn with the utmost seriousness, allowing them to stand in paradoxical relation to one another and refusing, therefore, to fall into one of the two major errors noted above. Balthasar believes that Christian theology needs to account for Christ Jesus, the Son, *in the form of God* (v. 6)— that is, in his equality with the Father—while also giving full and uncompromised credence to his emptying of himself unto death. In other words, both the equality and the emptying of the equality must be held together.

On this basis, Balthasar makes what is likely the foundational claim of his entire theological vision. In his view, the Father's eternal begetting of the Son and the Son's response to this gift—which is identical with this gift's reception—is the foundation of all truth, beauty, and good-ness.[82] Eternally, the Son allows himself to be begotten by the Father in not claiming this gift for himself, but instead offering the fullness of this gift back to the Father in love. The intra-Trinitarian drama is the tension of begetting and emptying between the Father and the Son. The distance between these two persons is the space of the gift and the return-gift of each person to the other, as well as the space for the unity between them. In this space of gift-and-response, the Spirit is spirated as the bond of union and the guarantor of difference. Balthasar recognizes this "sepa-ration," which is enacted in the economy, "as a mode of union" trans-posed from the immanent Trinity.[83] The eternal begetting of the Son in this manner is what Balthasar, borrowing from Sergius Bulgakov, calls the *Ur-kenosis*. This is the mystery of *the Lamb that was slain* (Rev. 13:8, RSV).[84] This primal gift, which is the heart of the very mystery of God, undergirds all other kenotic activity in the economy. As Balthasar memo-rably claims, "In this inner space all the world's salvation lies enclosed."[85]

Transposition in the Key of Obedience

The recognition of the *Ur-kenosis* permits Balthasar to offer a theologi-cally adequate response to the demands of the hymn in Philippians 2. With this theme, Balthasar is able to present the deepest meaning of cre-ation itself. Creation, for Balthasar, is a second kenosis subsequent to the eternal kenosis of the begetting of the Son, though of course not in any strictly chronological sense. Creation is itself a mark of the self-limitation of God, analogous to the self-giving of the Father to the Son.[86] The con-summate truth of creation will likewise be analogous to the return-gift of the Son to the Father. The drama of salvation history occurs within this very space.

The Incarnation is the decisive event in the history of salvation, though Balthasar's understanding of it is broad indeed. In taking on human flesh, the Son translates his person—that is, his distance from and relation to the Father—into time and creatureliness.[87] As ever, the personhood of the Son is not something that he grasps or claims as his own; instead, he receives his equality from the Father precisely in not clinging to it. His "I" is thus not the "I" of self-consciousness but the

"I" of mission.[88] This mission originates in the Father; it is spoken to, through, and from the Son, who allows himself to be spoken as the Father's Word. Translated into the economy, this mission takes on the form of obedience—what Paul described as *becoming obedient to death, even death on the cross* (Phil. 2:8, NAB)—bestowing meaning to the life of the Son as the Incarnate Word in accordance with the tuning of his human will to the divine will of his Father. The deepest truth of Jesus Christ, then, is the truth of his generation in the Father's love, so that he can say that *whoever sees me sees the one who sent me* (John 12:45, NAB). This obedient tuning of the human life to the Father's will culminates in the final abandonment of Jesus to his Father as expressed in his Passion, beginning in earnest in the Garden of Gethsemane, whereby he commits his entire existence not to his own will as if a private possession, but to his Father's will as a return-gift. In the culmination of his Passion upon the cross, the Son's active mission is thus complete: his entire existence-unto-death has been given over to the will of the Father.[89] He has withheld nothing for himself.

The Last Measure of Equality

It is precisely at this point that Balthasar's speculative theologizing reaches its highest pitch. Balthasar maintains that the active mission of the Son completed upon the cross leads to the final stage of the descent of the Word in the Incarnation. This final stage is the passive fall beneath dying and death into the state of being dead.[90] According to Balthasar, seeing the fullness of the revelation of God in the Son means seeing what is unable to be seen—in order to see the final form of the Son's obedient self-emptying, we must peer into the silent darkness of Holy Saturday.[91] Only here do we glimpse the total distance between God and God-forsakenness and, in a real sense, the centerpiece of Balthasar's Christology.

In the process of allowing his own person to be translated through the Spirit into time and creatureliness, the Son assumes the full spectrum of creaturely possibilities, including the state of being most separated from God. This means that Christ takes up the self-contradictory position of becoming completely passive, in the total creaturely distance from

the source of all life. His existence approaches the state of nonexistence—
that is, existence without life. In being dead, Christ becomes solitary, isolated, and noncommunicative. He enters into solidarity with the dead
in their desolation, thus bearing upon himself "the whole weight of the
world's sin as the uttermost consequence of his mission," allowing himself to take on creation's "No" to God as his own "without actually pro-
nouncing or confirming it himself."[92] However, in this silent solidarity
Christ also bears the hidden announcement of the fact of redemption he
achieved upon the cross.[93] At the Incarnation's nadir, the Son accepts in
the economy what is eternally his within the Godhead: full equality with
the Father in the distance between their persons so that, in obedience to
his Father's will, he assumes creation's extreme distance from its Creator.
In this state of being dead, the Father shows the Son his "special reserve":
hell, or the radical possibility of God-forsakenness that comes with the
forfeiture of God's gift of creaturely freedom. The Son accepts this last
drop of the Father's gift of self by turning away from the Father who gives
him this freedom, thus establishing the final translation of his person at
the utmost limit of creation in its self-negation. Christ makes his own
even the possibility of forsaking God, and in this his equality with God is
made fully manifest in creation, hidden under the veil of death on Holy
Saturday. All creaturely distance is thus held within the distance between
the persons in the Godhead.[94]

A Historical Parable of Hell

Throughout chapter 2 and implicitly at the beginning of this chapter,
I argued that misconstruing the seriousness of death hinders the ability
to appreciate the fullness of the gift that Christ embodies and confers in
the Resurrection, which is precisely the gift that establishes and enlivens
the communion of saints. At this point when I have utilized Balthasar's
work to claim that the full descent of the Word of God in the Incarnation goes to the extreme limit of creation in the grave—into the state of
being dead—it is important to attempt to clarify precisely how lifeless and
noncommunicative this state is. In doing so, I wish to help cleanse the
imagination of any residual Neoplatonism that conceives of some kind
of survival principle that abides by its own power after physical death.

The notion of death with which Christianity reckons—that is, death as sin, which moves toward the absolute breakdown of communication—is far more serious: it is the view of death that approaches creation's absolute zero in self-contradictory nonexistence. Since no one can report with authority on the nature of this state except Christ who died and was raised, we can only, in the end, look to him. All the same, in trying to understand what he shows us, we search for images that refract the infinite comprehensibility of his revelation. While we might appeal to a literary image of this emptiness like King Lear holding the lifeless Cordelia,[95] the most important account would be historical—and the most jarring such account of the move to the absolute breakdown of communication that is the disclosure of humanity's collective guilt is presented in Auschwitz. In terms of portraying the insanity and starkness of this dark moment of history, no one provides a more penetrating, personal, and astute testimonial analysis than the Jewish Italian Auschwitz survivor Primo Levi.

In his testimony spread across numerous books and essays—though most of all in his seminal work, *Se questo è un uomo*—Levi describes the horror of the concentration camps (the *Lager*) in terms of the calculated process of dehumanization through the deliberate breakdown of communication and the consequent diminution of life to solitary meaninglessness. While we are unable to attend to the full breadth of his testimony here, we can listen to a major message of his witness by looking at three intertwined phenomena. The first of these is the process of initiation into the *Lager*; the second is the manipulation of language within the *Lager*; and the third is the relationship between community (or its absence) and existence (or, conversely, nonexistence).

Levi describes the initiation process as a decisive rupture in time and space, leaving the prisoners—the *Häftlinge*—with no place, no time, and no meaning but the enclosed place, the empty time, and the meaninglessness of the *Lager*.[96] This process is intended to force the *Häftlinge* into a state of abject alienation. The *Lager* sought to sever the past from the present and to keep the present static—that is, absolutely separated from any real or potential future. The best way that Levi can find to describe the repurposing of time and meaning is to call this initiation a "baptism."[97] Levi experienced the destruction of his identity—that is, his name, his history, and his memory—when he "climbed down" into "an enormous empty room that [was] poorly heated," a room that he says was "on the bottom," in "hell."[98] In this movement, he is taught the new meaning of who he is: "*Häftling*: I have learnt that I am *Häftling*. My number is 174517; we have been baptized, we will carry the tattoo on our left arm until we die."[99] These numbers branded upon the *Häftlinge* tell the story of the *Lager*: a number tells where one comes from, when one came, and with whom.[100] This number is the symbol of the *Lager* as the ultimate and only point of reference: the path to the *Lager*, the date of entry, and the mass with whom one entered are the only distinguishing features one retains. Everything is directed toward the *Lager* as identities are locked into this place.

As long as the *Häftlinge*'s names remain confiscated, nothing behind the names—that is, nothing of the particular persons—is available to themselves or others.[101] Those names tell stories—personal stories. To have a name enables one to be invoked, to be addressed, to be available for relationship. Names are symbols that represent and present the one who has lived, is living, and will live; who has related, is related, and will relate to others; who is always the one, particular, dynamically relational yet specific individual.[102] The walls of the *Lager* closed in so tightly and the "baptism" of the initiation was so efficacious that Levi describes the possibility of remembering himself as all but impossible, saying, "it is as if I was trying to remember the events of a previous incarnation."[103] That "previous incarnation" is a life that is now, for all intents and purposes, gone. Memory fails. Levi's existence is all but completely confined to the space of the *Lager*.

As a neophyte in the order of the *Lager*, Levi is bluntly told, "There is no why here."[104] When "why" goes, so too go the symbolic framework for language, the concrete referents for concepts, and the inner logic of meaning. The intent of language is to make persons relational in multiform ways: to others, to the world, and to the greater, ineluctable meaning of things. But in the *Lager*, where references are restricted and ultimately directed only to the inevitability of death, persons are fatally delimited and narrowed to the point of erasure. Against this constant backdrop of annihilation, the multiple languages with which the *Häftlinge* entered the *Lager* were all confused. The *Lager* became "a perpetual Babel" in which language drove individuals into isolation rather than allowing them means for understanding one another or their situation.[105]

The only life with which the *Häftlinge* were left within the strict economy of the *Lager* was one whose sole aim was the chance at minimally prolonged survival. In the reduction of persons to the singular purpose of competing with others for the calories needed to survive another day, individuals were mechanically stripped of all that individualized them, with the distinctness of human subjects seriously blurred and moving toward negation. Seen through Levi's eyes, the *Lager* processed distinct individuals into a homogenous and unchanging whole that subsisted in a static time, in a closed space.

While the situation of the *Lager* that Levi describes is not fully devoid of communication, this tragic historical occurrence is likely the closest thing to the noncommunication zone of Sheol that is possible in this world. The human persons who either, like Levi, survived to witness to their fate or who, through the testimony of such survivors, are remembered at least in some specific way, represent humanity pushed to the limit of erasure. In the end, the situation of the *Lager* and the fate of the *Häftlinge*—or, even more, the *Muselmänner*[106]—is the product of both individual sin and the sin of humanity in its unwillingness to remain open to the source of life by creating its own order of meaning, reason for existence, and classifications for personhood. This historical example shows creation approaching self-contradicting negation: the choice for God-forsakenness. Its byproduct is an indistinguishable mass of solitary figures whose existence has become more like nonexistence.

Communicative Silence

When Ratzinger speaks of Sheol, he intends something like what Levi describes. Levi's testimony also points toward the sort of God-forsaken silence that Balthasar believes Christ assumed on Holy Saturday. Indeed, Balthasar's biblically anchored theological description of the shadowy nonexistence of the dead is reminiscent of how Levi describes the bleak and fading existence of the condemned of Auschwitz:

> To existence in death there belong darkness, dust, silence. From Sheol one does not return. No activity goes on there, there is no joy, no knowledge of what happens on earth. There is no more praise of God. Deprived of

all strength and all vitality, the dead are called *refa'im*, the powerless ones. They are as if they were not. They dwell in the country of forgetfulness. "And to there even Christ descended after his dying."[107]

In the silence of Holy Saturday, the Word of Life enters into solidarity with those for whom there is no living communication. On this day, the solidarity of Christ means "being solitary like, and with, the others."[108]

This paradoxical solidarity is held within the intra-Trinitarian relations and transposed into creation. Thus, one of the truly ingenious contributions of this theological understanding of the central day of the Paschal Mystery is that it opens up an account of the relationship of creation to God that permits God to be the foundation of creation without in any way being dependent on creation as a partner or as a moment of God's own self-becoming. The whole relationship is held within God's love alone. At the same time, this view crucially emphasizes the significance of history, which is given unparalleled dignity through the Son's assumption of the full measure of human nature, even unto its complete abasement.[109]

The ramifications of this theological account are profound indeed. If Holy Saturday guards the secret of the final consequence of the Son's filial obedience, then the love of God always outflanks even the most forsaken of creatures, even the greatest sinner and the powerless ones who bear the consequences of humanity's sin. No abyss is deeper than God's love, for God's love plumbs the full depths of death when the Son lies lifeless in the state of being dead between the crucifixion and the Resurrection. In him, the primordial "Yes" of the Son to the Father's gift of self embraces and breaks open the "No" that creation says to God in its sin.[110] On Holy Saturday, the Son's ultimate Word is his silence—the silence of obediently accepting the will of the Father even unto the absolute limit of creaturely existence: its annihilation. This Word—the most eloquent of all for Balthasar—judges every other word, regulates all thought and beauty and goodness, and is indeed the final standard upon which all else is measured.[111]

The Answer from Revelation

Tracing the revelation of God on Holy Saturday yields an answer to the tripartite question I articulated at the beginning of this section, a question that has motivated the explorations of this chapter from the outset. In response to the first part of the question, the Son's Incarnation shows that the range of God's offer of communication is objectively unlimited. There is no room to imagine a distance at which God's offer of life would not reach because Christ has gone beyond the last horizon.[112] As Balthasar attests, "However wide the dramatic acting area may become, we can have confidence that no abyss is deeper than God. He embraces everything: himself and everything else."[113] Through the transposition of the Son's eternally begotten person in creation, even the denial of creation's communication with its Creator has been drawn into the space between the Father and the Son in the bond of the Holy Spirit. More precisely, the most extreme distance between creation and Creator expressed in creation's unequivocal rejection of God has been shown, in the Son, to be always already bracketed within the distance of the divine persons.[114] The drama of creation, including humanity's fall through the death of sin, is played out within the mystery of God's love.[115]

As for the part of the question pertaining to the conditions for accepting God's offer of communication, the final passivity of the Son in his obedience to the Father's will as his own mission gives us an answer. In the Son's steady fidelity we see that it is in fact the openness to receiving God's gift of self rather than any meritorious action that constitutes the precondition for becoming God's dialogue partner. The only truly necessary action is contained in the ultimate decision to *not* resist God's love.[116] This *not*-doing paradoxically calls upon and constitutes the full measure of creaturely freedom.[117] Balthasar approvingly quotes first Gustave Martelet and then Ratzinger in support of this point:

> "Where God is concerned, there can never be those who are in any way deprived of his love, since he is Love itself. . . . The absolute refusal of life (which is hell) exists, therefore, only in the case of him who eternally acknowledges and affirms no one but himself; and it is inconceivable that God could have anything to do with this grotesque possibility." . . . "Christ allots perdition to no one. . . . He does not pronounce the fatal verdict. It happens where a person has held aloof from him. It comes about where man clings to his isolation."[118]

The final part of our question finds an answer in relation to the previous answer. Those who are candidates for inclusion in God's dialogue are those who allow themselves to become persons in the person of the Son. This is the heart of Balthasar's interpretation of Paul's *en Christoi*.[119] Personhood—and thus the capacity for sharing oneself and receiving the self-donation of another—is established in the pattern of the Son's receiving and giving as his identity. The Son gratefully acknowledges his indebtedness to the Father for everything by giving back to the Father all he is given; analogously, created persons accept their own personhood not in the self-manufactured pseudo-freedom of autonomous self-assertion, but in acknowledging their own "indebtedness, in ever new ways, to absolute freedom."[120] The candidates for inclusion in the dialogue are those who take up their own unique missions within the universal, all-embracing mission of Christ, who opens wide communication with the Father, outside of which there is no life. Eschatologically, those who take up these personal missions "in Christ" are the saints.[121]

Deep Calls upon Deep

Since Christ, in the absolute openness of his person, stretches himself communicatively from his eternally begotten origin in the Father all the way to the extreme limit of creation, he allows himself to become the space of life as communion. Upon this truth we may therefore state that, "in Christ," every site of alienation—even that *far country* (Luke 15:13) of life's dissipation—becomes a possible site of the creaturely acceptance of the divine Word. Christ does not eliminate death; rather, he transforms it through the obedient openness of his mission. As his mission from the Father is offered *pro nobis* all the way to his death and descent into hell, Christ draws to himself—*into* himself—the great many who fade listlessly in all manner of sin's alienation, thus creating a "mystical fellowship of death."[122] In doing so, Christ is the mercy that salves the wounds of sin's negation of life with God's efficacious will to bestow life in communicating himself. The reliance on this freely given gift is the fount of human freedom.[123]

By manifesting without remainder his desire to share the fate of sinners, Christ himself becomes the principle of communion among the dead. He personally communicates solidarity with the dead in assuming the *wages of sin* and personalizes nonpersons with the *free gift of God* that is his eternal life (Rom. 6:23, RSV). Christ is "the single word which resumes everything in itself," definitively establishing "the dialogue between God and creation" in the revelation of "the internal dialogue of God" now become "the world's affirmation of God," wiping "out every contradictory *no* . . . in the truly vicarious suffering for sinners on the cross."[124] It is the "Godmanhood" of the Son that makes possible the unique bearing of the total sin of the world,

> Yet not God together with just any man, but God, the absolutely unique, in that absolutely unique man who is unique because he is God, and who, for this reason and no other, can communicate a share in his Cross to his fellow human beings, with whom he is more profoundly solidary than any man can ever be with any other man, and can do that in death itself, where each man is absolutely alone.[125]

No other man can share fully in the isolation of human beings alienated from God: only he who chose this loneliness as his own purely out of love can become one with each human being in his "loneliest loneliness."[126] Sharing in this loneliness submerges death in the wellspring of life, cleansing isolation in the basin of communion.

Holy Saturday is the terrible, glorious last Sabbath of the old covenant. Upon this death, the body of the new covenant readies for birth. Having loved until the end (John 13:1), Christ shows that the mysterious heart of God is the will to love, which is even deeper than the will to create. Creation comes from love, not vice versa. In the beginning, God creates out of love rather than happening to love what is created. In the end, God re-creates out of love rather than simply loving what is worthy of re-creation. This love is bottomless. From this depth springs the whole symphony of the new creation as God's dialogue of love.[127] Therefore, by seriously confronting death in following Christ through the descent into hell, we prepare to allow the gift of the Resurrection to purify our vision of the lingering notions of autonomy and self-sufficiency that obscure the brilliance of God's "second gift" unto nothing, a gift that recapitulates and consummates the original gift of creation itself. Seeing through the absolute gift of the Resurrection illuminates the analogous relationship between the *resurrection of the body* and the doctrine of *creatio ex nihilo*.

Given to Nothing: Creation and Resurrection

The communion of saints is an eschatological dimension of the Christian faith that expresses the belief that those incorporated into the life of Jesus Christ freely and actively share in God's life as a redeemed and sanctified community. This article of faith is Christological in that it concerns the full meaning of the Incarnation, pneumatological in that it pertains to the Spirit's work of forming community in the bonds of charity, and ultimately Trinitarian in that it fundamentally entails the graced participation in the divine life of persons-in-communion. The doctrine of God therefore has everything to do with humanity's hope of fulfillment. In Balthasar's words, "the more Trinitarian (which is to say, the richer) our picture of God is, the more we are able to have a positive attitude to the eternal perfection of the world created and redeemed in God."[128] This truth also lies at the core of the Christology of Karl Rahner, who states that

> the fact that God himself is man is both the unique summit and the ultimate basis of God's relationship to his creation, in which he and his creation grow in direct (and not in converse) proportion. This positive nature of creation, not merely measured in relation to nothingness but also in relation to God, reaches its qualitatively unique climax, therefore, in Christ. For, according to the testimony of the faith, this created human nature is the indispensable and permanent gateway through which everything created must pass if it is to find the perfection of its eternal validity before God.[129]

If these statements are indeed true, then the approach to a full and proper understanding of the communion of saints as intrinsic to creedal faith requires the rejection of any notions of competition between God and the world—or, more to the point, between God and human flourishing, or between divine and human persons. These illusory notions come from the corrosive influence of sin. The path to appreciating the original vocation and final destiny of human beings is the continual discovery of our place in God's freely willed creation.

I have gone to great lengths in the previous chapter and especially in this one to argue that, in the Christian view, human death is a definitive end. Due to sin, this end approaches the total breakdown of communication from God, who is the source of all life. Through the Incarnation and specifically in the full descent of the Word of God to the noncommunication zone of the dead, the intra-Trinitarian communication of divine love embraces creation in all its dimensions. Therefore, in the Resurrection of Christ, the Father not only accepts the return-gift of the Son in which their unity proceeds in the Spirit, but he also welcomes creation itself into the very life of God, confirming its dignity before God who deems it *very good* (Gen. 1:31). The secret of creation is thus revealed only in the Resurrection of Christ, in virtue of whom God confers upon human beings a share in this eschatological glory through the *resurrection of the body*, which we may also call the *resurrection of the dead* (see 1 Corinthians 15).[130] As Brian Robinette acknowledges, "There is no greater testimony to God's love for creation in all its contingency and particularity than the resurrection. What creation institutes, the resurrection confirms and completes."[131]

In the light of the Resurrection of Christ, we discern that the doctrine of creation and the doctrine of the resurrection of the dead have at least one essential feature in common: they both have to do with the power of God's love over nothing.[132] This singular act of God *in* history and *for* history, which comes from *beyond* history, is for the Christian "the criterion in whose light tradition must be read."[133] In the Risen Christ, the God in whom all *those who share the faith of Abraham* believe is definitively revealed as the one *who gives life to the dead and calls into existence the things that do not exist* (Rom. 4:16–17, RSV). It is upon his gratuity that both the gift of creation and the gift of new life depend. By renewing our understanding of the gratuitous gift of creation that God calls forth *ex nihilo*, I hope to show how the freedom of those called into the new life of Christ in his Resurrection also depends on the freedom of God's love, so that we may begin to consider the communion of saints in terms of the reception of and response to this gift alone.

Truly Nothing

Christ's descent on Holy Saturday is God's move toward his creation as it brings itself to nothing. What Christ here obediently assumes is creation's disintegration into the formlessness from which God wills to call it forth. Christ thus enters into creation's *un*-creation. In doing so, the dead Christ incarnates what becomes of all creation, including and especially human beings, without the creative communication of God's life—that is, nothing. God's creative act is always given to nothing, with the recipient of the gift constituted by the giving of the gift itself.[134] This nothing without God is total, meaning that it is not only the absence of matter but also the absence of influence, need, and indeed being itself.

Thomas Aquinas attempts to clarify the relationship of creation to God as one of complete dependence when he reasons as follows:

> To every effect produced by God there is either something pre-existent or not. If not, the thesis stands, then God produces some effect out of nothing pre-existent. If anything pre-exists, we either have a process to infinity, which is impossible, or we must come to something primitive, which does not presuppose anything else previous to it. Now this primitive something cannot be God Himself, for God is not the material out of which anything is made: nor can it be any other being, distinct from God and uncaused by God.[135]

To think of God as a material out of which something is made or, alternatively, to think of God as having to resort to working on some pre-existent matter in order to create is, according to Aquinas, to think of something other than the God whom Christians profess in their creed. The God of the Judeo-Christian tradition is being itself: underived and perfect. The act of creating belongs to God alone.[136]

Summarily, Aquinas holds that all creatures—that is, creation as a whole and each part of it—come not from something pre-existing since "prior" to existing creatures would be in a state of non-being, so to speak. Uncreated creatures do not have existence either in actuality or in potentiality.[137] The agent who brings that-which-was-not into being can be none other than God, for God alone is the one who is being absolutely.[138]

It follows that no intermediary would be able to bestow being because nothing can give what it is not—that is, being itself.

In line with Aquinas, one must conclude that there is no "when" or "what" prior to *the beginning* of which Genesis 1:1 speaks. Though the first chapter of Genesis concerns the ordering of *the earth*, which *was without form and void* (Gen. 1:2, RSV), there cannot be any prologue to this chapter other than God since there is nothing of which to speak other than the absolute being of God *in se*. When John's Gospel opens with a meditation on the Eternal Word, it attests that all prologues are referred to God alone. There is nothing to speak of that does not come from the mystery of God.

While the doctrine of *creatio ex nihilo* is certainly about what precedes *the beginning*—or, more precisely, what does *not* precede it—it is also and perhaps even more crucially concerned with the question of creation's why. The question of why there is something—anything—and not nothing is itself implicitly addressed in the claim of *creatio ex nihilo*, even if it is commonly the second dimension of the question to be considered, if it is ever considered at all. And yet, this dimension is in fact the most important facet of the doctrine of creation, for it is the one that redounds to God's intention, God's motivation, or, to put it more sharply, to who exactly this God is in whom *we live and move and have our being* (Acts 17:28, RSV).[139]

In order to hold fast to the true meaning of the (Judeo-)Christian teaching about creation, it is essential to cling to what God fundamentally reveals about God: that God wills to create for no other reason than to establish a relationship with that which God creates. God creates by giving being to what has no being so that what comes into being may share in God's life. By this logic, the fullness of the revelation of God contains within it the hidden meaning of creation itself. As such, when Jesus Christ is raised from the tomb, he reveals, in his very person, the "God who calls unto eschatological life what has succumbed to the nonbeing and nondoing of death," thereby allowing the whole of creation to resound in him its dependence on God's summons for its own being.[140] In the Resurrection, the Father accepts the Son's gift of obedience unto death by *bestow[ing] on him the name that is above every name* (Phil. 2:9, NAB)—that is, God's very own name. In the Risen Christ, God translates the name he once gave to Moses—*I am who I am* (Exod. 3:14, RSV)—as "I am the one who saves you."[141]

The New Creation

The Resurrection of Jesus Christ is an event in the history of creation that does not in any way result from the power of creation itself. While the raising of Jesus from the dead is consistent with creation's deepest truth as God's freely given gift of life through relationship, the Resurrection is something that God does to creation, for creation, and in creation in the mode of irruption.[142] In his complete passivity on Holy Saturday, the Son remains in solidarity with noncommunicative creation to allow the Father to do for and in him what he does not do for himself under the weight of sin that he has accepted as his own.

The Resurrection allows creation to become what God intends it to be. Christ is the first fruits in whom those who have fallen asleep become a new creation (see 1 Cor. 15:20, 23; 2 Cor. 5:17). Left to itself, creation would cease to be, just as those who die do not retain life by their own power. Present and future existence come from beyond the limits of nature, as both the gift of creation itself and the promise of creaturely perfection originate in divine goodness.[143] Those called into being according to God's own image (Gen. 1:26–27) find their own truth in hearing themselves spoken as a "creaturely word which has its existence in [God's] eternal Word."[144] Partaking in the communication of God's life means receiving as one's own in the second gratuity of re-creation the original truth of God's gratuitous "being-for" as the foundation of one's very existence.

The gift pledged in creation and fulfilled in resurrection is the space to be "other" from God so as to enter into dialogue with God.[145] In the surprising expanse of "God's all-embracing Trinitarian love,"[146] God creates space for creaturely particularity from nothing other than his love. When creation cedes this space in its sin, God's re-creates this space for particularity through nothing but the fidelity of his love. In both instances, God's Word *gives life to the dead and calls into existence things that do not exist* (Rom. 4:17, RSV). In this Word, the "'let be' in absolute Otherness"[147] that characterizes the relations of the divine persons is communicated as the deepest truth of created persons.

This Christian vision of creation and the eschaton is sharply distinguished from Rilke's doctrine of absorption into the unity of being, which reverberates with an implicit Hegelianism. Likewise, the insufficiency of Moltmann's conception of human incorporation into the wholeness of creation in God's eternity is further disclosed since what he misses is precisely God's delight in the particularity of his creation.[148] Most important of all, this Christian view stands in prophetic opposition to the kind of violent homogenization of the *Lager* to which Primo Levi bore witness. What comes about in Christ is the preservation of the deepest dignity of creatures in God's will to redeem and perfect the freedom and subjectivity first given to them in creation.[149] Sharing in God's act of creation means learning to speak according to God's Word as it is freely given.[150]

The Word of Life

In this chapter, we have been concerned with the purification of the imagination through the serious confrontation with death that Christianity demands. This attempt at purification occurs between, on the one side, the obfuscations that modern secular or even atheistic approaches to death introduce in response to the commonplace denial of death, and on the other, the work of allowing a renewed eschatological imagination to conform to the mystery of the communion of saints, which I attempt in the subsequent chapters. Toward the beginning of this chapter, I appealed to Karl Rahner to sketch out the dimensions of a theology of death within a truly Christian eschatology. Joseph Ratzinger's thought then permitted me to locate the drama of the communication of God's life within salvation history while pointing the way from the faith of Israel to the person of Christ. The predominant Christology I employed for asking the question about communication in Christ then came from Hans Urs von Balthasar, whose goal was to perform the theological task according to the strictures of sacred revelation, even as he probed theologically undertreated areas of the Church's tradition. This path led us to Holy Saturday before moving on to a vision of creation in the light of the Resurrection.

All the while, my hope has been to deepen our exploration of the intrinsic nature of the communion of saints within the logic of the Christian faith. As an eschatological reality pertaining to the gift of creaturely participation in divine life, the question about the range of, conditions for, and candidates in God's communication of life is essential to my project. To that end, what Balthasar, in particular, helped me to uncover is that absolute receptivity without any activity is itself the baseline condition for becoming an interlocutor in God's symphonic dialogue with creation. This is true because Christ has made it so. Christ holds *the keys to death and the netherworld* (Rev. 1:18, NAB) because he has allowed himself to be spoken in the language of absolute silence in the state of being dead. This is God's definitive and most profound eloquence in creation. To approach an understanding of the communication of the dead among themselves, as well as the way in which the blessed dead address the wayfaring living in God's communion, we learn in Christ that we must prescind from our preconceived categories for worldly communication and listen afresh for God's voice—the voice that those living in Christ have made their own.

We cannot know the saints who live in Christ if we stay within the boundaries of reason alone. Seeing them requires the vision that grace alone can provide, a kind of seeing that often begins with a shock as commonplace ways of seeing according to our delimiting expectations are first exceeded and then transformed. Hearing them requires an openness that only the Holy Spirit can provide, a kind of hearing that starts with the purgation of our deafening presumptions about truth before tuning us to the pacific humming of divine desire. Speaking to them requires a new grammar, a kind of grammar that is sui generis in Christ who claims them and seeks us.

What the work of this chapter gives us are the thematic dimensions of a truly Christian eschatology. What we will be in Christ is neither identical to nor wholly different from what we are now, and the saints now abide within the space of that paradox. To orient ourselves eschatologically—both in theology and in prayer—we must hold fast to the permanent significance of history, and thus of embodiment and of relationality, because God delights in creation. In Christ, God has opened up the whole of creation, unto its utmost boundary, as the field for the communication of his life: there are no crevices too small, no chasms too deep for this Word of Life. And yet, this all-powerful Word expresses power in humility, respecting the freedom of those who would hear it, even though their capacity to hear is itself a gift. To speak in this Word is the delight God intends (cf. Ps. 81:10). The blessed ones are those who have allowed the Lord to open their lips so that they may proclaim his praise (Ps. 51:15).

My thesis is that this praise redounds to God's own desire, with which Christ himself was and is fully identified, and which the saints have accepted as their inheritance. The saints have consumed this desire, grown into it, and become personalized, particular echoes of it: in this harmony, God's will for creation is fulfilled as their sanctification. The saints resound with God's glory as they sing the hymn of the divine desire, a desire that first met them in the freedom of love. In receiving this gift, the truth of life as communication becomes their own truth. They witness to the mystery of Christ that *those who hear will live* (John 5:25, RSV).

CHAPTER 4

DISPOSSESSING DESIRE

Becoming Fully Human

All life depends on God's freely given gift. Nothing precedes this gift and, correspondingly, nothing would remain were this gift rejected. Aligned with this logic, I stated in the previous chapter that the true meaning of death for Christians is sin, for the willful breakdown in communication with the source of the gift of life is tantamount to forfeiting one's creaturely status. Positively stated, creaturely life intensifies in its activity according to the measure of openness with which the creature receives the divine gift.[1]

What God gives is primary; however, what I intend to argue in this chapter is that *what* God gives is inseparable from *how* God gives—with God, the content and the style of giving are presented as one to the creature for whom the gift is offered. As created persons progress toward their fulfillment in conformity to the person of Jesus Christ, they move from accepting God's freely given gift, to sharing this freely given gift through the freedom of their own creativity, to being transformed by and into the very manner in which this gift is given. Sanctification—that is, the graced activity of partaking in divine life through the agency of the Holy Spirit, to which Christians profess belief in the third part of the creed—is the process of created persons becoming reconstituted in accordance with the communication of God's life. The path of holiness and indeed eschatological beatitude is one of learning to love what and whom God loves according to the manner of God's love. In the life, death, and Resurrection of Jesus Christ, God's desire to love his creation is definitively revealed and proffered—it is an absolute and boundless desire. For those incorporated into Christ's life through the Spirit, this divine desire defines their own creaturely desire, which has become the essential truth of their lives as persons and the basis of their life together in communion.

From beginning to end, this chapter is chiefly concerned with how the communication of God's life enables the communication of life among the members of the communion of saints. In particular, I open up the prospect of the communication in Christ of the blessed to those still on pilgrimage, thus reading theological anthropology from an eschatological standpoint in a decisively Christological key.[2] This approach to more fully understanding the dynamics of this mystery of communication requires a deliberate progression in four stages.

In the first section, I theologically exegete the encounters with the risen Christ as recorded in the Gospels. I uplift these testimonies as both presenting the unrepeatable (trans-)historical event of the Christian faith and establishing the grammar for apprehending the new life that *those who have not seen yet believe* subsequently inherit (John 20:29–30, RSV). N. T. Wright, Joseph Ratzinger, Karl Rahner, Hans Urs von Balthasar, and Rowan Williams feature prominently in this section because each is, in his own way, concerned with both the narrative quality of these encounters and the relationship between the content and form of what is communicated. In this section, my direction is to move from the primacy of what God gives to the mode of reception necessary for receiving this gift.

In the second section, I move in the opposite direction—from the human struggle of discovering the truth of one's existence that points to a distinctive mode of apprehension, to the primacy of God's gift as *the way, and the truth, and the life* (John 14:6, RSV). Augustine's *Confessions* serves as my primary text for analysis because therein Augustine gives the narrative account of how the redemption of memory occurs through receiving the gift of mercy as the fulfillment of one's deepest desire. Moving in this direction, I argue that there is a foundational correspondence between what is given to humanity—and all of creation—in the Resurrection and who the human person essentially is.

I then use the third section to pivot from *what* God gives and *how* one receives this gift to *how* God gives and *what* transformation this way of giving effects in the recipients. I appeal to Henri de Lubac's modern retrieval of Augustinian theology to argue for a truly Christian (theological) anthropology in which destiny is constitutive of ontology. I argue that the natural desire for God precisely as gift is made known to us in Christ's fullness. In Christ, the dignity of creation as God's first gift is revealed and from his Resurrection the second gift of creaturely sanctification comes forth. The desire for God is ultimately a longing for God's way of loving, meaning that the One who creates this desire draws human persons into a new way of being.

In the final section I focus on how the transformation initiated by the divine gift builds communion among those who receive. Moreover, these recipients of grace are given the freedom to give what they receive, *grace upon grace* (John 1:16, RSV). The saint is thus the one whose desire is fulfilled in Christ as she willfully joins in the joy of Christ's giving. This is the way of communicating life from the side of eschatological fullness.

Encountering the Risen Christ: The Beginning of a New End

The eternal significance of humanity rises on Easter morning. This is the perpetual spring in which all creation is made new. Unlike the seasonal spring, Easter is not the revivification of what lay lifeless in the dead of winter, as if rekindling the memory of something forgotten but now unexpectedly recalled. More like a spring of water, this day gushes with the source of life itself, measuring all distance in terms of thirst and longing.[3] On this day creation beholds what it yearned for but never knew, what it reached toward but never grasped, what it waited for but never expected.[4] On this day the disciples meet their risen Lord, from whom their own fulfillment flows.

Encountering the risen Christ, the disciples confront an objective reality that draws them toward a distinctive mode of subjective apprehension. In order to meet Christ as he is, the disciples must accept a new way of knowing, seeing, remembering, and desiring. These encounters thus inaugurate a fundamental change in the disciples themselves. Moreover, those who rely on their testimony—that is, Christians—receive both the content of their proclamation of the risen Christ and their mode of perception and apprehension; in other words, the disciples who encountered Jesus in his resurrected glory communicate their belief in his Resurrection *and* the grounds for this belief.[5] To experience the risen Christ is to experience the one who died and who now lives in glory—this experience brought the first disciples in contact with the death they had to undergo in order to begin to live as redeemed persons freed for the sanctifying work of the Spirit. Subsequent generations of disciples must be similarly reconstituted through their encounter in faith with Jesus Christ, whom they come to know as the resurrection and the life (see John 11:25) through the apostolic witness.

Faith in History

In his extensive study on the biblical roots of the Christian belief in the Resurrection of Jesus, N. T. Wright defends the thesis that the tradition of the empty tomb and of the meetings with the risen Jesus have the actual historical event of Jesus's bodily resurrection as their necessary condition.[6] He asserts that not only is the Resurrection of Jesus historic, but in fact, according to the evangelists' testimonies, it is also properly *historical*.[7] Even as distinctive overtones are heard by each of the evangelists and echoed through their Gospels, their testimonies all move from and point back to a fundamental reality: that Jesus appeared to his disciples in the transformed physicality of his embodied life.[8]

To read the Gospels aright, one must accept the fact that the evangelists are presenting the bodily Resurrection of Jesus of Nazareth as an historical event. To stand with them in faith one must assent to the veracity of their historical claim. Moreover, this line of interpretation makes clear that the central conviction of the Christian faith is anything but speculative: it is absolutely bodily (see 1 Cor. 15:17). The first disciples' meetings with the risen Christ are irreducibly unique, while the testimonies of these meetings are incomparably privileged. Subsequent Christian experiences are analogous to but never identical with these events that *"will never happen again."*[9]

The witnesses to the Resurrection claim to have historically encountered the bodily life of him who fell into the void of death and was
raised on the third day. Concomitantly, it is God's action that comes
from nothing rather than the faith of these witnesses on whose testimony
Christian belief itself depends. Their faith comes from meeting the risen
Christ, who comes back from the dead by the power of God. What God
does is absolutely primary.

Shock and Seeing

John the Evangelist is particularly keen on establishing what all the Gospels hold as true: that what the disciples encounter in the forty days of
Easter are the first fruits of the new creation. John's theological vision begins with the Eternal Word who, in the Resurrection, unites the Creator with the new creation.[10] Easter is thus pure revelation: an historical
event that comes *to* but not *from* history itself. Any attempt to trans-
late the Resurrection event into a purely philosophical or scientific register, or even to explain it exhaustively according to a specific theological
system, is always bound to fail from the start. The Resurrection cannot
just fit in with preexisting worldviews; rather, it establishes the definitive
worldview.[11]

To submit the Resurrection to any independent procedures of verification or interpretation is to miss the central question with which this
singular event is concerned. This question is what each of the Gospels,
in their own way, attempts to address: who is this person, Jesus of Nazareth? The Resurrection offers the complete answer, one that is not deduc-
ible from other evidence alone. On the one hand, the risen Jesus is who
he was prior to death; on the other, a radical change has taken place. The
continuity and the discontinuity together signify the uniqueness of this
person, in whom the meanings of life and death, space and time, history
and salvation are hidden and revealed.[12]

Following Hans Frei, John Thiel punctuates the importance of the
continuity of Jesus's identity before death and in his resurrected glory.
In fact, Thiel supports the claim that Jesus is most himself in his Resurrection because he consummately embodies the words and deeds of his
entire life.[13] While his life from birth to death was a pledge of fidelity

to the salvific will of God, Jesus's return to his disciples in the Resurrection is the fulfillment of his promise to them and, through them, to all of creation. He is the Messiah—*the power of God and the wisdom of God* (1 Cor. 1:24, RSV)—who embodies the constancy of his character in the fulfillment of his promises—that is, as mercy.[14]

While the unanimous agreement of the Gospels to the constancy of character and continuity of identity of the risen Jesus is clearly evident, the diverse narrative traditions presented in the Gospels also recall the disciples' difficulty in recognizing him as the one they knew. While the Gospel of Matthew emphasizes the disciples' encounters with Jesus as leading them into worship (28:11, 17) and the longer ending of Mark's Gospel foregrounds the initial failure to believe (16:9–14) that preceded their reception of a new mission from Jesus (16:15–20), the two Gospels that consider the encounters with the risen Jesus at length—Luke and John—each highlight the subjective shift that the disciples must undertake in order to recognize Christ as he is. Within this "dialectic of recognition and non-recognition,"[15] these Gospels preserve the fact that for the first disciples, the experience of the Resurrection was a shock.[16]

The theme of surprise is one the author of Luke's Gospel develops in his account of the Resurrection, beginning with the announcement to the women (21:1–8), the proclamation to the Eleven (24:9–11), and Peter's arrival at the tomb (24:12), then followed by the two appearances: the first to the disciples journeying to Emmaus (24:13–35) and the second to the disciples in the upper room (24:36–49).[17] Of these episodes, the dialectic of recognition and non-recognition unfolds in greatest detail on the road to Emmaus, where Jesus draws near to the disciples. Luke tells his readers that the disciples do not see who Jesus is because their *eyes were kept from recognizing him* (24:16, RSV). There is something about them rather than Jesus that forces this failure of vision. It is only at the conclusion of the journey, when Jesus sits with them at table to take, bless, break, and give bread, that their *eyes were opened and they recognized him* (24:30–31, RSV). The reason they did not recognize him earlier is not that they had not known Jesus (24:19) or that they were unaware that his tomb was by then empty (24:22–24). The foolishness Christ confronted lay elsewhere.[18]

In the course of their testimony, the disciples divulge their insufficiency: *But we had hoped that he was the one to redeem Israel* (24:21,

RSV). Not only do they speak of their hope in the past tense, but they also admit that prescribed expectations conditioned their faith in Jesus. They believe the redemption of Israel has not been and presumably will not be accomplished because Jesus has died. They interpret the meaning of Jesus through their expectations rather than allowing Jesus to interpret and recast their expectations.[19] Had they truly clung to Jesus as their source of truth and of life, they would have been open and ready to make a new act of faith when he appeared to them, despite all expectations. The cure for their self-induced blindness occurs through exposing that which blinds them to the light of a radically new and unexpected experience of grace.[20] Jesus recasts their memories as he interprets the Scriptures through himself before presenting these disciples with the fulfillment of the Scriptures' promises in his own embodied fellowship with them (24:26–31). He prepares them to receive what they did not know they always desired. Only as they are shocked into recognizing him do they come to recognize their own desire for him in retrospect: *Did not our hearts burn within us while he talked to us on the road, while he opened to us the Scriptures?* (24:32, RSV). In this encounter, they themselves are changed according to what they desire and how they know.[21] The offer of mercy enables them to see and accept mercy.

John tells of a similar transformation in the narrative of Jesus's appearance to Mary Magdalene. She goes to the tomb *while it was still dark* (John 20:1, RSV) in search of the dead body of the one whom she had loved. She is unrelenting in her search for his corpse, even after she finds the tomb empty (20:2), encounters *two angels in white* (20:12), and eventually turns to stand face to face with Jesus, who issues a question of identity: *Whom do you seek?* (20:15a, RSV). She persists in her desire for the dead body and thus is prevented from seeing the Living One. But when Jesus speaks her name—*Mary*—she turns again (20:16). In the offer of her own name from the lips of the One who knows her, she recognizes the stranger she previously accused of hiding a dead body as the risen Lord himself.[22] Mary's cycle of storytelling is broken as she encounters the living body she sought among the dead. Seeing the Lord is, for Mary, a matter of recognizing the one she loved and beginning to see him anew in his fullness.[23]

Ratzinger observes that the full transformation for which this encounter calls actually concludes with the confession of Thomas the

Apostle. Whereas Mary went in search of a memorial, Thomas would only be satisfied with new hope if it passed through and did not disregard where his hope died, on Golgotha. It is worth pausing for a moment to consider the significance of Thomas's demand. While it is easy to consider him as the doubter who is culpably unwilling to believe, we might think more deeply about how the seriousness with which he takes death contrasts sharply with what we considered in the second chapter as the engrained tendency, especially in modernity, to deny death. The condition he sets for believing in this wholly unexpected possibility is that this proposed reality not arise from anything like a wish for anesthesia on his part. He cannot change his memory; his memory must be broken and then re-created. It is as if Thomas resists—in anticipatory fashion—the sort of cheap versions of hope that would lure us out of the painful realities of real loss for the sake of a more pleasant and palatable pseudo-reality—one that is, in the end, little more than the projection of a fantasy. Thomas looks hard at reality, holding with such firmness to what he knows as real that he will only move from it if a surpassing reality should break upon him, one that validates the truth he knows even as it surpasses it.[24]

For Thomas's sake, then, Jesus offers his wounds because Thomas will not forget the cross. That revolution of recognition that began with Mary and was later shared by proclamation and then as the gift of peace to fearful disciples hereby enters into the stage of completion. Thomas responds in unadulterated faith to the crucified, risen Jesus: *My Lord and My God* (20:28, RSV).[25] He has clung to no other wish and so now Thomas can cling in faith to the One who is the Incarnation of hope in his Resurrection. Here with Thomas, the first question Jesus asks in John's Gospel—*What do you seek?* (1:38, RSV)—finally elicits a fully appropriate response as the seeker implicates himself without reserve in naming what and whom he seeks. So it is that John arrives by way of narrative detail at the same conclusion at which Matthew arrives by way of narrative brevity: the Resurrection invites worship and issues a mission (see Matt. 28:9–10, 16–20; cf. Mark 16:15–20).[26]

On the narrative level, these accounts of Jesus's meetings with his disciples present a double shock. First, the disciples are shocked to recognize the unknown stranger as the One they have always loved, the One who was crucified. In the absorption of this first shock, the disciples themselves are shocked into a new way of seeing and being. They cannot accept Jesus according to their old expectations and assumptions, their previous limitations and preset ideas, or their unwillingness to accept themselves as the ones both guilty of unfaith and now offered mercy. The Resurrection's impact on them forces them to evacuate their sense of self in order to receive anew the gift of who the risen Christ calls them to be.[27]

Transmission and Transformation

In their own experience, the first disciples confronted the truth that the Resurrection of Jesus Christ cannot be interpreted according to any hermeneutic other than the one the event itself provides. Brian Robinette calls this the "resurrection hermeneutic," which opens up a "grammar" that is normative not just for the Gospels, but indeed for the form and content of the Christian faith itself.[28] By their testimonies, the witnesses to the Resurrection transmit two things at once: the objective reality of Jesus's Resurrection and the subjective condition necessary for them to apprehend that reality. The second follows from the first, but in the testimony of the apostles, these two are not easily distinguished.[29] Balthasar observes that "the disciples had to be transformed and raised up from a *carnalis amor ad Christi humanitatem*, that Christ who *videbatur esse quasi homo unus ex eis*, by being carried, entranced, into the sphere of the Spirit, to a *spiritualis amor ad eius divinitatem*."[30] The encounters with the risen Christ draw the disciples forward into the space of given freedom where they might receive the gift of new life through their humble acceptance of and willful response to God's unsolicited offer of love. Meeting Jesus in his Resurrection transforms their vision, capacitating them to gaze on the divine gift that Christ's humanity presents (see 2 Cor. 3:12–18). This way of seeing and apprehending is itself the gift of the Spirit, who opens the mystery of God *in se* to God's action in the world *pro nobis*.[31]

What did it mean for the first disciples to *see* Jesus in his Resurrection? What does it mean for those who receive their testimony—that is, Christians—to *see* him? Put simply, to *see* the risen Christ is to see that Jesus is the Son of God. Without recognizing him as such, one does not see *him*. What the disciples encounter as true in the Resurrection illumines the truth of which they were, at best, only partially aware earlier: that Jesus is, as Wright summarizes, "the one in whom the living God, Israel's God, has become personally present in the world, has become one of the human creatures that were made from the beginning in the image of this same God."[32]

Paul insists that if the seminal event of the Christian faith were not true, then all preaching and indeed the faith itself would be in vain (1 Cor. 15:14). The first disciples therefore pledge themselves to the truth of this event not merely as some brute fact, but rather as a personal event in which they themselves were involved. Their own testimony insists that Jesus is the Son of God, that he came to them in his Resurrection, and that they were changed—fundamentally changed—by the encounter. In their attestations to the historicity of this unique event, the disciples commit themselves to the consequences of such a claim. To recognize the risen Jesus as the same One whom they knew but who lives now in a way discontinuous with what they thought possible means that the disciples confess that the power of God is stronger than death. And this mode of seeing only became possible once they recognized that the risen One came *to them*, was given *to them*, and embodied mercy *for them* in the healing and renewal of *their* wounded humanity.[33]

This structure of belief is represented in the creed itself. The mysteries of the second part of the creed make manifest the ultimate truth of the first part: the life, death, and Resurrection of Jesus make God known as the Creator and Giver of life, the one who *calls into existence the things that do not exist* (Rom. 4:17, RSV). The apostolic witnesses preserved the memory of what they experienced as the mystery of Jesus's life from their own inspired position. In the "sphere of the Spirit," they both recognized Jesus for who he is and began to know the fulfillment of the promises of his meritorious sacrifice. Christ's gift of mercy is the ground upon which they come to understand. With their testimonies, they communicate not only whom they met, but also how they came to know him anew and thereby came to discover themselves in the encounter.[34] Since their witness is self-committing, accepting the content of their preaching means also inhabiting their sphere of belief (see 2 Peter 1:16–21).[35] Subsequent generations of Christians do not meet the risen Jesus in exactly the same way that the apostolic witnesses did; rather, they meet him in identity and otherness through the objective content of the apostolic testimony and in the embodied worship of the Church in its liturgy and sacramental life.[36] Later Christians do not simply repeat what the first disciples experienced, yet they *do* rely on that initial experience and enter into the space those disciples first received as their own in the historical encounter with the person of the risen Christ. Christianity's unavoidable reliance on the eyewitnesses to the Resurrection already casts light on the redemption of the communicative nature of the human community, and thus of humanity's original solidarity through the gratuitous gift of its eschatological fulfillment.[37] Augustine attends to this unexpected reality in *De doctrina Christiana*, where he concludes that God is pleased to save those who believe through the folly of preaching (see 1 Cor. 1:21), for God did not need to work through human ministry yet deigns to do so.[38]

Memory and Meaning

The Easter event itself and the order of its transmission through the first witnesses both preserves and communicates what Ratzinger calls "the most fundamental feature of Christian faith"—that is, "its personal character." Christianity's "central formula is not 'I believe in something,' but 'I believe in you.' It is the encounter with the man Jesus, and in this encounter it experiences the meaning of the world as a person."[39] This affirmation of belief in the personal communication of the person of Jesus Christ opens up for the believer "a new space of life, a new space of being in union with God."[40] This is nothing short of an ontological revolution, whereby the creature is manifestly oriented to her Creator.

The unfathomable newness of the risen Christ breaks like the swift sunrise upon the nighttime of stale certainties and nostalgic recollections. Encountering the risen Christ is not just a matter of remembering who he is; it is also and more significantly about receiving a new memory.[41] The Resurrection discloses the secret of the crucifixion as the end of impersonal and depersonalizing powers bent toward domination. The competition between disparate attempts to define the meaning of the world according to individualized or partial narratives leads, ultimately, to destruction and death, with no possibilities for sustaining life, let alone everlastingly enriching it. On Golgotha, Christ accepted these deceptions, the systems they create, and all their consequences. On Easter morning, he was raised as the embodied truth deeper than these fallacies: that God is the God of life. If "death is guilt made visible,"[42] then the risen Christ is forgiveness made personal. The truth of all creation, and especially of the human person, rises with him. Theological anthropology begins from his fullness.

Yielding to Easter as the central event of all creation entails, at one and the same time, the acceptance of a new way of being. It is paramount, however, that we understand that even though the new creation requires the purgation of selfish and delimiting ways of being, the life Christ offers is not instituted by force; rather, the new gift springing from Easter respects and preserves the dignity of the original gift of creation even as it fulfills and elevates it. The truth that Christ embodies and imparts in his Resurrection does indeed correspond to the deepest longing of creation itself and, more to the point, the deepest desire of the human person. If the disciples discover the wellspring of their own fulfillment on Easter morning, then they also accept the recovery of who they were always already called to be. Their memories of themselves and of each other, as well as of creation as a whole, begin to heal toward wholeness when they meet their eschatological destiny in the risen Christ. In him, the life to which Christians are called is revealed as profoundly embodied rather than disembodied. This embodied fullness repositions Christians in openness toward the whole of creation that God consummately embraces in Christ.

What we see on Easter in Jerusalem and Galilee is that the point of departure for the eschatological imagination is the Resurrection of Jesus. He is the life of God that undoes death, who comes personally to those bound for death with the offer of new life. As the embodiment of divine mercy, he discloses the unrivaled primacy of what God gives—a giving that is unsolicited, unprecedented, and unbound (see 2 Cor. 4:7–12). And while it is true that the encounter with the risen Christ enables one to discover the truth about oneself, the converse is also true: in seeking the truth about oneself, one will ultimately be referred to Christ so long as one does not end one's search prematurely. The quest for knowledge, for truth, and for the understanding of being itself will reach its end only if one fundamentally yields to the primacy of God's gift. This yielding unblocks the pathway to the discovery of oneself as one accepts the deepest truth of one's existence as hidden in the mystery of God's love.

In this chapter's first section, I have placed the decisive emphasis on the sheer revelation of the Resurrection, in which the deepest truth of the absolute freedom of God is made manifest in the risen Jesus. I have placed a secondary emphasis on the fact that the witnesses to the Resurrection were led into changing their very way of knowing and hoping in order to become accommodated to—and thus to accommodate—the gift of fullness and a future that Christ brings them in his person. At this point, I switch the direction of emphasis in order to show how the transformation the disciples undergo corresponds to their created nature. While the effects of sin and fear introduce into their conversions a shock that is almost violent as this radically new life comes to meet them, there is in fact a deeper harmony between this grace and their nature than the conflicts that arise from any sinful resistance. Only a rigorous, unrelenting search for the deepest meaning of one's existence will lead to this harmonious longing for the unanticipated gift that Christ brings. Therefore, we turn now to Augustine, who performs such a search most completely in his *Confessions*, where his anthropological investigations become an openness to the transcendent and to all of creation. The eschatological dimensions of *De Trinitate* and *City of God* will gently illumine my analysis in regards to the fulfillment of the mysterious natural desire Augustine discovers in *Confessions*. On the whole, Augustine presents, with incomparable acuity, what the movement into the "sphere of the Spirit"—the space of true freedom—entails. For it is Augustine who narrates his own (re)discovery of what T. S. Eliot once described as "a condition of complete simplicity (costing nothing less than everything)."[43]

At the End of All Exploring: What Augustine Found

I return to Augustine now after the work of the third chapter because there I attempted to show that Christianity adheres to a belief in the meaning of created beings that shares in the truth of the person of Christ. The beginning of this chapter was dedicated to exploring the biblical testimony as to how this works. By this rule of faith—which guides rather than derives from thought—existence and identity depend on the free gift of God unto nothing. This truth is definitively revealed in Christ's Resurrection, in which the meaning of creation itself—precisely as *creation*—is opened up. Phenomenology cannot suffice for Christology because it does not reach this depth; only the latter allows for a complete anthropology. When we ask about the *whole* human person, we must be open to seeing that the question of the being of that being for whom being itself is a question leads not just to how this being exists, but also to why. At the end of all exploring, this is what Augustine found. As he investigates his *memoria*,[44] he allows the examination of the "how" of his own being to press onward toward the "why" that is his beginning and his end. Contrary to all expectation, this path leads him to leave himself in order to find himself.

In chapter 2 I introduced Augustine's phenomenological interrogation of the question of his own being as that which Martin Heidegger assumed and then adapted for the intended purpose of asking the question of being *as such*. The Heideggerian critique is that Augustine shut down his process of discovery prematurely when he reverted to his Neoplatonic instincts and posited the idea of an immutable, eternal principle by which he could measure his own instability. Heidegger thus believes that in rejecting Augustine's error, he alone is free to pose the question of being in its entirety. As the conclusion of his process of existentially analyzing the human being—or *Dasein*—Heidegger claims that the individual's death is that which gives the definitive end to the being who questions being. Death definitively temporalizes the individual and thus gives it its concrete shape. Death is the shocking truth-bearer that each individual tends to avoid, thus obscuring the meaning of his being. Heidegger boasts of death as his end, which he thinks Augustine lacked the courage to accept.

The problem with Heidegger's method is that he begins with the assumption that the question of an individual's existence is restricted to the boundaries of the individual himself. The moment that Augustine's interrogation of his own self begins to point toward something other than what is strictly contained within this self, Heidegger cries foul. If Augustine were injecting something into his process of discovery that was foreign to the process itself, then Heidegger may indeed be justified in his critique on phenomenological grounds; however, if Augustine is truly following the method of strict phenomenological interrogation onto this path that leads beyond himself, then, ironically, Heidegger is the one guilty of the very charge he levels against Augustine. In this case, Heidegger would be importing a predetermined and self-asserted philosophical principle into the mode of discovery—a principle dictating that the individual cannot be constitutively relational. The crucial difference is that Augustine accounts for the manner by which he sees what he sees, whereas Heidegger asserts his paradigm of autonomy without accounting for its legitimacy.

By reading Augustine's treatment of *memoria* in book X of the *Confessions* more closely than Heidegger did, we come to find that faith does not begin with the suspension of the process of questioning one's life; rather, faith spurs on this questioning to its definitive conclusion.[45] In discovering that he is ontologically referred to something (and indeed *someone*) else, Augustine goes beyond what might be philosophically deduced. That to which he is referred is communicated to him through the unfathomable desire—the desire that has no ground and thus cannot be fathomed—at the bottom of his *memoria*. This is the desire for that which he has never known or otherwise imagined. What separates Augustine here from Heidegger is the experience of mercy and the willingness to take this mercy as the hermeneutical key to the entirety of his existence. But this mercy cannot be reified, for it is in fact a way and not an object. This way of mercy implicates Augustine in his quest from beginning to end, leaving nothing outside the scope of his examination, including his own starting point.

The Way of Discovery

The central question that Augustine takes up in book X of his *Confessions* concerns what he loves when he loves God (202–3 [X.9–7.11]).[46] That he loves God is certain (see 201 [X.6.8]); whom or what he loves when he loves God is anything but. Without understanding whom or what he loves, Augustine remains a problem to himself, for without the knowledge of that to which he directs his life and for which he spends his energies, he is unable to fully know himself: "What am I, then, O my God?

What is my nature?" (203 [X.17.26]). The question of his love for God thus structures his very existence.

Heidegger, of course, brackets the presence of "God" from the outset and, in the end, replaces "God" with death as the definitive point of orientation for an individual's existence. He wants the questioning Augustine performs without Augustine's addressee. The addressee, he believes, is a belated addition that deficiently recasts the true meaning of an otherwise useful existential analysis. Heidegger will take as sheer fact Augustine's observation that "human beings have the power to question" (203 [X.10]). Therefore, when Augustine's investigation of himself leads him to analyze how he questions rather than just what he questions,[47] Heidegger believes that beneath the falsely ornamented form of the question that Augustine asks—"How then am I to seek you, Lord?" (216 [X.20.29])—is a deeper question that asks, baldly, "How then do I seek?" The question of being resides in this manner of pure seeking without a presumed end. The referent for Augustine's question is, to Heidegger, both superfluous and distracting—it is the fatal flaw of metaphysics. What Heidegger fails to grasp, however, is that Augustine's question does not just aim at God, but in fact begins in and with God, and it is shaped throughout by God's mercy. The end of Augustine's quest reveals that Heidegger's fundamental error was with his beginning—that is, with the very hermeneutic he employs in reading Augustine.

With Heidegger's approval, the refusal to locate or identify himself with any particular object, faculty, or capacity for thought impels Augustine's search. When Augustine plunges into his *memoria*, he is first met with those things that remain as images in his mind, images that moved from the external realities they represent, through his senses, and into his *memoria* (203–5 [X.13–15]).[48] Behind these he finds intellectual powers that have entered his *memoria* through his liberal arts education, which are present to him not as images of external realities, but as the things themselves (207 [X.9.16]). Even deeper than these, though, are capacities that allow him to engage in such learning, the very operations of collecting thoughts and of thinking itself (207–9 [X.10.17–11.18]). These abilities belonged to his mind (at least latently) without entering from the outside, and yet they were scattered in disorder before he learned to remember and activate them.[49]

As his search touches on deeper complexities, Augustine discovers that he can recall how he learned what he has learned and that he can remember that he remembers (209–10 [X.13.20–14.21]). With this, he begins to detect how his mind at once contains these things he finds while also remaining somehow free from that which fills it since the emotions that accompany the memory of an emotion are often different from what is being recalled. Awestruck as he is with this discovery, he becomes truly perplexed when he discovers that he also possesses the ability to remember forgetfulness. Enigmatically, the presence of forgetfulness proves that he remembers that he has forgotten something, even though he cannot recall what he has forgotten (212 [X.16.24]). More troubling still, by remembering his forgetfulness he surmises that he does in some indescribable way remember precisely what he has forgotten because he knows, if and when he does recover it, that this item or thought was indeed what he was missing. In this respect, he is like a woman who has lost a coin and searches for it with a lamp: the coin is hidden in the darkness of obscurity and the light of the lamp is his *memoria* working to re(dis)cover it (214–15 [X.18.27]). In this way, that which is retained in the *memoria* points, like a clue, to that which has escaped from the field of memory. It is this remnant that makes the search for what is lost possible at all (215–16 [X.19.28]).

This confounding, seemingly endless seeking is precisely the sort of existential agitation Heidegger covets; the vigor of this manner of examination is all within the aegis of his interest. He can stand next to Augustine at this point to appreciate how "great is the faculty of memory, so great the power of life in a person whose life is tending toward death!" (214 [X.17.26]). Augustine's demonstration of the instability of his grasp of knowledge is evidence of a movement toward the question of the being of his being, a question that is typically obstructed by one prematurely settling for some thought, idea, or purported truth that is taken as certain and consequently becomes the foundation upon which one's life is inauthentically built. Augustine will perspicaciously document the ways in which this inauthentic grasping occurs when he treats the three forms of concupiscence. As I detailed in chapter 2, Heidegger makes much of these Augustinian modes of dissipation.

It is what happens in between the discovery of his memory of forgetfulness and his treatment of these forms of concupiscence that invalidates

Augustine's project in Heidegger's eyes. If Heidegger had his way, the kind of seeking without end that Augustine portrays between chapter 12 (X.8.12) and chapter 28 (X.19.28) would be accepted as the authentic manner of being. The treatment of the ways in which individuals fail to sustain this manner in their inauthentic dissipation, which Augustine begins in chapter 41 (X.30.41), would then follow immediately afterward. Augustine, however, describes a final stage of exploration whereby he discovers something at the base of his *memoria* that is even more enigmatic than the memory of those things he has forgotten. What he finds is something that he has never encountered, never possessed, and never forgotten, yet is still present to his *memoria*. In other words, he finds within himself something that *does not belong to him*. Heidegger considers this alleged discovery a falsehood arising from a wish for existential stability, inculpating Augustine of the crime of metaphysical thinking. To Augustine, though, this final discovery becomes the portal to the very source of his restlessness that also happens to be the end to which his entire quest is tending. Moreover, his approach to this portal occurs through the same rigorous phenomenological method that yielded his previous discoveries.

The Discovery of the Way

In the deepest part of his *memoria* Augustine finds something that does not, properly speaking, belong there. Augustine discovers desire. This desire has direction but no direct object. Even still, this desire abides in the *memoria* unlike anything else found there because it brings to bear something that was never present to the senses, or ever known once or forgotten, and thus not simply a matter for recollection—as the Platonist doctrine would dictate. What Augustine discovers is a desire for the *vita beata*—a "life of happiness" (216 [X.20.29]). This life of happiness is not itself something present to Augustine as a memory, and yet his entire *memoria* is directed toward it. It is this "immemorial" that he desires, and this desire, common to all, is constitutive of the very quest he enacts. This is the discovery that answers the question of the meaning of his existence, and yet this answer gives him no more rest than when he began his search; if anything, he becomes more restless since now he confronts anew the issue of how to seek.[50]

Augustine's discovery of this desire is thus the discovery of something imposed on him.[51] In recognizing this desire as the essential principle of his *memoria*, he begins to understand that his own being is constituted in and as a response to what he desires. He has explored all the space he might have warrant to claim for himself and he has not found, in any portion of it or in the entirety of that space, the fulfillment of the desire to which his whole life tends. All the experiences, memories, and hopes for delight (*delectatio*) that Augustine has entertained all point eventually to this deeper desire, that he might enter into a state of full, uninterrupted, perpetual enjoyment. In book XIII, Augustine will speak of resting in a way that modifies Aristotle's laws of local motion, which declare that, "drawn by their weight, things seek their rightful places" (310 [XIII.9.10]). For a human being such as him, his weight is his love, so that where he sets his heart there he will come to rest (see Matt. 6:19–21). By now he has learned that one who attempts to remain at rest in any moment of temporal enjoyment misplaces oneself in mistaking some mutable state of existence for the immutable life of happiness in which one ultimately desires participation. Yet, the only place where one will be able to rest as oneself—whole and entire—is where the good one desires gives a place where one "may have no other desire but to abide there for ever" (310 [XIII.9.10]). Augustine discovers that this end comes to him, not from him, and so *the way* there will be other than the way in which he has been traveling.[52]

Prior to the tension of a life pulled apart through the fragmentation of desire into illusory desires of the flesh, of the eye, and of the lust for prestige—similarly, before the woman in Eden judged the fruit as tasty, beautiful, and intellectually satisfying (see Gen. 3:6)—there is already an original, primordial, created, and good tension that concerns the drama of the human person following one's constitutive desire—beyond any fleeting happiness that can be grasped—into the boundless space of unending enjoyment, which alone gives one a place to set down one's weight and rest. The desire Augustine discovers in these chapters of book X that Heidegger found fanciful is, in fact, the ineluctably ungraspable element upon which the entire structure of his existence builds. It refers to a good deeper than the performance of his search itself and it is a drama more original than the one told according to his soul's dissipations. It is true that Augustine approached this portal through the powers of his mind, progressing by the powers of first exterior and then interior phenomenological observation to the very deepest part of his own *memoria*. What his intellectual quest offers him, though, is at first nothing more than an impenetrable sign—something that merely points beyond itself, for which his intellect does not possess the key that turns this sign into a portal for his passage.[53] The key he needs is the will to seek beyond himself, yet this will to transcend his own boundaries and the limits of his own powers is itself something that must be given to him, not achieved by him.

What is hidden from those who lean on their own understanding (see Prov. 3:5–6) is that by the time the Augustine of the "present" writes book X, he has already found this key. This is, most of all, what Heidegger neglected to see: that the perspective from which Augustine makes this examination is itself something that he receives rather than simply something he assumes through his own self-generated power. Heidegger comes to Augustine's text with a predetermined paradigm of autonomy in place, one that dictates that the answer to the question of the being of a particular being is discoverable through the eventual isolation of this being unto itself. What Augustine is demonstrating in this particular book of his *Confessions* is that the narrative preceding "the who" and "the what" and "the how" of his "now," is the very hermeneutic of his present quest. In telling the story of God's mercy on him, Augustine did not just testify to what he had seen or even to what he sees now—deeper still, he has testified to that light by which he sees (see Ps. 36:9). The search for who he himself is in the present begins with presently claiming as his own *memoria* the embodied experience—the particular history—of locating the certain good for which he has always longed. He did not make or achieve this good; it came to him, pierced him, shocked him, entered the confines of his heart, and he fell in love. He trusts this love (see 212 [X.6.8]). This love gives him a direction along which to look for the final answer he seeks: it is the gift that commands him to seek (223 [X.29.40]), one that would mean little if "not first carried out in deed as well" (200 [X.6]). As Augustine will consider with great sophistication in *De Trinitate*, his search is impelled by the sweet invitation to *seek his face always* (see Ps. 105:4).[54] This is the "why" of his exploration.

It is the memory of his own story that permits him to locate the "dwelling-place" of God. Augustine said to God that "it is to your mercy that I address myself" (6 [I.6.7]) in attempting "to give a coherent account of my disintegrated self" (25 [II.1.1]). His understanding of the story is thus shaped in this address to mercy. In willing for himself that which he has heard in this mercy, Augustine accepts this place of unending happiness as his truth (see 222 [X.28.29]). He learns to see and know himself only as he gives himself to seeing and knowing the mercy that came to him; he understands only to the extent that he begins from and continually returns to the acceptance of himself as the one to whom the mercy of God has addressed himself. Locating himself as such makes the issue of "place" meaningless (221 [X.26.37]), for the space in which he would perpetually find what (actually, *whom*) he seeks is nowhere but the entirety of his life: to him, this space is simply everything. Therefore, in order to discover the One he desires, Augustine must allow for the transcendence and transformation of the concept of space itself. As Augustine has already learned, he must allow *himself* to become the place of God's dwelling by making himself a space for praise.

The Matter of Space

The narrative that precedes book X of the *Confessions* paradoxically has both everything and nothing to do with space. In the search for the truth of his existence in the discovery of God, Augustine speaks geographically in depicting his movement away from God "to that far country" as opposed to that "peaceful homeland" he eventually seeks (21 [I.18.28]; 144 [VII.21.27]). He portrays himself in topographical terms as "a land of famine" (36 [II.10.18]) and he even topologically ponders the corporeal dimensions of God as he ventures toward the limit of spatial thinking itself (134–35 [VII.10.16]; cf. 90–91 [V.20], 100–101 [VI.4–4.5], and 130–31 [VII.7.11]). The story he tells is one in which he learns to abandon a spatially dominated imagination in order to encounter God in the space of his own life. The revolution in his seeking whereby he accepts that it is not God but he who dwells and it is not he but God who gives shelter opens Augustine to being filled with God by clinging to God with his whole being (222 [X.28.39]). The place of God—the location of the life of happiness—must be embodied in order to be known. Otherwise, the question of space in reference to God is without meaning (see 221 [X.26.27]).

The way in which Augustine offers an account of himself is crucial if one is to rightly apprehend the analysis of book X, in which he explores his *memoria* or, as he specifies in book XI, "the present of past things" (261 [XI.20.26]). Adherence to a truly phenomenological method requires that one attend to *what* appears in *the way* it appears. Therefore, the way in which Augustine appears to himself is the datum the preceding books offer. It is thus important that Augustine portrays himself according to the wandering of the lost son, who struts and slides toward destruction as he himself becomes the very land of famine that he inhabits at the farthest point from home (see Luke 15:11–31). Augustine likens his waywardness to walking the streets of Babylon, as if taking up residence in a country not his own, fleeing from both his mother's love and his own hope for true peace. Augustine remembers this period of waywardness as begetting the desertification of his soul, leaving him more and more starved of the food that he most deeply desires (36–37 [II.10.18–III.1.1]).[55]

As his lust for praise according to the admiration of the world increases, Augustine's descent into desolation intensifies as he moves to Carthage (37 [III.1.1]). It is here, though, that Augustine begins to see himself as a lost son hesitantly beginning the long, slow turn away from the far country in which he has been consumed toward the home he still does not know. The journey to this homeland only progresses as he learns to enjoy this home for what it is (cf. Heb. 12:14).[56] This requires of him nothing less than allowing himself to be remade as one who knows this place as his joy. As yet, though, he is still too proud to allow this change to take place.

Augustine is repeatedly thwarted in his search because his manner of searching is itself a denial of the One whom he seeks. Strive as he might to leave the barren land that he himself has become, he will not find his home until he breaks from his urge to do it himself, trying in vain to change God into something he can grasp and hold within himself (see 70 [IV.26]; cf. 121–22 [VII.2]; 89–91 [V.19–20]; and 125–26 [VII.5.7]). He is attempting to make a god who is dependent on the space of his own mind, one whom he can trace according to spatial dimensions (see 137 [VII.14.20]). What is in need of changing is the order of Augustine's seeking: in knowing God, Augustine will not contain God as he would through some idea; rather, Augustine will know himself as contained— or given—by God, and thus he will truly possess that which he seeks when he knows himself as God's creation.[57]

Having done everything but change his manner of seeking, Augustine, near the end of book VII, finds himself surveying the peaceful, beatific homeland but without a way to cross over into it (141–44 [VII.20.26–21.27]). At this point, the search is, in effect, at its end. There is no more searching for Augustine to do; all that is left is for him to allow this homeland he glimpses from afar to become the homeland he truly desires. Like the desire for the *vita beata* he finds at the base of his *memoria*, the view of this homeland only intensifies his restlessness. Having once set out to find a land of his own where he could order the world according to his own ways and be moved by the adulation of others, he is now at the threshold of his true homeland, and yet he has never felt farther from it. More to the point, Augustine is on the cusp of humility in his recognition that possessing God can never be an accomplishment that would puff up the proud, but instead can only be held as one beholds a gift (see 143–44 [VII.21.27]).[58]

All the would-be progress that Augustine has made in his journey home would persist for naught if not for the one thing that will make all the progress truly meaningful: sacrifice. Up to the events remembered in book VIII, his progress in intellect, passion, and yearning for truth has yet to be handed over to God in praise; it has all, instead, remained within his own grasp and been directed, ultimately, to his own purposes (see 72–73 [IV.30]). The sacrifice of his confession thus remains to be offered (see 75 [V.1.1])—it is, in itself, the whole of the journey home, the quickening of his spirit, and the clearing of a dwelling place for God. He receives what he seeks only once the walls of the smallish space of his own pride open up as he *put[s] on the Lord Jesus Christ* (Rom. 13:14, RSV) and offers himself as the very space of God's abiding love (see 168 [VIII.29]).

Augustine becomes capacious to God in the humility of Christ. It all happens very suddenly, as if it requires no effort or time, and yet, from the other angle, it requires the fullness of time and maximal effort.[59] Paradoxically, there was no distance to cover, and yet Augustine arrives; there was no reason to starve, and yet he is revived; there was no space capable of holding God, and yet he becomes that space (see 161 [VIII.8.19]).

The drama of book VIII is decisively relevant to the quest Augustine engages in book X. In book VII, he tells of the way in which what he finds at the end of his probing of *memoria* becomes meaningful as a new beginning. The desire he discovers resists the attempts of conceptual mastery—that is, it does not avail itself to understanding through intellectual query alone. What Augustine narrates in book VIII is how he came to taste of pure and unexpected joy when he laid down his lust for achievement to instead receive in humility the peace for which he had always longed. The humility of God's love in Christ is the shocking joy that flooded Augustine's heart with the light of conviction, announcing to him that he had at last found what he always wanted.[60] It was in accepting this humble love in his own humility—his "sacrifice of praise," as he recalls again at the beginning of book IX—that he recognizes Christ as the Lord, the Eternal Word who says to his soul, "I am your salvation" (170 [IX.1.1]; cf. 6 [I.5.5]). Augustine only knows what he most deeply desires because Christ already drew near to him as the freely given gift of mercy, speaking directly to his soul through the mediation of Scripture and the witness of the saints whose own stories wooed him.[61] In book IX, Augustine proceeds to tell of how he begins to inhabit his *"spacious freedom"* (176 [IX.8]), in which his "old nature" becomes a "new life" of joy as his desire attains to the singular joy that found him in the garden, a joy that consequently draws him more deeply into communion with others, above all, his mother (see 178 [IX.10]). Books XI–XIII reveal Augustine's graced and self-committed vision of the whole of creation as seen in its ultimate referral to God according to God's own humble speech in Scripture.[62] Augustine learns to see, hear, and move according to the measure of what he receives.

On Praise and Dialogue

One way to divide up the *Confessions* is to see books I–IX as the articulation of the great question of Augustine to himself, book X as the structural orientation of the question to its answer, and books XI–XIII as Augustine's response to his great question in a redeemed mode of questioning. The change that occurs in book X and that thus distinguishes the first nine books from the last three is that the earlier books contain both Augustine as narrator petitioning God for an answer and Augustine as wanderer who does not yet address God, whereas in the latter books there is only the one Augustine turned in wonder toward God who is the Answer.[63] In book X Augustine presents the very possibility of his understanding of himself—that is, his understanding of his *memoria*—as inextricably integrated with the light by which he has come to see the entire space of himself, both exteriorly and interiorly. This light is the experience of mercy that gives coherence to his incoherent existence (see 178 [IX.11]). There would be no tale to tell, no life to analyze, no self to interrogate if not for that which is offered to him in what he receives as his own *memoria*. His beginning comes from the end he seeks, for he only sees what God has capacitated him to see (304 [XIII.1.1]). That mysterious desire he discovers at the base of his *memoria* points always back to the freely given joy that seeks him first, that joy which he would never be able to claim or achieve on his own.

Augustine does not presume to be able to give an account of himself as if he were doing so from a position without presupposition. In examining who he is now he must account for who he is as questioner, not just who he is as the object of questioning. This is what separates Augustine from Heidegger. Heidegger acts as if he could, all of a sudden and on his own power, autonomously claim himself in self-motivated resoluteness and existentially examine the being of his being.[64] What his phenomenological method fails to account for is the observer of the phenomenon itself. The first nine books of the *Confessions* are Augustine's account of where he himself stands in order to see and question himself. Augustine's question drives far deeper than Heidegger's, for Augustine refuses to presume his own power for questioning and thus discovers that he is in fact a question to himself. There is no relief from this state except to allow himself to be referred to the one who gives and fulfills his desire.[65]

What Heidegger fails to hear is that Augustine never conceptualizes God as an object of his thinking. In fact, he does not *use* God at all; rather, he addresses himself *to* God; moreover, his address to God presupposes God's unsolicited address to him, an address that brings him into being. Therefore, Augustine never stands outside this address in order to judge himself or measure his insight. For Augustine, this "to God" (*a Deo*) accepts and responds to the truth of God's creation "out of nothing" (*ex nihilo*) (see 276–77 [XII.7.7] and 135 [VII.11.17]).[66] Augustine's own "self" comes-to-be in the dynamic of this dialogue— and so Augustine seeks to dispose himself fully in this dialogue, relinquishing a space of his own that would offer him independent stability. His stabilization—his rest—is in his openness and willingness to return in praise what he receives as mercy.

Augustine's doctrine of time corresponds to this reality. For him, claiming the present is a possibility approaching impossibility since any moment of self-possession and self-awareness would always already be an awareness of his own dispossession of self in relation to God (see 258 [XI.20]). Time is the measure of how he allows himself to be referred back to God as the "Truth who is shaping me to himself" (271 [XI.30.40]; cf. 267 [XI.26.33] and 336–37 [XIII.29.44]).[67] The time that Augustine remembers in books I–IX is like the duration one experiences in holding one's breath, waiting to exhale. It is a time of strain and tension, leading ultimately to the crisis of either breathing or not breathing, an "unprecedented agitation" (167 [VIII.27]). To release the stale breath of his pride is to make room for the fresh air of God's mercy, as Augustine will later express unambiguously in the fourth book of *De Trinitate*.[68] To hold this gift in without turning it out again in praise would again deaden his lungs, and so Augustine learns that his desire is not to take in the air of mercy alone but indeed to enter into the rhythm of mercy-and-praise, breathing in and out (see 248 [XI.3.5]).[69] In this way, Augustine is always speaking to God, never simply about God as if the subject of a contained thought. As Marion rightly observes, unless one speaks to God in praise, one is in fact not speaking of or to God at all.[70] Praise is the condition of the personal acceptance of the freely given gift of mercy. By this reckoning, the entire *Confessions* is itself an expression of a redeemed *memoria*, a new memory of mercy shaped in a desire to praise (see 3 [I.1.1] and 337 [XIII.31.46]).

Augustine allows his entire embodied existence to take its place within God's creation as he accepts the Word of Life as *the gift* that addresses him and *the way* in which he may truthfully address himself to God. Again, the fourth book of *De Trinitate* elucidates the deep meaning of the journey of the *Confessions*. In the one gift of Christ's death and bodily resurrection, the soul of the sinner that has become deaf and mute to God learns to hear and speak again through the glorious exchange of the mercy of forgiveness and the praise of repentance. This mysterious healing comes forth from the risen Lord who is the "sacrament" that effects the renewal of the *inner man* and promises the resurrection of the *outer man*, which is the physical body that has yet to die (see 2 Cor. 4:16).[71] The shock of mercy (dis)placed Augustine into a space where he could praise because he discovered again—as for the first time—the truth of his desire to enjoy by will that life of happiness that was unrecognizable to him until he encountered it and began to seek it always.[72] In *City of God*, he further develops what he earlier discovered to be true: that he was to learn to see this joy as the glory of the Lord by suffering to *will* this joy as his own good. While pride still weakened his eyes, he could not bear to look upon the foolishness of God's love—but when he allowed this foolishness to heal him, his *eyes were opened and* [he] *recognized him* (Luke 24:31, RSV).[73] This seeing enkindled his desire for the rest of the eternal Sabbath, from which the disturbing cravings to rest in oneself are exiled and in which the leisure of reposing harmoniously with all is the eternal peace of perfect praise.[74] This destiny alone gives meaning to human existence.

Ontology by Desire

"The desire to see [God] is in us, it constitutes us, and yet it comes to us as a completely free gift."[75] According to Henri de Lubac, what Augustine touched on in the depths of his *memoria* is the fundamental paradox of the human being: that he is constituted by a natural desire for a supernatural end.[76] The *way* in which God seeks to give himself as the fulfillment of human desire determines the nature of human desire itself. Contemplation on this mystery is impeded within much of modern theology and thus within the Church's understanding of the faith because the intrinsically referential nature of anthropology to Christology has been obscured. Since, however, the Resurrection reveals the original truth of creation through the gift of its fulfillment, any anthropology that does not ultimately refer to what Christ embodies and gives is deficient. Up to this point, I have emphasized—in two directions—the fundamental orientation of the human being to what God gives; now I begin to pivot on this desire that is constitutive of human nature in order to move toward an understanding of how the human being for whom this desire is fulfilled is himself transformed. This transformation in and through desire will lead me to my definition of the Christian saint and to her intrinsically communal character.

Eden: Before and After

De Lubac's twentieth-century retrieval of an authentic Augustinianism is part of a larger attempt to restore a lost balance to Catholic theology. As this project touches on the anthropological, de Lubac devotes his efforts to preserving anew revealed truths of the Christian faith, even as these truths exist together only in a state of tension. Above all, and especially due to the varied objections of his critics, de Lubac is committed to maintaining the absolute freedom and sovereignty of God.[77] Alongside this truth and in fact dependent on it, de Lubac seeks to articulate the inviolable dignity of man, whose own freedom is real but only as exercised in harmony with the will of the Creator. All the actions in the mysteries of salvation—from creation to eschatological consummation—are first of all taken on God's initiative, as Augustine teaches in *City of God*, as elsewhere: "the will of [the soul's] Creator makes the first move; whether to make the soul which did not yet exist, or to recreate it when it had perished through its fall."[78] Belief in the one true God accepts nothing less, for in professing God as Creator and source of all life, one also recognizes that "the whole earth is 'balanced on nothing.'"[79] God is never compelled but always acts in freedom.[80]

In order to satisfy the demands of the faith as served by Catholic theology, de Lubac's thesis must be shaped according to revelation. He believes a truly Catholic understanding of the relationship of human nature to the supernatural will intrinsically order nature to grace in such a way that human beings are always in need of grace to reach their final end. The emphasis on this point opposes Baius's errant Augustinianism whereby redeeming grace is merely a remediation intended to restore human nature to its pure state as experienced in the prelapsarian condition.[81] At the same time, de Lubac guards against the Jansenist position in which the failure of what was already a permanently infantile human will leads to an infralapsarian condition in which grace is left to rule over the ruins of human nature.[82] De Lubac thus wants to allow for the maturation of the human will without stipulating the possibility of its autonomy; he wants to recover the depth of the Augustinian sense of Original Sin without losing the Augustinian understanding of mercy. The question of divine initiative and human freedom hangs in the balance.[83]

De Lubac is also of the opinion that the solution accepted almost unanimously in the early part of the twentieth century—a solution that assumes the authority of Thomas Aquinas—in fact stifles the very mystery it hopes to respect. The extrinicism of the two-nature system in which human beings are purported to have two ends—one natural and one supernatural—is not only inadequate for accounting for the mystery of the human person as disclosed in revelation, but is also a misrepresentation of Thomistic teaching in reaction to what were wrongly considered to be the opinions of Augustine.[84] A conceptual construction such as this is wholly foreign to the tradition of the Church.[85] To rectify this intractable theological predicament, de Lubac seeks to retrieve the true dynamism of Augustine's thought, which he believes to be congruent with the teaching of Aquinas, in order to articulate in modernity a renewed understanding of the relationship of human nature to grace that will better represent not just the Catholic theological tradition, but indeed the Christian faith itself.[86]

De Lubac's argument first responds to the faulty sixteenth-century interpreters of Augustine, then to the reactionary system that developed out of interpretations of Thomistic thought in order to safeguard against these forms of Augustinianism. A crucial aspect of the critique of Baius is to note that in Augustine's view, nature never escapes the action of grace. Even Adam, who stood in the original condition before the fall, was dependent on grace at every moment, abiding in continual acceptance of the gift of grace, in virtue of which he persevered.[87] The grace of sanctification was not a right of man's entailed in the grace of creation, but in fact was given as a perpetually new gift. Whereas the gift of creation is a gift-unto-nothing, the gift of sanctification is equally gratuitous.[88] Therefore, the movement of human nature to its end was always in need of and in contact with the unmerited gift of grace, which alone provides what human nature seeks.

While Jansenius's insistence on nature's absolute dependency on the action of grace seems to square with de Lubac's interpretation of Augustine, de Lubac is quick to show the deficiency of Jansenius's claim with the assertion that the human will is itself God's gift.[89] Jansenius's teaching that perfect harmony of the human will with grace in the original condition indicates the negligibility of the human will's power is directly contrary to Augustine's actual thought. In the original condition thus construed, the human will would be merely in a mode of acquiescence rather than positive agreement with the divine will, such that after the breaking of this harmony, the operation of grace can only act *in spite of* human will. De Lubac believes this is not in keeping with the whole of Augustine's thought, for whom "man and God were not two powers in confrontation, nor two individuals who are strangers to each other," and for whom the mystery of nature within the unlimited horizon of the supernatural was a matter of inclusion, union, and transformation rather than annihilation.[90] Augustine insists on the necessity of grace, not the irresistibility of it.[91]

In order to elucidate the essential agreement between Augustine and Thomas on these matters, de Lubac must roundly critique the teachings of those who purveyed what he considers to be an inauthentic Thomism. In contradistinction to what Cajetan and Suarez represent, de Lubac argues that according to Aquinas, the human being has only one proper end, not two. The ultimate end of the human person is supernatural, the beatific vision.[92] Human beings naturally desire to transcend their own nature. Therefore, in what de Lubac considers to be not only consistent with Augustinian theology but also with Thomistic theology, he avers that the Christian faith reveals—and the tradition of the Church teaches—that human nature is indeed defined by a natural desire for a supernatural end.[93] This constitutive desire makes human nature what it is.

All the same, though, this desire does not belong to human nature as a rightful possession. To desire is precisely not to claim; rather, it is to stand in a position of radical openness and need.[94] Part of the makeup of the human being is thus precisely its inability to move on its own toward that which it seeks. Moreover, that which the human being naturally seeks is not something that could ever be grasped or possessed—there is no object or thing that fulfills this desire. What human nature naturally desires is God as *gift*.[95] That God would offer himself as the ultimate good of his creature depends completely on God's gratuity and grace, indeed a second gratuity that follows the first gratuity of creation, the latter no less radical than the original.[96]

The Strain of Truth

The paradox of the human being is held within this very tension: that what is most one's own is that to which one has no proper claim. With the creation of human beings, "there happens in time a new thing that has no end in time."[97] The revelation of this mystery of the human being depends entirely on God's gift. This gift that draws human nature into its fulfillment is just as unsolicited, just as unmerited, just as surprising as that original gift of creation itself, which is the very condition of the possibility of this second gift. And yet human nature was only shown to be what it always has been according to its constitution in God's creation beginning with "the good news announced to mankind one night at Bethlehem."[98]

If we are to speak meaningfully about the relationship and yet inerasable distinction between God and human persons as the latter enter into their eschatological fulfillment, then we must recover this properly theological account of who the human person is. What de Lubac calls the "ontological call to deification which will make of man, if he responds to it, a 'new creature'" is also that "second, wholly distinct, super-eminent gift" in which the full dignity of the first gift of creation is revealed.[99] The human person is defined by what she desires, and yet in sin this desire is wounded and hidden, such that the truth of creation *as* creation is obscured. And so this desire must be reawakened—reawakened by the kiss of its own fulfillment so that it may be known for the first time, so it may lead the will in search of its delight and never cease until it rests in that for which it longs (see Song 1:2).[100] Not only to complete us, but also first to awaken us we need the grace of our last end, for "it is by the promise given us of seeing God face to face that we really learn to recognize our 'desire.'"[101]

As Augustine demonstrated in his *Confessions*, following the pattern of spiritual seeing that the eyewitnesses to the risen Christ first enacted, there are "certain depths of our nature [that] can be opened only by the shock of revelation."[102] How would we know of the "best and greatest of all possible promises"—the promise that God "will be the goal of all our longings; and we shall see him for ever"—if not for God's revelation of this destiny to us?[103] And how will we learn to love this duty as our delight for all eternity if not for God shaping our desire to himself in order to fulfill us with his love? We come to know what it means to be human only in seeing the flesh of the Son of God, in hearing the words of God's Eternal Word, in witnessing the mysterious glory of his life, death, and Resurrection as the inexhaustible love that we desire.

Desiring God

"Do you know what is the most special good the blessed have? It is to have their will filled with what they long for," writes Catherine of Siena.[104] According to our positive engagement with de Lubac's thesis, Catherine's insight means that human beings become most fully themselves in beatitude. The shock the first witnesses to the Resurrection experienced allowed them to recognize their hearts burning within (see Luke 24:32); subsequently, with Augustine's search, we studied this as the pattern by which disciples come to know themselves only through the revelation of their ultimate desire fulfilled in God's mercy.[105] To be filled with what one longs for would thus suggest that the human person is perfectly himself only once that to which he is fundamentally oriented becomes his own possession—or more precisely, comes to fully possess him.[106] Without yet being filled with what we desire, *it does not yet appear what we shall be, but we know that when* [Christ] *appears we shall be like him, for we shall see him as he is* (1 John 3:2; cf. 1 Cor. 13:12, RSV). And still, were not his coming imprinted already upon our hearts, we would not know to look for him. As the mature Augustine explains, "So it is God the Holy Spirit proceeding from God who fires man to the love of God and neighbor whom he has given to him, and he himself is love. Man has no capacity to love God except from God."[107]

From God

In seeing the glory of Jesus Christ, we behold this whole drama in the grace of the Spirit; and it is the Spirit who gives us the words of praise to speak the mercy of Christ, *the power of God and the wisdom of God* (1 Cor. 1:24, RSV). Only in this vision and with this grammar can we recognize the blessed dead and hear their witness, redounding in praise to the mercy that abides them. They are more fully human in their union with God, revealing who we already are from the side of what we will become in response to Christ, God willing.

In claiming that the life of the blessed dead is communicable I must also reassert that death is a definitive end, as I argued in chapter 3. The life of the blessed *is hidden with Christ in God*; therefore, they appear in Christ who is their life and their hope (see Col. 3:1–4). The appearances of the risen Christ to his disciples thus take on additional depth of meaning: in disclosing the transformation the disciples had to undergo in order to start to recognize the Lord in his glory, the testimony to these encounters also suggests the transformation we must undergo if we are to recognize those whose life is hidden in this glory. What is true of the risen Christ is true of those united to him in God's love given unto the nothingness of death, as Ratzinger aptly articulates: "He no longer belongs to the world that is perceptible to our senses: he now belongs to the world of God, and hence one can see him only if he allows himself to be seen. And *this* act of seeing makes demands of the heart, the spirit, and the inner openness of man."[108] The blessed dead draw us forward to where they are in Christ—not back into what we might otherwise want, but into the truth, beauty, and goodness of the fullness we truly desire.

In Christ

If the desire for God as free gift is constitutive of human nature and if Jesus Christ fulfills that desire in offering human beings what God calls them to be, then human desire is for Christ. Moreover, in giving himself out of love, Jesus Christ at once reveals and institutes that which human beings desire, so that this desire ontologically (re)orients human beings to Christ in his person. We recall here Balthasar's view that the person of Christ is identical with his mission from the Father, which he lived out in the form of obedience in his life and death.[109] In keeping with this, the one whom human beings naturally desire as the gift of eternal life also draws them into the Father's very act of giving. In receiving their fulfillment in Christ, the blessed come to partake in God's own way of loving.[110] This indeed is the mystery of the image in which human beings are created: the mystery of God's own desire, which, unlike the created desire that yearns for it, expresses only plentitude.[111]

The *vita beata* is wrapped up in the mystery of God's desire to love creation into being and perfect it, a mystery that is itself contained within the mystery of God's Trinitarian life. In this abyss of charity, the human desire for God as gift is united to God's act of giving, so that the fulfillment of human desire is the gift of a way of giving. Since Jesus Christ is his mission, Balthasar espouses that "*en* becomes *syn*" for those who are *en Christoi* since they come to participate "in Christ's dying and rising and in his work (*synergoi*)."[112] Christ is the pattern and archetype of the new creation.[113]

God's way of loving in Christ is the shibboleth for the communion of saints. A saint is known as a participant in God's way of loving—one who offers praise for God's mercy by giving what one receives. In the acting area of his mission, Christ opens up the space for the action of his communion.[114] And in his High Priestly Prayer to the Father, Jesus speaks the mission he himself will fulfill:

> *I do not pray for these only, but also for those who believe in me through their word, that they may all be one; even as you, Father, are in me, and I in you, that they also may be in us. . . . Father, I desire that they also, whom you have given me, may be with me where I am, to behold my glory . . . that the love with which you have loved me may be in them, and I in them.* (John 17:20, 24, 26, RSV)[115]

In this, all the law and the prophets are contained: to love God and to love your neighbor (see Matt. 22:36–40). Out of love, God has made himself neighbor to his wounded creatures (see Luke 10:25–37); he loved us first and shapes our desire to himself (see 1 John 4:19). To live into this love is therefore to love in a manner like God's way of loving: to love gratuitously, without cost and without claim. The love with which the Father loves the Son—the unoriginate love of Absolute Mystery—is the love that Christ gives to his disciples with the command to *love one another as I have loved you* (John 15:12; cf. 13:20, 34–35, RSV).[116] This is the desire of the human heart. What is given could not have been solicited, for what is given in Christ is that *"spacious freedom"*[117] to love.

With the Holy Spirit

God fulfills the will of the blessed by freeing them to love their neighbors, and this gift requires nothing less than the whole drama of salvation. What is conferred between the mystery of Jesus Christ remembered in the second part of the creed and the mystery of life in the Spirit rehearsed in the third part is the graced freedom to embody the mercy that is given. The encounters with the risen Christ announce this transformation; with the Pentecost of the Spirit the meaning of all history is reconfigured to the life of grace. Here, the "why" of creation itself is revealed: that in giving himself, God might be the fulfillment of what he calls into being. The mercy that is God's embrace of his creation even unto death in Jesus Christ is the memory that reveals and inflames the desire of creation made new in the Resurrection. In handing over the Spirit for the life of the world, "the self-communication of eternal love" becomes, as Balthasar muses, "the pedal note which lasts through all the confused music of the world's time."[118] And as Ratzinger and Rahner both respectively conclude, history is now the time of responding to this gift in harmony with the absolute freedom of God, who makes space for the freedom of his creatures.[119] This end beckons and capacitates the wills of these creatures to turn (*conversio*) in the direction of the union of love given as their deepest desire.[120]

What the third part of the creed professes are the characteristics—the marks—of this new life in the Spirit as configured to the hope of the communion of all in Christ. The communion of saints is the eschatological image of the definitive shape of this new life, in which those who have been filled with forgiveness from the wellspring of God's mercy turn to give new life to their neighbors by forgiving them their debts (cf. Matt. 6:12; Luke 11:4; John 7:38; 4:10, 14; Isa. 12:3). The blessed forgive the shortsightedness of the wayfarers in lending their own vision of glory as the freedom to love as they are loved. In offering their own *memoria* of Christ's mercy as the deepest desire of their existence, the blessed offer medicine for our prideful wish to claim other ends for our lives;[121] they are raised up from within history as witnesses to creation's future in God, which surpasses what might be achieved within the bounds of history, yet nevertheless begins there.[122] We see in them that awaiting the resurrection of the body is awaiting the end of history, when all relations extended throughout time and according to space culminate, revealing at last the true significance of the humanity of each and all in the eternal significance of the Word that became flesh (see John 1:14).[123] Indeed, the humanity of Christ breaks through all silos of isolation through the charity of his embodiment, creating through his deeds the very desire for charity in those who touch the freedom to love that he embodies, as bridegroom and bride become *one flesh* (Gen. 2:24; cf. Eph. 5:21–33).[124]

On the side of humanity's fulfillment in Christ, the blessed communicate hope to us; they remember us before we remember them.[125] They have become echoes of the heart of Jesus's own prayer, *that they may all be one* (John 17:21). The gift they receive of being made one in Christ turns them to desire the completion of Christ's mission. The witnesses to the Resurrection first turned to embody—in word and in deed—the One who came to them in his own glorified body. Augustine received the proclamation of that word and the efficacy of those deeds in the space of his own body: his *memoria*. So too now the saints mediate this grace, re-presenting the body of the risen One in the presentation of their own word and deeds: their charity, hope, and memory. To heed their witness is to join in the word and deeds that sustain their harmony.

We see as much in the dynamics orchestrated from the pen of Dante, the poet of Christian eschatology. Without delving into the questions of the revelatory status of his (poetic) vision and the congruence of his work with biblical faith tout court, one may readily discern the way in which the communication from self-giving love through dispossessing desire moves the narrative itself, thus offering a strong Christian poetic response to the depersonalizing thrust of Rilke's eschatological poetry, which we examined in chapter 2.[126] For Dante, those blessed ones who find repose in the bloom of God's glory hasten to serve those still in exile. Indeed, Dante's own pilgrimage begins from its end, as his heart is disposed in keen desire from the call of the Virgin Mary that beckoned Lucy to release the love of Beatrice in search of that lost man in a dark wood.[127] Along the path her descending love blazed, Dante ascended toward "the end of all desires," where his will and desire turned in(to) harmony with Love Eternal.[128] The saints' memory of the sinner offers the sinner a new memory. The freedom to accept this call to new life is granted to the pilgrim as the cascade of grace fills up the reservoir of human freedom. Whether the (would-be) pilgrim exercises or negates this freedom becomes the central issue of the human drama, one whose mystery is inexhaustible.[129] The progress in harmony with the offer of grace coming from the side of eschatological fullness is one of increasing agency and growth in personhood, a kind of "thickening treatment"— as C. S. Lewis puts it in his own short eschatological work—that is quite the opposite of what Rilke envisioned.[130]

The encounter with the saint is the encounter with one who embodies the reception of the mercy Christ himself embodies. Christ makes God's love personal and this love makes the saints into theological persons. The saints thus communicate both the content of God's gift and the mode of acceptance—they are the pedagogues who teach by loving, who draw those of us as yet unable to see into the spacious freedom of recognizing Christ. A saint is who God calls her to be in Christ. She sees us as members of her beloved and she presents herself as the assurance of believing without sight. She desires for us to discover our deepest desire and she comes to us with the love that uncovers that desire. She speaks to us only God's mercy and helps us to speak in praise. The surpassing reality of her life only becomes recognizable to us once we are shocked free of our delimiting presumptions. As the first witnesses to the Resurrection stepped into the place of receiving Christ as mercy given *for them* and as Augustine received this healing mercy as the key to his memory, will, and understanding, so too have all the blessed who live in Christ entered into the unlimited freedom of being loved. They communicate only from that freedom and they call us forth into dialogue there. In this chapter I have striven to explicate this very mystery—that the eternal primacy of God's gift both demands and enables a wholly distinct mode of reception in God's beloved ones, by which they are transformed according to God's own way of loving so as to communicate this love gratuitously to their neighbors.

Concordantly, if we are to recognize the blessed dead now as *hidden in Christ* (Col. 3:3), we must recognize them according to their charity, their humility, and their desire to draw us into their bliss. It is not what we would otherwise expect but it is what we nonetheless desire. This means, moreover, that our response to them will not only take the form of calling upon them and trusting them with our needs—though it does mean this—but also in setting off as pilgrims to embody their blessed concern for us in our concern for others, the kind of care to which we have no right, can make no claim to, do not at all possess, and yet learn by faith to desire: *to love one another as I have loved you* (John 13:34).[131] The enigma of a saint is contemplated only in the key of Christ's sweet command, such that the unimaginable words of a dying Thérèse of Lisieux illumine the imagination of the faithful:

> I feel that I'm about to enter into my rest. But I feel especially that my mission is about to begin, my mission of making God loved as I love Him, of giving my little way to souls. If God answers my desires, my heaven will be spent on earth until the end of the world. Yes, I want to spend my heaven in doing good on earth. This isn't impossible, since from the bosom of the beatific vision, the angels watch over us. I can't make heaven a feast of rejoicing; I can't rest as long as there are souls to be saved. But when the angel will have said: "Time is no more!" then I will take my rest; I'll be able to rejoice, because the number of the elect will be complete and because all will have entered into joy and repose. My heart beats with joy at this thought.[132]

If what we desire is constitutive of our humanity, and the perfection of our humanity rests in the fulfillment of our desire, then the saints, who have entered into this perfection, refract our true humanity to us in their union with God in Christ by the power of the Holy Spirit.[133] In them, we see that the desire *for* God becomes the desire *of* God and holds together heaven and earth in the twin loves of God and neighbor. Only thus does the peculiar become familiar and even desirable, such that the final repose of our hearts might be the movement of love itself.

CHAPTER 5

BODILY MEMORY

A Fool's Errand?

Toward the end of the previous chapter, I briefly introduced the dynamics of Dante's *Commedia* to illustrate how the transformation of the pilgrim's desire begins on the side of eschatological fulfillment, where the saints reach down in charity to inspire the pilgrim's ascent toward "the end of all desires."[1] To many, invoking Dante in support of an understanding of the communion of the blessed ones with members of the pilgrim Church is a dubious prospect, to say the least. A prevailing opinion is that Dante's eschatological vision is fraught with rigidly hierarchical conceptions of human relations in the eschatological realms. These conceptions seem to fix and even exaggerate in the afterlife the very differences that exist between human persons on earth. Not only do the blessed abide at an unfathomable distance from the damned, but the blessed also stand separated from one another according to their merits, thus petrifying in heaven a caste system of holiness for all eternity.

It may seem doubly foolish, then, to begin this fifth chapter with a further appeal to the *Commedia*, especially since my primary objective is to argue that the *communio sanctorum* is the consummate union of heaven and earth, eternity and history. Moreover, in order to advance this claim, I defend rather than dismiss an understanding of the hierarchical ordering of relations within this communion. My contention is that the assumed dichotomy between hierarchy and communion is a false one; the pressing issue concerns the proper understanding of hierarchically ordered relations within the *communio sanctorum*.

In the following pages, I move from purgatory to paradise, from Baptism to Eucharist, and from the social order to the Body of Christ. The view I have been espousing throughout this work is that the saints are *more fully human* because they have come to accept as mercy given *for them* the redeeming gift of the new life of the Spirit in Christ. Their reception of this gift requires and invites them to become dispensers of this same gift to others. The *communio sanctorum* is thus at once a school for holiness and a school for humanity: human creatures still in need of redemption learn how to be fully human in the communication of the life of the Spirit within the one human body—the Body of Christ.

My defense of a renewed understanding of the hierarchical order of social relations begins in the middle of Dante's *Commedia*, with a small selection of specific episodes of the *Purgatorio* offering a key to understanding the movement of the whole work. These episodes highlight the importance of the conformation of the human will to the divine will through the reconfiguration of memory according to the transformation of desire. On the basis of what I unearth here, I then refine my understanding of the status of the hierarchical order that Dante imports into the deepest reality of the *Paradiso*: the Empyrean. The purpose of this section is not so much to rescue Dante's work from misinterpretation as it is to call into question the underlying suspicion of order—especially hierarchical order—in regards to both the final and the as-yet-incomplete forms of the *communio sanctorum*. In resetting this interpretation of the *Commedia*, I turn Dante from a liability into an asset based on a corrected understanding of the order of eschatological relations.

I leverage what I gain from the outset of the chapter when, in the chapter's second major part, I argue that the eschatological order of social relations reflects and indeed illumines the original social order of humanity according to God's act of creation. To this end, I examine aspects of both Augustine's and Karl Rahner's theologies of creation with attention to the consistent eschatological dimensions of their thought. My examination will position us to appreciate the inherent dignity of human nature.

In the third section of the chapter, I contemplate the journey from freedom to freedom—that is, from the mercy of God that frees sinners to the response of praise that constitutes human persons' willful participation in this freedom. I thus tie the question of creaturely dignity to the future to which God beckons those he claims. I double-back to Dante's *Purgatorio* for the first image of this journey before situating my thought in the biblical narrative of the Exodus and connecting it to the sacramental pilgrimage beginning in Baptism.

These first three major sections of the chapter lead to and, in many respects, culminate in the fourth and longest section of the chapter. In this section I bring my theological explication of the communion of saints into the closely related areas of sacramental and liturgical theology. Beginning with the pneumatological character of the Church, I pursue a deeper understanding of the Eucharist as the sign and instrument of the communion God establishes in creation through the gift of God's own communion. In the final section I move with the Eucharistic mystery to connect Christ's Ascension to Mary's Assumption so as to conclude this chapter's articulation of the meaning of "bodily memory." I thus arrive at the threshold of this work's conclusion in which I return to where I began with a deeper appreciation for the communion of holy persons who cling together with the charity of God in Christ.

Ordering the *Commedia*

In his recent book about the "last things" in the Catholic imagination—in which he ends with a reinterpretation of the communion of saints according to what he calls a "noncompetitive key"—John Thiel argues that the development of the doctrine of purgatory results from growing "eschatological anxiety" on behalf of primarily the laity who were forced to compare themselves rather unfavorably to the heroic holiness of martyrs, ascetics, and consecrated religious.[2] For those who could not compete with the extraordinary holiness of those who sacrificed their earthly lives to the rigors of ascetic living, the emergence of purgatory allowed for a prolongation of time for accruing merits to one's lived existence in order to secure a more favorable final judgment for life eternal. Undergirding this eschatological anxiety is an implicit conviction that one's life matters and that the ultimate meaningfulness or meaninglessness of such a life hangs in the balance.[3] Thiel believes the anxiety that gives rise to these notions is a scourge on the eschatological imagination of Christians, structured as it is according to a more competition-based spirituality. Hence, when Thiel looks at Dante's *Commedia*, he not only sees thirty-three cantos that vividly illustrate the consequences of such "eschatological anxiety" in the *Purgatorio* (not to mention the *Inferno*), but he also sees the poetic transposition of this anxiety-inducing vision into the heavenly realms of the *Paradiso*. On Thiel's reading, the poet of the Christian eschatological imagination is inscribing an order of hierarchical competitiveness upon eternal beatitude.[4] This suspicion of hierarchy is emblematic of influential strands of contemporary Catholic theology about the communion of saints.[5]

While I both appreciate and agree with Thiel's primary interest in having the Christian imagination reach toward the corporate nature of salvation, I do not share in his general suspicion of hierarchy per se as that which obstructs the emergence of a true communion for the saints. In due course, I will treat Thiel's proposal more fully as a whole, but first I attend to Dante's eschatological imagination, which Thiel plainly presents as supporting the commonplace understanding he wishes to challenge. What I intend to show is that while it is true that there is a hierarchical order to the relations among persons in the *Commedia*, this order in fact serves the true communion among the blessed themselves, between the blessed and those in purgation, and between those in purgation and the members of the Church on earthly pilgrimage. I begin my work of reappraisal with the central *cantica*—the *Purgatorio*—since the transformation most clearly under way there is the hinge of Dante's whole poetic and spiritual journey.

Paternoster *in the* Purgatorio

In the seventeenth and middle canto of the *Purgatorio*—and thus at the exact midpoint of the entire poem—Dante puts upon the lips of his guide, Virgil, a terse but telling commentary on the vices that the pilgrim has already encountered in his journey up the mountain's terraces.

Standing now on the fourth terrace (where sloth is purged), the follies of pride (first terrace), envy (second terrace), and anger (third terrace) are recounted. These three vices manifest related yet distinct ways in which obsessive self-regard comes at the expense of care for others. Pride is born of one's wish to keep others down so that one may excel by comparison (17.115–17);[6] envy comes from one spurning the success of others out of concern for losing praise for oneself by comparison (17.118–20); and anger arises from the urge to cause another harm as retribution for some grievance one has perceived as done to oneself (17.121–23). With each vice, an economy of competition is established wherein the good of others comes at one's own expense, and vice versa. The enactment of these vices thus drives would-be neighbors into isolation from one another. This habitual competitiveness is precisely what the journey through the *Purgatorio* means to remedy.

According to Dante's account, purgation consists of the chastening of desire, which leads to the redemption of memory. This chastening is much more a form of disciplining, directing, and reorienting than it is punitive in nature. More precisely, the punitive aspects of penance are all part of a rehabilitative and indeed transformative process through which the souls in purgatory come to will for themselves the good they most deeply desire. The beginning of the eleventh canto (on the terrace of pride) offers a glimpse of this rehabilitation of the will in concert with the transformation of desire in a most compelling fashion. The first lines of the canto present a revised version of the *Paternoster*, sung as Dante imagines it would be sung not on earth or in heaven, but precisely in purgatory. The community gathered here in prayer directs itself in longing toward "the heavenly spheres" (11.1) from which the peace they cannot attain for themselves comes down (11.7–8). They seek to sacrifice their own wills in praise to the divine will, as the holy angels do, so they may ascend in holiness toward the realm of their hearts' desire (11.10–15). And though they beg remission for the consequences of the sins they have committed and the harm they have caused while beseeching their Father to keep them from evil, they also recognize that they are now free from the snares of evil and from the possibility of sinning anymore (11.16–24). This seeming dissonance at the end of their prayer—where the penitents pray for freedom from evil and sinning but confess the fact of their freedom from falling again—would be nonsensical if not for their prayer's coda: "This final prayer is made, O dearest Lord, / not for ourselves (we now have no such need). / We speak for those behind us, who've remained" (11.23–24). To reinforce the point, Dante immediately states, upon the conclusion of the prayer, that their prayer was "for themselves and us" (11.25).

In one and the same prayer, then, this penitential community of souls prays both for themselves and for those still on journey in this life, before death. For them—within the context of the poem—these are not two separate actions but rather two movements of the same action. If sin is the denial of one's place within the created order such that an economy of competitiveness rends asunder those who come from a single *Pater*, then the course of treatment for these sins will be the refashioning of one's will toward the health of the whole communion as a single body. As presented in Dante's work, purgation consists of increasing one's freedom *from* the sinful inclinations toward isolating self-possession outside the communicative body of the human community; at the same time, it is also growing in freedom *for* the willful participation in the communion of this one communal body. Furthermore, this turning of one's will toward the good of others allows one's own growth in holiness to become a model, a spur, and an aid to the rehabilitation of those members of the one communion who are in greater need of mercy.

The vices of those in purgatory are being healed through the remembrance of the needs of others. They do not present themselves as having the power to meet those needs on their own; rather, they gather up the needs of others in their prayer to their *Pater* as if it were a prayer for themselves: "but free *us* from the one who is our goad" (11.21, emphasis added). They will attain full health when their strength of willing the good of others overcomes the lingering effects of the competitive tendencies in which they once indulged.

It becomes even more evident that this union of one's concern with the needs of others is a constitutive feature of prayer in the *Commedia* when the *Paternoster* is mentioned for a second time. In *Purgatorio* 26.127–32, one of the souls—Guido Guinizelli—asks Dante (the pilgrim) to say the *Paternoster* for him when Dante enters the heavenly realm. In the *Paradiso* not even the *effects* of sin remain, and so a

Paternoster offered there would be pure praise without any petition for one's own healing.[7] The only healing that would be sought would be the healing for another who is not yet in full health. While Dante does not compose an explicit *Paternoster* for the *Paradiso*, we may assume that such a prayer would keep to the same principle as the one uttered in the *Purgatorio*—namely, that the needs of others would be presented to the *Pater* as one's own needs.[8] Those in heaven—now fully free *for* the willful communion of the one communal body—would assume the needs of others as their very own. In this case, even though those in purgatory can no longer sin, they are still undergoing the process of separation from the effects of their sin. If one in heaven were to pray for one of these, it would be to express concern even for the struggle of one whose beatific end is assured. This brief request uttered in the *Purgatorio*'s twenty-sixth canto added to the extended recitation of the prayer in the eleventh canto shows that, in Dante's account, the blessed in heaven are united to those in purgatory by offering the merits of their prayers for those below, while those in purgatory seek heavenly bliss in praying for those still toiling on their earthly pilgrimage. The character of the blessed is expressed as care for those still learning to desire heavenly bliss, while those in the final stages of learning this desire are themselves being transformed through their growing concern for the ones still behind them. The ascent of holiness proceeds according to the descent of charity.[9]

This principle of proportionality between the sharing of concern and the growth in holiness is part of the fundamental logic of Dante's *Purgatorio* and, therefore, of the entire *Commedia*. Rather than extending the game of competitive spiritualities from earthly life into the afterlife, purgation in this account consists of healing unhealthy souls of their residual competitiveness. This healing process does not negate the distinctions among persons—even in regards to their degrees of holiness—but instead allows intensifying degrees of cooperation with divine grace to motivate particular persons to exercise their own agency for the good of others, especially those most in need. This is the state of the hierarchical order of Dante's *communio sanctorum* as seen from the *Purgatorio* and the essential character of this communion will persist once Dante contemplates the heavenly realm. As we will see, the order that Dante envisions in the *Paradiso* does not codify distances *from* holiness; rather, it orchestrates mediations *of* holiness.

Personhood in the Paradiso

The suspicious concern over the hierarchical ordering of beatific life is threefold. First, there is the issue of distance pertaining to how close or relatively far removed the blessed are placed from divine glory at the last judgment. Second, there is the issue of the final positioning of the blessed in relation to one another, where each is above some and below others according to the merits of the earthly actions of those who now dwell in heaven.[10] Third, there is the issue of only static and passive participation in heavenly life due to the fact that the specific location of each of the blessed is firmly determined according to the distance from divine glory and from one another; hence, there can be no suspense in such a still-frame image—there is neither movement nor dramatic busyness of agency among the blessed.[11] Based on this tripartite concern, John Thiel critiques Dante's poetic depiction of heaven as one that guarantees differentiation to the point of divisiveness among the saints. To Thiel, the ills of this hierarchical conception become especially clear when Dante's elevation to the Empyrean fixes in place those he has already passed to get there, thus emphasizing their distance at a remove from the fullness of glory and their subordination to those more closely united to God.[12]

The point of tracing Dante's presentation of the character of the penitential souls in relation to both earthly sojourners and the heavenly saints was to show that one of the key relational dynamics operating in the *Commedia* is that those "higher up" hasten to aid those "further and farther away" from the end of all desires. For the penitents, this sharing of concern impels their own progress; while for the blessed, the fullness of their character is expressed in their charity. Quite to the contrary of fixing distances between persons according to merit and forms of holiness that accrue divine favor, the whole point of the poem is that the distance between the human and the divine is to be traversed as the relations among human persons strengthen. While it is true that the vast majority of the cantos in the *Paradiso* deal with the ascent through the heavenly spheres—from the heaven of the moon to the *Primo Mobile*—the distances between these spheres, as well as between the souls Dante glimpses in abidance in each, are properly metaphorical. The stepwise progression through the *Paradiso* was given to Dante (the pilgrim) as a gift for his own understanding, and it is given through Dante (the poet) to the reader for the sake of one's own understanding. He and we are treated to a complex display of intelligibility. The brilliance of heaven is made intelligible for human minds that work through space and time, growing in understanding slowly through comparative mensuration.[13] All that Dante describes as existing *as if* it were in space and time in these heavenly spheres *in truth* exists eternally beyond space and time in the Empyrean, to which Dante finally ascends by contemplation in the thirtieth canto.[14] More to the point, space and time are redeemed, transformed, and sanctified in the communal life of the blessed ones.

When the pilgrim leaves the *Primo Mobile* for the Empyrean, Beatrice informs Dante that "We've left / the greatest of material spheres, rising / to light, pure light of intellect, all love, / the love of good in truth, all happiness, / a happiness transcending every rapture" (30.38–42; cf. 22.61–67; Rev. 21:22–22:5).[15] The spatial dimensions that Dante was given to ponder in his journey through the heavenly spheres trained his eyes to contemplate the ineffable glory in which the blessed share communion. The individuation of the saints is arrayed in the personalities of definite persons (31.43–51), whose undivided union gives the appearance of a rose in full bloom (30.100–126) in which the whole of salvation history is preserved (see 32.4–137). The order Dante willfully observes here abides as unbroken relationality, where the good of one is communicated through the communal body for the good of the many. Physical distance is meaningless in this communicative body, for Dante clearly attests: "Nothing's gained here or lost by 'near' and 'far.' / For where God rules without some means between, / the law of nature bears no weight at all" (30.121–23).

Although the Empyrean is beyond space and time, movement there perdures and in fact intensifies infinitely. This is the movement of love. Even without the explicit composition of a *Paternoster* for the *Paradiso*, at the very apex of beatific life Dante describes the fulfillment of the movement previously enacted in the prayers of the penitents from *Purgatorio*

11.[16] This movement of love takes place in the person of the Virgin Mary, to whom the final petitionary words of the entire *Commedia* are spoken, for the pilgrim's sake, from the lips of Bernard on behalf of many saints (33.1–39). Upon the completion of Bernard's prayer, the Blessed Mother turns with subtle gracefulness from attentiveness to another's desire, to the assumption of this desire as her own, to the offer of pure praise to the source and summit of charity:

> The eyes—which God both loves and venerates—
> attentive to these orisons, made clear
> how welcome to her were these holy prayers
> and then turned straight to the eternal light
> in which (we're bound to think) no creature's eye
> inwardly travels with such clarity. (33.40–45)

The harmonious movement of Mary's eyes from descending charity to ascending praise displays, with the utmost poetic elegance, that the hierarchical order that Dante envisions in heaven fosters the bonds of communion among the blessed saints and through them with those still on pilgrimage and in greatest need. This order expresses the movement of divine love itself.

What the journey through the heavenly spheres and finally into the Empyrean shows is that the objectification of a hierarchical order that segregates human persons subsists only so long as one desires to observe the order from a distance. The order itself is revealed as the matrix of grace once one commits oneself to entering into it, moving beyond one's addiction to measuring distances of space between persons and of counting time by the deferral of admiration that comes from judgments spawned from an urge for self-preservation. Dante's ascension to the Empyrean is coincident with the ongoing transformation of his will to love in harmony with those who have educated him in the heavenly spheres. Those saints who know this harmony of love through their own embodiment of it within the Empyrean came to the pilgrim even before he ascended to their realm of love beyond space and time. They condescended to him in love, speaking to him and teaching him in the ways that he was capable of understanding so that he might grow in the wisdom of love in order to willfully participate in their eternal communion. Even as he entered this communion, the order of communication—the order of mediations of love—did not pass away, even in the full bloom of beatific life; for this social configuration is the redeemed and sanctified communion for which *the Word became flesh and dwelt among us* (John 1:14, RSV).

As those created in the image of divine love grow into the likeness of this love, the whole human body becomes an instrument transfigured in and for this communion of love. Though there are undoubtedly elements to the *Commedia* that can obstruct the full flourishing of the Christian eschatological imagination—such as the very judgments that Dante executes on various historical personages in assigning them to the distinct eschatological realms—the logic of this hierarchically ordered communion is not one of them. Rather, this ordered work of love is a fecund image for the eschatological imagination in conformity with the demands of the Christian faith.

Alternatives to Order

The order of communion and communication that I have retrieved from the *Commedia* is one in which agency originates from the side of eschatological fulfillment and moves toward those in need for the sake of communion rather than dominion. For what do the blessed offer to those in need of healing but the space of their own souls as the sacrificial site for prayer and charity? This is a communion of servanthood where the blessed hasten to serve. While Dante does not offer a systematic theological account of the workings of the *communio sanctorum*, he does present us with an artistic rendering that opens the theological imagination to a more profound consideration of this article of faith. He illustrates how particular members build up the one communion through embodied works of mercy; and while these works are offered now for the sake of those in need, in the fullness of time when the needs for petitions pass away, this order of communication will remain as an instrument of praise. These bonds of mercy are more than merely an efficient cause of healing the one communal body because through these acts of communication the communal body itself is becoming what God has created it to be. I support this claim with Augustinian and Rahnerian resources below, but first I consider at least two alternative proposals concerning the shape and character of the *communio sanctorum*.

Elizabeth Johnson is keenly interested in the participation of all persons in the *communio sanctorum*. She is critical of what she calls the "patronage model" because she believes it functions to limit access to— or at least freedom of participation in—the one communion for ecclesiastically underprivileged members. In one sense, she wants to build upon Lawrence Cunningham's well-founded critique of the bureaucracy of the canonization process that tends to reflect the institutional ideals of powerbrokers more than the faith and holiness of the people.[17] In another sense, she accepts Rahner's observation that in modernity God is an unknowable mystery and then she goes on to claim that the investiture of canonized saints with certain privileges has contributed deleteriously to this distancing from God and thus also to the obfuscation of the particular histories and faith of actual persons, especially those who have been oppressed.[18] She proposes a "companionship model" in which the saints are known as *friends of God and prophets* (Wis. 7:27) who are not raised above the living in any way, but rather accompany and encourage the living even as the living remember the lives of those now dead and especially the injustices done to them. Together, the living and the dead strain forward in hope of reunion.

The distinctive virtue of Johnson's view is that it disrupts the hegemonies of the present time and of the powerful, calling for a re-envisioning of true life with God as opposed to the banal assumptions perpetuated through current structures of power.[19] The significant shortcomings of this view, however, are too steep a price to pay for what the proposal actually delivers. Most notably, Johnson substitutes a new socio-political paradigm—one relating to an egalitarian community—in place of the model she is critiquing and dismissing.[20] A more promising route would be to refrain from discrediting the hierarchical dimension of the *communio sanctorum* in full, and instead work toward reconceiving this hierarchy according to the order of love and mercy in place of misused power and domination. In the hierarchy of love and mercy that I am proposing, power is translated into service, authority into care, and holiness into sacrifice. Those who are higher up, so to speak, are also those who, in virtue of their abiding in Christ through the Spirit, bend down with Christ to serve those in greater need.

After highlighting the merits of Johnson's view, John Thiel also chooses to pursue a path that diverges from Johnson's.[21] Among the many gifts that his recent work on the eschatological imagination brings to bear is the seriousness with which he deals with acts of forgiveness and the rich, complex work of reconciliation. In his account of the *communio sanctorum*, the work of forgiveness becomes the shared work of all the saints. This corporate activity redounds all the more to beatific joy since "nothing," Thiel claims, "produces true joy more than does the reconciliation that follows upon forgiveness and repentance."[22] This ongoing activity of forgiveness among the saints ensures the continuity of their respective personal characters within the one human community.[23] Thiel helpfully conceives of the manifold ways in which forgiveness may occur and respects the specifically historical and social dimensions of these concrete acts of forgiveness and processes of reconciliation.[24] Moreover, Thiel observes the mysterious exchange between grace, which he terms "aneconmic," and human persons whose redemption occurs in an economic setting. This is the setting in which the "economy of grace does its business."[25] In the presence of grace, the economy of redemption opens space for processes of engaged reciprocity that enable forgiveness to truly affect personal relationships.[26]

According to Thiel, eschatological hope that respects the meaning of history must also respect sin's lingering effects. In this view, these remaining effects are the sad face that allows for the joy of heaven to show forth in contrast. The saints carry this sadness with them as they everlastingly "work toward an eschatological solidarity that is both universal and fulfilled in every imaginable way."[27] This would be a fine articulation of Christian hope if Thiel were speaking of the enduring—though not eternal—significance of purgatory; however, Thiel wants to erase the line between purgatory and heaven, thus allowing the effects of sin to continue on in eternal life.[28] Ironically, despite his efforts to dispatch with the anxiety-filled doctrine of purgatory, Thiel ends up redefining heaven as a perpetual purgatory.[29]

For all the positive contributions that Thiel's close attention to the eschatological imagination offers, the dialectic that he proposes between the workings of grace and the lingering effects of sin hides an especially crippling proposal. Namely, this view borders on granting ontological status to sin, at least transitively through the perpetual endurance of its effects. The veer toward this undesirable end begins with an incomplete anthropology, wherein the definition of human nature depends on an association with sin in order to be distinguished from the divine nature. While the effects of this anthropological principle are evident in the eschatological vision Thiel espouses, I argue that Thiel takes his lead from a view of human nature and the *communio sanctorum* that Bradford Hinze espoused in an essay published in 2000, to which Thiel approvingly refers.[30]

In his essay, Hinze wishes to consider the dialogical nature of revelation and the Church, as well as the sinfulness of the Church itself. In the course of undertaking this important study, Hinze distinguishes his ecclesiological proposal that foregrounds dialogue from an alternative view that he perceives as cherishing obedience. Hinze portrays Hans Urs von Balthasar as his primary antagonist, though Joseph Ratzinger, John Paul II, and Henri de Lubac are also implicated. Behind all of these figures is a certain Pauline and Augustinian understanding of the Church as the Body of Christ and therefore "the collective presence in the world of the incarnate Son of God and risen Christ."[31] This view, Hinze claims, promotes an inherent "ecclesial monophysitism or christomonism, a position unable to recognize the human role in ecclesial matters, one that discredits human agency both in moments of creativity and in matters of sin."[32]

In Hinze's account, the alleged monophysitism or christomonism of the ecclesiology he critiques holds to a robust Mariology in which Mary is revered as the type of the obedient Church, whose dignity is predicated on pure subjective receptivity to the objectivity of the Word in history.[33] As Hinze paints the picture, this Marian emphasis leaves the Church and humanity itself in a position of limp dependence on the absoluteness of divine agency. Hinze wants to defend a position in which humanity may be both responsive and nonresponsive to grace—cooperative and resistive to divine agency—but believes that those who protect the immaculate state of the Church on Marian grounds propound a view in which the divine ultimately absorbs the dignity of humanity. Since their error is in part due to the reluctance to admit of the sin of the Church, Hinze's solution is to emphasize its sinfulness. When Thiel follows Hinze's lead, he pushes forward toward an eschatological vision that cannot be anything but concerned with the ongoing forgiveness of sins, for the sins of humanity are constitutive of its character even in the Church triumphant—the eschatological fullness of the *communio sanctorum*. Eternity has been conditioned by history, rather than vice versa.

The crucial misstep in this line of argument occurred with failing to understand the view of human nature generally shared among those whom Hinze accused of fostering a too-lofty Mariology and a relatively non-dialogical ecclesiology. Though John Paul II is less theologically developed than the other three with whom he was mentioned (for John Paul, a personalist philosophy is the primary operator), Balthasar, Ratzinger, and de Lubac all operate with a basic Augustinian understanding that human nature is deeply wounded, with a human will in need of healing through the grace given in Christ. It is not the case for them that the divine element cancels out the human element; rather, the gift of grace seeks to make human nature surpassingly strong so as to respond freely to the divine gift.[34] Their understanding of the wounded condition of the human nature is not possible without being given a view of this humanity in its fullness. When they see Mary, then, they see her as fully free because they see her perfectly conformed to the grace given in her Son. A complete and truthful vision of humanity is possible in view of first its fullness, from which an understanding of its present unhealthy condition may be drawn. An appreciation of full health precedes and enables an accurate diagnosis of sickness.

It is a mistake to attempt to see the *communio sanctorum* as simultaneously the *communio peccatorum*, unless one has learned to see the latter as a state of pilgrimage toward the fullness of the former. Throughout this work, I have been advocating for an understanding of the *communio sanctorum* whereby sins—understood as the culpable failures to communicate life and blessing—are healed in the Word who is raised up from the silence of being dead. Sin has no ontological status, most especially in the *communio sanctorum*; rather, sin is only the "unontological" chaos out of which God creates anew. The saints promise and embody what God pledges to creation in Jesus Christ: that all who are given speech in what they hear spoken to them in Christ will share together in life ever-lasting.[35] Most profoundly, this fellowship does not erase history—it redeems, transforms, and sanctifies it. The created order is renewed so it may communicate blessing, not the curse. Moreover, the transcendent fulfillment of creation in and through the eschatological communion of created persons is absolutely free *for* this symphonic dialogue of communication, and therefore absolutely free *from* all the isolating effects of sin. The very wounds of the sins of many become the sites of the resurrection of the body, where new relationships based in mercy are forged among those who previously stood in enmity, suspicion, and hatred. In eschatological beatitude, the causes of those wounds and their pains are remitted, so that only the life that is created in those cavities of communicative love is remembered as mercy through praise. Human persons thus come to share in the divine work of bringing life out of death and creating out of nothing. In the exercise of charity, human persons become capable of looking into absence and depositing gratuity. The forgiveness of sins is one such act of charity and precisely one that is eschatologically accomplished. The fruits of that particular act remain for eternity, even once the activity of forgiveness is completed. Likewise, charity in response to need and want reaches its end in the fullness of time, while the charity of a communion of persons sharing in praise endures eternally.

In summary, I contend that the anthropological vision that Thiel draws from Hinze's ecclesiological proposal leaves human nature too dependent on sin for its essential definition, especially in contrast to the divine nature. Thiel is thus bound to imagine the communion of saints according to an ongoing process of forgiveness since the sins of human persons are constitutive of their character; in other words, Thiel allows what we are *now* to trap us eternally. Conversely, I claim that *what we shall be* frees us (see 1 John 3:2; cf. 1 Cor. 13:12), for life in the Spirit, to which the third part of the creed provides testimony, is *now* the process of our liberation in response to the merits of Christ, which *then* leads to the eschatologically consummated liberation wherewith human persons are finally and fully free. The *communio sanctorum* promises the fulfillment of human personhood where the saints are free to love as they are loved.

The Communicative Nature

In light of this conviction, I move now to bolster the argument of this chapter with an appeal first to Augustine and then to Karl Rahner, each of whom identifies the properly communicative nature of humanity as originally created. I seek to further demonstrate how *what we shall become* unveils the deepest truth of *what we are now*: our beginning is disclosed in our end. In other words, the original intention for humanity is only recognizable if seen from the vantage point of what the Christian faith promises we are to become in Christ with the Holy Spirit. Augustine's conception of the original solidarity and Rahner's notion of the holy *pneuma* offer distinct yet complementary Catholic understandings of this foundational character of the human community. After I treat these two notions relatively briefly, I proceed to treat the biblical and the sacramental understanding of the formation of human persons into one communal body of sacred memory. The Exodus narrative and the Sacrament of Baptism will present to us the gateway to the Church as *communio*, in which we will explore the Eucharistic character of this one communion that holds together heaven and earth, eternity and time.

Augustine's Original Solidarity

There is nothing to look at if one looks at sin. The attempt to gaze at sin derives from "a hostile intelligence" by which one supposes that there is some force independent of God that works against God.[36] Sin is the privation of the good, the deprivation of life. Dwelling on sin distorts the viewer, for the absence that is evil disorders gawkers. Moreover, if one does not recognize sin as passing away in Christ, then one does not see Christ. To see Christ in terms of sin is blind madness, but to see sin against the fullness of Christ is healing. True sight comes from seeing in the Holy Spirit, while true understanding comes from knowing things by the Spirit that gives life. With this belief, Augustine penned some of the more celebrated lines in his vast corpus:

> It is different for people who see creation through your Spirit, for you are
> seeing it through their eyes. Thus when such people see that these things

are good, you are seeing that they are good; whatever created things please them for your sake, it is you who are arousing their delight in these things; and anything that gives us joy through your Spirit gives you joy in us.[37]

It is impossible to see the truth of creation without seeing creation in the light of faith. In the language I employed above, it is impossible to diagnose oneself in a state of illness when one cannot remember a time when one was not sick, or, alternatively, if one does not at least have some sense of what full health would be. Only once one is given the gift of a glimpse or foretaste of full health, which is itself already the beginning of healing, may one begin to know the truth about oneself. The narrative of the *Confessions* that I traced in detail in chapter 4 tells of how Augustine tasted the mercy that uncovered his deepest desire. When he sought to understand the desire that he discovered, he learned that the final end of his existence is to enjoy without end the peace he had been given. As with anyone who recognizes his own fragile mortality as "a person whose life is tending towards death,"[38] Augustine found two options for living his life (aside from a third quasi-option that would be to deny the fact of death itself, which is the distinctively modern position that I documented in chapter 2).

The first option for one who takes death seriously is to attempt to claim one's life as one's own, which is a practice that inevitably comes at the expense of others. Heidegger anachronistically represented this option in my Augustinian exploration. The other option would be to trust in the gift of life beyond all expectation, even as one admits that all powers for preservation that one possesses will come to an end in death. According to Paul, Abraham exercised this will when *he believed, hoping against hope* (Rom. 4:18, NAB) that life would come from God despite all evidence to the contrary. With significant emphasis, Augustine described a trust like this as being the supernaturally infused gift of faith that sees Christ as that "ineffable mercy" in whom "death, which all agree to be contrary to life, has become the means by which men pass into life."[39] Even in that which is simply evil—that is, death, the total breakdown in communication—God has wrought his exceedingly good work of creation in Christ. To see life in Christ against the extreme vitiation of life which is death is to see by faith beyond all expectation (see 2 Cor. 5:7). The full strength of this faith grows, as with Augustine, through the persistent belief in the inestimable power of the gift of mercy one receives, on the basis of which one begins to see and interpret all of creation "through the Spirit." This way of seeing and knowing opens the imagination to contemplating the final end to which the saints are called, an end that everyone naturally desires. Only from the perspective of that beatific end—the end that is the fullness of health beyond the lingering effects of the sickness of sin—can we contemplate with Augustine the original truth of the creation of man, trusting all the while in the God who, from beginning to end, is ever-faithful to his promises.

Augustine describes the end that all desire as the eternal Sabbath: peace without end. This is the unending enjoyment of life with God, the gift and pledge of whom put on human flesh and was raised out of the grave clinging to that same-flesh-now-glorified. By the grace of this un-solicited gift, human beings learn to not just desire to dwell in this rest, but, according to Augustine at the conclusion of *City of God*, to become this Sabbath themselves. In resurrected bodies transfigured to praise, we will be "filled by him when he will be all in all" (see 1 Cor. 15:28).[40] In light of this end without end, we come to see—by contrast—that the only evil is *not* to will this end as one's own and another's good—that is, the common good. Though one cannot comprehend evil on its own, one can observe it as the negation of what should be. Therefore, when Augustine turns to treat the allegorical interpretation of paradise—and thus to consider our original created condition that is now inaccessible to sight and to knowledge—he measures how we are now according to how we will be in Christ, on the basis of Christ's promise given in the Spirit. With this view, "it is certain that if man ignores God's will he can only employ his own powers to his own destruction; and thus he learns what a difference it makes whether he gives his adherence to the good that is shared by all, or finds pleasure only in his own selfish good."[41] The only and original evil is to turn away from the good that God wills for us and to strive, in vain, to claim one's life as one's own possession.[42]

Since God is unchanging and ever-faithful to his promises, the sin that we call "original" is not proper to God's intention in the act of crea-tion. The original solidarity that God wills for his free creatures precedes the corrupted human will that pursues its own selfish interest. Seeing through the Spirit in whom the end promised in Christ begins even now, the full meaning of the scriptural account of the creation of man is revealed. Distinct from all other creatures, man alone is created as one individual, out of whom the genesis of human society is drawn.[43] Out of the single human a partner is made for the sake of companionship so that human persons may will for themselves the communion God wills for them in his intentional act of creation.

The primordial truth undergirding the account of the creation and fall of man in Genesis 2–3 is that the human person is created for communion. This is God's will and our good: *that they may all be one*, as Jesus prays in John's Gospel (17:20, RSV). This ultimate good for the human person means that, against the eschatological horizon, the multitude of divisions among persons in the world resolve to only two ways—what Augustine names as the way of the Heavenly City and the way of the Earthly City. Those who abide by the former cling to one another in clinging to God in Christ, while those of the latter separate from one another in clinging to their own self-serving wills.[44] The story of the fall tells of how human persons—created for and living in communion—relinquish the gift of clinging to God as they cling to what pleases them according to their own standards.[45] Their original solidarity then works to pull down rather than build up the one communal body of humanity that was created as a single individual. The first community—created in and for mutual companionship—lusts after companionship of their own making without God. So closely bound in partnership was the first couple that the falling away of one leads the other to choose the comforts of companionship rather than sacrificing his will for the sake of his own and another's good—the common good of persevering in God.[46] Rather than stretch himself from God to his fallen companion, the man (later named Adam) consummates the fall as he seeks to claim as his own the fellowship that was given as gift. The communion of human persons in God is thus exchanged for the non-communion of selfish wills. Death enters when the communion of persons breaks down because communication ceases among those who isolate themselves from their own and the other's good. The "good news" of Jesus Christ is good not simply because life is given where once only death reigned, but also because the original goodness of creation is recovered as it enters into fulfillment in

Christ, thus enabling those isolated in sin to see the good, to begin to delight in it, and to enter into the joy of the Spirit that they have been created to desire.[47]

Augustine's theology of creation is eschatologically conditioned. Since Christ inaugurates humanity's supernatural end in the fullness of the Paschal Mystery and the handing over of the Spirit, the original truth of creation itself is hidden and revealed in what Christ gives. While almost all would agree that sin is treated with the utmost seriousness in Augustine's theology, the intrinsic connection between his eschatology and theology of creation grants sufficient warrant to the claim that the age of sin and all its effects is nothing more than an interregnum. While sin and its effects persist, sin appears to reign and a community of sinners appears to form; once the mercy of God in Christ comes into view, though, sin is stripped of its illusive power and the community of sinners is exposed as a sham. The future that is opened in Christ recasts human nature as created for communication. In sin, human nature has existed in a state of contradiction as it communicates its own addiction to noncommunication. Redemption in Christ—the Eternal Word—restores truth to human nature by making it communicative of life even in its total collapse in death. By the Holy Spirit, the grace of Christ first heals and then sanctifies: the principle of communication is renewed and then the communal body is perfected in communicating the charity that calls it into being. The intrinsic harmony of the original solidarity and the eschatological communion of the blessed does not ignore the history of salvation that unfolds between them; instead, history is restored to its deepest truth as the gift of solidarity is freed *from* its self-negation and freed *for* the fullness of communion through the graced maturation of human wills.

Rahner's Holy Pneuma

Karl Rahner's theology of death contrasts with Augustine's in certain important respects. Most notably—as I discussed at length in chapter 2—there is something of a positive valence to death for Rahner since this real end to finite human life secures the eternal significance of the freely determined actions of the creature.[48] As Augustine treats it, death is *only* evil, and yet it is also that which God has made into an instrument of his mercy in Christ.[49] Even though Rahner attempts to preserve a partially Irenaean view of death, he also expresses the same Pauline emphasis on the victory of divine life of grace over that which is its contradiction: sin and death.[50] Despite the fact that Rahner's notion of the resurrection of the body is less remarkable than Augustine's as commensurate with the respective severity of their notions of death, this agreement as to the triumph of Christ's communication of grace in the noncommunication of death points to a more fundamental form of harmony between the two.

In his own way, Rahner articulates a defense of the inherently communicative nature of humanity that is reminiscent of Augustine's. Furthermore, Rahner ties this character to God's intention in creating human persons, stressing its primordial status in contradistinction to the contingency though universal corruption of humanity's fallen state. Also like Augustine, Rahner conceives of the redemption of the original dignity of humanity's communicative nature as concomitant with human sociality serving as the very instrument through which sanctification is wrought. In order to explicate Rahner's theological vision, it is helpful to offer an account of his understanding of Original Sin from the starting point of his conception of concupiscence.

Briefly put, concupiscence is the experience of an absence of "something that ought to be." For Rahner, this sense of contradiction pertains not to a person's "'nature' but [to] his supernatural and yet undeniable determination."[51] What is not there but should be is the unexacted preternatural gift of integrity.[52] Concupiscence influences those who do not possess the gift of original integrity, by which a person's free decisions would be fully expressive of her nature. The freedom entailed in these free decisions would not primarily be a freedom *from* the "sluggishness" of nature that is characteristic of concupiscence, but rather a freedom *for* "an exhaustive engagement of . . . being in a personal decision directed to the good."[53] The sin of Adam (*peccatum originale originans*) results in the fissure between person and nature because this originary free decision was against disposing totally of oneself as subject and thus was the genesis of Original Sin (*peccatum originale originatum*), which affects all those who come after.[54]

The loss of integrity through the *peccatum originale originans* entailed the loss of the divinely intended quality of humanity to be a medium of divine life. In accordance with God's self-consistent universal salvific will, God created humanity as unified with the intention that sanctification by the holy *pneuma* of the whole race would progress through human generation, as I discussed already in chapter 3.[55] By losing its original integrity, humanity lost the communicatory quality of its original blessedness. The remnant of solidarity in humankind signifies God's intention that each person should be saved through his association with the others in the one community of humanity. Redemption in Christ is thus achieved by way of imparting the holy *pneuma* upon humanity, thereby bringing about the restoration of the intended communicatory quality of humanity through the humanity of the Word. In Christ, human nature becomes what it was intended to be: the sacrament of salvation.[56]

The anthropological-cum-social implications of Rahner's Christology allow him to draw out decisive eschatological dimensions of the Christian faith. These eschatological dimensions are consistent with and indeed definitively interpret the created nature of humanity as such. In his essay "The Church of the Saints," he argues that when Christians venerate the saints, they are acknowledging the real, historical efficaciousness of God's grace in Christ. These acts of veneration do not only recognize the effect of this grace on certain human persons in isolation, but also and indeed most especially these are eschatological statements of faith whereby the living Church attests that in Christ the human nature in which all share has become the instrument of salvation. Moreover, the instrument of our humanity is not being transfigured outside the confines of history—as if to abstract the good from the messy complications of life in the world—rather, this transfiguration occurs in the midst of history itself.[57]

The holiness of the saints is more essential and more original to the definition of the Church and to the truth of human persons as God's creatures than are the sins and sinfulness of the Church, its members, or human beings on the whole. Bradford Hinze, whose ecclesiological proposal I explored above in connection with the anthropological and eschatological conceptions Thiel assumes, also drew from Rahner in constructing the argument that I critiqued. While it is certainly true that Rahner posed serious questions about the sinful state of the Church,[58] a broader consideration of his theological outlook enables one to see that the holiness of the Church in virtue of its saints—who witness to the victory of Christ over sin and death—is always primary, even in its state of historical incompleteness. The truth of creation must ultimately be defined either according to the victory or failure of Christ to redeem the original integrity of human nature and thereby transform the embodied human community into the instrument of sanctifying grace. While the history of sin is evident, it is contextualized within the bounds of the grace of creation and the grace of redemption and sanctification. Though sin and its lingering effects cannot be ignored, we must also refrain from elevating them to the status of ontological substantiality and granting them a home in eternity. Fallen humanity is to be distinguished from humanity as originally created, as well as humanity redeemed and sanctified in Christ through the Spirit, and so "the Church is meant to be and to appear as the community of eschatological salvation and of victorious grace."[59] The free communication of this victorious grace within the human community *as such*—that is, humanity as restored and renewed in Christ—is the path to and the prize of eschatological salvation.

Graced Human Nature

Despite the distinctiveness of their respective soteriologies, Augustine and Rahner offer compatible and even mutually reinforcing views of the insuperable original dignity of human nature as discerned from the end for which Christ frees us. In their own ways, they present grace as building upon nature, but only as grace first heals human nature of its chronic addiction and fatal illness. Indeed, grace heals nature in order to perfect it. With an eye fixed upon what we hope to become as a beatific communion in Christ, the reality of humanity's distance from what it should be—and from what it was in fact created to be—becomes apparent. In these views, history and creation are interpreted eschatologically.

As the gift of Christ's eternal life definitively manifested in the Resurrection, life in the Spirit grants redeemed human persons not only the freedom to hope for what they will become but also grants the freedom to remember—indeed, for the first time—who they were originally created to be. Christ is the love that gives us hope and restores our memory. In him, we are reclaimed as good and given the grace to believe that this goodness is the most original truth of our being as God's creatures.[60] As Augustine put it, we see creation through the Spirit.[61] This goodness, though, never was nor can it ever be claimed as a private possession, for the good for which we are intended is the common good—that is, the good that we share with others. More to the point, this common good constitutively commands and invites each person to will the good of others and so share together the gift of communion in Christ. This is the joy that everyone naturally desires.

What Augustine and Rahner help us to see is that the belief in the *communio sanctorum* expresses both the Church's horizon of hope and its pilgrimage of memory. On the basis of participating in the hope of what Christ calls us to become, we remember the truth of who God created us to be; conversely, in neglecting the former we forget the latter. The task of the Christian life is to cling to the gift we have received as the sole, defining truth of our existence. As Dante illustrated in the *Purgatorio*, the struggle of clinging to this truth looks like charitably offering the space of one's own soul for the good of others while also entrusting oneself to the charitable care of those who are free to give of themselves. In short, Dante sketched out the basic dimensions of a communion of charity. As I continue to build my argument for an understanding of the *communio sanctorum* as a communion of charity that embodies what we might call the "logical narrative conclusion" to belief in the Triune God as presented in the creed, I return briefly—and for the last time—to Dante's *Commedia* in order to study a poetic image of the journey toward the bodily memory that defines the Christian pilgrimage of sanctification. I then locate the sacramental origin of this bodily memory in Baptism, its ecclesial apogee in the Eucharist, and, as we approach the final chapter, in its eschatological communion of the glorified human body.

The Space of Freedom

Between Lethe and Eunoe

When earlier I appealed to Dante's poetry I attended to the way in which his hierarchically ordered community stretches across distinct spheres of existence and works through the downward movement of charity to draw upward those members further removed from their final beatific end. I identified the *Paternoster* in *Purgatorio* 11 as an exemplar of how purgation and charity comprise two movements of the same action in building up a single communion in which the common good is realized in the non-competitive mutuality of concern among members. While I contend that these two movements do indeed attain to one complete action, I also recognize that the two movements are distinct and non-redundant. This becomes most apparent in the concluding cantos of the *Purgatorio*, where Dante presents a final stage of his purgatorial pilgrimage that recapitulates the entire journey up the mountain's terraces—a journey that occurred through exterior ascent and interior reorientation. In the immeasurable space between two bends in the same river, the drama of human sanctification unfolds.

Atop the Mountain of Purgatory, Dante approaches the threshold of the Earthly Paradise. He stands on the banks of a river (28.25–27)[62] in which his reflection brings back to him all the shame of his life's sins in the presence of his beloved Beatrice, whose stern pity illuminates Dante's failings (30.73–81). This is the River Lethe, which flows down "from God's own will / . . . with all its power / to take the memory of sin away" (28.125, 127–28; cf. *Inferno* 14.136–38). The happiness the Earthly Paradise promises is not attainable for one still gripped by the shame of sin, and so this water removes from one's memory all the presumptions of self-constructed identities in which one has indulged. This cleansing separation removes one from one's own history and indeed leaves one exiled from any historical memory.

If the passage through Lethe returns one to something like the Edenic state, this separation from one's history embodied as personal memory indefinitely suspends the significance of human life. Such an invalidation of history does not accord, however, with the eschatological vision of the *Commedia*. Even before Dante (the pilgrim) passes through the waters of Lethe, Dante (the poet) has Matilda explain that this river of forgetfulness later curves to hold the border of the far side of the Earthly Paradise, and in that part the river takes on another name: Eunoe. Whereas Lethe strips away the memory of sin, Eunoe restores the memory of "all good done" (28.129; cf. 33.124–32, 142–45). Significance is restored to history before one moves from the Earthly Paradise to the Heavenly Paradise, and this restoration occurs in the mode of redemption.

Dante is twice plunged as he passes through the Earthly Paradise: once for cleansing and once for reviving. In separating these moments and even naming the river differently for each passage, the poet is demonstrating the distinctiveness of the two movements of the same act that I identified earlier. This entire journey through purgatory concerned the negation of the effects of human persons' obsessive self-regard, which always comes at the expense of other persons in the human community. Throughout purgatory, movements of affirmation accompanied these negations as the penitents learned to will the good of others, uniting the wellbeing of others with their own. The space these penitents open up through the dispossession of their self-interest becomes the space for charitable self-giving. In the Earthly Paradise—specifically between Lethe and Eunoe—Dante has paused in the disappearing moment between these two movements, as if to contemplate the meaning of breathing from the stillness of lungs just emptied and about to fill.

In the space between these two immersions, we discern the twin dimensions of freedom that I have stressed in these pages. In Dante's account, the fact of the forgiveness of sins is already accomplished for those even on the base of the Mountain of Purgatory. What happens at the top, then, is that the fulfillment of the remediation for these sins is effected so that the power of death is definitively overcome. This everlasting freedom *from* sin is consummated in Lethe; the freedom *for* beatific life is then distinguished as distinct yet conjoined. The wholly positive dimension of freedom is accomplished alongside the work of remitting guilt throughout the purgatorial journey; thus, even as purgatory is about the separation of souls from the memory of their sins, it is also about claiming aright a redeemed memory. On the basis of this positive reengagement and integration with history, the gift of beatific life begins. Quite to the point, Dante presents himself—the pilgrim turned poet—as the beneficiary and executor of such a memory when he sets out to write his poem according to "the good that I found there"[63] as tonic for "a world that lives all wrong."[64] His eschatological vision presents the truth of the human person and human community as fundamentally oriented to the eternal rhythm of mercy-and-praise, which is ultimately and absolutely free from the ongoing reference to sin or the enduring association with its effects. Essential to beatific life is the freedom *from* forever having to say "I'm sorry" so that redeemed persons may together dispose themselves to *forgetting what lies behind but straining forward to what lies ahead* (Phil. 3:13).

Between the Red Sea and the River Jordan

Moving forward from this reading of the *Commedia*, I argue that sanctification consists of forgetting histories devoid of a future so that those *straining forward* move with a historical memory of future blessedness. Without a memory conformed to the gift of mercy, attempts at progress are foiled—or, in the words of Dante's *Paternoster*, "all travel backwards who strive forwards most."[65] Immediately preceding these words of the eleventh canto, Dante refers to *manna* (*Da oggi a noi la cotidiana manna*, 11.13), reminding the reader of Israel's desert food. This food was provided each morning from the hand of the One who led the Israelites out of Egypt, so that receiving this food always entailed remembering what was done for Israel. For Israel, *manna* received *today* was a memory of history conformed to mercy. Moreover, the desire for this food—or, conversely, the lack of desire for it—was correlative to Israel's identification with its own liberation. Flagging zeal for this gift is at once a failure of memory for what has occurred and a failure of hope for what is to come. It is not surprising, then, that when Dante alludes more directly to the Exodus, he does so on purgatory's terrace of sloth, where healing occurs as the fullness of desire impels true progress.[66] Dante recalls the Israelites' grumbling against the Lord and their subsequent failure to inherit the land promised to them: "before the river Jordan saw their heirs, / all those for whom the sea had opened, died!" (cf. Num. 14:1–35).[67] With their desire directed back to the captivity from which they had come, the Israelites cannot remember who they are called to become. This biblical witness is crucial to understanding the connection between memory and desire. Moreover, the journey from the Red Sea to the River Jordan typifies the meaning of freedom for that *communio sanctorum* that inhabits the Heavenly City, a community which, as Augustine envisioned, "will be freed from all evil and filled with all good, . . . yet will not forget its own liberation, nor be ungrateful to its liberator."[68]

On the other side of the Red Sea, the Israelites are absolutely free and, at the same time, profoundly unfree. Even though God's liberating deed has been performed, the Israelites cannot simply step into their very own land and possess what they are promised; rather, they must accept their identity as a free people so they might become free in the land the Lord provides.[69] But freedom is hard work. In the face of hunger, the Israelites flee their liberator and cling to the fleshpots of Egypt (see Exod. 16:2–3). In this, the remembrance of the land of their captivity is not itself the issue; *how* they remember Egypt is the problem. They identify themselves with the relative comfort they experienced in their captivity instead of staking their identity on the wondrous deed of the One who led them out of that captivity. The memory that should constitute their identity and open up their future still lags behind the liberation God has already accomplished.[70] Were they to enter the land promised them forgetful of the Lord's wondrous deeds and clinging instead to their perverse memories of captivity, their homeland would be spoiled and they would despise what they always desired (see Ps. 106:21–24).

There is something like a double-movement to Israel's one passage through the Red Sea: the objective freedom *from* the Egyptians and the subjective freedom *for* accepting a new identity that leads to Israel's future. Israel's song of salvation (see Exod. 15:1–18) as well as the *Shema* itself contain the very key to its growth as a people. On Sinai, Israel receives the prescription for and description of its new identity—indeed, it is inscribed upon Israel.[71] In the habitual rehearsal of who it already is because of what God has done, Israel grows into who God calls it to be: a free people living in a promised land of freedom.[72]

The passage through the Red Sea is thus only completed once the desire for Egypt is itself cast into the sea (cf. Exod. 15:19). Another water crossing marks the death of this perverse desire, so that what was objectively given in the Red Sea is subjectively consummated in the Jordan (see Deut. 28:63–30:20; cf. Rom. 11:1–10). In the biblical witness, these two water crossings are two movements of the same action, separated by forty years and a vast desert. In the tension between these two movements of freedom, the reorientation of desire changes a memory closed in upon a history of captivity into a memory of liberation for a history of salvation. The conformation of the truth of Israel's identity to its rightful memory is a matter not of forgetting its history but of remembering its whole history according to the mercy God offered there. The desert journey is the historical parable of Israel's entire earthly pilgrimage: the breaking of a perverse memory and the acceptance of the memory of redemption.

Between Baptism and Glory

The Christian Sacrament of Baptism assumes all the implications of this typological prefiguration.[73] In the waters of Baptism, the deed of salvation is accomplished for the baptized as the once-for-all sacrifice of Christ touches the sinner. The baptized have already died with Christ and now receive the offer of everlasting life in the communion of the Holy Spirit, and yet the freedom of the Christian life is hard work as the neophyte must continually cling to this freedom and embody it. The power of God *who gives life to the dead and calls into existence things that do not exist* (Rom. 4:17) is given freely to the baptized as the sole power of their existence; for the baptized, life is assured with God in Christ. And yet, the drama of the *vita humana* unfolds in the immeasurable space between the deed of salvation and the willful conformity with this deed. The issue of Christian living concerns coming to fully desire that which the baptized have been given and to which they have been called.

For the Christian who is freed from Original Sin, the effects of Original Sin remain for a time. The tendencies toward isolating self-possession persist, thwarting the full exercise of charity that would characterize a communion of persons in which members act together for the good of the whole body. Those baptized but not yet consummated in glory (see 2 Cor. 1:21–22; cf. 2 Cor. 3:17–18; 5:5; Eph. 1:11–14) experience a sluggishness to their freedom as their desire to be remembered in mercy is fragmented, leaving the will in a state of lingering disorder relative to the common good of salvation. Put another way, the memory of the members of the communal body is not yet fully conformed to the good of the whole body because the members struggle to fully desire the good of others as their own good. The failure of desire and the failure of memory intertwine as the beneficiaries of the gift of liberation from sin do not yet stake themselves fully on the mercy God has freely given in Christ.

The pilgrim Church abides in the time and space of already belonging in holiness to the life of the Spirit and not yet fully willing to live in this spacious freedom (see Phil. 3:12–16; cf. 1 John 3:12). It exists in the disappearing moment between the meaninglessness of history in a world that is passing away and the eternal meaningfulness of history secured in God's embrace.[74] Balthasar interprets Augustine's doctrine of time as reckoning with this eschatological tension. The strain between what is definitively given and what is willfully accepted is relieved only in the ongoing *conversio* that is "the renewed practice of cleaving in love to God" through which one transfers one's heart to "where the heavenly Jerusalem lives."[75] History is meaningful because, "as an event of divine freedom," God has definitively acted in history in Christ.[76] The body of the risen Christ redeems time from the meaninglessness of death, and the Christian raised out of the waters of Baptism is ordered to the memory of this body (see Col. 3:1–4). The journey from those waters to the glory of the Heavenly City is thus tread "through time toward the risen Christ."[77] Those who have become more practiced in the memory of the indelible identity of this one body testify to the deepest truth of the one people whose life is given in the Spirit. This bodily memory holds the mystery of the Church as one people in which the fullness of God's wondrous deed is communicated from those who rest in this memory to those who are still restless for it.[78] The greatest witness the saints give on behalf of the uninterrupted communion of this one body is the charity they exercise for the good of the members still striving to embody the memory of God's gratuitous mercy. So long as any members of this one communal body remain in the process of purgation and spiritual growth, the whole body participates in purgation and growth in the name of charity.

To speak of the saints in heaven sharing in the purgatorial activities and spiritual growth of those still on pilgrimage on earth or in purgatory seems, at first, to contradict the teaching of Benedict XII's bull of 1336, *Benedictus Deus*.[79] In continuity with what I argued in chapter 4, however, I claim that the fulfillment of salvation is achieved in the saints' sharing the way of God's love in Christ. Until the final resurrection of the dead, the saints' sweet unrest in charity is already their eternal rest in God's love precisely as God's love still works through the Spirit on the one communal body of the whole Christ. This definitive emphasis

on charity—on which I further expound below—enables us to recon-
cile what Henri de Lubac has recognized as Christianity's "undying belief
in the essentially social nature of salvation" with the beatific life of the
blessed dead.[80]

Both for unique persons and for the whole communion of persons
in Christ, what is accomplished in Baptism is completed in the resurrection of the dead. The sacramental communion in Christ into which
Christians are initiated at Baptism is eschatologically realized when
Christ's members communicate—through the unimpeded free exercise
of their wills—the gift of God's incarnate love that overcomes death. The
charity that prompts and marks growth in the freedom of holiness does
not cease once the effects of sin have been purged; rather, the eternal significance of this charity ripens into the communal life of the saints, upon
whom the story of salvation is written.[81] The blessed dead are those who
have even now crossed the Eunoe into the memory of "all good done,"[82]
who live even now in that promised land of freedom across the Jordan,
and whose own praise beckons the rest of those who share in their communal body to remember themselves in God's mercy through a sacrifice
of praise.

For those still on pilgrimage, this sacrifice is twofold. On the one
hand it is, as Nathan Mitchell has put it, "an act of dying, a surrender
of that obsessive impulse to dominate others, to destroy their freedom,
to secure our own lives by taking the rest of the world hostage."[83] This
death occurs in Baptism when neophytes are united to Christ's death,
and then the lingering effects of that old way of being are cast into the
saving waters through every act of liturgy, every purgatorial act of self-
dispossession. On the other hand, the pilgrim affirmatively gives the
space of herself—of her time, her prayer, her works—in sacrifice for the
good of others. For now, this charity comes at a cost, for one always loses
something when one gives to others in the competitive economy of this
world. And yet, *the love of God [that] has been poured out into our hearts
through the holy Spirit that has been given to us* (Rom. 5:5; cf. 8:14–17,
NAB) underwrites this loss so that the return on investment is everlasting life in God.[84] The free gift of God's life in the Spirit *as* and *for* the
bond of communion is charity—first, charity as mercy from God to his
creation given from the fount of God's very life, then charity as praise

from creation in response to God and, further, charity as service within the one communal body hidden in Christ (see John 15:12; cf. 13:20, 34–35). The mystery of the Church as communion is at once what gives meaning to and draws meaning from the Christian belief in the *communio sanctorum*. This principle of communion that stretches across death and forms wayfarers, penitents, and the sanctified into one body is always first the *communio* of God (see 1 John 4:7–21). This is an ecclesiological statement aptly expressed in Augustinian theology and more recently expounded in the thought of Joseph Ratzinger with his version of the so-called *communio* ecclesiology, in which the Eucharistic character of the Church comes to the fore. To this Eucharistic ecclesiology of communion, we now turn.

The Church's Oblation

Holy Spirit as Communio

In the opening paragraph of *Lumen gentium*, the council declares that "the church, in Christ, is a sacrament—a sign and instrument, that is, of communion with God and of the unity of the entire human race" whose "nature and universal mission" are orientated to drawing all people into "full unity in Christ."[85] This communion at the heart of the Church is the cornerstone of Joseph Ratzinger's ecclesiology, which depends heavily on his interpretation of Augustine's pneumatology and Eucharistic theology. In short, Ratzinger reads Augustine—especially but not exclusively according to book XV of *De Trinitate*—as identifying the Church's own sacramental principle of communion with the person of the Holy Spirit. While this theme is prevalent as early as in Ratzinger's doctoral dissertation,[86] it is presented clearly in a consolidated and sharpened form in an essay that appeared in the journal *Communio* under the title "The Holy Spirit as Communion."[87]

In Ratzinger's essay, his entrée to Augustine's ecclesiology comes by grappling with the particularity of the Holy Spirit. Unlike the Father and the Son whose very names point to the distinctive characteristics of these respective persons, the name of the Holy Spirit is essential to God as such and does not appear to directly indicate the particularity of this person. It is precisely in this dilemma, however, that Augustine discerns the Holy Spirit's particularity. "When [the Holy Spirit] is named by that which is the divinity of God," Ratzinger comments, "by what the Father and Son have in common, then his essence is just that, the *communio* of Father and Son. . . . His particularity is being unity . . . mutuality itself."[88] Only in seeking the Holy Spirit according to the personal nature of the unity and distinction of the persons of the Trinity rather than attempting to conceptualize the Holy Spirit as "derived from a universally metaphysical substance" is this particularity made manifest.[89] Spirit is thus defined, for Augustine, as *communio*—that is, as "the unity which God gives himself," the unity in which "the Father and the Son give themselves back to one another."[90]

Based on this crucial preliminary work of understanding the "name" of the Holy Spirit as *communio*, Ratzinger then proceeds to interpret Augustine's treatment of 1 John 4:7–19 in *De Trinitate* XV. Toward the end of the previous chapter, I already cited the conclusion that Augustine draws from his reading of John's first epistle, namely, that "Man has no capacity to love God except from God."[91] This love with which man loves God must first be given to man as the gift of God. The question Augustine applies to 1 John 4 then is, basically: Of which Person of the Trinity does this epistle speak when it says that the love with which we are to love one another is the love of God given to us from God (see 4:7)? By attending closely to the text itself, Augustine rules out the Father—who "is God in such a way that he is not from God"—and the Son, who is the one in whom God *himself loved us* (v. 10); Augustine then recognizes that "it is the Holy Spirit of which [God] has given us that makes us abide in God and him in us," and therefore the one by whom we love one another.[92] The Holy Spirit is the very gift of charity that unites us to God and enables us to love our neighbor.[93] By this gift—that is, the *communio* of God—what Ratzinger describes as "the basic criterion of love" is disclosed: "Love in the full sense can only exist where constancy exists. Where abiding exists. Because love has to do with abiding, it cannot take place anywhere except where there is eternity."[94] Or in Paul's pithy expression: *love never ends* (1 Cor. 13:8, RSV).

The full meaning of the Church's essential character as given out of and always referring back to the mystery of the Triune God becomes even clearer for Ratzinger as he reads Augustine on the Donatists.[95] If the Holy Spirit is the presence of God precisely as *communio*, then breaking love—that is, refusing to abide with others and remain united with them, even for the sake of pursuing the most exalted idea of perfection—signifies removal from the presence of God. When the Donatists left the Church, they left that abiding, that constancy, that bearing with one another that is *caritas* as given in the Holy Spirit. Those who join together in schism reenact the fall of Adam, who chose solidarity in sin over the self-sacrificial solidarity that stretches one between communion with God and union with one's neighbor. Even though the Donatists retained everything else, in leaving *caritas* behind they left everything.[96] While clinging to the Church does not guarantee charity, breaking from the Church does guarantee charity's absence. In proclaiming that the Church is essentially love, Augustine is therefore laying down a dogmatic ecclesiological thesis. "As a creation of the Spirit," Ratzinger explains, "the Church is the body of the Lord built up by the *pneuma* and thus also becomes the Body of Christ when the *pneuma* forms men and women for 'communio.' This creation—this Church—is God's 'gift' in the world, and this 'gift' is love."[97]

The love that God poured out as the Spirit into the heart of the Church recovers the original gift of creation in the mode of redemption and also sanctifies the world through this second gift of love. De Lubac's relentless emphasis on the social nature of humanity and the common destiny of mankind further illumines the point that Ratzinger makes on the basis of Augustinian pneumatology. In no uncertain terms, de Lubac claims that the Catholic faith has always maintained that "the human race is one. By our fundamental nature," he continues, "and still more in virtue of our common destiny we are members of the same body [so that] the life of the members comes from the life of the body."[98] Salvation is never simply a matter of the salvation of individuals but always concerns the salvation of the entire body, the whole communion of members. Without following this teaching into a doctrine of *apokatastasis*, it is possible and indeed necessary to contend that the Church is the sacrament of Christ for the whole world, bound as one in God through the *caritas* of the Holy Spirit. The Spirit that brought into existence what was not in creation is the same Spirit that comes down as the "fire of universal charity" to reunite the fragmented body of humanity.[99] The Church's missionary character derives from its fundamental identity in the sacrament of charity.[100] Indeed, the Spirit assembles the *communio sanctorum* by re-membering the body.

The Gift of Prayer

In the same chapters of *De Trinitate* XV that I treated above, Augustine applies the fruits of his exegetical work on 1 John 4 to interpret the "Holy Spirit" in Paul's Letter to the Romans: "So the love which is from God and is God [1 John 4:7–8] is distinctively the Holy Spirit [1 John 4:13]; through him the charity of God is poured out into our hearts [Rom. 5:5], and through it the whole triad dwells."[101] This same Spirit ensures our hope (see 5:5; 8:24–25) since hope does not stand upon any power belonging to the world on its own but only upon the power of the Spirit of life who sets captives free (see 8:14–25). When Paul goes on to acclaim that *the Spirit too comes to the aid of our weakness* (8:26a, NAB), we may extend the Augustinian pneumatological doctrine to hear that "God's *communio*"—that is, the *caritas* of God— comes to heal our failures in love. Furthermore, *the Spirit [who] intercedes with inexpressible groanings* (8:26b; cf. 8:22, NAB) gives us who *wait for adoption* (8:23; cf. 8:15, NAB) the prayer to purge us from *slavery to corruption* (8:21; cf. 8:2–3, NAB) and free us for *the glorious freedom of the children of God* (8:21; cf. 8:1–14, 19, NAB).[102] As de Lubac reminds us, Paul's context here is the social rather than individualistic standpoint, bringing into view the communion of the whole body (see 12:3–20; cf. 1 Cor. 12:12–27).[103] Strictly speaking, there is no such thing as an individualistic standpoint within Christianity because the Spirit that teaches us to pray is *communio* and therefore "prayer is essentially the prayer of all for all."[104] Personhood and communion grow in direct proportion to one another.

Every authentic Christian spirituality is, in the end, an ecclesial spirituality.[105] The Holy Spirit praying in us leads each one out of the private chambers of our "closed inward-looking self" toward others in communion with God in Christ.[106] The Son who historically embodies his communion with the Father in *becoming obedient to death* (Phil. 2:8) and who was later raised from the dead as the glory of the Father's unfathomable will to love, opens himself to those whom the Father gave him. His prayer—*ut unum sint* (John 17:21)—becomes the lifeblood of this communion.[107] He makes us sharers in his relationship with the One he called "*Abba*, Father" (Rom. 8:15; cf. John 20:17, 28, NAB).[108] To live in his communion first demands purgation so we might freely speak the most profound affirmation. As Ratzinger comments, to say "*Our Father*" necessitates the denial of self-preserving preferences as we "strip ourselves of what is merely our own, of what divides."[109] This struggle to detach from our obsessive self-regard frees us to charitably affirm the good of others as our own good, unto "the communion of the children of God," in harmony with Christ Jesus, who assumes all creation in his "Yes" to the Father (cf. 2 Cor. 1:19–22).[110]

Bent as humanity was in its fallen condition toward the self-negating isolation of sin unto death, Christ took on our fallen humanity and turned it into an affirmation of the life of God. He makes our humanity his prayer to the Father in the *communio* of the Holy Spirit. Christ gives the peace that does not come from this world (John 14:27), but is given in the world as the pledge and foretaste of that eternal Sabbath when God will be all in all (1 Cor. 15:28). This is the gift of peace on which Dante mused when, in the *Paternoster* of *Purgatorio* 11, the penitents asked that peace come down to them from the heavenly realm.[111]

This gift called down from heaven as the Son's communion with the Father is the vertical axis of salvation history. Just as the *Ur-kenosis* of the Father's eternal begetting of the Son undergirds all kenotic activity in the economy,[112] so the Spirit as *communio* is the basis of all true solidarity in history.[113] The Holy Spirit is given as Christ's way of being in the world, and life in the Spirit bears the fruits of Christ's glorious sacrifice: the holiness of the church, the communion of saints, the forgiveness of sins, the resurrection of the body, and life everlasting. Life in the Spirit proclaims the deepest logic of the world as *created*, so that those who are re-membered in the liberating gift of God's mercy in Christ come to embody *caritas* as a testament to the ultimate truth about the world and the God who created it.[114] The Spirit in whom we pray—or, better, the

Spirit who prays in us—is the power of God working within and upon history to communicate the new life that springs from the Resurrection of Christ.[115] The Spirit who communicates new life in Christ is the protagonist of history who mediates grace in the Sacraments of the Church, especially the Eucharist.[116]

The Memory of Communion

The Eucharistic assembly abides in the space between the memory of Christ's Paschal Mystery and the fullness of life in the Spirit; this convocation journeys from the "tremendous event" of God in history to the final transformation of history's consummation.[117] While the Eucharistic liturgy is rightly the work of the Church (*opus ecclesiae*), this is only true because this liturgy fundamentally depends on the work of God (*opus Dei*). As the primary Sacrament of the Church, the Eucharist preserves the priority of agency in history: although the Church "makes" the Eucharist, this power is predicated on the gift of God in Christ, who gave himself for the life of the world without provocation—that is, freely and completely gratuitously. Indeed, the Eucharist is the living memory of the One who *first loved us* (1 John 4:19, RSV).[118] This chronological and ontological priority in love opens up a future for the Church that is oriented to the freedom for full participation in the communion offered in the sacrament. The eschatological dimension of the Eucharist calls for the transformation of the assembly into one communion of charity that unceasingly draws its life from the *communio* of God who comes to it.[119] The Eucharist is the bridge of eternal love stretching between memory and hope, and the gift of Christ's sacramental presence safeguards both the meaning of what is given and the fulfillment that is to come.

Recently, Jean-Luc Marion has sought to provide philosophical clarity to Christ's presence in the Eucharist. He believes that preserving the real ontological difference in the meeting place of the sacrament uniquely maintains the *distance* necessary for the Church to worship and commune with the One who is not in any way the product, extension, or projection of a consciousness otherwise determined. The Eucharist thwarts any and all attempts at "collective self-satisfaction" whereby God would be reduced to the dimensions of the community—that is, its memory of itself as derived from something other than God's action.[120]

What Marion is at pains to observe is that the sacrament does not hold Christ within the confines of the community's present time but rather permits the Church entry into the eternity of Christ's Resurrection. The descent of charity that the sacrament makes present can be neither demanded nor possessed; it must be respected in an assent of praise that will, necessarily, require the charitable activity of the communicants. The bread and the wine now become Christ's body and blood are viatic for the members of the communion as they traverse the *distance* between who they are and who Christ calls them to be in him.[121] When properly observed in thought and in practice, Christ's Eucharistic presence reconfigures the present as the space between the memorial of Christ's sacrifice and the *epektasis* of the Church's growth toward and into God. This sacred present holds in tension what has been given and what is promised.[122]

Interpolated between God's merciful gift definitively given in Christ and the freedom to embrace this gift in the life of the Spirit, the Church exists as the mystery of that which is not God but to which God has shared the gift of divine life. In substantive agreement with Marion, Louis-Marie Chauvet has argued that observing this distance between God and the world is indeed necessary for God's communication with the world and, subsequently, creation's return address of praise to God.[123] Even though the Eucharistic assembly traverses this distance, it does not abolish it.[124] *Distance* is an essential element to sacramental presence, for what is made present is precisely that which cannot be contained or delimited: the supernatural *caritas* of God. This gift also offers *direction* since the reception of this gift requires the recipient to become what he receives in the Body of Christ.[125]

Consumption of the Eucharist is thus intricately connected to being opened up. This opening up is marked as service to and charitable self-giving for others. To truly receive the self-gift of the Son—who receives and is himself the Father's self-gift—the communicant must allow the *caritas* of God to be translated into his own life. As Benedict XVI stated in his first encyclical,

Worship itself, Eucharistic communion, includes the reality both of being loved and loving others in turn. A Eucharist which does not pass over into the concrete practice of love is intrinsically fragmented. Conversely . . . the "commandment" of love is only possible because it is more than a requirement. Love can be "commanded" because it has first been given.[126]

The openness of the Eucharist is double-sided: it is an openness to the Other who gives himself freely to the communicant and to the others to whom the communicant is called to give of himself.[127] In this exchange of charity, one becomes what one receives and truly receives what one is. By receiving the gift of God's *caritas*, one becomes a concrete person in Christ's communion and when one gives oneself for others in response, one recognizes oneself as free to love while also demonstrably professing that others are children of the same "*Abba*, Father."[128]

Participation in the Eucharistic movement of charity embodies a commitment to the basic and ultimate meaning of the world. In memory of Christ Jesus who forges the communion of God and humanity in his person, the members of his communion press on toward their eschatological fulfillment as one communion of charity.[129] In this sacred memory is hidden all those who have died to this world and live in Christ. As the Church offers its oblation of praise, this memory becomes its own.

Within the Action

In introducing the etymological roots of the term *communio sanctorum*, I noted in chapter 1 that especially in the East the primary meaning of the term's Greek equivalent pertained to the "participation in the Eucharistic elements."[130] In the West, the meaning of this term fluctuated more over the course of the centuries, but by the time it was incorporated into the Apostles' Creed it primarily signified "fellowship with holy persons."[131] These two meanings of *communio sanctorum* are held together to this day in the expression uttered in the Byzantine liturgy, when the priest elevates the consecrated gifts and proclaims, "Holy things for the holy people!"[132] In this final turn before the final chapter and conclusion of this book, I seek to identify the meeting of these two meanings in the Roman Catholic liturgy, specifically in the Eucharistic Prayer. While we have been predominantly concerned with the communion of holy persons throughout these many pages, the full meaning of this communion departs from and returns to the Eucharistic liturgy in which the unity of the human race flows from the divine communion poured into the world.

At the heart of the Eucharistic liturgy is an image of the eschatological fulfillment of the Incarnation.[133] Because the Word took on human flesh, this human flesh is transformed as it shares in the Son's *communio* with the Father. The Church's Eucharistic Prayers testify to this belief, especially in the Roman Canon (i.e., Eucharistic Prayer I).[134] The structure and content of this prayer in which a split epiclesis surrounds the anamnesis presents the union of the blessed dead with the wayfarers who gather at the altar.

Leading into the Roman Canon's first moment of epiclesis is the hierarchical arrangement of saints in the *Communicantes*, in which "the glorious ever-Virgin Mary" leads her spouse and a company of "blessed Apostles and Martyrs" (§86). After the second moment of epiclesis that occurs on the other side of the institution narrative and consecration, anamnesis, and offering, the prayer moves to remember those "gone before us with the sign of faith" (§95). In the sacrament, the community asks to remain united with those who have died, so that together they may share in fellowship with the heavenly company in which John the Baptist leads a host of fourteen martyrs "and all your Saints" (§96, the *Nobis quoque*).[135] Through these two moments of invoking the Holy Spirit, the communion of saints is drawn into the sacred memory of Jesus Christ, arrayed like a rose in bloom.[136]

Indeed, *memory* is fundamental to this sacramental action. At the beginning of the *Communicantes*, the Church prays, "In communion with those whose *memory* we venerate" (§86). The second list of saints—in the *Nobis quoque*—follows the petition to "*remember*" the dead with the living in the company of the saints in heaven (§§95–96). Between these two movements of memory is the centerpiece of the whole action: "Do this in *memory* of me" (§90). This is the "mystery of faith" (§91) by which the Church celebrates "the *memorial* of the blessed Passion, the Resurrection from the dead, and the glorious Ascension into heaven of Christ, your Son, our Lord" (§92). The memory of Christ is the heart of the Church, and in this memory the Spirit forms his members into one body.[137] In the drama of the liturgy, the Eucharistic community is being conformed to the gift it receives.[138]

At this point, perhaps the most important question of this book comes to the fore. If the memory of Christ is the central mystery of the Church in which the *communio sanctorum* is formed, then whose memory is this? Who remembers Christ and his saints? In regards to those "whose memory we venerate" it might at first seem as if the community at prayer is the agent of memory, perhaps even in response to the memory by which those saints remember themselves and us. Likewise, when the community asks the Lord to "remember, also [those] who have gone before us," it might sound as if it is the community that first remembers the dead and then beseeches the Father to also remember them. Furthermore, when the words of Jesus himself are spoken, they come to the community with the sound of a command or at least an invitation, such that out of the community itself will come the agents who "Do this in memory of me." In each of these moments of the liturgical action, it is certainly true that the Eucharistic community engages in an act of memory, but based on what I have attempted to explicate in these pages, this act of memory is not nor could it ever be attributed first of all to the community or any members of it.

In chapters 2 and 3, I argued that death is creation's absolute zero as self-contradictory nonexistence. It is the collapse into nothing of that which was created out of nothing; this is the full meaning of death with which Christianity reckons. Toward the end of chapter 3 and more squarely in chapter 4, I then argued that the gift of life that overcomes this unmitigated catastrophe is given in history but does not come from history—this gift is the Resurrection of Jesus Christ. In him, the Word of God that entered into the solitary silence of being dead speaks a new creation in the risen One, who embodies mercy as the truth of creation and the gift of new life in the Holy Spirit. From this it follows that if we were to consider the power of memory to which the liturgy appeals as primarily belonging to those saints the Church names, then the problem of death would still haunt us. When these persons died, they died as whole persons—no powers or potentialities remained in them, for them, or to them. If we can speak now of their memory, then we must acknowledge that their memory is dependent on that which does not, first of all, come from them. Correlatively, if the power of memory is attributed primarily to the community that gathers in the liturgy, so too is this community made up of members who will, in time, die. Their impending deaths testify to the contingency of their own powers and agency; the coming of death seals the ephemeral status of creatures limited by time, space, and even sentiment, not to mention the effects of sin. The memory that any creature maintains is limited, faulty, and, in the end, bound for erasure in death.

When the Church venerates its saints, remembers the dead, and enacts the memory of Jesus Christ in the Eucharist, it only ever does so within God's own memory of history.[139] The way in which God knows history and remembers his creation is through "the blessed Passion, the Resurrection from the dead, and the glorious Ascension into heaven of Christ." In the Eucharistic liturgy, God's own memory is given to the Church so that the Church can make this sacred memory its own. This memory does not come from the Church but is given to the Church so that the Church may come to be. The Church discovers itself in this sacred memory the more it desires to know and love itself and all creation through this memory alone; the Church, as one body, at once asks and accepts that the Lord will *remember no more the sins of my youth* and instead *remember me only in light of your love* (Ps. 25:7, NAB). When receiving this memory in the sacrament, communicants taste what they ultimately desire and they (re)discover this desire as the basic truth of their own existence. Without the memory that is given, creation is bound by the nothing from which it comes and the death to which it goes. When the Church names its saints and seeks union with them through the celebration of its "mystery of faith," it engages in an efficacious action as it performs what it seeks and seeks what it is given: a *communio* of persons in the holy gift of Christ, the Father's own self-gift. In the sacrament, the eternal significance of the humanity of Christ becomes the everlasting truth of humanity itself, which was created as one body, redeemed from sin, and, in the Spirit of the risen Christ, freed to live according to the charity of God.[140] Belief in the *communio sanctorum* absolutely depends on belief in the Triune God, and, conversely, belief in the Triune God blossoms into the *communio sanctorum* as the Christian faith moves toward its consummate form, as the Apostles' Creed attests.

Gazing upon that one communion of saints assembled in two companies and united to the sacred memory of Christ by the Holy Spirit, the Church at prayer in the Roman Canon glimpses its own dignity and destiny. Pondering the mystery of life in this Church, the communicants might come to realize that the saints presented with the ever-Virgin Mary and John the Baptist do not pray for themselves since they have been glorified and thus are not in need of anything, including the forgiveness of sins.[141] Rather, they pray for the others, for those still in need, for the whole of humanity—or, in short, for the sinners partaking in the sacrament of salvation and all those for whom that blessed charity will be shared through these communicants.[142] The heavenly saints' participation in and petition for the offer of mercy in Christ is itself the proper expression of their beatific life. Their joy attains to communicating God's mercy throughout the one communal body as an unending hymn of praise. Indeed, the communion of saints is the eschatological symbol of the Word of Life spoken through the noncommunication zone of death.

Ascension, Assumption, and the Resurrection of the Body

This Eucharistic image is the revelation of the eschatological dimension of all liturgical action as the fulfillment of the truth of bodiliness. In the center of this ordered arrangement is the Incarnate Word, whose bodily resurrection is the redemption and glorification of the very flesh that underwent the passion of a sinful creation and fell into the silent finality of death. In one pithy expression, Irenaeus captures the drama of the body in regards to death and resurrection: "For what is more ignoble than dead flesh? Or, on the other hand, what is more glorious than the same when it arises and partakes of incorruption?"[143] If *the wages of sin is death* (Rom. 6:23, RSV), Irenaeus contemplates what death signifies, how it stings, and what life given in the Resurrection of Christ means. In his reflection on especially 1 Corinthians 15, Irenaeus discerns that death is wrought upon the mortal body, which loses its vital power in death and falls incommunicably into isolation. All that the flesh touched and expressed is lost in the catastrophe of death; if any significance to the activities of living appeared secure in the course of the life of that flesh, that significance is dissolved as the body decomposes in the grave. As I argued in especially chapter 3, this is the very end Christ assumes, which the silence of Holy Saturday guards. When Christ rises on the third day, he clings to that very flesh that lay ignobly in its solitariness, that which was seemingly bound for corruption. In the appearances to his disciples, this flesh now glorified is at first unrecognizable until it is suddenly apprehended as the gift of new life that has overcome the unbridgeable separation of bodies from one another due to sin. The significance that was lost is rescued, redeemed, and perfected in the glorious flesh of the risen One. This is *the victory through our Lord Jesus Christ* (1 Cor. 15:57, RSV) in which Irenaeus observes the bond of charity as the new rule of mortal bodies made spiritual through "the Spirit's instrumentality."[144]

What the Church rehearses in the Eucharistic liturgy is the living memory of this glorious gift. It is at once the efficacious memory of the one in whom this entire drama unfolded and it is the proleptic memory of the completion of that very same gift in the re-membering of bodies torn apart in sin and death. When sin infused irresolvable disorder in death the Lord of Life reordered the meaning of the body by holding to the flesh he shares with those created in his image. And lest this wholeness be construed as a merely noetic reality, the dogmatic statement of the bodily Assumption of Mary in connection with the Ascension of the Lord illumines this whole mystery of salvation as a fully and permanently somatic relationality.[145]

In the person of Mary was already what Dante glimpsed as accomplished at the top of the Mountain of Purgatory, what the Israelites journeyed toward between its two water crossings, and what every Christian seeks in participating in the life of the Church: the holy freedom "from every stain of sin" as one who "freely cooperat[es] in the work of human salvation through faith and obedience."[146] Mary is the first to participate in and embody the redeemed order of creation, in which her bodily existence in the world is only ever an instrument of blessing, wholly conducive to the grace brought forth in her Son. She is redeemed not as sinners are redeemed—"as a liberation from a stain already contracted"—but rather as being wholly preserved from the stain itself. In her, the Redeemer has warded off the wound of sin whereas for all others he heals that wound.[147] Mary allows herself to be wholly united to the perfect sacrifice of her Son, and in the glorious exchange of this union of flesh he communicates to her, first of all, the blessing of divine love.

When the Church pronounces Mary of Nazareth's glorious Assumption as a truth of the one faith, it claims that what was assumed into heaven is nothing less than the whole history of the Blessed Mother—that is, her embodied life in full.[148] In the concluding chapter of *Lumen gentium*, the Church employs a typological reading of Scripture to recall, in brief, the full portrait of the first of all redeemed creatures who, in the particular and historical contours of her own life, responds affirmatively to the address of her Son. To employ Rahner's language, she who was without even the sluggishness of concupiscence that marks the lingering separation of person and nature, freely offers the whole of her life as a return-gift to the gift of Divine Love who assumed her flesh. It is the flesh that she shares with her blessed Son that is "taken up body and soul into heavenly glory."[149] She is the mystery of human freedom on which Dante mused when he presents her in the form of the subtle gracefulness moving from mercy to praise within the complete action of charity. This movement is the expression of her whole person in perfect harmony with the human nature redeemed in her Son.

The dogma of Mary's bodily Assumption is not only a statement of belief about the holiness of Mary or even the promised destiny of humanity itself; even more, it is a declaration about the truth of the eternal significance of the humanity of Christ. In the transposition of his divine personhood into creaturely terms, the Son of God become human establishes and definitively reveals the rule of created personhood. The divine pattern for created personhood is openness to the movement of love, resisting any special claim for oneself through the perpetual affirmation of the reception of the gift of life from the gratuity of divine grace. The body—as I argued throughout chapter 3 and into chapter 4—is the instrument of this relationality; even more, the body is the symbol of this truth in and for creation. To be embodied is to be connected and to be ordered to relationship.

At one and the same time, the Son of God accepted and instituted this truth of creatureliness as patterned on the truth of divine love itself, thus freely yielding himself to dependence on human bodiliness (see Phil. 2:5–8 and John 1:1–14). Therefore, to conceive of the ascended

Christ as solitary at the *right hand of the Father* would be to fail to contemplate him as clinging to his humanity, and thus one fails to contemplate Christ at all.[150] In sharing in human bodiliness, the Son of God gave himself over—permanently and inseparably—to sharing in the bodiliness of the members of which he is head. When the Church proclaims the mystery of Mary's bodily Assumption it assents to the truth of faith and hope that the humanity of Christ is eternally united to his divinity. The perfect reception of his Blessed Mother into heaven proclaims the fruitfulness of the symphonic dialogue of Creator with creature, unhindered by sin and full of graced freedom, through the instrumentality of the one sacred Body of Christ in whom salvation is achieved.

In the Eucharistic liturgy when the memory of this one sacred body emerges at the center of the members of the human community—bonding together Mary and all the saints—the Church receives from its Lord the eternal promise of its bodily acceptance into the divine communion. The Spirit makes room for creation in divine life, just as the Spirit makes room in creatures for the indwelling of divine life. The Body of Christ becomes the site of mutual hospitality for the gift and response of Creator and creature unto life everlasting. When the Church professes faith in the *resurrection of the body*, it announces what it receives in the bodily memory of the Son: that bodiliness—with all its potential for and acceptance of relationality, with all its history of wounds and healing—is the dwelling place of divine love within the order of creation.

CHAPTER 6

WORK OF LOVE

Hastening to Wholeness

This chapter deals with training in holiness—that is, the way in which God confers his way of perceiving and acting upon his people so that they may come to share in his glory. Whereas the previous chapter focused ultimately on God's memory of creation in Jesus Christ through the power of the Holy Spirit, this chapter focuses on how that memory is communicated as the pattern of life for those being drawn into communion. Similarly, as the preceding chapter culminated in the bodily action of the Church in its Eucharistic liturgy unto the resurrection of the body, so this chapter culminates with a brief meditation on how liturgical training slowly forms the people of God in the grammar of communion, leading to a renewed emphasis on the particularities of persons bound together in charity.

We are seeking to understand the communion that the saints share with a form of inquiry that requires discipline and openness. Augustine invited his readers to a similar approach in regards to growing in the understanding of Scripture when he wrote that "the mind should be cleansed so that it is able to see [the divine light] and cling to it once it is seen. Let us consider this cleansing to be as a journey or voyage home."[1] As with the reading of Scripture as the grammar of revelation, seeing the holiness of a saint is not simply a matter of the one who is presented but also a matter of the one who perceives—not just *what* is seen but *who* sees and *how*. Likewise, the belief in the communion the saints share and make present is not only a question of presentation but also of apprehension. We thus seek to allow the saints to teach us how to see them in the light of Christ and, through and with them, to begin anew to see ourselves as a due part of God's beloved creation.[2]

That creation is beloved is another way of saying that the *caritas* of the Spirit is the logic of creation itself. The Church professes that Scripture is the continuous manifestation of that logic summed up and perfected in the Word made flesh. To see creation *as creation* is inseparable from addressing God *as God*. Christ is the keynote of this address—an address not delivered merely as a statement but as initiation into the divine logic. In order to recognize the communion of saints as the fruit of the narrative logic of the Church—the reading of the logic of creation according to the logic of God incarnate in Jesus Christ and handed over in the Holy Spirit—we must return in the end, with "cleansed minds," to the logic of Scripture. In the very words of Scripture the *Logos* himself is made present and what the Church discovers is the movement of charity. The meaning of creation and of each creature is bound up in its question to its Creator, "Who are you?"—and, as Joseph Ratzinger succinctly expresses, "God's answer is not an explanation but an action."[3]

Illuminating the divine logic of Scripture will take place in both aesthetic and pedagogic terms. I begin with an exegesis of the prologue to John's Gospel, attentive to the movement described therein. In turning to Christ as the hermeneutic of all of Scripture, the movement of the Incarnation quickens our gaze to perceiving the ascent of holiness according to the descent of mercy. Divine beauty dwells in and as this movement; by coming to move accordingly, human persons are drawn into God's glory. Among other ways, the Synoptic Gospels display this logic through Jesus's Transfiguration, which I subsequently exegete. From that vantage point, I look back upon Moses as a type of Christ who incites this movement toward glory in the people. I then connect what we see in Moses by way of anticipation of Christ to what we see in the saints who reveal Christ as the archetype of holiness and humanity. The saints do not just know this divine logic but conform themselves to it and become living witnesses of it; in fact, they witness to each other and their witness is efficacious. I attend to but one strand of the communion of saints that will stand as a representation for the whole—that strand that includes two Carmelites—Thérèse of Lisieux and Teresa of Avila—and gathers up two relatively contemporary figures: Teresa of Calcutta and Dorothy Day. In them we will gaze upon the unique beauty of holiness and the pedagogy of transformation that is oriented to the fullness of glory in the movement of mercy for the sake of building communion.

The communion of saints embodies what the Church's liturgy practices: the renewal of creation according to divine logic. In the final turn, then, I come back to the central problem with which I began this work: the Christian claim to communion running through the definitive interruption of death. I comment on the theological issue of the "intermediate state" before attending to selected prayers with and for the dead in the Church's liturgy. That momentum from the liturgy will bring us ultimately to the particularity of devotional practices in the life of the faithful. All throughout, I seek to contemplate the logic of the communion of saints as persons becoming whole in their hastening toward one another.

The Coming of the Lord

By learning to see the person of Jesus Christ we come to know the meaning of salvation history, and by studying the particularities of salvation history and its scriptural grammar, the dimensions of Christ expand. The light of the gospel reveals the Old Testament's fulfillment, and the Old Testament portrays what the gospel of Jesus Christ fulfills (cf. Luke 24:27; 1 Cor. 15:4).[4] Jesus Christ comes as gift and yet this gift is itself a summons, so that resting in Christ is the freedom to move in and with him, to accept in his gift the way of giving itself. The climactic verse of the prologue to John's Gospel is a hymn of praise to this mystery: *And the Word became flesh and dwelt among us, full of grace and truth; we have beheld his glory, glory as of the only-begotten Son from the Father* (John 1:14, RSV). The *Logos*, the Word, the pattern hidden in God comes to dwell among the people—that is, he tabernacles with us.[5] Looking back to that which prefigures Christ before looking ahead to those who are configured to Christ the archetype opens up the significance of God drawing near (John 1:14), of the prophet who comes before him following after him (John 1:6–8, 15), and of those who receive him being changed in him (John 1:12–13). This is the pattern the Lord showed to Moses on Sinai, which Moses carried down with him to the people and according to which they constructed God's dwelling place in their midst. Though Moses glimpsed this pattern, its mystery cannot be anticipated: God's move precedes understanding. And what is true for Moses in the mode of anticipation is true for the saints in the mode of fulfillment.[6]

The structure of John's prologue mirrors the disclosure of God's Name in Exodus. In Exodus 3 God hands over his Name: *I Am Who I Am* (v. 14, RSV), or, as it is alternately translated, *I Will Be What I Will Be*. The substantiality of God's Name is expressed in the reliability of God's action: God reveals himself in what he does. Thus, on the other side of the Red Sea when Israel has been delivered from Egypt, it names YHWH as such: *He is become my deliverance . . . Lord is His name* (Exod. 15:1–3, JPS). In John's prologue, the Word (*Logos*) is identified with God (1:1–3) and in due course this Word is named *Jesus Christ* (v. 17). In between these two moments of naming, the action that gives the Name its meaning is acknowledged: *And the Word became flesh* (v. 14, RSV). As with Exodus, where the meaning of YHWH is translated through his action, so here the meaning of the Word henceforth known as Jesus Christ is translated through the action of taking on flesh and dwelling. The Word who is before and above the world comes to the world and in doing so reveals who God is: he is the One who hastens toward, in mercy that perceives and acts.

This "bold and brief statement of the fact of the Incarnation"[7] does not remain locked within a Platonic paradigm, such that the Form abides above and the enlightened one who ascends reports about it to those down below. What remains hidden from the wisdom of the philosophers is that that which is hidden above is the mystery of God's bending down. What there is to contemplate above is the descending mercy of God, which is God's glory. In *coming into the world* (v. 9, RSV), the Word of God discloses that God is what God does, and his identity cannot be observed without responding to this movement—objectifying God for the purpose of conceptual mastery is ruled out.

Stuck within philosophical categories alone, Augustine "could not even begin to guess what a mystery was concealed in the Word made flesh."[8] In all he read in the Platonists, he found all the ideas about the logic that dwells above but he did not find who Jesus Christ is: the incarnate logic of God's own bending down, who comes to dwell with us.[9] He could not study this because he was not yet moving according to this movement of God. What is true of Augustine at that stage is also true of all those who know him not: without opening up to a responsive participation in God's own pattern, his identity remains hidden. But to take this pattern as the very logic of the world itself means to follow after him, learning how to descend in mercy according to God's own descent. Receiving divine mercy and moving with it are united.

By focusing on the movement of the Incarnation, each Gospel shines as testimony to who this person is according to who he has shown himself to be as coming from and going to the Father. To perceive his glory means learning to receive and respond to what he reveals in what he does. To gaze upon Jesus Christ is to gaze upon the fullness of the God who bends down and to learn to see this action as the meaning of all creation. In other words, the beauty of the Lord's glory is pedagogic since the movement that Christ reveals is the pattern into which he draws others, who must learn to move in this manner.

In this way, what John presents in his prologue parallels the other Gospels' respective presentations of Jesus's ascent of and descent from Mount Tabor. The Transfiguration demonstrates, in brief, the divine pedagogy embodied in Jesus that trains the disciples for the transformation of holiness. Moreover, what occurs in and around Jesus in this episode fulfills what was prefigured in and around Moses as he led the people out of Egypt, and then ascended and descended Mount Sinai on behalf of the divine mission to forge a covenant of freedom with the newly liberated Israel.

To help illumine Jesus's movement in light of the movement Moses prefigures, it is helpful to place the two narratives side by side using Mark's account. On the surface, there are at least six important points of connection: both Moses and Jesus ascend after six days (Exod. 24:15; Mark 9:2a); three of Moses's companions are named as are three of Jesus's disciples (Exod. 24:1, 9; Mark 9:2a); both ascend the mountain

(Exod. 24:9, 12–13; Mark 9:2b); as Moses's face shines in glory so is Jesus himself transfigured in glory (Exod. 34:29; Mark 9:2b–3); the cloud of God's presence appears (Exod. 24:15–16, 18; Mark 9:7b); and God's voice comes forth from the cloud (Exod. 24:16; Mark 9:7b).[10] Noting these parallels, Jean Daniélou argues that the Transfiguration is an episode that fulfills the Old Testament figure of the Feast of Tabernacles, which recalls the Israelites dwelling in tents in their desert pilgrimage. Daniélou further claims that this feast, which was indeed a figure of past events, also becomes a symbol of the future to which God calls Israel, when the just will dwell forever within God's protection. Thus, the eschatological hope of Israel is represented in this feast, and in the Transfiguration this hope's realization emerges.[11]

Peter's request to *make three booths* (Mark 9:5; Matt. 17:4; Luke 9:33) strengthens the connection to the Feast of Tabernacles.[12] The cloud that descends upon this mountain points back to the cloud that covered both the top of Sinai (Exod. 24:15) and Israel's tabernacle in the desert (Exod. 40:34; cf. 33:9). In each instance, the cloud delivers the presence (*shekinah*) of the Lord.[13] As if directly in response to Peter's search, the voice from the cloud directs attention to Jesus, saying, *This is my Son, my Chosen; listen to him!* (Luke 9:35–36, RSV). When the disciples look up afterward, they see only Jesus, for he is God dwelling in their midst. Peter and the other disciples are left gazing upon Jesus while their understanding lags behind the revelation—his identity still remains a mystery to them.[14] Significantly, then, the very next verse in each of the three Synoptic Gospels explicitly describes the movement of Jesus and his disciples: they come down the mountain (Mark 9:9; Matt. 17:9; Luke 9:37). Peter sought dwelling above but he ends up descending with Jesus, according to Jesus's own action.

The very next scene—suspended momentarily by the conversation about Elijah and John the Baptist in Mark (9:9–13) and Matthew (17:9–13), respectively—has Jesus returning to the "disciples" (Mark) or the "crowd" (Matthew and Luke). The first request he heeds down below is for healing by exorcism. Jesus perceives well the suffering of the young boy and heals him in haste, with precision. While there is also an important element of the particularity of mercy here to which I attend at the end of this chapter, for now it is sufficient to note that in response to a world closed in upon itself in neglect of the God who hastens and beckons, the mercy of God descends to drive out and open up, re-creating his people to the freedom of worship in constructing something beautiful. The freedom to receive and respond to the glory the Lord bestows is not possible when hearts are in thrall to other powers that become idols. This recalls Exodus 32, where the idol fills the space reserved for worship and clogs up the hearts of the people. In the narrative of Exodus, the mercy that Moses himself assumes channels the mercy of God, driving out what is false and opening up the closed hearts of the Israelites.[15] What Moses prefigures, Jesus fulfills.

Rather than interpreting the healing of the boy with a demon as a separate episode from the Transfiguration, reading across Scripture to and from Jesus Christ invites us to more fully recognize the very glory of divine presence that was displayed on the mountaintop above in the movement of mercy that occurs down below. In the deepest sense, Peter was not wrong to want to make dwellings while gazing upon the image of Jesus in glory, but what he did not yet understand was that dwelling in and with the Lord who was in their midst meant following behind his glory as he hastens in mercy to those in need. Turning back to the book of Exodus will enable us to apprehend what Jesus fulfills and what he opens up for his saints. The Lord's glory dwells in the pattern of movement that Moses and Israel anticipate, and those called into communion with God and one another in Jesus Christ are oriented to the beatific rest he gives when they praise accordingly.[16]

A Beautiful Pattern: The Aesthetic Pedagogy of the Book of Exodus

In the book of Exodus, Moses is at once a figure of Christ and a figure of the communion Christ establishes. Moses points to the whole drama of salvation, as the pedagogy of descending mercy and ascending praise configures Moses to divine desire and confers upon him a new memory that is efficacious for the people. In the role he assumes, Moses is ordered to Christ, and by the transformation Moses undergoes and incites in others, he anticipates the holiness of the saints who share in Christ's communion.[17]

God's entrance into the historical narrative inaugurates this pattern; in fact, God's entrance into the narrative *is* the pattern. The import of God's approach establishes the basis of the doctrine of mercy, which is predicated on perceiving well the suffering of another and then acting in response.[18] These are the terms with which God is introduced in 2:23–25, and, even more significantly, they are the terms by which God introduces himself in 3:7–8 (cf. Acts 7:34).[19] From the first mention of Moses's movement by his own power, he is described as taking on what will eventually be portrayed as the very movement of the Lord (Exod. 2:23–25): Moses perceives suffering and acts (2:11–12), which is the basis of his own beauty (see 2:2; Acts 7:20; Heb. 11:23).[20] Moses's configuration to this pattern will approach completion through his ascending and descending of Sinai, and ultimately when he leads Israel to construct a dwelling place for God's mercy (see Exod. 39:32–43).

In the theophany of Exodus 3, the Lord hands over the divine Name and gives himself as the One known to the patriarchs and the One who will be known as Israel's liberator from Egypt (vv. 6–10, 16–17). The memory of Israel's forefathers will unite with the deed that Israel will remember henceforth: the deliverance from slavery. Moses receives the commission to announce this divine memory of past and future things before Israel, using the speech of his brother, Aaron, before whom the Lord makes Moses like God (4:16–17).[21] Since Aaron is the one who will speak, Moses's mission in likeness of God is more than a message delivered in words—his mission is to embody the message of salvation in action. Moses hastens to the people in their suffering, to deliver them.

Even as Moses is portrayed in the likeness of God, he is also portrayed in the likeness of the people, not simply as they will be but as they are at present. When the first request is presented to Pharaoh to let Israel go into the desert to worship, and Pharaoh, rather than complying, increases the burden of labor, the people curse Moses and Aaron for intensifying their suffering (5:20–21). As he turns from the people to the Lord, Moses despairs of his commission because his own labor has not been effective (5:23). Here, Moses is the image of the fickle trust of the people, conditioned as it is by a miotic reading of the present conditions.[22] The Lord responds to the slackening trust of his prophet with the recitation of the divine memory, with which the Lord has identified himself. God bends down to Moses to hand over his Name as the Lord of his forefathers, the Lord of the covenant, the Lord who heard the cry of the people, the Lord who has come to his own, the Lord who will lead Israel out of bondage into the land he promised to them and prepares for them (6:2–8). The Lord pledges himself as the response to the grumbling and cursing of his people. Moses turns back to deliver this memory to the people.

The Lord confirms Moses in his mission when he anoints him *as God to Pharaoh* with Aaron like a prophet to Moses as Moses is prophet to God (7:1, RSV). When Moses appears repeatedly before Pharaoh, he appears on behalf of the Israelites' suffering, which God has personally observed, and he comes in person to alleviate their suffering, according to his divine commissioning. As Pharaoh's heart is hardened through the habitual neglect of the plight of the Israelites, Moses's heart is strengthened as he continues to act on the mission of relieving Israel's pain.[23] In this way, the ensuing plagues do not just constitute the continuing failure of Pharaoh to heed the Lord's command, but the plagues are also a form of an ongoing dialogue between God and Moses. As God instructs Moses, so Moses speaks to Pharaoh; God then acts in fidelity to what Moses has declared until Moses reports back to God and God relents. When Pharaoh hardens his heart again, the cycle of dialogue between God and Moses resumes. As Pharaoh spirals into deafness before the Lord, Moses exercises listening and delivering, perceiving and acting, coming and going from word to deed and back again. This is divine pedagogy working through dialogue.

The consequence of Moses's exercise in dialogue with the Lord becomes apparent when, at the critical moment of deliverance on the banks of the Red Sea, Moses responds to the complaints of the people with encouragement in trust (14:13–14). Moses, who has been immersed in the living pedagogy of God's word becoming action, is now, unlike earlier (see again 5:22–23), the one who gives the people his own trust in the Lord. Moses has come to know that the God who was—the God of Joseph, son of Israel, whose bones Moses is carrying out of Egypt (13:19)—is the God who is now working. Moses has learned to remember the Name of God: the One who perceives and acts.[24]

Even as Moses acts as intercessor between God and the people, Moses's transformation is still in process. In his ongoing role as mediator,

Moses is indeed a type of Christ, but as one whose desire continues to be shaped in God's own desire, Moses is a type for the saints coming into communion with one another in Christ. When the Israelites murmur against God, Moses not only echoes the cries of the people to God (see 16:25) but also begins to absorb the complaints himself (17:2–4). Moses does not pass blame along to the Lord as he did in Egypt (see again 5:22–23) nor does he directly respond to their doubt with encouragement (see again 14:13–14), but now he identifies the charge against God with a charge against himself, and seeks not to exonerate himself or flee from the people, but recognizes himself as implicated in the grumbling against God. He whom the Lord had made *as God* (4:16–17; 7:1) is stepping into the consequences of that designation. His own acting area is becoming the space of the covenant between God and his people.

The transformation of Moses according to the movement of the Lord is most apparent as Moses ascends Mount Sinai to meet the descending God. From that height, Moses himself will descend to the people to bring God's word. Though Moses's ascending and descending of Sinai covers the majority of the remaining chapters of Exodus, the lynchpin dynamic of the ongoing dialogue is succinctly captured in just two verses: *And the Lord came down upon Mount Sinai, to the top of the mountain; and the Lord called Moses to the top of the mountain, and Moses went up. And the Lord said to Moses, "Go down"* (19:20–21, RSV). Moses's ascent is in response to God's descent, and Moses's own descent follows God's command. To recall what we observed at the beginning of Exodus, God bends his ear to the cry of the people, coming to them to save them, and Moses is first portrayed in resemblance to this movement. This is the leitmotif of Exodus and, indeed, of salvation history: the movement of charity begins in God's mercy to redeem and save, while the sanctification of creation is learning to move in this pattern.[25]

The Law that Moses receives on the mountain and which he is to carry back to the people is itself the manifestation of God's mercy. Through the Law, the Lord who *came down upon Mount Sinai* (19:20, RSV) enters into the life, customs, and culture of his people, shaping them and setting for them a straight path to himself. The thoroughness of the details in the following chapters of Exodus—not to mention Numbers and Leviticus—is, by this reading, a rendering of the excessive care of God for the people. Mercy's perception is precise, its response particular, and in the specificity of the commands given to Moses for the people, the Lord who perceives and acts discerns the needs of his people and responds directly for their own good.

The consummation of these commands will be in the construction of the tabernacle, for which God himself will provide the pattern (25:9). This pattern is certainly in the details of the vision Moses bears according to God's instructions regarding the tabernacle's design, but to count only the details and not the source and summit of the tabernacle itself is to risk missing the meaning entirely. The tabernacle will house the ark of the covenant, the top of which will be the mercy seat. As the perpetual Sinai, this will be the meeting place for God who descends to the people to call them to ascend to him. This is the pattern of the tabernacle, which holds the covenant: the mercy of God come down to his people, calling them forth in praise to share in the movement of his mercy. In fact, the tabernacle itself cannot begin without an openness to this mercy, for it is *from every man whose heart makes him willing* that the materials for the tabernacle will come forth (25:2, RSV; cf. 35:5). The tabernacle is itself the occasion of dialogue, where heart speaks to heart (cf. Jer. 31:31–35; Heb. 8:10; 10:16).[26]

The Lord's desire for dialogue is immediately contrasted with the vanity of the people in lusting after gods of their own making (Exod. 32:1–6). The merciful descent of Moses will now, because of the offense, bring wrath rather than comfort. God's wrath can erase this people and God offers Moses the privilege of separating from the people so God may make from him alone—rather than from the people themselves—the great nation that will be God's own (32:10). The power is given to Moses to exalt himself at the expense and abandonment of the people. This temptation is of divine proportions (see, e.g., Isa. 54:8–10; Jeremiah 31; Matt. 24:26; Mark 10:38; Luke 22:42; John 18:11).

It is at this point that the transformation of Moses according to the divine pattern of mercy enters into its final stage. Rather than cut the people away from himself and from God, *Moses begged the Lord* (Exod. 32:11, RSV), not for himself, but for the people.[27] In his plea before God, he appeals to the very memory that God himself gave to him (32:13, RSV). He remembers that he is speaking to the One who brought this people *forth out of the land of Egypt with great power and with a mighty hand* (32:11, RSV). The memory of the God of Israel's forefathers is united to the memory of the deliverance from Egypt. Moses remembers when it seems that God himself has forgotten. Moses is now the bearer of this memory, and he opens this memory before the One who identifies himself with it. Moses persuades God with God's own logic. The memory proves efficacious.

When Moses does turn to go down the mountain (32:15–16), he is going to the people rather than away from them. As God swallows his vengeance, so does Moses swallow his burning anger when, in response to Aaron's plea, Moses calls Israel back into God's company through the gate of the camp (32:25–26). Having driven out what was false and drawing together those who would open their hearts to ordain themselves to the service of the Lord (32:29), Moses holds this people to himself when he returns to God to make atonement, offering himself in place of the guilty (32:32).[28]

Moses's movement with and for the Lord has shaped his character, such that the height of his prayer is now for the Lord to come down, and the soul of his prayer is his desire for mercy for the people. As Moses continually beseeches the Lord to come down and cling to this people, he is begging the Lord to do what the Lord has shown himself to do already, what the revelation of the Lord in fact is, and what the Name of the Lord has been translated to mean. The Lord is mercy to this people. Moses has been stretched to desire this mercy, to beg for it, even when it seems as if it has been justly removed, even when mercy is folly (see 1 Cor. 1:18, 23; 3:19). In being conformed to the desire of the Lord, Moses is acting according to the glory of the Lord—and that manner of acting *is* the Lord's glory. Moses cannot see this glory because it is only there in his performance, not for his viewing. It cannot be objectified: it is the holy darkness of divine love, and it overshadows him (see Exod. 33:17–23; cf. 13:21).[29]

In the radiance of God's mercy, Moses abides with the people for whom he sacrificed himself, and according to the pattern impressed upon him, he appeals anew to those with *generous hearts* to bring forth *an offering to the Lord* to construct a dwelling place for God's mercy (35:5, RSV; cf. 25:1–9, 21–22). We may therefore consider everything that occurs in the following verses of Exodus 35 through the end of Exodus 39 as done according to movements of the heart: out of *generous hearts* responding to the bending down of the Lord God, the tabernacle is constructed, in all its exquisite detail. In the end, it was *the sons of Israel* who did all the work, not according to their own reckoning and yet with their own skill, with their own materials, with their own labors *according to all that the Lord had commanded Moses* (39:32, 42, RSV). Moses sees not just what has been constructed, but also all those who built it. They are the ones who moved according to the pattern of God's mercy, offering praise from their *generous hearts* to the One who bent down to them, who remembered them, who liberated them.[30]

And Moses blessed them (39:42b, RSV). Moses grows into the dimensions of God's beauty as he is trained to move from, as, and back to God's mercy. In the end, the consummation of Moses's own beauty before God (Acts 7:20; cf. Exod. 2:2; Heb. 11:23) is his conferral of blessing upon the Israelites in their own resemblance to God's mercy.[31] Moses blesses the people with God's own blessing (see Exod. 39:42; Deut. 33:1–29).

Interlude: Glory as Dwelling, Dwelling as Communion

In terms of the movement involved in the book of Exodus, at least three things are clear. First, God makes the first move. God never loses sight of the Israelites in their bondage; he hears their cries and moves with compassion. God remembers them and is mindful of his covenant first of all. Second, Moses's training proceeds according to God's own movement. God comes down and beckons Moses upward in order to send him back down to the people. The pattern of glory that God exhibits is the template for the glory Moses inhabits and bestows. Moses becomes beautiful in the Lord's beauty. Finally, Israel inherits its identity and destiny to the extent that it begins to move in response to and as God moves, in and through Moses. Israel receives its own name in the bestowal of the divine Name: Israel is the one God has remembered and to whom he *is* deliverance and salvation (see Exodus 15; cf. 3:13–14).

This narrative of salvation signifies and makes present the beautiful pattern of God through which Moses and Israel come to share in the glory of the Lord, which always goes before them. This pattern exists first of all in God alone but, through God's mercy, takes form in and through Israel in the construction of the tabernacle (see 25:9, 40; cf. Acts 7:44). That tabernacle constructed in the desert is the symbol of the whole drama or pattern that is the key theme of Exodus: it is where God's mercy comes to dwell, where the fruits of Moses's training in holiness ripen, and where the responsive generosity of Israel becomes something beautiful. It points to the fulfillment of God's dwelling among his people in the flesh.[32]

Jesus Christ configures all creation to the pattern he makes incarnate, and he trains his disciples in the beauty of his own movement. Christ's pattern is not something available for mere conceptualization, but rather invites knowing God *as God*, of entering into creation *as creation*, and, ultimately, of coming to embody the beauty of holiness in and *as communion*. In him alone may we discern "the divine economy that governs all things."[33]

If Moses and the history of Israel prefigure Christ, then the Church and its saints "postfigure" him.[34] What is glorious and true about God and humanity in Jesus Christ measures the glory and truth of those who are fulfilled in him. Therefore, I now seek to take the pattern I have discerned in reading Scripture through the person of Jesus Christ and interpret the saints accordingly, attending especially to how the saints learn to perceive and act for others. In the fullness of time, the communion the saints construct is the eschatological tabernacle the New Moses blesses.

Thérèse of Lisieux and the Beauty of the Earth

At the end of chapter 4, I described the saint as the one who comes to embody the mercy incarnate in Jesus Christ. The saint's mode of receiving divine mercy is to become configured to what she receives: a gift that institutes a way of giving, which I traced in my scriptural exegesis. According to the pattern of love poured out in Christ, the desire for God that is both inbuilt in and impressed upon the beloved creature is, in the saint, transformed from a desire *for* God into the desire *of* God. The saint is the one who learns to love and is united with what her Beloved loves. As an example of this mysterious union, I recited the words of the dying Thérèse of Lisieux, whose final desire was to rest in the movement of heaven to earth according to the mission of the Son, who hastens to those *still a long way off* (Luke 15:20, NAB).[35] In her enigmatic words, we already passed by the "postfigured" pattern of Christ's divine mercy.

In what follows, I seek to expand my vision of Thérèse through the portal her last words provide. To the extent that we are capable of perceiving the movement of Christ, we will know what to look for in his saints. While there would be no theological error in stating that in looking closely at a saint we are looking for a "miracle," we prepare ourselves better to gaze upon the particularity and peculiarity of holiness if we are willing to attend to grace working in and through human elements rather than searching for grace without mediation. The willingness to see Thérèse in this light will permit us to see her in a way reminiscent of how the book of Exodus invites us to see Moses: as one who is trained in holiness through movements following God's own pattern of entering into the condition of his people. The transformation in holiness for Moses and then Israel that accompanied the extraordinary events of Exodus prefigures what takes place through the ordinariness of Thérèse's life and spirituality, which are keyed to the figure of Christ. And just as Moses was inseparable from the people and, in fact, served this union himself through his own willingness to sacrifice for them (Exod. 32:11–32), so Thérèse gives herself over to communion with others throughout her life and she desires to do so even in her death. In her, as with all saints, we find more than a solitary figure of holiness—much more, we find evidence of a culture of holiness: a kind of formation, the fruits of which become efficacious in forming others in the logic in which she herself was inculcated. In reading a particular saint's life according to the logic of divine love and recognizing the way in which that logic is enacted in the witness of the saint herself, we become ever more capable of imagining what sanctity is and how it is inseparable from the promise of communion. Seeing Thérèse for who she was and how she became who she is, one learns to see the dimensions of a Trinitarian faith—that is, the sign of the cross that the creed itself enshrines.[36] Holiness is its own beauty.

The life of Thérèse of Lisieux—even from her earliest years—speaks to her belief that human desire is fulfilled in divine desire. With careful attention, it even becomes apparent that the fulfillment of human desire in divine desire is the vocation at the heart of the Church. In short, the doctrine captured in the life of Thérèse of Lisieux is an ecclesiological doctrine of desire for communion.

In *Story of a Soul*, Thérèse provides much detail about her earliest years with her family, prior to entering Carmel. To the casual reader, these years may seem quaint and of minimal importance; more poignant still, her whole testimony may disappoint the one in search of greatness because all one finds are repetitions of littleness, sometimes bordering on the melodramatic.[37] To the careful reader, however, those early years enable the dynamism of her latter years, as a concert pianist's private lessons are hidden within her concert performance. Moreover, appreciating the beauty of the whole performance requires training in a taste for holiness.[38] The seemingly obsessive regard for all the little things in early life—in which Thérèse deems just about every minute detail meaningful and necessary—testifies to both the capacity for and the education in a keenness of perception that will free her to later follow the Way of the Cross so closely. About those early years Thérèse herself confessed, "God was instructing me in secret."[39]

In his address naming Thérèse a Doctor of the Universal Church, John Paul II identified her "eminent doctrine" as the simple truth of her life, which is perhaps the most basic truth of the gospel: "God is our Father and we are his children."[40] She was trained in this truth from a young age and her holiness grew from this primary conviction. As a consequence of this trust, she believes that what is promised to her—that which is given to her as her own desire—will be fulfilled, for what father, if his child asks for bread, will give a stone instead? (Matt. 7:9–11; cf. Luke 11:9–13; Mark 11:24; John 15:7; 16:23–24; 1 John 5:14). She learns this trust and allows it to shape her desire all throughout her early life, so that her own desire is slowly conformed to what God desires to give her (see James 4:3). Her lifelong spiritual disposition is aptly captured when she reflects on the trip to Rome in the last year before she entered Carmel: "I was acting toward Him like a child who believes everything is permitted and looks upon the treasures of its Father as its own."[41]

In the first relationships of Thérèse's young life, her whole life's drama abides *in nuce*: her own father's love is the symbol of God the

Father's love and affection for her. Her sisters are the living symbol of the communion of the Church that will structure her spirituality. In the suffering she experiences in the illness and death of her mother, she brushes against the suffering that will ultimately draw her from confidence to courage as she follows Christ's suffering on the cross to give herself as a sacrifice of love to others.[42] Even in a childhood filled with compassion and companionship, there is a real darkness that refines and ripens her conviction of belovedness and leads her deeper into the mystery of that love which embraces her. She begins, in other words, abiding in the belief in *God, the Father Almighty,* as her loving Father and sets out to love not just the fact that she is loved but indeed the very way in which she is loved in *Jesus Christ, the Father's only Son.* By the *Holy Spirit* she is transformed according to what she learns to love and desire.

This love and desire was first shaped in Thérèse's family, which was devoted to "a way of becoming *holy* through fidelity in little things."[43] As the daughter of two skilled artisans, she grew up in a household that attended to intricate details and worked delicately in daily life. Her father, whom she loved with a special affection, was especially instrumental in schooling her in Christian discipleship, most of all through the way his own habits and dispositions influenced hers. Perhaps no episode is more telling of the importance of this hidden formation than the one she recounts from shortly after the death of her mother:

> During the walks I took with Papa, he loved to have me bring alms to the poor we met on the way. On one occasion we met a poor man who was dragging himself along painfully on crutches. I went up to give him a coin. He looked at me with a sad smile and refused my offering since he felt he wasn't poor enough to accept alms. I cannot express the feeling that went through my heart. I wanted to console this man and instead I had given him pain or so I thought. The poor invalid undoubtedly guessed at what was passing through my mind, for I saw him turn around and smile at me. Papa had just bought me a little cake, and I had an intense desire to give it to him, but I didn't dare. However, I really wanted to give him something he couldn't refuse, so great was the sympathy I felt toward him. I remembered having heard that on our First Communion Day we can obtain whatever we ask for, and this thought greatly consoled me. Although I was

only six years old at this time, I said: "I'll pray for this poor man the day of my First Communion." I kept my promise five years later, and I hope God answered the prayer He inspired me to direct to Him in favor of one of His suffering members.[44]

This small event that is hardly even worth mentioning in the grand scheme of world history appears significant for the one who discerns Thérèse according to Christ the archetype. She tells us that her father habitually formed her in a view of the world when he made almsgiving a part of their regular routine. Formed to see and act in a certain way, she sets out to offer her alms, but in this case she meets unanticipated resistance. Confounded and distressed, she is left to discern more deeply how to respond in this particular situation, for this particular man, whose particular suffering turns out to be beyond her ability to grasp. In the end, the young Thérèse innovates in the pattern of her father's almsgiving and in response to both the man's suffering and his gesture of consolation. She pledges to offer him the gift she will receive years later in her First Communion. In this interaction she practices the very movement that will grow into the pattern that will define her life.

Thérèse stretches according to this pattern as she contemplates the cross of Christ and its implications for her life. Upon recalling the "*night of light*" that she recognizes as the beginning of a new period of her life, she remembers Jesus coming to her "mercifully" and instilling within her "a great desire to work for the conversion of sinners." She describes this as "*charity* enter[ing] into my soul," and then immediately connects this memory with another:

> One Sunday, looking at a picture of Our Lord on the Cross, I was struck by the blood flowing from one of the divine hands. I felt a great pang of sorrow when thinking this blood was falling to the ground without anyone's hastening to gather it up. I was resolved to remain in spirit at the foot of the Cross and to receive the divine dew. I understood I was then to pour it out upon souls. The cry of Jesus on the Cross sounded continually in my heart: "*I thirst!*" These words ignited within me an unknown and very living fire. I wanted to give my Beloved to drink and I felt myself consumed with a *thirst for souls*. As yet, it was not the souls of priests that

attracted me, but those of *great sinners*; I *burned* with the desire to snatch them from the eternal flames.[45]

Thérèse's characteristic intensity of piety and drama may strike modern ears as bluster. Balthasar argues that the more "sober-minded" and "rational" who would dismiss moments such as this as merely the pious ravings of an eccentric religious, may in fact be guilty of presuming to "know too much" and have thus become incapable of reading the saint as an icon.[46] But an icon is precisely what Thérèse is presenting here: she is writing herself according to the image of the cross upon which she gazes. She sees in this cross more than a relic of deeds accomplished—she sees the merciful desire to rescue others from suffering and torment. In "snatching" them, she will fulfill Christ's own desire.

In the following paragraph Thérèse tells of what she considers God's confirmation of and response to her desire to share in Christ's desire to save. She recalls the convicted murderer Henri Pranzini, for whom "everything pointed to the fact that he would die impenitent."[47] Perceiving this man's plight according to the criterion of cruciform desire, she brings forth all she has to offer for his benefit. As she confesses, there was nothing that was properly hers that would bear any power for him, and so she offers that of which she herself was a recipient and in which she was a participant: "the infinite merits of Our Lord, the treasures of the Church, and finally . . . a Mass offered for my intentions."[48] When it is reported to her that prior to his execution Pranzini "*kissed* the *sacred wounds [of a crucifix] three times!*" she interprets this according to the parable of the lost sheep, in which the shepherd leaves the flock to hasten to rescue the one gone astray (Luke 15:3–7). Consistent with the doctrine John Paul II discerned in her, she comes to bless Pranzini as one of God's beloved children, going so far as to call him "my *first child*."[49]

In these two incidents, Thérèse provides a consistent witness. Before both the poor man and the condemned man, Thérèse welcomes and seeks to act upon a deep desire for communion. In both cases, however, she confronts the limits of her own power: she cannot produce communion with the poor man even when she practices the almsgiving she was taught, just as she cannot make the condemned man penitent. At the crossroads of her limited power and her boundless desire, Thérèse offers herself as oblation to the power of Christ entrusted to the Church. She allows herself to become the space within which the communion of God and neighbor is efficacious in the Spirit. As she practices her desire for communion for these two men, we are given a glimpse of what will, in the end, be her sole and ultimate desire: to unite herself to the everlasting mercy of Christ, who is himself the communion stretched through the powerlessness of death.

Already resembling the movement of the Lord in her perceptivity before suffering and her willful actions to respond, Thérèse approached the fulfillment of her desire when she set out to "climb Mount Carmel" on April 9, 1888.[50] Coming to dwell in Carmel was, for Thérèse, the visible sign of her spiritual journey to give her whole life, without remainder, to the service of her Beloved. Within the cloister walls, she intended to dwell ever more deeply in the love of Christ.[51] In line with what we pondered earlier in regards to dwelling with the divine leading to a certain way of moving, Thérèse testifies that, "upon entering Carmel," the Lord set about teaching her

> that science hidden from the wise and prudent and revealed to *little ones* (Mt 11:25). The little flower transplanted to Mount Carmel was to expand under the shadow of the cross. The tears and blood of Jesus were to be her dew; and her Sun was His adorable Face veiled with tears. Until my coming to Carmel, I had never fathomed the depths of the treasures hidden in the Holy Face. . . . You called me and I understood. I understood what *real glory* was. He whose Kingdom is not of this world (Jn 18:36) showed me that true wisdom consists in "desiring to be unknown and counted as nothing," in "placing one's joy in the contempt of self." Ah! I desired that, like the Face of Jesus, "my face be truly hidden, that no one on earth would know me" (Is 53:3).[52]

Both Balthasar and Dorothy Day draw attention to Thérèse's identification of Isaiah 53 as the heart of her spirituality in devotion to the Holy Face of Jesus.[53] He in whose teaching she comes to rest instructs her in the mystery of "*real glory*," which bends down low, seeking not to exalt in oneself but to forget oneself for the sake of those below (see Phil. 2:6–11). As Thérèse ascends in holiness upon Carmel, she enters more deeply into the glory of downward-moving mercy.

It is easy and perhaps fashionable to ascribe this dynamic of holiness to Thérèse as the exception rather than the Christian rule. The position I have been developing in this chapter runs counter to such an opinion. While it is indisputably true that this pattern of holiness is clearer and more pronounced in Thérèse than it is in the multitudes, what is revealed in her is the logic of Christ: the divine logic in whom creation comes to be and through whom redemption and sanctification are accomplished. Even for Carmel, Thérèse is exceptional only to the extent of the vividness of her witness.[54] This is not to discount the saint; rather, it is to exalt her as a gift for the Church.

Teresa of Avila and the Beauty of Carmel

The culture of Carmel was founded upon and ordered to the very movement to which Thérèse gave witness. Carmel is a culture initiated in the prophet Elijah, the de facto founder of the order, who in fleeing from Mount Carmel to Mount Horeb was met by the divine presence descending upon him. What was given to Elijah as he dwelt in the presence of the Lord was the command to *Go, return on your way* (1 Kings 19:15, RSV). To rest in the Lord was to begin to move in his mission.

This basic rule became the structural logic for Carmel itself when its second founder, Teresa of Avila, reformed the order for the spiritual practice of contemplating the mystery of divine love. It is Teresa's spiritual doctrine that allows us to see Thérèse's own dwelling in glory as the fruit of the Carmelite culture in which the Little Flower grew. Though the immediate intended audience for her masterpiece was composed of her sisters and daughters in Carmel, that to which Teresa testified in *The Interior Castle* is not simply the property of Carmelites because the realms of intimacy she describes therein are of universal application since they concern the contemplation of God's presence.

As one of her early biographers reports, Teresa saw the whole of the work she would create in one flash of insight.[55] Like Moses glimpsing the heavenly tabernacle on Sinai, Teresa saw at once that which was to be the pattern for the contemplative life—that is, the life oriented to dwelling in the presence of the Lord. It is according to the pattern of heavenly dwellings that she conceives of the soul before God: "we consider our soul to be like a castle made entirely out of a diamond or of very clear crystal, in which there are many rooms, just as in heaven there are many dwelling places" (see John 14:2).[56]

This theme of "dwelling-with" that Teresa introduces in the beginning and continues throughout, reaches its climax in her meditation on the seventh and final dwelling place, where contemplation becomes undivided spiritual union. Teresa explains that "just as in heaven so in the soul His Majesty must have a room where He dwells alone. Let us call it another heaven."[57] The Lord gives a dwelling to the soul in the deepest dwelling place of the soul itself, recalling, by other means, that mystery of mutual indwelling in the Empyrean about which Dante mused. What this meeting concerns is not simply the soul that ascends to the logic above, but rather the logic above as coming to dwell in the soul itself. It is the descent in mercy of the Lord God that one encounters at the peak of contemplation. "For in lowering Himself to commune with such miserable creatures," Teresa writes at the end of the sixth dwelling, "He wants to show us His greatness."[58] To consider the distance traveled is to begin to grasp the immensity of the gift—as Simone Weil puts it, "We cannot take a step toward the heavens. God crosses the universe and comes to us."[59] The only secret that is ever revealed is the secret of the Word of God hastening to take on human flesh (John 1:14). The end of contemplation is the Incarnate Word, Jesus Christ: he is the height of unity of God and creature, the one in whom true freedom begins.

The effect of contemplating this gift is, first, to forsake all else so as to desire this gift most of all and, second, to accept all suffering that comes for the sake of clinging to Jesus Christ's presence. Dwelling with him means stretching toward the dimensions of his person. Glory, then, "lies in being able some way to help the Crucified."[60] This growth in desire according to the measure of the desire of the Crucified is, in the end, the absolute guard against any form of spiritual elitism. To rest in Christ and be filled with him is to receive the One who *did not count equality with God a thing to be grasped, but emptied himself* (Phil. 2:6–7, NAB). To dwell in him who dwells in the deepest dwelling of oneself is to set out in his mission to reach those estranged from the dwelling he provides. There is nothing abstract, nothing mystical, about this: it means, as Sarah Coakley describes it, being "thrust back into the repetitive hurly-burly of the kitchen or the marketplace,"[61] or, as Teresa puts it, to begin not with "desiring to benefit the whole world but [concentrating] on those who are in your company."[62] The point, Teresa instructs, is to move with Christ whose glory is coming to dwell in our flesh, to redeem and sanctify. For the saint, dwelling is moving is loving.[63]

The desire for the desire of the Lord gives way to what, in retrospect, is the germ of Thérèse's Little Way. "In sum," Teresa writes,

> What I conclude with is that we shouldn't build castles in the air. The Lord doesn't look so much at the greatness of our works as at the love with which they are done. And if we do what we can, His Majesty will enable us each day to do more and more, provided that we do not quickly tire. But during the little while this life lasts—and perhaps it will last a shorter time than each one thinks—let us offer the Lord interiorly and exteriorly the sacrifice we can. His Majesty will join it with that which He offered on the cross to the Father for us. Thus even though our works are small they will have the value our love for Him would have merited had they been great.[64]

In her encouragement for the living of the day-to-day, Teresa translates the wisdom that is her final rest.

Knowing Teresa from the heart of her prayer is also a way of coming to know Thérèse more deeply. The holiness of Thérèse was not merely due to the infusion of unmediated grace, like a miracle that wholly disregards the created capacities of human life; rather, in looking back upon Teresa and considering Thérèse's growth within her own family, Thérèse appears as one who trained in holiness within particular cultures ordained to a common end. From the Martin household to Carmel, Thérèse passed from one microculture of the Church to another in which God's hastening to her in love was to be translated into her own hastening to others in Christ. With great theological erudition and spiritual sophistication, Teresa elucidated the basic pattern that enlivened the routine education in which Louis and Zélie immersed their children: perceive all things in the light of the Incarnate Word and act in him to forge communion where communion is incomplete. For Thérèse, this immersive education meant seeing and acting for the poor man, seeing and acting for the condemned man, seeing and acting for her sisters in Carmel, seeing and acting in prayer for priests and missionaries, and—as the logical narrative conclusion of divine logic dwelling in human flesh—desiring to see, hasten to, and draw into communion all those in exile from the dwelling of God-with-us. The enigmatic desire to "spend my heaven doing good on earth" and to move with Christ until all are at rest becomes the fulfillment of one who is trained in the movements of communion. Thérèse's dying words testify to desire refined through the practices of communion that marked her life. The saint emerges from this training as the one who is consummately free to cling to this earth with the heavenly mission to love unto the end.

To see a saint as a saint means learning to identify her according to the efficacious desire of Christ, her Beloved. Through their common though personalized witness of ascending in praise to the Lord descending in mercy, Teresa and Thérèse passed over into the beauty of divine glory. Hastening to others for their own good is, paradoxically, the way in which the saint herself is adorned with the glory of the Lord, like a "beautiful dress enriched with priceless stones."[65] To give oneself as the space of creation in which the bond of communion is forged is to allow the world to be configured to that heavenly pattern and to make something beautiful for God.

What makes the saints holy is what makes them into bonds of communion, and vice versa. For the saints to serve as points of light that help illuminate the deepest meaning of creation, one must allow oneself to pass over from analyzing them to apprehending them, with the difference of the latter being that the one who perceives begins to move as the saints move. The saints present themselves as mirrors before those who gaze upon them, allowing those whom they encounter in word, deed, or witness to rediscover themselves as created, redeemed, and called to sanctification according to the pattern the saints themselves have embodied. As examples of this transformation in holiness that passes from the communication of the saint to the one who learns to perceive and act accordingly, we now turn to two contemporary figures who themselves learned to move by the movements that Thérèse learned in the Martin household and in Teresa's Carmel, in the pattern of the Word made flesh. These descendants are Teresa of Calcutta and Dorothy Day.

Mother Teresa and the Beauty of Calcutta

The beauty of the saints is the freedom of their *generous hearts*. Despite concerns about exalting the saints at the expense of others, the true exaltation of the saints is in seeing their desire to expend themselves for the good of others. This, of course, is the pattern given from the Sacred Heart of Jesus, from whom comes the paradox that *whoever seeks to gain his life will lose it, but whoever loses his life will preserve it* (Luke 17:33; cf. 9:24; Matt. 10:39; 16:25; Mark 8:35; John 12:25). To remove themselves from the human community would be antithetical to the logic of Christ that the saint has taken as her own. The saint who is transformed in Christ hastens to give this freedom to those still behind. Learning to give is the path of holiness itself and, as Teresa of Calcutta testifies, receiving the gift of Christ communicated through the saints always already entails participating in giving this gift to and for others.

As confounding as Thérèse's dying words may be, the private confessions of Teresa of Calcutta are perhaps even more jarring. In a 1962 letter to her spiritual director, Mother Teresa disclosed that "The physical situation of my poor left in the streets unwanted, unloved, unclaimed— are the true picture of my own spiritual life, of my love for Jesus, and yet this terrible pain has never made me desire to have it different.—What's more, I want it to be like this for as long as He wants it."[66] After more than a dozen years of hastening with the light of Christ to the "dark holes of the poor"[67] as a Missionary of Charity, following decades of serving the Indian poor in other ways as a Sister of Loretto, Teresa had identified herself so much with her mission that the condition of those to whom she brought communion through feeding, healing, and accompaniment became her very own spiritual condition. Her interior life was a map of the streets of Calcutta, with every path leading to one of its many slums.[68]

In this darkness is her beauty, but it is a beauty one must learn to see according to its own measure. This is where her devotion to Thérèse is illuminating. Like her patroness, Teresa not only sought to give herself over in haste to the needs of those suffering and in need—no matter how small those needs might be at any given time—but she was also assenting to this movement, by her words and deeds, as the very desire of Christ taking hold of her. In the manner of Thérèse, who gazed upon the

Crucified and contemplated his desire for communion with those separated from him, Mother Teresa instructed her own sisters as follows:

> "I thirst," Jesus said on the Cross when Jesus was deprived of every conso-
> lation, dying in absolute poverty, left alone, despised and broken in body
> and soul. He spoke of His thirst—not for water, but for love, for sacri-
> fice. Jesus is God: therefore, His love, His thirst is infinite. Our aim is to
> quench this infinite thirst of a God made man. Just like the adoring angels
> in Heaven ceaselessly sing the praises of God, so the Sisters, using the four
> vows of Absolute Poverty, Chastity, Obedience and Charity towards the
> poor ceaselessly quench the thirsting God by their love and of the love of
> the souls they bring to Him.[69]

The culture of the Missionaries reproduced the culture of Carmel but in
a distinctive place and through distinctive means. The pattern of glory of
Jesus Christ—who is divine mercy bent down low even under the darkness of death, who is communicated through the community of his disciples unto Teresa of Avila and Thérèse and Teresa of Calcutta—appeals
to *generous hearts* for a beautiful offering to construct a dwelling for communion. If Teresa of Calcutta and her Missionaries are exceptional, it is
because they do not cling to exceptionality but practice moving with and
in Christ, who is God's own perception of suffering and action as mercy.

Teresa of Calcutta's testimony to the fulfillment of her own desire is
strikingly similar to the desire expressed in Thérèse's dying words. Teresa
writes, "If I ever become a saint—I will surely be one of 'darkness.' I will
continually be absent from heaven—to light the light of those in darkness on earth."[70] The pattern she seeks to follow all the way to the end is
not one in which something is reserved for oneself, in an urge for self-
protection, but one which, beyond all manner of reckoning, opens up to
a participation in the divine glory of giving space for communion with
others.[71]

To look back upon Mother Teresa, one is often tempted to see her removed, set apart, with a holiness unreachable and inimitable. It is like seeing the face of Moses aglow in the glory of the Lord and considering one's
own face as a shadow by comparison. What is missing in such a glance of
envy or excuse is the recognition of precisely what allows for the glorious

resemblance such a figure bears. Without doubting that sharing in this glory is a gift of the Lord, it is still true that the beauty of Teresa emerges out of her merciful hastening to the poorest of the poor just as Moses's radiance grew through his habit of ascending to God and descending in mission to the people. Each of them took a first step and many others to follow. What is common is that the steps were in response to a gift and the way of receiving that gift was learning to sacrifice oneself for others.[72] In the end, Teresa is more integrated and consistent than she is exceptional (at least if exceptional is supposed to mean detached from the ordinary). The logic to which she clung became the logic of her life and witness. And just as Moses refused to be set apart and learned instead to offer himself for the people, so too Teresa of Calcutta—as with Thérèse and Teresa of Avila before her—contemplated the pattern of Christ well enough to recognize that the dwelling he gives is the gift of joining in his mission. This sharing in Christ makes one holy, and therefore fully human.

Dorothy Day and the Beauty of New York

That this participation in the life and the movement of Christ and his saints is at once a school for holiness and a school for humanity was the central conviction of another one of Thérèse's spiritual children: Dorothy Day, a prolific writer among many other things. One of the most well-known lines she ever penned appears in the epilogue of her autobiography: "We have all known the long loneliness and we have learned that the only solution is love and that love comes with community."[73] What is less apparent at first and certainly less well-known is the subtlety and depth of her own contemplation of the person of Christ, for which she is in large part indebted to that nineteenth-century French Carmelite with whom she shared very little otherwise. In her company, Dorothy studied the meaning of Christ in communion.

Dorothy Day was born about a month after Thérèse of Lisieux died, in 1897. Needless to say, Dorothy never knew Thérèse, at least not until she lay in the maternity wing of Bellevue hospital, holding her newborn daughter, Tamar Teresa. Not yet Catholic, Dorothy could still find the appeal of a great figure who did great things, like the great reformer,

Teresa of Avila, after whom she named her own child. What she was not prepared to take seriously was a quaint "young nun with a sweet insipid face,"[74] who seemed to obsess over minutiae that paled in comparison to the major conflicts of the day. And yet the woman in the bed next to Dorothy mistook Tamar's middle name for the name of the Little Flower and thus gave Dorothy the medal of the saint she had in her pocket, instructing her to pin it on the newborn child's gown. After initially protesting, Dorothy accepted the gift of this new saint—not because she was fond of the saint but because her love for her own child demanded a gesture of largesse. Dorothy decided that she would give her child not one but two saints: from the older saint she would give a name and from the younger one she would give a "novice mistress, to train her in the spiritual life."[75] Thus began Dorothy's own relationship with Thérèse of Lisieux, whose holiness required Dorothy to grow in order to cherish it.

To read the spiritual biography of Thérèse that Dorothy authored is to receive Dorothy's own witness to the gift she found in this little saint previously unknown to her. In Thérèse, she came to recognize the universal human desire to grow in love and the response to the universal human problem of not knowing how to do it.[76] Dorothy studied Thérèse—not just according to biography or reputation, but according to the nuances of her spirituality in practice, which forced Dorothy to suspend her biases in order to grow in understanding. What slowly captured Dorothy's imagination was the littleness and attentiveness that led Thérèse to wholeness in love—this is what Dorothy discovered she wanted for herself, not to mention for her child. She who at first wanted to find the answer to her longings in the great upheavals of history and the overturning of intractable power structures was forced, in gazing upon Thérèse, to meditate on the mundane.

Dorothy paid close attention to that first culture in which the Little Flower grew: the Martin household. She discovered two parents who, as skilled artisans, exercised exquisite skill in crafting their familial life. Through their guidance, the obscure and routine work of domesticity, which remains hidden from the world but for the one who looks closely for it, was patterned on the intricacies of abiding together in love and remaining open to others. Even the care they took to live modestly and save their earnings was, when examined well, done in the interest of, as Dorothy put it, creating the "kind of home where it would be easier to be good."[77] In other words, Thérèse's parents invested in the economy of the household as the place where love was to be practiced, where mutual concern was to be the rule, and where the praise of God was expressed in multiform ways. It is telling, then, that Dorothy found in the Martin household the basic insight that she grew to love in Peter Maurin's vision for the Catholic Worker movement, "to make that kind of society where it is easier to be good."[78] Dorothy's close attention to the smallness of Thérèse—to the intricacies and minutiae of the culture that first formed her—revealed to Dorothy an aspect of that great good to which she would seek to orient her life.

In the account of the death of Thérèse's mother Zélie, Dorothy again closely observes the way in which a culture fosters communion and communicates it. In this case, she witnessed it in the definitive interruption to communication between persons that the death of a loved one brings. In a family where liturgical feasts marked time, it was not insignificant that the family hosted a party on August 24 for the feast of Saint Louis, which they celebrated to honor their own father who bore the same name. Even as their mother lay on her deathbed about to receive last rites, the family opens itself to the company of the saints. When Zélie is anointed, the priest prays through the intercession of "Mary, St. Joseph, all the angels, archangels, patriarchs, prophets, apostles, martyrs, confessors, virgins, and all the other saints."[79] When she is sent forth from the world, Zélie is bade a happy journey in the name of these same angels and martyrs and saints, "through Christ our Lord, Amen."[80] Dorothy then lists Thérèse and her sisters as participants in the requiem Mass, united to this great company just invoked. When it is said elsewhere that Thérèse's early life was a "festival of communion,"[81] this exemplifies what is meant. The good home her parents created was one in which communion was practiced, even at the hour of death.[82]

Likewise, when Thérèse offers her First Communion for the poor man, Dorothy takes notes. She discerns in this the fruits of what Louis and Zélie taught their children: "that it is a privilege to serve the unfortunate with our own hands and do the works of mercy directly."[83] When Dorothy—the revered practitioner of the Corporal Works of Mercy—then

exalts the Spiritual Works as "spiritual weapons to save souls, penance for
luxury when the destitute suffer, a work to increase the sum total of love
and peace in the world,"[84] she testifies to her own education in learning to
desire that depth of love in which what one does for the perceived needs
of the neediest is united with how one gives oneself as a participant in the
sacrificial offering of Christ for the life of the world. Her works of mercy
became more than altruistic gestures, more even than efforts on behalf of
justice—indeed, in continuity with Thérèse, Dorothy was formed to see
all the Works of Mercy as practices in the presence of God, whereby one's
own vision of the world is transformed.[85]

In attending closely to Thérèse, Dorothy was learning how to cherish the small things, to see their incalculable significance and dignity and
worth. "There is never too small an incident for Thérèse to mention in
her memories," Dorothy writes, "knowing that we can all of us match
them, but not, perhaps, draw the same lesson."[86] By this education in
following the way of love, Dorothy's own interior life was transformed,
slowly becoming a map of the streets of New York, with every path leading to the place of the poor.

Along with the inspiration of Peter Maurin and the witness of
Thérèse of Lisieux, it was ultimately in obedience to Christ that Dorothy
sought to draw near and salve the wounds of those suffering from poverty
and injustice.

> Christ lived among men. That great mystery of the Incarnation, which
> meant that God became man that man might become God, was a joy
> that made us want to kiss the earth in worship, because His feet trod that
> same earth. . . . His teaching transcended all the wisdom of the scribes and
> Pharisees, and taught us the most effective means of living in this world
> while preparing for the next. And He directed His sublime words to the
> poorest of the poor, to the people who thronged the towns and followed
> after John the Baptist, who hung around, sick and poverty-stricken at the
> doors of rich men. He had set us an example and the poor and destitute
> were the ones we wished to reach.[87]

In response to Christ who had drawn near to dwell with and among
those he loved, Dorothy sought to draw near to dwell with and among

those she learned to love in him. "One must live with them," she writes, "share with them their suffering, too. Give up one's privacy, and mental and spiritual comforts as well as physical."[88] This decisive movement of coming to share in the condition of those who suffer—with the hope of bringing relief in whatever form possible—was all a way of living "as though we believed indeed that we are all members one of another, knowing that when 'the health of one member suffers, the health of the whole body is lowered.'"[89]

As Dorothy learned from Thérèse, who contemplated the presence of the Lord both at home and in Carmel, learning to dwell in the movement of mercy requires practice. One is trained to perceive and act upon the urgent necessity of establishing communion where communion is broken. "Sometimes it takes but one step," Dorothy acknowledges, before confessing that this first step leads to many others that "are very small affairs," and which together shape one into a way of being. This education, which she associates with learning to bear the ugliness of two lepers she once kissed, capacitates one to become more graceful in embracing what at first repels, taking the good of another for one's own good "and especially to subordinate our own impulses and wishes to others."[90] These things are hard, they do take practice, and they stretch one toward the reaches of Christ, who goes beyond the limits of abandonment. In Dorothy's case, it meant learning to perceive well the particular sufferings of those in whose midst she placed herself, with the sort of attentiveness that does not overlook the bills and receipts that tumble onto a kitchen table, symbolizing the burdens of an impoverished mother named Felicia for whom there is little to do but wait together for spring to warm her apartment and her children.[91] Communion with Felicia and with her children is the divine pattern remapping the streets of New York.

The legend of Lawrence, the third-century Roman deacon, is apropos here. Lawrence was responsible for the Church's treasury in Rome, principally in terms of distributing alms to the poor. Ordered to gather up all of the treasures of the Church throughout the city and hand them over for the emperor's use, Lawrence asked for a reprieve of three days to accomplish the task. On the third day he returned as ordered but with the poor and sickly of the city and announced, "Here are the treasures of the Church!"[92]

Whether or not the legend is entirely factual has very little to do with its truth. In the witness of Thérèse, Teresa of Avila, Teresa of Calcutta, and Dorothy Day, a common truth emerges: to contemplate (or dwell-with) Jesus Christ is to move with his salvific desire to forge bonds of communion. In Christ, this bond is his very body, raised again on the third day. Those who enter into his communion make his body present in the bonds they create through hastening to others in the manner in which he hastens to them. To dwell in the glory of the Lord is to follow him in like manner and thereby come to resemble that which is praised.

To return again to Exodus, the wealth that the Israelites handed over to Moses for the construction of the tabernacle was the very wealth they had taken from the Egyptians (3:21–22; 11:2–3; 12:35–36; Ps. 105:37; cf. 32:2–4; 35:4–29). In Thérèse, who gave her prayer and desire for the poor man and the condemned man as an offering of communion; in Teresa of Avila, who returns to the everyday from the heights of mystical union; in Teresa of Calcutta, who became the light for those in the "dark holes"; and for Dorothy Day, who went to dwell in the midst of poverty because Christ comes to dwell in ours—opening up and refusing to hoard the gift received is itself the expression of the glory of the Lord. Saints give themselves as the space for God's movement of mercy in the world. In and through them, the bonds of communion are established. They hold others together in themselves and teach those others how to give themselves as space for communion in turn. In the interlocking charity of the blessed, the whole edifice of God's everlasting dwelling among men is constructed. We call this the Body of Christ.

The jewels of the saints are the poor to whom they hasten. The challenge to those in every age is in *not resisting* being recognized as one of the poor of Christ, to whom the love of God hastens. The sin of the rich man who did not feed Lazarus was not simply his failure to feed, it was his failure to become empty and feed on what the Lord gives, which is at once a way of giving (Luke 16:19–31).[93] Through the Spiritual Works that announce good news in desolate places and the Corporal Works that heal illness and injury, those who move with the descent of divine mercy construct a dwelling in the pattern of Jesus Christ (see Matt. 4:23–25; 9:35; Mark 1:39; Luke 6:17–18).

The Intermediate State and the Beauty of Wholeness

The position I have developed in this chapter presents, by extension, a theological opinion about the disputed question of an "intermediate state."[94] In chapter 5 I commented briefly on Benedict XII's bull, *Benedictus Deus*, which declares that the souls of the blessed dead already share in the beatific vision in advance of the general resurrection of the body. Following the work of chapter 4, I proposed that the "sweet unrest" of the saints is their dwelling wholly within the mission of the Son, on whose behalf the Spirit works until the end of time to draw the Mystical Body to completion. What I said in part then I have said in full throughout this chapter: that dwelling in the Lord is—according to the logic of Scripture culminating in and flowing from the person of Christ—coming to move as the Lord moves in the descent of mercy. As a dimension of divine charity, God's mercy is his perception of suffering and action in response. Those who enjoy the beatific vision even now share in this glory, which means they live in the movement of mercy that seeks to forge and complete the eschatological communion of all the saints. The intermediate state observes the social nature of salvation, guarding the truth that none of the blessed ceases desiring the healing of the whole body until all are joined together in communion.

Joseph Ratzinger most clearly articulates the importance of the issues involved in considering the intermediate state: "History would be deprived of its seriousness if resurrection occurred at the moment of death."[95] What he is defending bears upon the meaning of the whole Christ. To sever the blessed dead from the ongoing drama of history would be to declare that, ultimately, history is at best tangential to their beatitude. The entire force of the Christian witness counters this, however, since God's definitive action upon history is in the Word who became flesh and, having suffered, died, and entered into the state of being dead, was raised again on the third day clinging to that same flesh, now glorified, with which he ascended to the right hand of the Father. Upon that very flesh are the wounds of history, now transfigured in glory. The three days in the tomb are a period of waiting, when, according to what I attempted to explicate in chapter 3, Christ himself seeks out the lost by falling into solidarity with their silence in death. The harrowing of hell is thus a symbol of the intermediate state, for the answer to death is not private salvation but communion. This is the answer—the action—in which the blessed dead participate: Christ bears the wounds of love and Christ loves the wounds he bears.

That there is a period of waiting for the fullness of joy squares with the consistent biblical witness to the salvation of a people, not merely of individuals. Rather than those still on pilgrimage or those not yet converted to communion holding the rest of the body hostage—including and beginning with Christ, the head—the joy in which the saints already participate is the desire for the others to be fulfilled with them.[96] If nothing else, this is what saints themselves—even while living among us—bear witness to. Throughout their transformation through the exercises of mercy, each saint provides an eschatological testimony to the communion of saints as the true dwelling of the Lord in our midst.

As for the doctrine of purgatory, then, the position that develops hereby is that purgatory is that dimension of the period of waiting for the whole body to be complete in which those whose desires are not yet oriented to the full communion of the one body of humanity in Christ are purged of their claims to private possessiveness through exercises that teach them how to desire the good of others. Purgatory forms *generous hearts*. The sluggishness of human desire is healed and trained for communion—this is what our examination of Dante's *Purgatorio*, beginning from the eleventh canto, helped us recognize. In recent history, Dorothy Day's kisses upon lepers are apt images of this training, "subordinating our own impulses and wishes to others."[97]

In the end, the social dimension of salvation in and as the communion of saints is in fact about safeguarding the seriousness of history. In the saints we examined, this meant taking seriously the crippled and the condemned, the Martin family and the sisters of Carmel, those in the "dark holes" of Calcutta's slums, and those without heat in the winters of New York. In the movement of these lives, we are given a glimpse of eschatological fulfillment. Christ hastens toward all these little ones in his saints and with his saints we are remembered in the communion of his body. The charge of those touched by mercy is to remember ourselves and others accordingly.

The decisive and permanent difference between Rilkean mysticism and Christian eschatology is most apparent here. For Rilke, the dead dissolve into undifferentiated oneness. Thérèse would cease to be troubled about this earth just as Mother Teresa's map of Calcutta would blur. In doing so, they would cease to be the persons they are, and that is precisely Rilke's point: all are to become the *energy* of loving rather than *persons* who love and who come to fulfillment in *being loved*, who fulfill their creation in *loving others*, and who embrace the sufferings and longings of love in order that this love may be complete rather than that we might become unbothered. The disquietude of the saints is indeed a sweet unrest: they are not anxious for themselves, they are anxious for us. They are anxious with the anxiety of God—if we may speak in such terms—who waits in hope for us. God's hope, as the poet Charles Péguy portrays, is God's weakness: he yields himself to *our* power.[98] That is the darkness of God: it is God's glorious light: *Darkness is not dark for you* (Ps. 139:12, NAB).

Before moving on to the final section of this chapter, one lingering issue should be addressed. In selecting the small strand of communion we examined in this chapter, I identified three canonized saints (Teresa of Avila, Thérèse of Lisieux, and, the very recently canonized, Teresa of Calcutta) and one Servant of God (Dorothy Day). Treating them together is not an attempt to canonize the last one by association, nor is it intended to diminish the importance of canonization (or beatification). I highlighted a very modern saint in Teresa of Calcutta and, especially, Dorothy Day as examples of what it means to heed the witness of the saints, who give reliable testimony to the pattern of Christ through their lives and teaching, in and through both the practices of attentiveness to what the saints reveal holiness to be (rather than what it is assumed to be) and the practices of receiving this gift of holiness through their own response in kind. If Teresa of Avila and Thérèse of Lisieux dwell in the presence of the Lord and Teresa of Calcutta is now known to join them there, then the proper response of those who hear the Lord's call through them is, like Moses and Elijah and the disciples on Tabor, to "Go."[99]

Liturgical Training and the Beauty of Prayer

This drama of communion is God's memory of creation—a memory preserved at the heart of the Church's liturgy. The memory of communion is always given first as God's work, but what happens in the liturgy is the source of the renewal of all of creaturely life, such that the training received therein becomes the way of moving, believing, and imagining all throughout creation thereby redeemed and sanctified. The drama of Exodus culminated in Israel becoming free and learning how to worship, and worship entails receiving the gift of the Lord who perceives and acts, and being transformed according to this pattern. Whereas Moses delivered this heavenly pattern to the Israelites and invited their assent on God's behalf for the construction of the tabernacle, the saints testify to Christ in their desire for communion with those who do not enjoy the desire for this communion in full. The tabernacle the saints construct is the completion of Christ's bodily communion.

To recognize the saints who enjoy beatific life in communion with the glorified Christ is to accept their desire for communion with us. To pray for the wellbeing of our own beloved dead is to beg God to mercifully draw them into this same glory and therefore for them to become wholly configured to the desire for the communion of the whole body. Lastly, to engage in this liturgical prayer is to yield ourselves to a desire that is given to us, which completes us, but which requires the death of our own selfish aims and individualizing concerns. The liturgy thus forms *generous hearts*.

Since the crucial moment for the Israelites to whom Moses descended was their conversion from hoarding their wealth for their own aims to offering it for the purposes of the Lord (see again Exod. 25:1–8; 35:4–29; cf. Luke 17:33; 9:24; Matt. 10:39; 16:25; Mark 8:35; John 12:25), we will examine one of the moments of the Eucharistic liturgy where this is represented and fulfilled: the Prayer Over the Offerings. This is a moment of suspended animation, where the possessions the congregation has brought forth are offered to the Lord for blessing so that they may be fashioned into something beautiful.[100] This is the moment of Thérèse offering her First Communion for the poor man and of beseeching the treasures of the Church for the condemned man. This is where Teresa of Avila moved from the third to the fourth dwelling place, where all the efforts she might have made become, at most, preparation for the Lord's work to begin. Moses climbed Sinai to meet the descending Lord, and when he descended Sinai he presented Israel with the invitation to begin their ascent in praise. In listening closely to the Prayer Over the Offerings from the Solemnity of All Saints, the Commemoration of All the Faithful Departed, and both a funeral Mass and an anniversary of death Mass, the Church's training in the pattern of Christ becomes more apparent.

From the outset of this study I have claimed that the theological work undertaken was in service of explicating what the Christian faith professes and revealing again what has always been proclaimed. In seeking to tie together more tightly belief and understanding, prayer and doctrine, practice and intention, I have attempted to allow the full doctrinal quality of the faith to renew worship and devotion on behalf of the communion of saints. By this point, my work of diagnosis, theological construction, and argumentation has concluded, and so as we turn to these elements of liturgical prayer, we seek to listen anew, more attentively and with revived imaginations, to what is being expressed.

The first brief prayer to which we listen comes from the Solemnity of All Saints (November 1), in which the merits of all the saints are celebrated at once. In the Prayer Over the Offerings on this day, the Church prays:

> May these offerings we bring in honor of all the Saints be pleasing to you, O Lord, and grant that, just as we believe the Saints to be already assured of immortality, so we may experience their concern for our salvation. Through Christ Our Lord.[101]

As the Church brings forth its gifts this day and asks for the Lord's blessing, it includes in its prayer one concession and one request. The Church concedes that there is no need to harbor concern for the everlasting life of those celebrated in this Mass—both those whose names are known and the anonymous saints—for they already share in the eternal glory of God. In connection with this, the members of the pilgrim Church assembled for this feast therefore ask that we "may experience *their* concern for *our* salvation." The Church recognizes in its prayer that those who rest in glory are the same ones who trouble themselves with the salvation of those yet to come—that is, those pilgrim members caught up in the work of the liturgy. Recognizing the glory of the saints and celebrating their merits is inseparable from apprehending their concern for the completion of the bodily communion. For the pilgrim members to "experience their concern" means not only apprehending the blessed saints as they are, but also and at the same time apprehending something about ourselves—namely, that we are the object of the saints' desire.

The second prayer comes from the next feast on the liturgical calendar: the Commemoration of All the Faithful Departed, or All Souls' Day (November 2). Over the gifts on this day, the Church prays,

> Look favorably on our offerings, O Lord, so that your departed servants may be taken up into glory with your Son, in whose great mystery of love we are all united. Who lives and reigns for ever and ever.[102]

Whereas on the previous day the prayer was offered for those about whom the pilgrim Church is not concerned, the prayer this day is offered for those for whom it continues to exercise concern. In other words, the Church commends to God's mercy and does not abandon those who have gone before. What the Church at prayer asks is that those who have died may live forever in that same glory of the Lord in which the saints share. If we carry forward the logic of the previous day, we will appreciate more fully the depth of meaning of the identification of the Son's glory with the "great mystery of love [in whom] we are all united." For the faithful departed to share that glory is for them to desire as the saints desire: that the whole body will come to dwell in Christ. In short, for the faithful departed the Church prays that they may be conformed to that prayer for the salvation of others, including those who now pray. The pilgrim Church thus prays that the faithful departed will become glorified in learning how to pray for the pilgrim Church and, at the end of time, to enjoy the communion of charity with the whole body. In this sense, the pilgrim members beg that, in his mercy, the Lord may make the faithful departed hasten in mercy toward them—these very pilgrims who now pray.

The next two occasions of prayer correspond to the logic contained within the first two prayers. In the Prayer Over the Offerings at a funeral (B. Outside Easter Time), the Church prays as follows:

> Be near, O Lord, we pray, to your servant (N.), on whose funeral day we offer you this sacrifice of conciliation, so that, should any stain of sin have

clung to him (her) or any human fault have affected him (her), it may, by your loving gift, be forgiven and wiped away. Through Christ our Lord.[103]

In placing itself within the action of the "sacrifice of conciliation," where all enmity in creation before God is swallowed up in the communion of Christ, the pilgrim Church dares to offer one of its own members from whom it is now separated by death. Those gathered at prayer have no power whatsoever to bond together what death has now rent asunder, and so all the assembled body can do is offer its concern over to the One who took this concern upon himself in his own death. In the end, "any stain of sin" or "human fault" has to do with either the failure to receive mercy or to offer it, which are ultimately two sides of the same mystery. As Romano Guardini states, "The high 'art of dying' is to accept the life that is leaving us, and by a single act of affirmation put it into God's hands."[104] What, then, is the stain of sin or human fault but the culpable failure to achieve this sole task? The pilgrim Church experiences the effects of this sin and fault in the pain of separation it endures, and yet it offers over this pain to the Lord as it begs that the sin and fault of its own member will, "by your loving gift, be forgiven and wiped away." What is wiped away is not merely an individual's impertinence, but the breaking apart of the communion of persons itself. To continue with Guardini, "the real antonym of community is not the individual and his individualism, but the egoist and his selfishness."[105] The pilgrim Church prays that the incurving of concern in which both this separated member and those still living indulge will be healed and transformed into mutual concern for one another.

The last Prayer Over the Offerings inculcates the assembly in this same grammar of communion. For a Mass on the Anniversary of Death (A. Outside Easter Time), these words are spoken over the gifts:

Look with favor, we pray, O Lord, on the offerings we make for the soul of your servant (N.), that, being cleansed by heavenly remedies, his (her) soul may be ever alive and blessed in your glory. Through Christ our Lord.[106]

In light of what has come before, we might pause to ponder the significance of the "heavenly remedies" here invoked. In the previous chapter, I argued that Dante gave us a glimpse of these "heavenly remedies" in the middle of the *Purgatorio*, while in this particular line of prayers we have listened to how the glory of the Son and the saints' concern for the salvation of others are united. We might say, then, that the "heavenly remedies" are the means of coming to abide in a new memory, one that sees the good of the others as one's own good and frees a creature to desire the communion God desires (see again John 17:20–26). Only "heavenly remedies" can heal the fatal wounds of creation's definitive foreclosure in sin. To be "ever alive and blessed in [the Lord's] glory" is therefore to be healed of the toxic attempts to live on one's own, for oneself, and according to one's own design, and instead to come into life according to the divine pattern. As I have said above, this soul's share in glory will have been mapped out in advance in the movement of mercy of the Word made flesh.[107]

In these prayers, we hear that when we pray in memory of the saints, we ask that we ourselves may be offered through their *generous hearts*. We hear that when we pray for the faithful departed, we ask that they be healed in mercy so that they may remember with *generous hearts*. And in reciting these prayers and growing into the space that they offer us to abide in, those who pray begin to practice mercy and are thus trained to receive what we ask for: *generous hearts*.

God's People and the Beauty of Particularity

Through the practice of the liturgy, the Church is to become what it receives and sets out as sign and instrument of unity.[108] Those who are inculcated in the liturgy's pattern of worship and who are trained to believe what the prayers of the saints and for the dead express, slowly learn to assent to these truths in the creative practice of their lives. For those who seek communion across all forms of alienation, the sublime promises of the liturgy are balm to wounded imaginations, and these promises are grafted on to the lives of the faithful in the humble practices of personal devotion.

It might seem counterintuitive to begin a discussion of personal devotion with a magisterial document, let alone a section of a magisterial document that quotes another magisterial document. Yet, in *Evangelii gaudium*, Francis appeals to Paul VI's words in recognizing that popular piety "'manifests a thirst for God which only the poor and the simple can know [, making] people capable of generosity and sacrifice even to the point of heroism, when it is a question of bearing witness to belief.'"[109] Popular piety is an antidote to the pride of enlightened thinking; it is the gift of the poor and the simple. At the beginning of this work, I traced how the devotional practices of Gallic Christians between the fourth and fifth centuries for venerating the blessed dead led to the incorporation of *communio sanctorum* as an article of faith in the Apostles' Creed. There as elsewhere Christian belief moved from the life of faith to the declaration of faith—that is, from prayer to doctrine. Out of the *generous hearts* of the poor comes that beautiful return gift of trust in the God who acts beyond explanation. These are the ones who place their cares into the hands of the Lord, giving themselves over rather than thinking themselves into certainty. As Francis confesses, "I think of the steadfast faith of those mothers tending their sick children who, though perhaps barely familiar with the articles of the creed, cling to a rosary; or of all the hope poured into a candle lighted in a humble home with prayer for help from Mary, or in the gaze of tender love directed to Christ crucified."[110] The challenge of Christianity, especially to the modern person, is to resist the temptation to exalt oneself above such simplicity and instead allow oneself to learn this humble posture. The Catholic genius consists in embracing rather than apologizing for the clinging to the concreteness of this devotional life of faith, born of God's work in the liturgy and guaranteed in the glorified body of the risen Christ.

Francis goes on to connect the concreteness of popular piety to the missionary power of intercessory prayer. Francis heeds the words of the Letter to the Philippians in which the Apostle to the Gentiles, through prayer, makes room in his own heart for the particular persons given to his care (1:4, 7). Like Thérèse after him, his prayer is a festival of communion "since authentic contemplation always has a place for others." And like the Blessed Mother whom Dante imagines standing between himself and the Blessed Trinity, Paul becomes the space where attentiveness to the needs of others is offered in gratitude *to my God through Jesus Christ* (Rom. 1:8, RSV). This prayer of intercession opens one's heart, frees one from self-absorption, and conforms the one who prays to the desire for the good of others.[111] Through the intercession of one member for others, that beauty of the Lord's perception of and action for the specific needs of the needy ones becomes the beauty of the one who sees and acts accordingly.

Far from an abstract pious thought, Francis's understanding of the centrality of concrete devotions and intercessory prayer is rooted in his own experience of practicing the Catholic faith. In particular, he gives himself as one of the spiritual children of that great saint of simplicity: Thérèse. It was Thérèse who not only desired to spend her heaven doing good on earth, but who also pledged to bring a shower of roses through her prayer. In her dialogue with her Beloved Christ, she promises to strew the flowers of her small sacrifices before his heavenly throne. These flowers are the many acts of love on her Little Way, in which she accepts the concerns and needs of others as blossoms in her own heart. She trusts that the littlest hearts of the poor ones—those in need—will became a beautiful bouquet that will please the Lord. She trusts that as these flowers "pass through Your own divine hands, O Jesus," the "Church in heaven . . . will cast these flowers, which are now infinitely valuable because of Your divine touch, upon the Church Suffering," to heal it.[112] The flowers that Thérèse gathers while on earth, she offers to the Lord and trusts that the saints in heaven will return them for the good of the suffering ones from whom they came. By the same logic, she pledges to spend *her* heaven showering roses back upon the earth. From both positions the economy is the same: the particular needs of particular persons are offered as intercessions to the Lord, in whom the desire of the saints is to join him in healing what impedes communion. From earth, Thérèse interceded for the poor man for whom she gave her First Communion and for Pranzini for whom she prayed for contrition. From heaven, she seeks the "souls to be saved", and Jorge Bergoglio, who would become Pope Francis, has long offered himself as a candidate for her care.

As one of three heavenly intercessors to whom Francis has habitually appealed, Thérèse is the one to whom he turns when under pressure or worried: "When I have a problem, I ask the saint, not to solve it, but to take it in her hands and help me accept it. And as a sign, I almost always receive a white rose."[113] These white roses, strewn across his life, are a scandal even to those who might trust in the particularity of God's concern and believe in the attentiveness of the saints because Francis does not mean metaphorical roses. No, he is referring to instances such as when he is pursued by "anonymous rose-givers" and in which he is physically rejuvenated when an unknown bystander hands him the flower.[114] These instances do not concern great ideas but rather humble prayers in search of personal love. When he uplifts popular piety in *Evangelii gaudium*, he is in part appealing to those devotions that he himself learned in the culture of his own family and in the other communities in which he was formed.

What pierces through in the prayer of the saints is the truth that nothing about God's care for creation is generalized except for the fact that God's care is unrelentingly particular. The antidote to what Francis calls "theistic gnosticism" or "airspray theism" is the "concrete Catholic thing"—that is, the practices that form the life of faith according to the incarnational impulse of Christianity.[115] What begins and returns to the liturgy permeates Catholic life. In place of general prayers to an abstract god, the authenticity of Christian faith is found in particular prayers to a personal God, who remembers particular persons in Jesus Christ.

Augustine provides an elegantly simple testimony to this truth. After all his attempts to exalt himself in his vainglorious pursuits of the intellectual life, in book IX of his *Confessions* Augustine speaks to the practices of humility he embraced in giving himself over to the concreteness of remembering his mother Monica. He recalls that she asked for only one thing of him: "'that you remember me at the altar of the Lord wherever you may be.'"[116] Through bouts of grief over the separation from her that her death inflicted, it was the opening of his heart to the devotional practice she prescribed that became his balm. In offering his mother within his address to God, he begins to pray both in thanksgiving and in lament before the mercy of the Lord. In one sweep of prayer, he cries out,

> Hear me through that healing remedy who hung upon the tree, the medicine for our wounds who sits at your right hand and intercedes for us. I know that she dealt mercifully with others and from her heart forgave her debtors their debts; do you then forgive her any debts she contracted during all those years after she had passed through the saving waters. Forgive her, Lord, forgive, I beg you, and do not arraign her before you. Let mercy triumph over judgment, for you, whose utterances are true, have to the

merciful promised mercy. Since their very power to be merciful was your gift to them in the first place, you will be showing mercy to those with whom you have yourself dealt mercifully, and granting pity to those toward whom you have shown pity first.[117]

In this intercessory prayer, Augustine makes space for her who made space for him in her life of prayer. Within the action of Christ performed upon the altar, mother and son entered into a condition of mutual indwelling within the "*spacious freedom*"[118] of the Church's memory.

Augustine's confidence in his mother's holy concern for him in the love of Christ inspires his confidence in remembering two others whose deaths he also recounts in book IX: his friend Nebridius and his son Adeodatus. Not yet with the same vibrancy or intimacy of his memory of his mother, Augustine confesses his belief that Nebridius enjoys life in God though, at the same time, he also believes without understanding that Nebridius is mindful of him "since you, Lord, from whom he drinks, are mindful of us."[119] The memory of his son is offered in delicate brevity. He praises his son, not for what he himself contributed to the boy, but for what the Lord made his son to be. In this act of praise of God and not himself, he embraces the confidence of one who trusts in a mercy that exceeds his own power and, as a fruit, "fear[s] nothing whatever for that man."[120]

In this one figure, then, we glimpse the training of a holy memory in process. By his way of remembering Monica at the altar, Augustine also begins to find the space to remember his friend and his son on behalf of communion. Finding that space means continuing to address himself to God, whose mercy comes down upon the altar in the Word made flesh— flesh now raised in glory. To remember *his* beloved dead means learning to remember them according to that mystery, and in that mystery they hasten toward him even as he longs for them. As he glimpsed with his mother at Ostia and sought to elucidate later at the end of *City of God*, the completion of that work of hastening will come when all attempts to separate from one another are overcome in graced freedom.

In place of those efforts to pull apart, in the fullness of time we will cling to one another in charity within the Lord who clings to us. Even now, particular acts of communion are ordered to that end according to the pattern of divine love united to creation in Christ. Within the one holy communion, the saints seek out those still in via to heal and inspire them, most of all through teaching them how to open themselves to desiring the good of others, in word and in deed. By the Spirit who communicates this movement of charity, those of *generous hearts* construct the communion of saints as the Lord's everlasting tabernacle. In hastening toward one another, we become a beautiful work of love.

CONCLUSION

In professing the *communio sanctorum* as intrinsic to its faith, the Church both witnesses to humanity's common good and begins to desire it. It recognizes that this communion is built up, for a time, through the purgation of all that separates persons from one another, as well as through each member's sacrifice of accepting the death of one's own isolation in order to yield to the gift of becoming one people. This sacrifice, which begins in the renunciation of what leads away from life, is everlastingly consummated in charitable activities among the members of the one communion in praise of God, whose mercy freed them from sin and death. The Church can never tire of proclaiming that *we love because he first loved us* (1 John 4:19, RSV).

The full proclamation of this love resounds in a new creation conformed to the capaciousness of God's gift of love in Christ. Therefore, my task has been to explicate the *communio sanctorum* according to the eschatological dimensions of the Incarnation. In Christ are hidden both the meaning of creation and its future beatitude; the Church thus knows and becomes itself only as it contemplates the mystery of Christ. This contemplation is given through the Holy Spirit, who both imparts the fruits of God's love in Christ and teaches those who have become a new creation the meaning of the gift they receive and the glory to which they are called. As the faithful of the Early Church grew into the gift of life conferred in the Spirit, the Church apprehended the communion of the living and the dead first through practices of veneration and later through the profession of an article of the one faith into which all Christians were baptized. As it began to claim and name its saints, the Church proclaimed the permanent validity of the humanity of Christ as the definitive way by which the redemption and sanctification of humanity itself is accomplished. On the basis of its belief in the Triune God, the Church perpetually discovers the fullness of its own identity within the Incarnate Word in whom the communication of God's life passes through death.

The true quality of Christian hope springs from the faith that even though death is indeed the end of creaturely life, God's communion with creation in the Passion, death, and Resurrection of Jesus Christ turns this end into a new beginning. In the light of this new beginning, the meaning of history itself is definitively reinterpreted. The God who assumed even death in his own Word as the consequence of sin draws even creation's God-forsakenness into the realm of mercy. God has dealt with death in utter seriousness; without taking death seriously, Christians cannot contemplate the fullness of hope that the Resurrection of Christ promises.

Yet, as I argued especially in chapter 2, this forgetting of death is precisely what the social regimens of modern (Western) society typically dictate. The customs that guard this denial both lead to and are nurtured by the modern penchant for isolating individuals, whether ritualistically, philosophically, or otherwise. In addressing this defining characteristic of the modern milieu, I sought to confront two issues arising from the neglect of death. On the one side, there is the epistemological issue of treating death as a strict boundary for verifiable truth, which thereby restricts the confidence that faith seeks to provide for trusting in the promises of Christ. On the other side, there is the theological issue of the commonplace, insubstantial, and imprecise notions of God as hovering above modern man without any real point of contact. Rather than beginning with Christ who plumbed the depths of death and established the truth of creation through his actions, death has been permitted to delimit truth and push God out past the periphery. In pursuit of the communion that God creates among the living and the blessed dead who share in the life of Christ, I have thus sought to contribute to the revival of the Christian eschatological imagination by beginning with God, who establishes his own criterion in revelation.[1] The seriousness of death is disclosed when the Word of God enters into and overcomes it. The practice of contemplating the mystery of what God has done in Christ heals the wounded mind and awakens the soporific spirit. The mystery of Christ's person establishes the truth of human persons, created and redeemed for sanctification as one communal body.

The neglect of death and the alienation of the living from the dead go hand in hand, and together these are symptomatic of the narrowing of Christian hope for salvation to an almost exclusively individualistic concern. With a cautious assist from Rilke, I heeded the critique that modern religions too quickly allow the comfort of pious wishes to relieve the tension of holding communion with the dead. Ultimately, the consequences of this concern drive far deeper in Christianity than in Rilke's thought since ignoring communion with the dead signals a break in the connection to and responsibility for the history of which the living are a part. The eschatological dimension of the Christian faith secures—rather than loosens—the belief in God's love for *this* life, for *this* world, for *this* one beloved creation that will be made new at the end of the age. God remembers history in the Paschal Mystery—that is, God both recalls what has been and joins again what has been rent asunder. The freedom of man and his responsibility in the world are not erased with death; more profoundly, the eternal significance of man's freedom is preserved in the memory of the crucified Lord, who bears the scourges of sin and communicates the healing mercy of God in his own body. In this glorious exchange, the history of suffering, pain, and loss is offered unto creation as the memory of forgiveness, liberation, and mercy. The saints are those who embrace this memory as the fulfillment of their deepest desire and who, in conformity with this blessed memory, communicate the mercy they receive as charity for the good of others. Sanctification of one member of Christ's communion is inseparable from the desire for the eschatological consummation of the whole communion.

As I have presented the case, this is all a matter of memory. Memory is never neutral: at minimum, memory (Augustine's *memoria*) beholds a judgment about history. Memory assents to some order—indeed, a *logic*—as true and it allows all things on which it touches to be rendered according to this order. The absolute priority of God's memory is the heart of the communion of saints because the conferral of the sacred memory illumines all of creation in the redemption wrought in Christ. To assume this sacred memory as one's own is to partake in the sanctification of the world as it turns mercy into praise all within the movement of charity. There is no neutral position here because the fundamental decision in regards to charity is a self-committing declaration about the truth of the world.

Charity is a logic unto itself. To enter into the way of charity is to humble oneself in order to be helped by others, to open oneself to the needs of others, and to allow the good of others to become one's own good. This is a reckless way of being, one that is unwise by all manners of accounting, save one. Only in the foolishness of God that is Christ, who gives without need and beyond measure, is the economy of charity underwritten. Through his one complete action, Christ establishes the meaning of the world, and because of him *the love of God has been poured out into our hearts through the Holy Spirit that has been given to us* (Rom. 5:5; cf. 8:14–17, NAB). The saints wager themselves on this investment in word and in deed: their word is their witness to this truth, even unto death, and their deed is the efficacious desire to share this truth with the whole human body, in Christ. To profess belief in the communion of saints as intrinsic to the Christian faith is to begin to wager oneself not just in word but also in deed to the good of all unto the reunion of all in the communion of Christ. This logic of charity is always first given in God who re-members what he created and re-creates in order to call his creatures into the holiness of life in communion.

Why, then, should Christians venerate the saints and pray for the dead? Because the very meaning of our salvation in Christ is wrapped up in our communion with one another.[2] And *how* do Christians exercise this communion? By entrusting our needs to the prayers of the saints and offering our own prayers for those in need, including the dead undergoing purgation; by accepting the charity of others and offering charity to others, all as an expression of the fundamental belief in the *caritas* of God as the foundation of life itself; and above all by participating in the body of the Church, convoked in the sacred memory of God in Christ, to whom the Spirit joins the saints in heaven with those still on pilgrimage.

The Christian, therefore, has the duty of *not* simply releasing the dead—or oneself, for that matter—to the mercy of God, for Christian salvation necessarily entails the consummation of the desire for communion with both the living and the (blessed) dead in God's mercy. To receive the love of God is to pass over into love of neighbor toward the final horizon that is the full assembly of the saints. In the Sacrament at the heart of the Church, God offers the gift of his memory of the whole communion in Christ as the Holy Spirit unites the members of the communal body to this sacred memory. This gift of God's *communio* begets the unity of human persons, *so that God may be all in all* (1 Cor. 15:28, NAB).

NOTES

Chapter 1. Indefinite Article

1. Jaroslav Pelikan, *Credo: Historical and Theological Guide to Creeds and Confessions of Faith in the Christian Tradition* (New Haven, Conn.: Yale University Press, 2005), 187.

2. J. N. D. Kelly, *Early Christian Creeds* (New York: Longman, 1972), 389–90; Susan Wood, "Sanctam Ecclesiam Catholicam, Sanctorum Communionem," in *Exploring and Proclaiming the Apostles' Creed*, ed. Roger Van Harn (Grand Rapids, Mich.: Eerdmans, 2004), 228; Berard Marthaler, *The Creed: The Apostolic Faith in Contemporary Theology*, 3rd rev. ed. (New London, Conn.: Twenty-Third, 2007), 330.

3. Nicholas Ayo, *The Creed as Symbol* (Notre Dame, Ind.: University of Notre Dame Press, 1990), 133.

4. Kelly, *Early Christian Creeds*, 394. Francis John Badcock holds a different position from Kelly on this point. Badcock is mostly concerned with the original meaning of the phrase *communio sanctorum* and, not unlike Kelly, attributes the origin of the phrase to the East, in particular to Asia Minor. Badcock then takes the Eastern meaning of the "participation in the holy things"—that is, —the Sacraments—to be the definitive meaning for the inclusion of the phrase in the Apostles' Creed. It bears remembering, however, that Kelly does not refute the Greek origin of the phrase, nor does he refute the original Greek meaning. Kelly's argument is that the meaning associated with the phrase when it is incorporated into the creed, not when it first appears in the Christian West, pertains to "fellowship with holy persons": a meaning established, as we will see below, in the Gallic regions (see Francis John Badcock, *The History of the Creeds* [New York: Macmillan, 1938], 243–72, especially 271). For more on this and related topics, see Emilien Lamirande, "The History of a Formula," in *The Communion of Saints*, trans. A. Manson (New York: Hawthorn, 1963), 15–38; and Heinz Kruse, "Gemeinschaft der Heiligen: Herkunft und Bedeutung des Glaubensartikels," *Vigiliae Christianae* 47, no. 3 (1993): 246–59.

5   Kelly, *Early Christian Creeds*, 398–400, 430–34.

6. Ibid., 388.

7. Ibid., 396–97.

8. Ayo, *The Creed as Symbol*, 132.

9. Pelikan, *Credo*, 85.

10. See John Henry Newman, "The Orthodoxy of the Body of the Faithful During the Supremacy of Arianism," in *The Arians of the Fourth Century* (Eugene, Ore.: Wipf & Stock, 1996), 445–68.

11. Pelikan, *Credo*, 341.

12. Ibid., 374; see also Jaroslav Pelikan and Valerie Hotchkiss, eds., *Creeds and Confessions of Faith in the Christian Tradition*, vol. 1, *Early, Eastern, and Medieval* (New Haven, Conn.: Yale University Press, 2003), 7–9.

13. Pelikan, *Credo*, 376.

14. Badcock, *The History of the Creeds*, 271. Even as Badcock is cited approvingly here, I must also duly acknowledge that he refutes the interpretation of the creedal article of *the communion of saints* that I am hereby advocating according to the narrative logic of the creed. Badcock worries that "a sort of semi-pelagian subjectivism" (271) is at work in any interpretation that would see the creed as imputing any importance to the actions or responses of Christians themselves. To him, the creeds are hymns of thanksgiving that, arising out of the milieu of the Early Church, were concerned solely with "God and His mighty works which the Christian was exhorted to study" (272) and not with the works of creatures themselves. "Our minds," he says of moderns, "are dwelling disproportionately on what we can or ought to do" (272). Though Badcock's caution is certainly worthy of serious consideration, it is also important to consider the understanding of grace with which Badcock is operating. It would appear as though he is operating with a contrastive notion of grace vis-à-vis nature, whereby human activity would minimize or in some way jeopardize the absolute agency of God. To interpret the inner logic of the creed as having anything to do with human agency or the active reception of the merits of Christ would be tantamount to equivocating on the absolute priority of God's work in Christ and through the Spirit. However, with an understanding of grace as non-contrastive—as I espouse later in this work—the bestowal of grace through the agency of the Holy Spirit is precisely intended to capacitate its recipients for agency. The third part (or third paragraph) of the creed would therefore speak to the one Spirit who communicates the work of salvation accomplished by our Lord precisely through making those who are not God sharers in the divine life. This would, of course, be the graced process of sanctification.

15. Pelikan, *Credo*, 378. Ayo offers a view of the third part of the creed that accords with the view I am espousing in *The Creed as Symbol*, 133. For another essay

on the interconnectedness of the last six articles of the Apostles' Creed with special consideration given to the communion of saints, see Rose Hoover, "The Communion of Saints: Lest the Journey Be Too Long," *The Way* 30 (1990): 216–30.

16. See Thomas Aquinas, *Summa Theologica*, Complete English Edition
(Westminster, Md.: Christian Classics, 1981), Ia.36.2.

17. Pelikan, *Credo*, 188.

18. Austin Flannery, ed., "Lumen Gentium: Dogmatic Constitution on
the Church," in *Vatican Council II: Constitutions, Decrees, Declarations*, rev. ed.
(Northport, N.Y.: Costello, 1996), §49.

19. Ibid., §48.

20. Ibid., §51.

21. Ibid.

22. Ibid., §50.

23. Ibid., §50 (emphases added).

24. Ibid., §49.

25. Karl Rahner, "Why and How Can We Venerate the Saints?" in *Theological Investigations*, trans. Cornelius Ernst et al., vol. 8 (Limerick, Ireland: Mary
Immaculate College, 2000), 4.

26. A word of caution from Pelikan supports the important role of theological explication on Christian doctrine, though in more severe and dramatic
terms: "By implication, unfaithfulness to this sum of doctrine [as contained in
creeds and confessions] amounts to disloyalty toward Christ, because the history of the church shows that it is a theological anomaly, or at best a fortunate
inconsistency, for a true personal faith as *fides qua creditur*, 'the faith with which
one believes,' to rest on false teaching as *fides quae creditur*, 'the faith which
one believes.' That is at any rate the conviction underlying the sharp condem-
nations of false doctrine in so many creeds and confessions from all the major
confessional traditions" (*Credo*, 75). Pelikan's point is that right doctrine is important for right belief, whereas I am averring a corollary of this position: that
the proper understanding of doctrine motivates and informs the full exercise of
faith.

27. Sarah Coakley touches on the necessary interconnection between the
development of orthodox doctrine and a real assent to such belief in the spiritual practices of the Church: "My own reading of this early patristic period, then,
neither reduces the history of the development of trinitarian doctrine to non-
theological forces, nor assumes that the achievement of classical orthodoxy is the
arrival at some stable place of spiritual safety. 'Orthodoxy' as mere propositional
assent needs to be carefully distinguished from 'orthodoxy' as a demanding, and
ongoing, spiritual *project*, in which the language of the creed is personally and pro-
gressively assimilated" (Sarah Coakley, *God, Sexuality, and the Self: An Essay "On*

the Trinity" [Cambridge: Cambridge University Press, 2013], 5 [emphasis in original text]).

28. In chapter 4 I offer a systematic defense of this claim.

29. I elucidate this claim in chapter 5.

30. Karl Rahner, "The Church of the Saints," in *Theological Investigations*, trans. Cornelius Ernst et al., vol. 3 (Limerick, Ireland: Mary Immaculate College, 2000), 93, 96 (emphasis in original text). While acknowledging the importance of the Church's action to canonize its saints (especially when these saints are the result of the vox populi [56]), Lawrence Cunningham also tempers views such as the one noted here that might otherwise seem to offer unmitigated praise for the Church's canonization mechanisms: "We must also understand that [the canonized saints'] position in the Church is the result of the particular care the institutional church has taken to make them 'their own.' In the history of sainthood in Catholic Christianity, the saints have been bureaucratized. Like all products of bureaucracy, they have become somewhat sanitized." Lawrence Cunningham, *The Meaning of Saints* (San Francisco: Harper & Row, 1980), 32. For additional recent works that seek to portray holiness and saintliness without the apparent confines of official canonization processes, see Michael Plekon, *Hidden Holiness* (Notre Dame, Ind.: University of Notre Dame Press, 2009); and Michael Plekon, *Saints as They Really Are: Voices of Holiness in Our Time* (Notre Dame, Ind.: University of Notre Dame Press, 2012).

31. Karl Rahner, "The Eternal Significance of the Humanity of Jesus for Our Relationship with God," in *Theological Investigations*, trans. Cornelius Ernst et al., vol. 3 (Limerick, Ireland: Mary Immaculate College, 2000), 44 (emphases in original text).

32. See Karl Rahner, "All Saints," in *Theological Investigations*, trans. Cornelius Ernst et al., vol. 8 (Limerick, Ireland: Mary Immaculate College, 2000), 27.

33. Consider the following lines from the council: "Sitting at the right hand of the Father [Jesus Christ] is continually active in the world in order to lead people to the church and through it to join them more closely to himself; by nourishing them with his own Body and Blood, he makes them sharers in his glorious life. The promised and hoped for restoration, therefore, has already begun in Christ. It is carried forward in the sending of the holy Spirit and through him continues in the church in which, through faith, we learn the meaning of our earthly life while . . . we hope for the benefits which are to come" (Flannery, ed., "Lumen Gentium," §48).

34. "In the lives of those companions of ours in the human condition who are more perfectly transformed into the image of Christ (see 2 Cor 3:18) God shows, vividly, to humanity his presence and his face" (ibid., §50).

35. Rahner, "The Eternal Significance of the Humanity of Jesus," 45. Rahner poses a challenging and pertinent question to all (Catholic) theologians, and perhaps especially to ones who attempt to study and expound on the communion of saints: "Every theologian should allow himself to be asked: have you a theology in which the Word—by the fact that he is man and in so far as he is this—is the necessary and permanent mediator of all salvation, not merely at some time in the past but now and for all eternity?"

36. "The speculative man becomes entangled in mysticism where his reason does not understand itself and what it wants, and rather prefers to dote on the beyond than to confine itself within the bounds of this world, as is fitting for an intellectual inhabitant of a sensible world; for reason, because it is not easily satisfied with its immanent, that is, its practical use but likes to attempt something in the transcendent, also has its mysteries" (Immanuel Kant, "The End of All Things," in *On History*, ed. Lewis White Beck, trans. Robert E. Anchor and Emil L. Fackenheim [Indianapolis: Bobbs-Merrill, 1963], 79); quoted in John Thiel, "For What May We Hope? Thoughts on the Eschatological Imagination," *Theological Studies* 67 (2006): 518.

37. Rahner, "Why and How Can We Venerate the Saints?" 6.

38. James Corkery proposes that remembering and staying connected to the ones a person has personally known but who have died helps such a person to move toward knowledge of and communication with the unknown saints, including the canonized saints of the Church. In brief, he states that the habit of attending to those who were once visible helps one learn to see the ones who are invisible. Corkery thus recommends a pedagogy of incremental attentiveness to heal the wounds that death inflicts on the imagination. See James Corkery, "The Communion of Saints," *The Way* 36, no. 4 (1996): 285–93.

39. Rahner, "Why and How Can We Venerate the Saints?" 6–7.

40. See Thiel, "For What May We Hope?" 518–19. Though Thiel ultimately critiques Rahner as a theologian who exercises undue Kantian restraint in his own eschatology (a charge that I refute, albeit obliquely, in chapter 3 as part of a larger section on the hermeneutics of eschatological assertions), what Thiel says in general about modern theologians regarding their eschatologies is applicable to the point I am making here regarding the imaginative and devotional modesty of modern Christians: "It is both expected and surprising that modern theologians have followed Kant's lead in their attention to eschatology. On the one hand, Kant's position on the limitations of knowledge has become axiomatic in modern theories of interpretation. Embraced theologically, it issues in the expected refusal of theologians to speak flourishingly about the afterlife. On the other hand, this epistemological modesty is somewhat surprising when one recalls that assertions

about the afterlife are not claims for knowledge but claims made in faith. It is surprising that many modern theologians have chosen to observe the Kantian strictures on knowledge, since the understanding they construct is measured (or should be!) by faith in the Christ event as revealed in Scripture and tradition."

41. Rahner, "Why and How Can We Venerate the Saints?" 7.

42. Ibid.

43. Ibid.

44. Ibid., 8.

45. Rahner, "The Eternal Significance of the Humanity of Jesus," 39–41.

46. Ibid., 41–42. The following lines are particularly relevant to my project: "We today are in danger of honoring God (or at least of trying to honor him) and of letting the world itself be God-less. The Christian attitude, however, would be to honor the world as something willed and loved by God, and to do this in a properly balanced way, since this love given to the world is itself of varying degrees; hence, it would be Christian to pay a truly religious veneration where the world has already found the finality of its eternal validity before God in the morning and evening summits of its spiritual history, i.e., in the angels and the saints" (41–42).

47. See Karl Rahner, "The Life of the Dead," in *Theological Investigations*, trans. Cornelius Ernst et al., vol. 4 (Limerick, Ireland: Mary Immaculate College, 2000), 347–54. I treat this topic to a significant degree in chapters 4 and 5.

Chapter 2. Solitary Confinement

1. See again Flannery, ed., "Lumen Gentium," §49. The second view noted above is related though not identical to the Platonic doctrine of the immortality of the soul, which holds that the soul is freed from the body at death. From a Christian perspective, this doctrine is insufficient due to its disregard for creation and history. I deal with this view in the following chapter in relation to the doctrines of *creatio ex nihilo* and the resurrection of the body. For now, I simply stipulate that this view is not only inadequate for the fullness of Christian hope, but also that it comes under attack from modern philosophy, which often takes this view as standard for Western religions, especially Christianity.

2. Philippe Ariès, *Western Attitudes toward Death: From the Middle Ages to the Present*, trans. Patricia Ranum (Baltimore: Johns Hopkins University Press, 1975), 85.

3. Philippe Ariès, *The Hour of Our Death: The Classic History of Western Attitudes Toward Death over the Last One Thousand Years*, trans. Helen Weaver, 2nd ed. (New York: Vintage, 2008), 580.

4. For a concise yet compelling overview of popular Christian approaches to death characteristic of the Patristic period, see Jaroslav Pelikan, *The Shape of Death: Life, Death, and Immortality in the Early Fathers* (New York: Abingdon, 1961). Jacques Choron also attempted a general survey of the conceptions of death in the Western tradition, starting with the pre-Socratics and ending with twentieth-century existential philosophers (see Jacques Choron, *Death and Western Thought* [New York: Collier, 1963]).

5. Ariès, *Western Attitudes toward Death*, 14.

6. Ariès, *The Hour of Our Death*, 22; see also Ariès, *Western Attitudes toward Death*, 7–25.

7. Ariès, *Western Attitudes toward Death*, 32–37.

8. Ibid., 37.

9. Ibid., 51–52.

10. Ibid., 55–58; see also Ariès, *The Hour of Our Death*, 28, 473–74.

11. Ariès, *Western Attitudes toward Death*, 59; see also 70.

12. Ariès, *The Hour of Our Death*, 300.

13. Ibid., 560.

14. Ibid., 587.

15. Ibid., 583. In a highly influential essay, Geoffrey Gorer argues that the taboos regarding death and mourning are equivalent to those related to sex and pornography in the Victorian era. At the conclusion of his essay, he avers that "people have to come to terms with the basic facts of birth, copulation and death, and somehow accept their implications; if social prudery prevents this being done in an open and dignified fashion, then it will be done surreptitiously. If we dislike the modern pornography of death, then we must give back to death—natural death—its parade and publicity, readmit grief and mourning" (Geoffrey Gorer, "The Pornography of Death," in *Death, Grief, and Mourning* [New York: Arno, 1977], 192–99, excerpt from 199).

16. Ariès, *The Hour of Our Death*, 580.

17. Thomas Long and Thomas Lynch, *The Good Funeral: Death, Grief, and the Community of Care* (Louisville, Ky.: Westminster John Knox, 2013), 184–85: "The living gather at their convenience to 'celebrate life' in a kind of obsequylite at which therapy is dispensed, closure proclaimed, biography enshrined, and spirits are, it is supposed, uplifted."

18. Ariès, *Western Attitudes toward Death*, 88–89.

19. Ariès, *The Hour of Our Death*, 94.

20. Long and Lynch, *The Good Funeral*, 60; see also 184–86.

21. Quoted in Ariès, *Western Attitudes toward Death*, 94; see also Jacques Maritain, *Reflections on America* (New York: Gordian, 1975). Thomas Lynch argues that ignoring the humanity and the appropriateness of grief renders the

commonplace modern approach to death inauthentic, as he approvingly cites Richard John Neuhaus's opinion that "The worst thing is not the sorrow or the loss or the heartbreak. Worse is to be encountered by death and not to be changed by the encounter. There are pills we can take to get through the experience, but the danger is that we then do not go through the experience but around it" (quoted in Long and Lynch, *The Good Funeral*, 231).

22. As he affirmatively summarizes Ariès's own diagnosis of the modern situation relative to the approach to death, Lawrence Samuel writes that "With the rise of the modern self, death became separated from the traditional, religious view predicated on it being a normal part of life. . . . Efficient, orderly (literally), and professional, the hospital of the late twentieth century depersonalized death by repressing its less attractive aspects" (*Death, American Style: A Cultural History of Dying in America* [New York: Rowman & Littlefield, 2013], 124).

23. See Jessica Mitford, *The American Way of Death* (New York: Simon and Schuster, 1963); and Jessica Mitford, *The American Way of Death Revisited* (New York: Alfred A. Knopf, 1998).

24. Long and Lynch, *The Good Funeral*, 189; see also 232. The PBS *Frontline* episode featuring Lynch and Sons funerary practice offers a rare glimpse into the dignified manner in which this family of funeral directors plies their trade within and on behalf of their particular community. See Miri Navasky and Karen O'Connor, "The Undertaking," *Frontline* (PBS, 2008); see also Thomas Lynch, *The Undertaking: Life Studies from the Dismal Trade* (New York: W. W. Norton, 2009).

25. Ariès, *The Hour of Our Death*, 613.

26. Ibid.

27. The origins of Rilke's story may well lie with a movement Ariès observed as once again granting cemeteries a place in the city, thus signaling a new kind of interest in the relationship between the living and the dead: "A new concept of society was born at the end of the eighteenth century; it developed during the nineteenth century and found its expression in Auguste Comte's positivism, an intellectualized form of nationalism. It was thought, and even felt, that society is composed of both the dead and the living. The city of the dead is the obverse of the society of the living, or rather than the obverse, it is its image, its intemporal image. For the dead have gone through the moment of change, and their monuments are the visible sign of the permanence of their city" (Ariès, *Western Attitudes toward Death*, 73–74). Cf. Romano Guardini, *The Last Things: Concerning Death, Purification after Death, Resurrection, Judgment, and Eternity*, trans. Charlotte E. Forsyth and Grace B. Branham (Notre Dame, Ind.: University of Notre Dame Press, 1965), 17–18.

28. See Rainer Maria Rilke, *Letters of Rainer Maria Rilke, 1910–1926*, trans. Jane Bannard Greene and M. D. Herter Norton (New York: W. W. Norton, 1969), 314–16. Rilke possessed an aversion to "Christian conceptions of a Beyond" because he believed them to "contain above all the danger not only of making those who have vanished more indistinct to us and above all more inaccessible—; but we too, drawing ourselves yonder in our longing and away from here, we ourselves become thereby less definite, less earthly" (314–15). He charges Christianity with propagating deficient views of the dead that consequently obfuscate present life with the disillusioning emphasis on the blessedness of the glorified dead who serve as objects of longing for the living. To Rilke, this understanding of the afterlife fallaciously separates the dead from the living and causes the living to disassociate from the world in their desire to go beyond it. By so starkly separating the dead from the living, the Christian view is yet another symptom of the modern impulse to ignore death and to exclude it from life. To the modern person and especially to the modern Christian, death has "turned more and more into something alien, and as we have kept it in the alien, something hostile" (316). Unlike Christianity, which he sees as denying and avoiding death by covering it up with hypotheses of guilt and atonement, Rilke seeks to welcome death and thereby to become open to those who were thought to have vanished. With this agenda, Rilke is close to the goal of my present study, except he has no place for the Christian narrative, let alone the intention of allowing that narrative to unfold in its fullness.

29. *Wer, wenn ich schriee, hörte mich denn aus der Engel Ordnungen?*

30. Romano Guardini, *Rilke's Duino Elegies: An Interpretation*, trans. K. G. Knight (London: Darwen Finlayson, 1961), 11.

31. See ibid., 302.

32. "Basic to Rilke's poetry is the will to shed the transcendence of Revelation and to ground existence absolutely on earth" (Romano Guardini, *The End of the Modern World*, trans. Elinor Briefs [Wilmington, Del.: ISI, 1998], 103).

33. In an essay concerning the communion of saints, Elizabeth Koenig decries the modern illusion of community as really nothing more than an aggregate of "shared emptiness." Though she is not commenting on Rilke per se, Koenig does signal a concern similar to the one that I attempt to draw out through the remainder of this chapter (see Elizabeth Koenig, "Keeping Company with Jesus and the Saints," *Theology Today* 56 [1999]: 18–28).

34. Rilke, *Letters of Rainer Maria Rilke, 1910–1926*, 316; see also 373.

35. Guardini, *Rilke's Duino Elegies*, 122.

36. Ibid., 46.

37. *Streifen Fruchtlands zwischen Strom und Gestein.*

38. We wildly collect the honey of the visible, to store it in the great golden hive of the invisible (my translation).

39. Rilke, *Letters of Rainer Maria Rilke, 1910–1926*, 374.

40. Guardini, *Rilke's Duino Elegies*, 262–63.

41. Rilke's thought on the matter is definitively summed up in the following excerpt from one of his letters: "Affirmation of life-AND-death appears as one in the 'Elegies.' To grant one without the other is, so it is here learned and celebrated, a limitation which in the end shuts out all that is infinite. Death is the side of life averted from us, unshone upon by us: we must try to achieve the greatest consciousness of our existence which is at home in both unbounded realms, inexhaustibly nourished from both. . . . The true figure of life extends through both spheres, the blood of the mightiest circulation flows through both: there is neither a here nor a beyond, but the great unity" (Rilke, *Letters of Rainer Maria Rilke, 1910–1926*, 373).

42. According to Guardini, "if we take into account [all the] Elegies, death is the only reality" (*Rilke's Duino Elegies*, 282).

43. See ibid., 218.

44. Ibid., 219.

45. Ibid., 175; see also 178. These are the same essential characteristics as the Overman on whose behalf Nietzsche's Zarathustra prophesies: the one who will say "Yes" even to the eternal return of the same (see Friedrich Nietzsche, "Thus Spoke Zarathustra," in *The Nietzsche Reader*, ed. Keith Ansell Pearson and Duncan Large [Oxford: Blackwell, 2006], 278).

46. Martin Heidegger, "What Are Poets For?" in *Poetry, Language, Thought*, trans. Albert Hofstadter (New York: Harper Perennial Modern Classics, 2001), 138.

47. Guardini, *Rilke's Duino Elegies*, 178.

48. Peter Fritz, "Sublime Apprehension: A Catholic, Rahnerian Construction" (Ph.D. diss., University of Notre Dame, 2010), 172.

49. For Guardini's penetrating description of Rilke's angel, see Guardini, *Rilke's Duino Elegies*, 21–22; cf. 203.

50. Rilke, *Letters of Rainer Maria Rilke, 1910–1926*, 375.

51. Reflecting on the deep and intense impression the Spanish landscape of Toledo made on him, Rilke writes to one of his correspondents: "External world and vision everywhere coincided as it were in the object, in each a whole inner world was displayed, as though an angel who embraces space were blind and gazing into himself. This world, seen no longer with the eyes of men, but in the angel, is perhaps my real task—at least all my earlier experiments would come together in it" (ibid., 145–46).

52. Rainer Maria Rilke, *Duino Elegies & The Sonnets to Orpheus*, trans. Stephen Mitchell (New York: Vintage, 2009), 11 (emphasis in original text).

53. Guardini, *Rilke's Duino Elegies*, 58.

54. See ibid., 59, where Guardini describes Rilke's notion of human existence as "an outflowing without return."

55. Rilke, *Duino Elegies & The Sonnets to Orpheus*, 11.

56. Guardini, *Rilke's Duino Elegies*, 62; see also 208.

57. Rilke, *Letters of Rainer Maria Rilke, 1910–1926*, 373.

58. Guardini, *Rilke's Duino Elegies*, 22. Fritz capitalizes on the Nietzschean resonance on this point: "Again, Rilke and Nietzsche, the poet and the thinker, resemble each other, for in desiring to rid themselves of the self-sealing thought of the subject, both believe that examining the 'uttermost limits of being as a whole . . . must at the same time proceed . . . through the human being's loneliest loneliness" (Fritz, "Sublime Apprehension," 172); see also Martin Heidegger, "Nietzsche, Volume II: The Eternal Recurrence of the Same," in *Nietzsche: Volume I: The Will to Power as Art and Volume II: The Eternal Recurrence of the Same*, trans. David Farrell Krell (New York: HarperOne, 1991), 25.

59. Guardini, *Rilke's Duino Elegies*, 23.

60. Ibid., 24.

61. Ibid.

62. Nietzsche, "Thus Spoke Zarathustra," 273 (emphasis in original text). Elsewhere, Nietzsche writes that "A strong and well-formed man digests his experiences (including deeds and misdeeds) as he digests his meals, even when he has hard lumps to swallow" (Friedrich Nietzsche, "Genealogy of Morality," in *The Nietzsche Reader*, ed. Keith Ansell-Pearson and Duncan Large [Oxford: Blackwell, 2006], 24); cf. Friedrich Nietzsche, "Twilight of the Idols," in *The Nietzsche Reader*, ed. Keith Ansell-Pearson and Duncan Large (Oxford: Blackwell, 2006), 470; Friedrich Nietzsche, "Human, All Too Human," in *The Nietzsche Reader*, ed. Keith Ansell-Pearson and Duncan Large (Oxford: Blackwell, 2006), 224; and Friedrich Nietzsche, "The Gay Science," in *The Nietzsche Reader*, ed. Keith Ansell Pearson and Duncan Large (Oxford: Blackwell, 2006), 219.

63. Guardini, *Rilke's Duino Elegies*, 30.

64. Rilke, *Duino Elegies & The Sonnets to Orpheus*, 5.

65. "That *Present* which is held in authentic temporality and which thus is *authentic* itself, we call the '*moment of vision.*' This term must be understood in the active sense as an ecstasis. It means the resolute rapture with which *Dasein* is carried away to whatever possibilities and circumstances are encountered in the Situation as possible objects of concern, but a rapture is *held* in resoluteness"

(Martin Heidegger, *Being and Time* [New York: Harper Perennial Modern Classics, 2008], 387–88 [emphases in original text]).

66. Martin Heidegger, *The Phenomenology of Religious Life*, trans. Matthias Fritsch and Jennifer Anna Gosetti-Ferencei (Bloomington: Indiana University Press, 2010), 152–70.

67. There is a connection between the sort of detachment the Christian saint attains and the indifference Rilke is here defining. The resemblance will become clearer in chapter 4 when I move with Henri de Lubac to draw out an Augustinian ontology of desire. The crucial difference between Rilke's lover and the Christian saint is that impersonal, noncommunicative ecstasy characterizes the former while the latter becomes the embodiment of gratitude.

68. Guardini, *Rilke's Duino Elegies*, 113.

69. Ibid.

70. Ibid., 158–59.

71. Ibid., 192–93.

72. Ibid., 193.

73. Ibid., 304.

74. In an attempt to oppose and correct Rilke's view, Guardini asserts that "One of the mysteries of the human personality is that it only awakens to real life of its own when it has left the self for the sake of someone else. Man cannot really say 'I' until he has said 'Thou'" (ibid., 81). In an essay discussing Guardini's theological anthropology, Robert Krieg argues that Guardini critiqued Rilke's claim to the priority of self-autonomy because, in addition to being false to the human person, this self-reliance eventually becomes tiresome, thus leading to a heteronomous reliance that eventually opens the door to totalitarianism. The move away from theonomy is therefore the first and most decisive step toward the breakdown of human personhood (see Robert Krieg, "Romano Guardini's Theology of the Human Person," *Theological Studies* 59 [1998]: 457–74).

75. Guardini, *Rilke's Duino Elegies*, 303.

76. Ibid., 17. As noted above, Ariès considers the breakdown of community and the atomization of individuals to be a hallmark of modern life (see Ariès, *The Hour of Our Death*, 613).

77. Guardini, *Rilke's Duino Elegies*, 102.

78. Ibid., 280–81 (emphasis in original text).

79. Ibid., 116; cf. 87–88. Guardini offers a rather developed critique of modernity's denial of revelation and the concomitant evacuation of human personality in *The End of the Modern World*, 95–113.

80. In a Christian framework, we would need to qualify the meaning of the self since this notion could very well be associated with inauthentic human personhood due to the self-affirming sin of pride. In this instance, however, Rilke

is talking about the human person as such. Though he does have a sense of human beings as somehow fallen in their distractedness in the world and their preoccupation with transient things (the end of the *Eighth Elegy* makes this clear), his underlying premise is that there is not any substantiality to human persons as such. The Christian narrative would actually propose the opposite: that in seeking to become substantial on their own terms, humans have actually forfeited their substantiality as persons. I deal more fully with this fundamental disagreement between Rilke's narrative and the Christian narrative at the close of this section.

81. Guardini very helpfully summarizes the way in which the first seven elegies deal with the human person, whom Rilke is analyzing for the constitutive capacity of being genuinely influenced by another "person" in the *Seventh Elegy*: "In order to woo an individual person one would have to presuppose the presence of such a person with a self of his own. But from the earlier Elegies it is abundantly clear that Rilke does not believe in the existence of such a being. In fact, for him the whole fulfillment of existence lies in renouncing any claim to such a person. The First Elegy shows Man as a creature who is capable neither of 'using' nor of 'being used' by another. The Second Elegy deals with the evanescence of our Being. The Third attempts to show that it is only possible to exist as a person in the limited world of the conscious. As soon as this conscious existence is relinquished everything else vanishes with it. The Fourth Elegy divides Man up into the two aspects of observer and observed. The Fifth shows him in the grip of an impersonal force which treats him like part of a machine. The Sixth portrays the Hero with whom we can have no contact because he passes through the world like a star in the sky. And the Seventh Elegy states that no 'wooing,' not even the 'purest,' could possibly call forth a response from another human being" (Guardini, *Rilke's Duino Elegies*, 190) (emphases all in original text).

82. Rilke, *Duino Elegies & The Sonnets to Orpheus*, 49.

83. Generally, the dominating figure of the angel stands in the place where one might have otherwise expected to find God.

84. Guardini, *Rilke's Duino Elegies*, 238.

85. This view relates to Nietzsche and Heidegger—as well as Marx—all of whom see the vision of a divine person who is the guarantor of substantial existence as the objectified projection of a subjective lack within the human person himself. Nietzsche calls this the idol man creates to compensate for his own sense of nothingness, while Heidegger blames Augustine and all of Western thought after him for losing nerve and resorting to Neoplatonic ideals. For his part, Marx sees this divine being as the self-projected figure of alienation that lords it over the unhappy conscience. For a lucid treatment of Nietzsche's critique of the Christian belief in God, see Henri de Lubac, *The Drama of Atheist Humanism*, trans. Mark Sebanc (San Francisco: Ignatius, 1995), 42–58.

86. Guardini, *Rilke's Duino Elegies*, 238.

87. Ibid.

88. Ibid., 239.

89. Ibid., 251.

90. Rilke, *Letters of Rainer Maria Rilke, 1910–1926*, 374 (emphasis in original text).

91. Guardini, *Rilke's Duino Elegies*, 250.

92. Rilke, *Duino Elegies & The Sonnets to Orpheus*, 59 (emphasis in original text).

93. Guardini, *Rilke's Duino Elegies*, 251.

94. Ibid., 297.

95. Quoted in Heidegger, "What Are Poets For?" 89.

96. Albert Hofstadter, "Introduction," in *Poetry, Language, Thought* (New York: Harper Perennial Modern Classics, 2001), xv.

97. Consider Jacques Derrida's opinion on the matter: "The individualism of technological civilization relies precisely on a misunderstanding of the unique self. It is the individualism of a role and not of a person" (*The Gift of Death & Literature in Secret*, trans. David Wills, 2nd ed. [Chicago: University of Chicago Press, 2007], 37 (emphases in original text).

98. Heidegger, "What Are Poets For?" 114.

99. Ibid., 110–12.

100. Ibid., 90, 95.

101. Hofstadter, "Introduction," xv.

102. Heidegger, "What Are Poets For?" 94.

103. Ibid., 122 (emphasis in original text).

104. Martin Heidegger, "The Origin of the Work of Art," in *Poetry, Language, Thought*, trans. Albert Hofstadter (New York: Harper Perennial Modern Classics, 2001), 79; see also 54–55.

105. See, for example, Heidegger, *Being and Time*, xv.

106. Ibid., 32.

107. Ibid., 33.

108. Heidegger, "What Are Poets For?" 113.

109. Ibid., 106.

110. Martin Heidegger, "Nietzsche, Volume I: The Will to Power as Art," in *Nietzsche: Volume I: The Will to Power as Art and Volume II: The Eternal Recurrence of the Same*, trans. David Farrell Krell (New York: HarperOne, 1991), 3–7.

111. Fritz, "Sublime Apprehension," 171.

112. By assessing Heidegger's judgment of Rilke alongside Fritz's judgment on behalf of the Christian tradition, we see that each finds Rilke incomplete or inadequate for precisely the opposite reasons (see ibid., 171–72).

113. Theodore Kisiel, *The Genesis of Heidegger's "Being & Time"* (Berkeley: University of California Press, 1993), 200.

114. Heidegger, *Being and Time*, 374.

115. Augustine, *The Confessions*, trans. Maria Boulding (New York: Vintage, 1998), 261 [XI.20.26].

116. Heidegger, *Being and Time*, 416; see also Sean McGrath, "Alternative Confessions, Conflicting Faiths: A Review of 'The Influence of Augustine on Heidegger,'" *American Catholic Philosophical Quarterly* 82, no. 2 (2008): 319.

117. Augustine, *The Confessions*, 204–14 [X.8.12–17.26].

118. Ibid., 212–13 [X.16.24–25].

119. Ibid., 216–18 [X.20.29–31]; see also Heidegger, *The Phenomenology of Religious Life*, 132–41. I give this mysterious desire extended treatment in chapter 4.

120. Heidegger, *The Phenomenology of Religious Life*, 141 (emphases in original text).

121. Augustine, *The Confessions*, 222–23 [X.28.39]; see also Heidegger, *The Phenomenology of Religious Life*, 152.

122. Augustine, *The Confessions*, 223–32 [X.30.41–53]; see also Heidegger, *The Phenomenology of Religious Life*, 155–65.

123. Augustine, *The Confessions*, 233–35 [X.35.54–57]; see also Heidegger, *The Phenomenology of Religious Life*, 165–69.

124. Augustine, *The Confessions*, 235–40 [X.36.58–39.64]; see also Heidegger, *The Phenomenology of Religious Life*, 169–80.

125. Heidegger, *The Phenomenology of Religious Life*, 178–80.

126. "For Augustine, having received oneself coincides with the discovery that this self is for another, and it is precisely in the tension of this relation that the unique sense of the historicity of being is to be found. Heidegger, however, translates (and so perhaps reduces) the Augustinian relation between the self and another self, between the 'I' and God—an intrinsically historical relation, since the 'I' is itself only insofar as it is for another—as an endogenous shift, a self-generated inversion of life, when life is no longer directed towards specific contents, but is turned towards itself and is enacted in its original and necessary mode of having-oneself, in a dynamic of pure self-possession. And I say 'pure' since what comes to be possessed is not an individual, personal, spiritual, or even psycho-biological identity; indeed, it is not any determined thing, but is the very movement of receiving-oneself, without a giver but also without a receiver" (Constantino Esposito, "Memory and Temptation: Heidegger Reads Book X of Augustine's 'Confessions,'" in *A Companion to Heidegger's "Phenomenology of Religious Life,"* ed. Sean McGrath and Andrzej Wiercinski [New York: Rodopi, 2010], 293–94).

127. Ibid., 294.

128. Heidegger, *The Phenomenology of Religious Life*, 123.

129. Ibid., 209; see also 174, 194–95; Kisiel, *The Genesis of Heidegger's "Being & Time,"* 204.

130. Sean McGrath comments on this Heideggerian accusation in two separate articles: "In Heidegger's view, Augustine loses his way as a 'hermeneutician of facticity' when he resolves the restlessness of human existence into the *tranquillitas* of the *visio beatifica*, the timeless vision of God" (McGrath, "Alternative Confessions," 324). And again, "For Heidegger, this is the decisive interjection of Greek metaphysics into Augustine's thinking, which blossoms into Scholasticism, the substitution of *contemplatio* for the *expectatio* of Christian faith. Augustine replaces the temporalizing being-toward-an-absent-God with the aesthetic enjoyment of an eternal principle and thus initiates both the forgetfulness of history in the Middle Ages and the reign of theory in Western philosophy" (Sean McGrath, "The Young Heidegger's Problematic Reading of Augustine's Ontological Restlessness," *Journal for Cultural and Religious Theory* 4, no. 1 [2002]: 8). A third comment on this same point comes from Matthias Fritsch, who discerns that "what is most indebted to Greek metaphysics in Augustine, according to Heidegger, is the axiological and ultimately aesthetic theory of value which equates God with being, goodness, and beauty. In addition, the concept of God as eternal being betrays what we might call, following the later Heidegger and Derrida, an onto-theological metaphysics of presence" (Matthias Fritsch, "Cura et Casus: Heidegger and Augustine on the Care of the Self," in *The Influence of Augustine on Heidegger: The Emergence of an Augustinian Phenomenology*, ed. Craig de Paulo [Lewiston, N.Y.: Edwin Mellen, 2006], 7).

131. McGrath, "The Young Heidegger's Problematic Reading," 8.

132. Heidegger, *The Phenomenology of Religious Life*, 195. "The definition of God as supreme being is the ontotheological proposition that Heidegger rejects when he speaks of the originary and essential responsibility of the Dasein" (Derrida, *The Gift of Death & Literature in Secret*, 33).

133. Heidegger, *The Phenomenology of Religious Life*, 178–80.

134. Nietzsche, "Genealogy of Morality," 421.

135. In chapter 4 I argue that Augustine's method is in fact more rigorously phenomenological than Heidegger's.

136. Heidegger is, of course, not quite as colorful in lambasting the Bishop of Hippo as was his predecessor: "Saint Augustine and the leaders of the Christian movement—oh they are shrewd, shrewd to the point of holiness, these Church Fathers! . . . Nature was neglectful when she made them—she forgot to endow them with even a modest number of respectable, decent, *cleanly* instincts" (Friedrich Nietzsche, "The Anti-Christ," in *The Nietzsche Reader*, ed.

Keith Ansell Pearson and Duncan Large [Oxford: Blackwell, 2006], 497) (emphasis in original text).

137. Heidegger, "What Are Poets For?" 139.

138. Heidegger, *Being and Time*, 294.

139. Ibid.

140. Ibid., especially 303–8.

141. Ibid., 310.

142. Ibid., 311; see also 298.

143. Ibid., 345–48.

144. Ibid., 387–88.

145. McGrath, "Alternative Confessions," 328; see also Fritsch, "Cura et Casus," 19.

146. Esposito, "Memory and Temptation," 293–94.

147. Although Fritsch's understanding of Augustine's "self" is not sufficiently developed and accords too closely with the overly Platonic notion of the self that I rebut in chapter 4 when I return to Augustine on desire, he does offer a helpful summative comment regarding this juxtaposition of Heidegger and Augustine: "Hence, Augustine's confession to God is a dialogue with a personal, loving God and savior. Heidegger's philosophical intentions in reading *Confessions*, however, sever the confessional, singularizing relation, the relation that allows the self to soar above the social and material worlds, from such an expectation. Hope becomes emptied of a transcendent content: *vita beata, veritas, fruitio Dei*: eternal life in God's proximity. What remains is the focus on one's factical self-enactment, as brought to light in genuine self-concern. The action of God, the giving of face, becomes 'naturalized' in the existential care of the self" (Fritsch, "Cura et Casus," 18). Although I concur with McGrath in judging that Heidegger is in fact saying the opposite of Augustine in his unrelenting appeal to an analysis of factical existence devoid of reference to a personal God, I do not accept McGrath's conclusion that "Phenomenology and theology mutually occlude one another" (McGrath, "Alternative Confessions," 329).

148. Ariès, *The Hour of Our Death*, 613.

149. Iain Thomson suggests that Heidegger may not be completely agnostic about "the other side" of death, though his existential analytic does stipulate that death is the horizon of experience; see Iain Thomson, "Can I Die?: Derrida on Heidegger on Death," *Philosophy Today* 43, no. 1 (1999): 29–42. Jacques Choron also offers an interesting comment in regards to the firmness of Heidegger's belief in what his philosophy indicates about death: "In view of Heidegger's emphasis on the anxiety of death, it is only natural to ask whether he is not himself obsessed by the thought of death and the fear of it. Does not what Guardini says about Rilke, with whose thought and feeling Heidegger shows such deep affinity,

apply also to Heidegger, that in spite of his original glorification of death 'one can hear how little he believed his own message and how intensely he was afraid of death'?" (Choron, *Death and Western Thought*, 240).

150. See de Lubac, *The Drama of Atheist Humanism*, 305.

151. Guardini, *Rilke's Duino Elegies*, 304.

152. Derrida, *The Gift of Death & Literature in Secret*, 17.

153. Ibid., 32–35; once again, a reference to Nietzsche's critique of "Christianity's stroke of genius" is in order (see Nietzsche, "Genealogy of Morality," 421).

154. Derrida, *The Gift of Death & Literature in Secret*, 45–53.

155. Furthermore, Augustine himself surpasses Heidegger on strictly phenomenological grounds. In chapter 4 I show the depth of Augustine's phenomenological method with the use of Jean-Luc Marion's reading of the *Confessions* in light of Augustine's unceasing *confessio* alongside Henri de Lubac's appreciation for Augustine's willingness to question himself about the mysterious desire at the base of his *memoria* that ontologically constitutes Augustine outside himself. In this view, Heidegger rather than Augustine forecloses on the process of phenomenological interrogation.

156. Rilke, *Letters of Rainer Maria Rilke, 1910–1926*, 316.

157. Karl Rahner claimed as much in his famous essay on the topic, which I treat in the following chapter.

158. In the preface to his *The Drama of Atheist Humanism*, de Lubac offers a nuanced and direct assessment of the atheistic humanist attempts to conceive of reality—including life and death—without God: "It is not true, as is sometimes said, that man cannot organize the world without God. What is true is that, without God, he can ultimately only organize it against man. Exclusive humanism is inhuman humanism. . . . The earth, which without God could cease being a chaos only to become a prison, is in reality the magnificent and painful field where our eternal being is worked out" (de Lubac, *The Drama of Atheist Humanism*, 14).

159. Guardini, *The Last Things*, 27–28.

Chapter 3. Word of Life

1. See Karl Rahner, *Hearer of the Word: Laying the Foundation for a Philosophy of Religion*, trans. Joseph Donceel (New York: Continuum, 1994), 137.

2. Fritz, "Sublime Apprehension," 73; see also Rahner, *Hearer of the Word*, 98.

3. "The basis of flight from the world constitutes the intrinsic possibility of Ignatian acceptance of the world. . . . Ignatian piety is piety towards the God who is beyond the whole world and who freely reveals himself. In this . . .

is to be found at once the reason for flight from the world and the possibility of an acceptance of the world" (Karl Rahner, "The Ignatian Mysticism of Joy in the World," in *Theological Investigations*, trans. Cornelius Ernst et al., vol. 3 [Limerick, Ireland: Mary Immaculate College, 2000], 283).

4. Karl Rahner, *Spirit in the World*, trans. William Dych (New York: Continuum, 1994), 186.

5. Rahner, *Hearer of the Word*, 35, 70.

6. See ibid., 50–51; cf. Fritz, "Sublime Apprehension," 66–67.

7. Kant's comments on grace are indicative here, for he asserts that "our use of the concept of cause and effect cannot be extended beyond the objects of experience, and hence beyond nature" (Immanuel Kant, *Religion within the Boundaries of Mere Reason: And Other Writings*, trans. Allen Wood and George Di Giovanni [Cambridge: Cambridge University Press, 1999], 72); see also Immanuel Kant, *The Conflict of the Faculties*, trans. Mary Gregor (New York: Abaris, 1979), 75.

8. "The one and true religion contains nothing but laws, i.e., practical principles, of whose unconditional necessity we can become conscious and which we therefore recognize as revealed through pure reason (not empirically)" (Kant, *Religion within the Boundaries of Mere Reason*, 164; see also Kant, *The Conflict of the Faculties*, 133).

9. Rahner defines freedom as "the capacity to make oneself once and for all, the capacity which of its nature is directed towards the freely willed finality of the subject as such" (Karl Rahner, "Theology of Freedom," in *Theological Investigations*, trans. Cornelius Ernst et al., vol. 6 [Limerick, Ireland: Mary Immaculate College, 2000], 183; see also 186); see also Karl Rahner, "The Comfort of Time," in *Theological Investigations*, trans. Cornelius Ernst et al., vol. 3 (Limerick, Ireland: Mary Immaculate College, 2000), 152; Karl Rahner, "The Theological Concept of Concupiscentia," in *Theological Investigations*, trans. Cornelius Ernst et al., vol. 1 (Limerick, Ireland: Mary Immaculate College, 2000), 361; Karl Rahner, "The Dignity and Freedom of Man," in *Theological Investigations*, trans. Cornelius Ernst et al., vol. 2 (Limerick, Ireland: Mary Immaculate College, 2000), 246–47; Karl Rahner, "Guilt-Responsibility-Punishment within the View of Catholic Theology," in *Theological Investigations*, trans. Cornelius Ernst et al., vol. 6 (Limerick, Ireland: Mary Immaculate College, 2000), 200; Peter Phan, *Eternity in Time: A Study of Karl Rahner's Eschatology* (London: Associated University Press, 1988), 51.

10. See Rahner, *Hearer of the Word*, 87, 94, 98.

11. "The end to which the free decision is orientated is that everything which is in man (nature), hence the involuntary act as well, should be the revelation and the expression of what man as person wishes to be; thus that the

free decision should comprehend, transfigure and transfuse the spontaneous act, so that its own reality too should no longer be purely natural but personal" (Rahner, "The Theological Concept of Concupiscentia," 365; cf. 360–61).

12. Karl Rahner, "Theological Considerations Concerning the Moment of Death," in *Theological Investigations*, trans. Cornelius Ernst et al., vol. 2 (Limerick, Ireland: Mary Immaculate College, 2000), 318.

13. See Karl Rahner, "Being Open to God as Ever Greater," in *Theological Investigations*, trans. Cornelius Ernst et al., vol. 7 (Limerick, Ireland: Mary Immaculate College, 2000), 42.

14. Rahner, "Guilt-Responsibility-Punishment," 202.

15. See, among others, Karl Rahner, "The Concept of Mystery in Catholic Theology," in *Theological Investigations*, trans. Cornelius Ernst et al., vol. 4 (Limerick, Ireland: Mary Immaculate College, 2000), 36–73.

16. Jürgen Moltmann, *The Coming of God: Christian Eschatology*, trans. Margaret Kohl (Minneapolis: Fortress, 2004), 75.

17. "If the dead are no longer in the time of the living but in God's time, then they exist in his eternal present. So how long is it from a person's death in time to the End-time raising of the dead? The answer is: just an instant! And if we ask: where are the dead 'now,' in terms of our time?—the answer has to be: they are already in the new world of the resurrection and God's eternal life" (ibid., 102).

18. See, among others, Richard Bauckman, "Eschatology in 'The Coming of God,'" in *God Will Be All in All: The Eschatology of Jürgen Moltmann*, ed. Richard Bauckman (Edinburgh: First Fortress, 2001), 17–18.

19. Richard Bauckman, "Time and Eternity," in *God Will Be All in All: The Eschatology of Jürgen Moltmann*, ed. Richard Bauckman (Edinburgh: First Fortress, 2001), 159–73.

20. At the same time, Moltmann believes that God will complete the good work he has begun when a life is cut short and thus does not reach its fulfillment. Moltmann's view is certainly more theocentric than to hold that a person's history is frozen in eternity upon death, though he leaves much to be desired in terms of speaking of how this completion in God occurs. See Jürgen Moltmann, "To Believe with All Your Senses," in *The Catholic Theological Society of America: Proceedings of the Sixtieth Annual Convention*, ed. Richard Sparks (Berkeley, Calif.: Newman Hall, 2005), 7.

21. Bauckman, "Eschatology," 7.

22. Moltmann, *The Coming of God*, 70–71, 102.

23. Rahner, *Hearer of the Word*, 28, and throughout the work since this is the book's basic thesis.

24. This is not, of course, to suggest that Rahner and Moltmann have anything like antithetical notions of time, but rather that the decisive emphasis in

each is placed on importantly different notes. The resonance between the two comes through in Phan, *Eternity in Time*, 55, before Phan moves on to specify Rahner's notion of time and eternity in relation to freedom and subjectivity.

25. Rahner expresses this view with particular clarity in the following passage: "In every decision we decide about ourselves, not about an action or a thing. . . . We do not merely string out without any connection single actions one after the other. But in every action we set down a law of our whole activity and life. We do not simply perform good or bad actions: we ourselves become good or bad" (Rahner, *Hearer of the Word*, 86; see also Rahner, "Guilt-Responsibility-Punishment," 201; and Rahner, "The Comfort of Time," 151, 157).

26. See Rahner, "The Dignity and Freedom of Man," 247; cf. Phan, *Eternity in Time*, 83, 107. Nicholas Adams argues that Rahner was far too willing to accept his former teacher's understanding of death and the correlative way in which it makes human beings constitutively futural. In Adams's view, Rahner's reliance on Heidegger forces him to take God out of the equation from the outset, without any recourse to substantive retrieval (see Nicholas Adams, "Eschatology Sacred and Profane: The Effects of Philosophy on Theology in Pannenberg, Rahner, and Moltmann," *International Journal of Systematic Theology* 2, no. 3 [2000]: especially 297). While Adams is certainly right to identify the ways in which Rahner's thought draws on Heidegger's existential approach to death, Adams overreaches in his indictment. Rahner's Christologically dependent anthropology makes all the difference when his eschatology is juxtaposed with Heidegger's. For Heidegger, the possibilities for a dialogical constitution of the human person are ruled out from the start, leaving him with an autoteleological entity who closes in on death, whereas Rahner's understanding of the human person builds from the central conviction that he is constitutively the "hearer of [God's] Word."

27. Karl Rahner, *On the Theology of Death*, trans. C. H. Henkey, 2nd ed. (New York: Herder and Herder, 1967), 49. Rahner develops his thoughts on the disintegration of the fallen (albeit perhaps also redeemed) human person especially in his treatment of concupiscence and human freedom (see 47–50); see also Rahner, "The Theological Concept of Concupiscentia"; Rahner, "Theology of Freedom"; and Karl Rahner, "The Sin of Adam," in *Theological Investigations*, trans. Cornelius Ernst et al., vol. 11 (Limerick, Ireland: Mary Immaculate College, 2000), 247–62.

28. Rahner, "Being Open to God as Ever Greater," 37–39. See also Rahner, "The Comfort of Time," 144; cf. Guardini, *The End of the Modern World*, 120–26.

29. Moltmann, *The Coming of God*, 66; cf. Moltmann, "To Believe with All Your Senses," 5. For a dismissal of the doctrine of purgatory, see Jürgen Moltmann and Elisabeth Moltmann-Wendel, "Love, Death, Eternal Life: Theology of

Hope—the Personal Side," in *Love: The Foundation of Hope: The Theology of Jür-gen Moltmann and Elisabeth Moltmann-Wendel*, ed. Frederic Burnham, Charles S. McCoy, and Douglas M. Meeks (San Francisco: Harper & Row, 1988), 13; as well as Moltmann, *The Coming of God*, 97–101; cf. Pierre Benoit, "Resurrec-tion: At the End of Time or Immediately after Death?" *Concilium* 60 (1970): 103–14.

30. See, for example, Karl Rahner, "The Intermediate State," in *Theologi-cal Investigations*, trans. Cornelius Ernst et al., vol. 17 (Limerick, Ireland: Mary Immaculate College, 2000), 114–24; Moltmann refers to Rahner's reservation in *The Coming of God*, 103. I take up the issue of the "intermediate state" more fully toward the end of chapter 6.

31. Moltmann is much more leery of granting any permanent value to human freedom; see, for example, *The Coming of God*, 109.

32. Karl Rahner, "The Body in the Order of Salvation," in *Theological Inves-tigations*, trans. Cornelius Ernst et al., vol. 17 (Limerick, Ireland: Mary Immacu-late College, 2000), 84–88. See also Rahner, *Hearer of the Word*, 87; cf. Phan, *Eternity in Time*, 162.

33. Cf. Moltmann, "To Believe with All Your Senses," 10; and Moltmann, *The Coming of God*, 70–77.

34. Rahner, "The Theological Concept of Concupiscentia," 369; see also Rahner, "The Sin of Adam," 257. I pick up this line of thought again with in-creased intensity in chapter 5.

35. Rahner, "The Sin of Adam," 256, 259–60.

36. Ibid., 258 (emphasis in original text).

37. Rahner, *On the Theology of Death*, 49.

38. Karl Rahner, "The Resurrection of the Body," in *Theological Investiga-tions*, trans. Cornelius Ernst et al., vol. 2 (Limerick, Ireland: Mary Immaculate College, 2000), 214.

39. Dietrich Bonhoeffer speaks of sin in a similar manner, albeit in a some-what incomplete, derivative Augustinian framework in his doctoral dissertation, later published as *The Communion of Saints: A Dogmatic Inquiry into the Sociol-ogy of the Church*, trans. Ronald Smith (New York: Harper & Row, 1963), espe-cially 71–85.

40. Karl Rahner, "Ideas for a Theology of Death," in *Theological Investiga-tions*, trans. Cornelius Ernst et al., vol. 13 (Limerick, Ireland: Mary Immaculate College, 2000), 184.

41. Joseph Ratzinger, *Eschatology: Death and Eternal Life*, ed. Aidan Nichols, trans. Michael Waldstein, 2nd ed. (Washington, D.C.: Catholic University of America Press, 2007), 69–70.

42. Ibid., 72; see also Moltmann, *The Coming of God*, 50–57; and especially Guardini, *The End of the Modern World*, 111, which is an endnote to page 97.

43. In his book on literature, theology, and eschatology, Paul Fiddes argues that an understanding of death allows one to grasp more of the organization and meaning of life (and what one hopes for in the afterlife) in ways similar to how reckoning with the end of a drama allows one to understand the entire story that the end completes. See Paul Fiddes, *The Promised End: Eschatology in Theology and Literature* (Oxford: Blackwell, 2000), especially 69.

44. Gary Anderson, *Sin: A History* (New Haven, Conn.: Yale University Press, 2009), 198.

45. Ibid., 194; cf. 197.

46. Joseph Ratzinger, *Introduction to Christianity*, 2nd ed. (San Francisco: Ignatius, 2004), 282.

47. Anderson, *Sin*, 199.

48. Joseph Ratzinger, *Dogma and Preaching: Applying Christian Doctrine to Daily Life*, ed. Michael Miller, trans. Michael Miller and Matthew O'Connell (San Francisco: Ignatius, 2011), 257.

49. Ratzinger, *Eschatology*, 80–81; see also Ratzinger, *Dogma and Preaching*, 247–48.

50. Ratzinger, *Eschatology*, 82.

51. Cf. Hans Urs von Balthasar, *Mysterium Paschale: The Mystery of Easter*, trans. Aidan Nichols (San Francisco: Ignatius, 2000), 152: "It is true that the Old Testament knows of no 'commerce' between the living God and the realm of the dead. It knows very well, however, the power of God over that realm." It appears, at this point, as though Ratzinger and Balthasar may stand at odds with one another regarding the status of Israel's religious understanding of God's power over death.

52. Ratzinger, *Eschatology*, 83.

53. Ibid., 86.

54. Rowan Williams, *On Christian Theology* (Oxford: Blackwell, 2000), 67–68; cf. Moltmann, *The Coming of God*, 67.

55. Brian Robinette refers to this passage from Williams and proceeds to make a further point about the connection between the experience of life in a situation of lifelessness and the development of the doctrine of creation: "We know from biblical scholarship that the stories of creation were composed subsequent to the events of exodus and covenant, and that only from the point of view of Israel's historic liberation and lived fidelity/infidelity does there emerge a theology of God as creator of the universe. The stories of creation themselves reflect the grammar of exodus and covenant" (Brian Robinette, "The Difference Nothing Makes: 'Creatio Ex Nihilo,'" *Theological Studies*, no. 72 [2011]: 547). Here, as with the articulation of the "communion of saints" as an article of faith, we see how the experience of lived faith clarifies and indeed contributes to the definitive articulation of the original faith that gave context to the experiences themselves.

56. Ratzinger, *Eschatology*, 90–92.

57. Ibid., 89; cf. Moltmann, *The Coming of God*, 79.

58. At this point, the small fissure mentioned above between Ratzinger and Balthasar seems to be healed; see Balthasar, *Mysterium Paschale*, 152. For a masterful study of the hope of resurrection in Israel on the basis of Scripture, see Jon Levenson, *Resurrection and the Restoration of Israel: The Ultimate Victory of the God of Life* (New Haven, Conn.: Yale University Press, 2006).

59. Rahner makes a point about the development of the monotheism of the Jewish religion based first of all on Israel's experience of God's deeds in "Theos in the New Testament," in *Theological Investigations*, trans. Cornelius Ernst et al., vol. 1 (Limerick, Ireland: Mary Immaculate College, 2000), 93–94.

60. See Ratzinger, *Eschatology*, 95–103; cf. Rahner, "The Sin of Adam," 256, 258, 260; and Rahner, "The Resurrection of the Body," 214.

61. Ratzinger, *Eschatology*, 93.

62. See especially Ratzinger, *Introduction to Christianity*, 293–301.

63. See Balthasar, *Mysterium Paschale*, 148.

64. See Ratzinger, *Eschatology*, 156, where he comments on this point in relation to Genesis 3.

65. See Ratzinger, *Introduction to Christianity*, 298–301.

66. Rahner, "Theos in the New Testament," 125.

67. One of the many places in which Balthasar critiques Rahner's soteriology is in a footnote to a passage in which he is speaking of the uniqueness of Jesus to vicariously bear the collective sin of the world. The entire section seems to be a critique of Rahner, whose own view is first rehearsed by proxy and then exceeded in decisive fashion to move toward more "sufficient christological depth" (Hans Urs von Balthasar, *The Glory of the Lord: A Theological Aesthetics, Volume VII: Theology: The New Covenant*, ed. Joseph Fessio, trans. Brian McNeil [San Francisco: Ignatius, 1990], 218). Another critique of Rahner's soteriology occurs in an endnote to a chapter on Good Friday (the note refers back to page 137) where Balthasar accuses Rahner of purveying "a minimalist interpretation" of several texts, including 2 Corinthians 5:21, to which I refer momentarily, thus seeming to limit Christ's solidarity with us and the power of his filial obedience to the Father that secures the glorious exchange in the union of natures in Christ's person. Balthasar believes that Rahner's view unduly portrays the descent into hell as more of a "cosmic Spring-time" than the final pitch of obedience suffered in love on behalf of the Son (see Balthasar, *Mysterium Paschale*, 146–47).

68. Hans Urs von Balthasar, *Theo-Drama: Theological Dramatic Theory, Volume V: The Last Act*, trans. Graham Harrison (San Francisco: Ignatius, 1998), 120.

69. Hans Urs von Balthasar, *New Elucidations*, trans. Mary Theresilde Skerry (San Francisco: Ignatius, 1986), 115–16; Balthasar, *Mysterium Paschale*, 119.

70. That Balthasar engages in speculative theologizing is beyond dispute. What matters is how he engages in such speculative enterprises, as well as the safeguards he observes to keep his probative work faithful to the living tradition of the Church. Jennifer Newsome Martin provides an excellent, concise summary of the four principal ways in which Balthasar maintains the requisite balance between the "'fixed' and 'mobile' aspects of the living Church tradition" (18), thus protecting his theology from illegitimate speculative modes. The four ways that Martin enumerates are as follows: (1) Balthasar scrupulously grounds his theology in biblical exegesis; (2) Balthasar starts his theology with and self-consciously constrains his theology by what is given in sacred revelation; (3) Balthasar refuses to manipulate the "hard data of Christianity" with any "ahistorical, abstracted human constructions of, say, natural religion or philosophies of history" (19); and (4) Balthasar objects to speculative doctrines of God that make God and creation coincident (Jennifer Newsome Martin, "Hans Urs von Balthasar and the Press of Speculative Russian Religious Philosophy" [Ph.D. diss., University of Notre Dame, 2012], 18–21); see also John Thiel, *Senses of Tradition: Continuity and Development in Catholic Faith* (New York: Oxford University Press, 2000), 197; Hans Urs von Balthasar, *Theo-Logic: Theological Logical Theory, Volume III: The Spirit of Truth*, trans. Graham Harrison (San Francisco: Ignatius, 2005), 167–84, 429; Balthasar, *Theo-Drama V*, 13–14; Hans Urs von Balthasar, *Theo-Drama: Theological Dramatic Theory, Volume III: The Dramatis Personae: The Person in Christ*, trans. Graham Harrison (San Francisco: Ignatius, 1993), 508; Hans Urs von Balthasar, *Theo-Drama: Theological Dramatic Theory, Volume II: The Dramatis Personae: Man in God*, trans. Graham Harrison (San Francisco: Ignatius, 1990), 419; Hans Urs von Balthasar, *The Glory of the Lord: A Theological Aesthetics, Volume V: The Realm of Metaphysics in the Modern Age*, ed. John Riches, trans. Erasmo Leiva-Merikakis (San Francisco: Ignatius, 1991), 44–50, 207–9, 228, 248; Balthasar, *Glory of the Lord VII*, 15; and Hans Urs von Balthasar, *The Glory of the Lord: A Theological Aesthetics, Volume I: Seeing the Form*, ed. John Kenneth Riches, trans. Erasmo Leiva-Merikakis (San Francisco: Ignatius, 2009), 165.

71. Anne Hunt argues that Balthasar's main contribution to modern theology is in rigorously thinking of God as love rather than God as being, meaning that Balthasar seeks to pattern his theology on the content and logic of sacred revelation rather than attempting to make God fit into a predetermined philosophical framework (Anne Hunt, *The Trinity and the Paschal Mystery: A Development in Recent Catholic Theology* [Collegeville, Minn.: Liturgical, 1997], 82); see also Hans Urs von Balthasar, *Love Alone Is Credible*, trans. D. C. Schindler (San Francisco: Ignatius, 2005), 47–60.

72. Balthasar describes theology's responsibility to revelation thusly: "Theology possesses in the form of revelation itself the unmistakable pattern for its

own structure. . . . The proportions of revelation should be those of theology . . . [with] a delicate sense of all [revelation's] nuances" (Hans Urs von Balthasar, *Explorations in Theology, Volume 1: The Word Made Flesh*, trans. A. V. Littledale and Alexander Dru [San Francisco: Ignatius, 1989], 196); see also Graham Ward, "Kenosis: Death, Discourse, and Resurrection," in *Balthasar at the End of Modernity* (Edinburgh: T & T Clark, 1999), 45–46. Guardini articulates a strikingly similar opinion in *The End of the Modern World*, 143.

73. The most forceful critique of Balthasar's theology of Holy Saturday comes from Alyssa Pitstick, who asserts that Balthasar not only went against the Church's tradition with his work, but in fact did so knowingly and willingly. Edward Oakes rebuts these accusations in a two-part debate with Pitstick (see Edward Oakes and Alyssa Pitstick, "Balthasar, Hell, and Heresy: An Exchange," *First Things: A Monthly Journal of Religion and Public Life* 168 [2006]: 25–32; and Edward Oakes and Alyssa Pitstick, "More on Balthasar, Hell, and Heresy," *First Things: A Monthly Journal of Religion and Public Life* 169 [2006]: 16–18). In her book-length treatment of Balthasar's theology of Holy Saturday, Pitstick goes into greater detail regarding what she believes to be Balthasar's fundamental errors. While a full engagement with Pitstick on these critical points would take more space than I am able to allocate in this study, it is worth noting that while Pitstick's criticisms appear to have some merit when taken in isolation, their power significantly attenuates when set against the whole of Balthasar's work. While Balthasar is certainly probing uncharted territory with his theology of Holy Saturday, he is doing so in accordance with what he believes is his vocation as an ecclesial theologian—albeit at the rim of permissibility for such a theologian—in attempting to systematically think through that which has been revealed, especially where that revelation is most difficult to understand and is least well treated (for Pitstick's full argument, see Alyssa Pitstick, *Light in the Darkness: Hans Urs von Balthasar and the Catholic Doctrine of Christ's Descent into Hell* [Grand Rapids, Mich.: Eerdmans, 2007]). Other notes of concern regarding Balthasar's treatment of the descent into hell include a reservation from Hunt, who thinks that Balthasar may in fact give sin some ontological status in Christ's *visio mortis* (see Hunt, *The Trinity*, 73). John Saward is concerned that Balthasar's Christ is passive in death and does not preach, although Balthasar would respond that Christ does indeed preach through the silent obedience of his solidarity with the solitary dead (for Saward's reservation, see John Saward, *The Mysteries of March: Hans Urs von Balthasar on the Incarnation and Easter* [Washington, D.C.: Catholic University of America Press, 1990], 123). Ward thinks Balthasar is vulnerable in relation to the *filioque* and that he at times appeals to knowledge of the Trinity that is beyond the data made available in the economy (see Ward, "Kenosis," 50–51).

74. See especially Balthasar, *Theo-Drama V*, 224–26, 243–46; and Balthasar, *Mysterium Paschale*, 62; cf. Ward, "Kenosis," 32–49.

75. Balthasar, *Theo-Drama V*, 168–75, 227–29; see also Hans Urs von Balthasar, *Theo-Drama: Theological Dramatic Theory, Volume IV: The Action*, trans. Graham Harrison (San Francisco: Ignatius, 1994), 323–24.

76. Balthasar, *Theo-Drama IV*, 336; cf. Ward, "Kenosis," 26–27; and for an account of the influence of Luther's theology of the cross on the anthropocentric thrust of Protestant theology, see Balthasar, *Mysterium Paschale*, 139–40.

77. Balthasar, *Theo-Drama III*, 526–27; Balthasar, *Theo-Drama IV*, 320–24, 336. When Balthasar claims that he is attempting to understand eschatology in theocentric and Trinitarian terms, rather than in anthropocentric terms, one is reminded of his varied critiques of Rahner's eschatology, especially when one refers back to Balthasar's comments about Rahner's Trinitarian theology in *Theo-Drama III*, previously cited in this note (see also Balthasar, *Theo-Drama V*, 244).

78. Balthasar, *Mysterium Paschale*, vii–viii.

79. In order to recover the necessary tension required of the orthodox doctrine of God's immutability, Balthasar recurs to Patristic teaching in which "God is both impassible and (in the Son) passible" (216). The nuanced teaching of the fathers distinguishes between involuntary influences that act on God from the outside and freely chosen passivity in God that depends on "some prior, 'active', free decision" (222). This view exceeds the distinctions between "immutability" and "mutability" since the real issue becomes divine freedom. In God's absolute freedom, God can "suffer" according to God's own free election (see Balthasar, *Theo-Drama V*, 216–23, 243–46); see also Balthasar, *Mysterium Paschale*, 28, 35; cf. Ward, "Kenosis," 43.

80. See Balthasar, *Theo-Drama V*, 67.

81. Among others, see Balthasar, *Mysterium Paschale*, 23–24; Balthasar, *Theo-Drama V*, 256–59; Balthasar, *Glory of the Lord VII*, 211–13; and Hans Urs von Balthasar, *Credo: Meditations on the Apostles' Creed*, trans. David Kipp (San Francisco: Ignatius, 2005), 46.

82. See Hunt, *The Trinity*, 59.

83. Balthasar, *Theo-Drama V*, 256–58; cf. 249–51, 261. See also Balthasar, *New Elucidations*, 123–24; cf. Jean-Luc Marion, *God Without Being: Hors-Texte*, trans. Thomas A. Carlson (Chicago: University of Chicago Press, 1995), 142.

84. Balthasar, *Mysterium Paschale*, 34–35.

85. Ibid., 72; cf. Hunt, *The Trinity*, 72.

86. Balthasar, *Glory of the Lord VII*, 214; cf. Martin, "Hans Urs von Balthasar," 256.

87. Balthasar, *Theo-Drama V*, 120.

88. Balthasar goes to great lengths to show the inseparability of Christ's mission and person in *Theo-Drama III*, 149–201.

89. Balthasar, *Mysterium Paschale*, 88–91, 100–107; Balthasar, *Explorations in Theology I*, 93; Balthasar, *Theo-Drama V*, 106. Elsewhere, Balthasar tellingly contrasts the Son's manner of being to that of a capitalist who clings to possessions as his own private reserve (see Balthasar, *Credo*, 46).

90. Juan Sara, "Descensus ad Infernos, Dawn of Hope: Aspects of the Theology of Holy Saturday in the Trilogy of Hans Urs von Balthasar," *Communio* 32 (2005): 552.

91. On this day Christ expresses his communion with the Father through the "obedience of a corpse" (Saward, *The Mysteries of March*, 120).

92. Sara, "Descensus ad Infernos," 561; compare this statement with these words from Balthasar: "the entire abyss of man's refusal of God's love has been crossed over: in other words, that God is solidary with us not only in what is symptomatic of sin, the punishment of sin, but also in co-experiencing sin, in the 'peirasmos' of the very essence of that negation—though without 'committing' (Hebrews 4:15) sin himself" (Balthasar, *Mysterium Paschale*, 137). The imagery of loading the weight of sin upon the Son calls to mind the religious function of the scapegoat in Leviticus 16:21–22 (see Anderson, *Sin*, 6, 15–16).

93. Balthasar, *Mysterium Paschale*, 159.

94. Balthasar, *Theo-Drama V*, 245, 267–68; cf. Saward, *The Mysteries of March*, 115–16.

95. See Fiddes, *The Promised End*, especially 65–74.

96. In his essay on "Shame," Primo Levi testified that as *Häftlinge*, "We had not only forgotten our country and our culture, but also our family, our past, the future we had imagined for ourselves, because, like animals, we were confined to the present moment" (Primo Levi, *The Drowned and the Saved*, trans. Raymond Rosenthal [New York: Vintage, 1998], 75).

97. In his essay "Argon," Levi translates "baptized" as "literally, 'destroyed'" (in Primo Levi, *The Periodic Table*, trans. Raymond Rosenthal [New York: Everyman's Library, 1996], 16). The emphasis on destruction by means of Baptism redounds on the marred history of Christian-Jewish relations, especially up to and including the early twentieth century. A habitual, reflexive tendency to force Baptism on Jews—at least in the discursive sense whereby the Christian standards of evaluation would be used to categorically measure and find wanting the dignity of the Jews, typically for self-interested or apologetic purposes—finds an echo here. The Christian treatment of Jews by way of instinctive contempt is possibly tantamount to a tradition of dictating a restricted and restrictive identity to the Jews. See Jules Isaac, *The Teaching of Contempt: Christian Roots of Anti-Semitism*, trans. Helen Weaver (New York: Holt, Rinehart and Winston, 1964), especially 21–33.

98. Primo Levi, *If This Is a Man*, trans. Stuart Woolf (London: Abacus, 1987), 28.

99. Ibid., 33.

100. Ibid., 34; see also Edith Wyschogrod, *Spirit in Ashes: Hegel, Heidegger, and Man-Made Mass Death* (New Haven, Conn.: Yale University Press, 1985), 207–10. In his last completed book, Levi describes the tattoo and the erasure of the name: "The operation was not very painful and lasted no more than a minute, but it was traumatic. Its symbolic meaning was clear to everyone: this is an indelible mark, you will never leave here; this is the mark with which slaves are branded and cattle sent to slaughter, and that is what you have become. You no longer have a name; this is your new name" (Levi, *The Drowned and the Saved*, 119).

101. Levi, *If This Is a Man*, 33.

102. Ratzinger, *Introduction to Christianity*, 133–35, 158–60; Joseph Ratzinger, *The God of Jesus Christ: Meditations on the Triune God*, trans. Brian McNeil (San Francisco: Ignatius, 2008), 21–25. Ratzinger is acutely attuned to the importance of names and the corresponding catastrophic danger in performing the debasing act that the *Lager* repeated for millions of *Häftlinge*—that is, the violent act of erasing a name. In commenting on this point of contact between Levi and Ratzinger—who is (not insignificantly) both German and the former pope—I am not seeking to appropriate Levi to the Christian narrative, a narrative that Ratzinger is self-consciously articulating. Rather, the import of such a connection, fleeting though it may prove to be, is at the very least the elucidation of the fact that the *Lager* experience to which Levi testifies is not contained within the *Lager*; here and now, the fear is repeated and confronted, even by the ecclesial head of the Church. The assault on names that occurred in an efficient and direct manner within the *Lager* is manifestly a threat to the world as a whole today through less readily discernible means.

103. Levi, *If This Is a Man*, 112.

104. Ibid., 35.

105. Ibid., 44.

106. See ibid., 96; cf. Giorgio Agamden, *Remnants of Auschwitz: The Witness and the Archive*, trans. Daniel Heller-Roazen (New York: Zone, 2002), 47.

107. Balthasar, *Mysterium Paschale*, 162–63. This passage is replete with biblical citations (more than thirty), which I have removed for ease of reading. See Balthasar's text for the complete list.

108. Ibid., 165.

109. Ibid., 251; see also Balthasar, *Theo-Drama III*, 508–9.

110. Balthasar, *Theo-Drama IV*, 338; see also Jean-Luc Marion, *The Idol and Distance: Five Studies*, trans. Thomas A. Carlson, 2nd ed. (New York: Fordham University Press, 2001), 215.

268   Notes to Pages 91–93

111. Balthasar, *Mysterium Paschale*, 79; Balthasar, *Glory of the Lord VII*, 234; and Hans Urs von Balthasar, *A Theological Anthropology* (Eugene, Ore.: Wipf & Stock, 2010), 240; cf. Ward, "Kenosis," 47–48; Sara, "Descensus ad Infernos," 561; and Hunt, *The Trinity*, 59.

112. Hereby we approach the deepest meaning of the triad of Lukan parables to which Charles Péguy refers in his poem on the virtue of hope, to which Balthasar gives extended treatment in *Theo-Drama V*. Through a Balthasarian lens, we glimpse the God who personally goes in search of his lost sheep (Luke 15:1–7), who sweeps her house for her lost coin (Luke 15:8–10), and who stands in wait and in hope for the return of his lost son (Luke 15:11–32). God comes for us, God searches for us, God waits for us. Christ embodies this profound urgency of love. See Balthasar, *Theo-Drama V*, 186.

113. Balthasar, *Theo-Drama III*, 531.

114. Ibid., 508–9.

115. Ibid., 514.

116. Balthasar gives eloquent articulation to this paradoxical precondition for being God's dialogue partner in *A Theological Anthropology*, 229.

117. Balthasar, *Theo-Drama IV*, 328–32.

118. Balthasar, *Theo-Drama V*, 278. We might also add words from C. S. Lewis regarding this all-important choice not to refuse God: "There are only two kinds of people in the end: those who say to God, 'Thy will be done,' and those to whom God says, '*Thy* will be done.' All that are in Hell, choose it. Without that self-choice there could be no Hell" (C. S. Lewis, *The Great Divorce* [San Francisco: HarperOne, 2000], 75).

119. See Balthasar, *Theo-Drama III*, 245–50.

120. Ibid., 36.

121. Ibid., 249; cf. 509.

122. Ibid., 245.

123. Ibid., 245–46. At this point, it is possible and perhaps even fitting to initiate a very important discussion about Baptism in relation to dying with Christ and into Christ's life; however, in order to properly emphasize the intrinsic connection between death with Christ in Baptism and the sharing in Christ's mission in the Eucharist, I postpone this discussion until chapter 5, at which point I will also be able to make use of the "ontology by desire" that I develop in chapter 4. It is also important to briefly address the charge of supporting "apokatastasis," to which Balthasar has on occasion been subjected. The unlimited offer of the gift of salvation does not imply that it will be universally accepted (see ibid., 36). Likewise, when Balthasar appeals to Edith Stein's meditation on God's persuasiveness, he is marveling at the gentle power of God's love in juxtaposition to our feeble attempts to resist such love. That God would allow such

acts of resistance to oppose his good will is absurd, and yet God's love is so deep that it will not force itself (see Hans Urs von Balthasar, *Dare We Hope "That All Men Be Saved?"; With, A Short Discourse on Hell*, trans. David Kipp and Lothar Krauth [San Francisco: Ignatius, 1988], 218–21).

124. Balthasar, *A Theological Anthropology*, 240.

125. Balthasar, *Mysterium Paschale*, 138.

126. The depth of this "loneliest loneliness" that Christ assumes in love far exceeds that which Heidegger tried to philosophize after Nietzsche (see Heidegger, "Nietzsche, Volume II," 25; cf. Fritz, "Sublime Apprehension," 172).

127. Balthasar, *A Theological Anthropology*, 233; cf. Augustine, *The Trinity*, ed. John Rotelle, trans. Edmund Hill (Hyde Park, N.Y.: New City, 2012), 417 [XV.4.22]; and Augustine, *City of God*, trans. Henry Bettenson (New York: Penguin, 2003), 451–53 [XI.21].

128. Balthasar, *Theo-Drama V*, 506.

129. Rahner, "The Eternal Significance of the Humanity of Jesus," 43.

130. See Ratzinger, *Eschatology*, 116.

131. Brian Robinette, *Grammars of Resurrection: A Christian Theology of Presence and Absence* (New York: Herder and Herder, 2009), 382; see also Robinette, "The Difference Nothing Makes," 545–46.

132. Robinette, *Grammars of Resurrection*, 361.

133. Ratzinger, *Eschatology*, 113; cf. Robinette, *Grammars of Resurrection*, 41, 47.

134. Marion, *The Idol and Distance*, 166.

135. Thomas Aquinas, *Of God and His Creatures: An Annotated Translation of "The Summa Contra Gentiles" of Saint Thomas Aquinas*, trans. Joseph Rickaby (Whitefish, Mont.: Kessinger, 2010), 85.

136. See Thomas Aquinas, "Appendix A: Summa Theologiae 1.45.5," in *Aquinas on Creation*, trans. Steven Baldner and William Carroll (Toronto: Pontifical Institute of Medieval Studies, 1997), 111–12.

137. Thomas Aquinas, "Writings on the 'Sentences' of Peter Lombard 2.1.1," in *Aquinas on Creation*, trans. Steven Baldner and William Carroll (Toronto: Pontifical Institute of Medieval Studies, 1997), 75.

138. In book XII of his *City of God*, Augustine argues this point with great sophistication (see Augustine, *City of God*, 471–509).

139. The question of "why" is the very question that Nietzsche asserts is born of the most perverse mythology: the mythology of "God," who is imagined to be the guarantor of meaning, purpose, and intention. Among other sources, see Nietzsche, "The Gay Science," 219. Augustine takes precisely the opposite position, arguing that questioning the world is proper to the fundamental character of the world and that all questions about the world ultimately lead back to God's

intention in creating the world. He presents this line of questioning in especially compelling fashion in book XI of *City of God*. Denys Turner touches on the decisive difference between an atheist like Nietzsche and a believer like Augustine (see Denys Turner, *Faith Seeking* [London: SCM, 2012], 11). For more on God's absolute freedom in regards to the act of creation, see Robinette, *Grammars of Resurrection*, 362; and James Alison, *The Joy of Being Wrong: Original Sin Through Easter Eyes* (New York: Herder and Herder, 1998), 99.

140. Robinette, "The Difference Nothing Makes," 545–46.

141. Ratzinger, *The God of Jesus Christ*, 24; see also Benedict XVI, *Jesus of Nazareth, Part I: From the Baptism in the Jordan to the Transfiguration* (New York: Doubleday, 2007), 133; and Ratzinger, *Introduction to Christianity*, 133; cf. Williams, *On Christian Theology*, 73–74.

142. See Robinette, *Grammars of Resurrection*, 41.

143. Balthasar, *Theo-Drama V*, 375; cf. Robinette, "The Difference Nothing Makes," 555.

144. Balthasar, *A Theological Anthropology*, 233; cf. Ward, "Kenosis," 45–46.

145. See Robinette, *Grammars of Resurrection*, 162, 374.

146. Balthasar, *Theo-Drama V*, 331.

147. Ibid., 502.

148. Balthasar, on the other hand, does not miss this note (see Balthasar, *Glory of the Lord I*, 155).

149. On this point, Robinette presents a Rahnerian view of freedom and human subjectivity in regards to both creation and resurrection (see Robinette, *Grammars of Resurrection*, 161, 381).

150. See Williams, *On Christian Theology*, 76; and Balthasar, *Theo-Drama V*, 485–87.

Chapter 4. Dispossessing Desire

1. See Augustine, *City of God*, 473 [XII.2]; cf. 572 [XIV.13].

2. Karl Rahner defends this coordination of theological categories in "The Hermeneutics of Eschatological Assertions," in *Theological Investigations*, trans. Cornelius Ernst et al., vol. 4 (Limerick, Ireland: Mary Immaculate College, 2000); see especially 335.

3. See John 4:7–26; 6:24, 35; 7:38–39; Isaiah 44:3–4; 55:1–3; 58:10–14; Psalm 1:3–4.

4. Something of this same sentiment is captured powerfully in Teresa's acclamation: "Here this great God, who holds back the spring of water and doesn't allow the sea to go beyond its boundaries, lets loose the springs from

which water in this trough flows. With a powerful impulse, a huge wave rises up so forcefully that it lifts high this little bark that is our soul" (Teresa of Avila, *The Interior Castle*, trans. Kieran Kavanaugh and Otilio Rodriguez [New York: Paulist, 1979], 134).

5. Karl Rahner, "Experiencing Easter," in *Theological Investigations*, trans. Cornelius Ernst et al., vol. 7 (Limerick, Ireland: Mary Immaculate College, 2000), 164; see also Rowan Williams, *Resurrection: Interpreting the Easter Gospel* (New York: Pilgrim, 1984), 42.

6. N. T. Wright, *The Resurrection of the Son of God*, Christian Origins and the Question of God: vol. 3 (Minneapolis: Fortress, 2003), 717; see also 706.

7. Ibid., 680.

8. Ibid., 682; see also Benedict XVI, *Jesus of Nazareth, Part II: Holy Week: From the Entrance into Jerusalem to the Resurrection* (San Francisco: Ignatius, 2011), 266–68.

9. Wright, *The Resurrection of the Son of God*, 658 (emphasis in original text).

10. Ibid., 667; cf. Balthasar, *Mysterium Paschale*, 205.

11. Benedict XVI, *Jesus of Nazareth II*, 274–75; cf. Rahner, "Experiencing Easter," 165; and Karl Rahner, *Foundations of Christian Faith: An Introduction to the Idea of Christianity* (New York: Crossroad, 1994), 277.

12. See Wright, *The Resurrection of the Son of God*, 712, as well as 680–82; cf. Benedict XVI, *Jesus of Nazareth II*, 242–43.

13. John Thiel, *Icons of Hope: The "Last Things" in Catholic Imagination* (Notre Dame, Ind.: University of Notre Dame Press, 2013), 46–47; see also Thiel, "For What May We Hope?" 534.

14. Thiel, *Icons of Hope*, 44; see also Thiel, "For What May We Hope?," 531–32. Balthasar observes the importance of the establishment of Jesus's identity in the resurrection appearances in *Mysterium Paschale*, 218–19; cf. Hans Urs von Balthasar, *A Theology of History* (San Francisco: Ignatius, 1994), 83–93.

15. Benedict XVI, *Jesus of Nazareth II*, 266.

16. The appearances to Paul will not be treated here alongside the appearances in the Gospels; therefore, I refer the reader to ibid., 263–65; Wright, *The Resurrection of the Son of God*, 375–98.

17. See Wright, *The Resurrection of the Son of God*, 657.

18. See Benedict XVI, *Jesus of Nazareth II*, 254; and Ratzinger, *The God of Jesus Christ*, 99–101; cf. Louis-Marie Chauvet, *Symbol and Sacrament: A Sacramental Reinterpretation of the Christian Experience*, trans. Patrick Madigan and Madeleine Beaumont (Collegeville, Minn.: Liturgical, 1995), 164–66.

19. See Balthasar, *Mysterium Paschale*, 220.

20. Augustine speaks of this blindness in relation to Christ's power. Christ eludes the disciples' recognition as they fixate on other details so as to reveal

himself to them as he refreshes and redeems what they are looking for and the way in which they look (see Augustine, *City of God*, 1061 [XXII.19]; cf. Balthasar, *A Theology of History*, 85).

21. See Wright, *The Resurrection of the Son of God*, 659–61.

22. Williams, *Resurrection*, 44–45.

23. Balthasar speaks of the transformation that occurs with Mary whereby this spark of presence changes empty absence of the search for the dead body into fulfilled absence of her ungraspable teacher (see Balthasar, *New Elucidations*, 58–60). Augustine speaks of the sacramental relationship between the Lord's bodily resurrection and our inner resurrection in regards to the way in which we seek and desire, specifically in reference to this episode with Mary Magdalene (see Augustine, *The Trinity*, 158 [IV.6]).

24. I refer the reader back again to the meditation on death and Christian hope that Guardini provides in *The Last Things*, 27–28.

25. Ratzinger claims that the entire Gospel builds toward this moment when sensing becomes worship at the recognition of God's glory (see Ratzinger, *Dogma and Preaching*, 303); cf. Luke 24:36–43, in which Jesus offers his wounds to the disciples so they might recognize him.

26. For the decisiveness of "mission" in the Easter event, see Balthasar, *Mysterium Paschale*, 224–25; cf. Balthasar, *A Theology of History*, 89–90.

27. See Williams, *Resurrection*, 34–35 and 88–89; cf. Robinette, *Grammars of Resurrection*, 76–77.

28. Robinette, *Grammars of Resurrection*, 7; cf. Pheme Perkins, *The Resurrection: New Testament Witness and Contemporary Reflection* (New York: Doubleday, 1984), 18; Northrop Frye, *The Great Code: The Bible and Literature* (San Diego: Harcourt, 1982), 171–72; Rahner, "Experiencing Easter," 165; Rahner, "The Hermeneutics of Eschatological Assertions," 342–43; and Balthasar, *Mysterium Paschale*, 189–290.

29. Rahner, "Experiencing Easter," 164.

30. Balthasar, *Mysterium Paschale*, 214.

31. See Robinette, *Grammars of Resurrection*, 348–49.

32. Wright, *The Resurrection of the Son of God*, 733.

33. See ibid., 717; and Williams, *Resurrection*, 120.

34. Ratzinger's definition of faith is relevant here since he says that "Faith is thereby defined as taking up a position, as taking a stand trustfully on the ground of the word of God" (Ratzinger, *Introduction to Christianity*, 69).

35. See Rahner, "Experiencing Easter," 166.

36. I deal with these matters in far greater detail in chapter 5.

37. This is in fact the main topic of chapter 5.

38. Augustine, *Teaching Christianity: De Doctrina Christiana*, trans. Edmund Hill (Hyde Park, N.Y.: New City, 1996), 111 [I.12] and 219–20 [IV.16.33]; see also Benedict XVI, *Jesus of Nazareth II*, 276.

39. Ratzinger, *Introduction to Christianity*, 79.

40. Benedict XVI, *Jesus of Nazareth II*, 274.

41. See Williams, *Resurrection*, 83; cf. Henri de Lubac, *The Mystery of the Supernatural*, trans. Rosemary Sheed (New York: Herder and Herder, 1998), 224–25.

42. Rahner, *On the Theology of Death*, 49.

43. T. S. Eliot, *Four Quartets* (New York: Harcourt, 1971), 59; cf., among other similar constructions, Augustine's analysis of the change in his desire from its dissipation in many things to its concentration in the one simple and necessary thing: "I had offered sacrifice, slaying my old nature, and hoping in you as I began to give my mind to the new life, there you had begun to make me feel your sweetness and had given me joy in my heart. As I read these words outwardly and experienced their truth inwardly I shouted with joy, and lost my desire to dissipate myself amid a profusion of earthly goods, eating up time as I was myself eaten by it; for in your eternal simplicity I now had a different wheat and wine and oil" (Augustine, *The Confessions*, 178 [IX.10]).

44. I will continue to employ the Latin term *memoria* rather than the English translation "memory" so as to remain cognizant of the fact that that which Augustine treats is broader and richer than what the English term typically communicates.

45. See, for example, Augustine, *The Confessions*, 202–3 [X.9–7.11].

46. Throughout this section, I include citations for *The Confessions* parenthetically within the body of the text itself. I continue to rely on Maria Boulding's 1997 translation, published in 1998 by Vintage, which I have cited previously within this present chapter as well as in preceding chapters.

47. The turn "inward" into the fields of memory marks the beginning of this particular quest (see Augustine, *The Confessions*, 204 [X.8.12]).

48. I use "memory"/*memoria* and "mind" somewhat interchangeably throughout since Augustine ultimately claims that "Mind and memory, however, are one and the same" (210 [X.14.21]). Jean-Luc Marion offers a more nuanced interpretation of this apparent tautology when he corrects what might otherwise be the typical way of giving some order to these two things in considering the *memoria* as one faculty of the *mens*. "For Saint Augustine," he says, "the 'cogito' . . . does not encompass 'memoria' as one of its many modes (imagination, sensation, will, understanding, etc.); rather, 'memoria' encompasses all the 'cogitatio' because it alone assures to it the unity of its flux by temporalizing

it" (Jean-Luc Marion, *In the Self's Place: The Approach of Saint Augustine*, trans. Jeffrey Kosky [Stanford, Calif.: Stanford University Press, 2012], 72). The way in which this temporalization occurs is through the memory of the immemorial that is the end and guiding element of Augustine's quest, but I delay discussion of this matter until later in this section.

49. The status of Augustine's Platonic pedigree comes into play here, with Phillip Cary going so far as to claim that Augustine's dependence on Plotinian thought led him to essentially invent the idea of an "inner self" centuries before Locke and Descartes would codify such an opinion (see Phillip Cary, *Augustine's Invention of the Inner Self: The Legacy of a Christian Platonist* [Oxford: Oxford University Press, 2000]). A direct rebuttal of Cary's claim appears in John Cavadini, "Review of Phillip Cary's 'Augustine's Invention of the Inner Self: The Legacy of a Christian Platonist,'" *Modern Theology* 18 (2002), especially 428; and even more forcefully in John Cavadini, "The Darkest Enigma: Reconsidering the Self in Augustine's Thought," *Augustinian Studies* 38, no. 1 (2007): 119–32; cf. Gerald Schlabach, "Augustine's Hermeneutic of Humility: An Alternative to Moral Imperialism and Moral Relativism," *Journal of Religious Ethics* 22, no. 2 (1994): 315–16. For Hans Urs von Balthasar's elucidation of how Augustine borrows from yet decisively exceeds the teaching of Plotinus, see Balthasar, *A Theological Anthropology*, 20–27.

50. Cf. Augustine, *City of God*, 371 [X.1]; and Marion, *In the Self's Place*, 92–96. Here and throughout, when I employ the term "desire" I intend the definition of the term in the general sense (*desiderium*) as the direction of the will toward some end. According to moral theology, I would also stipulate that this end is worthy of being sought (see Michael Figura, "Concupiscence and Desire from the Point of View of Theological Anthropology," *Communio*, no. 27 [Spring 2000]: 9).

51. Marion attempts to articulate the paradoxical quality of Augustine's desire in *In the Self's Place*, 83.

52. See Augustine, *City of God*, 557 [XIV.7]; cf. Jean-Luc Marion, "Resting, Moving, Loving: The Access to the Self According to Saint Augustine," *Journal of Religion* 91, no. 1 (2011): 36–38; and Marion, *In the Self's Place*, 265–82.

53. For Augustine's theory of signs (both natural and conventional), see Augustine, *Teaching Christianity: De Doctrina Christiana*, 129f. [II.1.1]; cf. Augustine, *The Trinity*, 408 [XV.9.15]; and Cavadini, "The Darkest Enigma," 125–26. Although I will not engage Henri de Lubac's Augustinian retrieval for the renewal of the Catholic understanding of the relationship between nature and grace until later, on this particular point it is worth referring the reader to de Lubac's comments on human desire and the inability of reason without

revelation to understand this desire; see de Lubac, *The Mystery of the Super-natural*, 207–15.

54. Augustine, *The Trinity*, 68 [I.3.5; see also IX.1.1 and XV.2.2]; cf. Khaled Anatolios, "Quest, Questions, and Christ in Augustine's 'Confessions,'" *Logos: A Journal of Catholic Thought and Culture* 3, no. 2 (2000): 67.

55. Cf. John Cavadini, "Book Two: Augustine's Book of Shadows," in *A Reader's Companion to Augustine's "Confessions,"* ed. Kim Paffenroth and Robert Kennedy (Louisville, Ky.: Westminster John Knox, 2003), 26–27.

56. One might recall the famous sermon of John Henry Newman—an Augustinian thinker in his own right—in which he contends that, "even suppos-ing a man of unholy life were suffered to enter heaven, 'he would not be happy there'; so that it would be no mercy to permit him to enter" (John Henry New-man, "Holiness Necessary for Future Blessedness," in *Selected Sermons, Prayers, and Devotions* [New York: Vintage, 1999], 6).

57. See Marion, *In the Self's Place*, 238.

58. Of course, the distance between pride and humility is immeasurable, which makes the truth of grace at once awe-inspiring and dreadful as it beckons and accuses in the same breath (see ibid., 112–13).

59. The repetition of the word *subito* throughout book VIII, as well as the intentionally quickened and urgent pace of the moments of "conversion" within the stories contained within this book are indicative of the immeasurability of freedom and the suddenness with which the abysmal gap between the will in conflict and the will in harmony is traversed.

60. Cf. Anatolios, "Quest, Questions, and Christ," 72; see also 51.

61. Such stories structure book VIII, most notably that of Antony of Egypt. See also Augustine, *Teaching Christianity: De Doctrina Christiana*, 110–11 [I.10.10–11.11]; 131–32 [I.6.7–8]; cf. Anatolios, "Quest, Questions, and Christ," 60.

62. See Augustine, *Teaching Christianity: De Doctrina Christiana*, 111–12 [I.12–14.23]; cf. John Cavadini, "The Sweetness of the Word: Salvation and Rhetoric in Augustine's 'De Doctrina Christiana,'" in *Augustine's De Doctrina Christiana: A Classic of Western Culture*, ed. Duane Arnold and Pamela Bright (Notre Dame, Ind.: University of Notre Dame Press, 1995), 164–81; and Marion, *In the Self's Place*, 195.

63. Anatolios and Marion both distinguish these sets of books in similar, though not identical fashion. In any event, the ambiguous nature of book X in relation to the other books only highlights the fact that the answer to the ques-tion of Augustine's "being" is not a matter of objectification or conceptualiza-tion, but rather of his original and ultimate orientation to God. See Anatolios,

"Quest, Questions, and Christ," 60, 68; Marion, *In the Self's Place*, 37–38; and, for a clearer statement regarding Augustine's "self-definition" as fundamentally the referral of his being to God, see Marion, "Resting, Moving, Loving," 25–26; cf. Augustine, *Teaching Christianity: De Doctrina Christiana*, 113 [I.17.16].

64. See Esposito, "Memory and Temptation," 293–94.

65. See Marion, *In the Self's Place*, 164–65, 169, 241–43; cf. 107, 151.

66. Cf. ibid., 245–46.

67. Cf. Balthasar, *A Theological Anthropology*, 23, 25.

68. See Augustine, *The Trinity*, 153 [IV.1–1.2].

69. This dynamic is evident in the beginning of Augustine's approach to Genesis 1, in which he humbly asks to listen so that he may understand.

70. Marion, *In the Self's Place*, 11–20, 43, 47, 210; see also Jean-Luc Marion, "Sketch of a Phenomenological Concept of Sacrifice," in *The Reason of the Gift* (Charlottesville: University Press of Virginia, 2011); cf. de Lubac, *The Mystery of the Supernatural*, 113–14.

71. Augustine, *The Trinity*, 153–59 [IV.1.2–6]; see also 391–92 [XIV.17.23]; cf. Augustine, *City of God*, 511–12 [XIII.2] and 1075–76 [XXII.24].

72. Augustine, *The Trinity*, 442 [XV.50].

73. Augustine speaks of the perfection that all seek as that which all must learn to recognize in the Body of Christ after his resurrection (see Augustine, *City of God*, 1061 [XXII.19]).

74. Ibid., 1090 [XXII.30].

75. De Lubac, *The Mystery of the Supernatural*, 167.

76. De Lubac identifies the claim to this orientation as "the fundamental affirmation at the basis of Christian anthropology"; see Henri de Lubac, *Brief Catechesis on Nature and Grace*, trans. Richard Arnandez (San Francisco: Ignatius, 1984), 17; elsewhere, he insists that to think otherwise is to think of something other than a human being (see de Lubac, *The Mystery of the Supernatural*, 59).

77. A full treatment of the twentieth-century debates in which de Lubac was engaged exceeds the scope of my present study, although the questions that this debate aroused, particularly in regards to the relationship of nature and grace as well as the status of Thomism and Scholastic philosophy, will be touched on in part below. For more on the specific issues in play and the critique that the encyclical *Humani generis* may or may not have lodged against de Lubac's thesis, see the following: Joseph Komonchak, "Theology and Culture at Mid-Century: The Example of Henri de Lubac," *Theological Studies* 51 (1992): 579–602; Gustave Weigel, "The Historical Background of the Encyclical 'Humani Generis,'" *Theological Studies* 12 (1951): 208–30; Georges Chantraine, "The Supernatural: Discernment of Catholic Thought According to Henri de Lubac," in *Surnatural: A Controversy at the Heart of Twentieth-Century Thomistic Thought*, ed. Serge-Thomas

Bonino, trans. Robert Williams and Matthew Levering (Ave Maria, Fla.: Sapientia Press of Ave Maria University, 2009), 21–40; David Braine, "The Debate Between Henri de Lubac and His Critics," *Nova et Vetera* 6, no. 3 (2008): 543–90; Hans Urs von Balthasar, *The Theology of Henri de Lubac: An Overview*, trans. Joseph Fessio and Michael Waldstein (San Francisco: Ignatius, 1991), 63–73; Stephen Duffy, *The Graced Horizon: Nature and Grace in Modern Catholic Thought* (Collegeville, Minn.: Liturgical, 1992), especially 83–84; and John Milbank, *The Suspended Middle: Henri de Lubac and the Debate Concerning the Supernatural* (Grand Rapids, Mich.: Eerdmans, 2005), especially 15–47.

78. Augustine, *City of God*, 523 [XIII.15], cf. 1065–66 [XXII.22].

79. Augustine, *City of God*, 530 [XIII.18]; cf. de Lubac, *The Mystery of the Supernatural*, 236.

80. Balthasar, *The Theology of Henri de Lubac*, 72.

81. Henri de Lubac, *Augustinianism and Modern Theology*, trans. Lancelot Sheppard (New York: Herder and Herder, 2000), especially 23–25.

82. Ibid., 68; cf. xiii.

83. See ibid., 32, 38.

84. De Lubac, *The Mystery of the Supernatural*, 68–74; see also de Lubac, *Augustinianism and Modern Theology*, 233–34; de Lubac, *Brief Catechesis*, 37–38; cf. Chantraine, "The Supernatural," 29; Braine, "The Debate Between Henri de Lubac and His Critics," 57.

85. De Lubac, *The Mystery of the Supernatural*, 37–38. For a succinct summary of the central historical thesis of *Surnatural* on which de Lubac's whole argument depends, see Komonchak, "Theology and Culture at Mid-Century," 585–86.

86. De Lubac notes the importance of reclaiming the ultimate end of human nature in the supernatural for the very drama of human existence in de Lubac, *The Mystery of the Supernatural*, 54; and especially de Lubac, *The Drama of Atheist Humanism*, 399–468 (cf. 14), in which he devotes an entire essay to the precariousness of the modern predicament and the hope that Christianity bears for man and the world; cf. Chantraine, "The Supernatural," 21.

87. De Lubac, *Augustinianism and Modern Theology*, 44.

88. De Lubac, *The Mystery of the Supernatural*, 75–79; see also de Lubac, *Augustinianism and Modern Theology*, 91.

89. De Lubac, *Augustinianism and Modern Theology*, 49; cf. Augustine, *City of God*, 568–70 [XIV.11].

90. De Lubac, *Augustinianism and Modern Theology*, 68–69; see also Chantraine, "The Supernatural," 23.

91. De Lubac, *Augustinianism and Modern Theology*, 24–28 and 51–52; see also de Lubac, *Brief Catechesis*, 122; cf. Milbank, *The Suspended Middle*, 97.

92. De Lubac, *The Mystery of the Supernatural*, especially 56–58; cf. Duffy, *The Graced Horizon*, 78.

93. For de Lubac's comment on the inadequacy but seeming unavoidability of the term "natural" to describe this desire, see de Lubac, *The Mystery of the Supernatural*, 229; cf. 58; cf. de Lubac, *Brief Catechesis*, 13.

94. De Lubac, *The Mystery of the Supernatural*, 113–14.

95. Ibid., 75–100.

96. The pronounced emphasis on this "second gratuity" in *The Mystery of the Supernatural* likely represents a response by way of clarification to the demands of *Humani generis* (see ibid., 236). In a similar vein, de Lubac is much more careful in his later work than he was in *Surnatural* to distinguish between Aquinas and his interpreters, thus exculpating Aquinas himself while also critiquing the two-nature system for which others claim his authority; cf. Duffy, *The Graced Horizon*, 68–70. The relatively gentle objection from Karl Rahner to de Lubac's thesis will not be treated here due to the necessary limitations of my project and because, on the whole, I stand in agreement with de Lubac's opinion that Rahner does not actually fundamentally disagree with him and that the proposition of a "supernatural existential" only delays the crucial question at hand.

97. De Lubac, *The Mystery of the Supernatural*, 133; cf. Augustine, *City of God*, 487–88 [XII.14].

98. De Lubac, *The Mystery of the Supernatural*, 131; see also 82 and 130.

99. Ibid., 76; cf. de Lubac, *Brief Catechesis*, 132–33; Milbank, *The Suspended Middle*, 44–47.

100. Cf. Bernard of Clairvaux, "Sermons on the 'Song of Songs,'" in *Bernard of Clairvaux: Selected Works*, trans. G. R. Evans (New York: Paulist, 1987), 212 [Sermon I.III.5].

101. De Lubac, *The Mystery of the Supernatural*, 215; see also 207 and 211; cf. Augustine, *The Trinity*, especially 424–25 [XV.31–18.32] and 441–42 [XV.50].

102. De Lubac, *The Mystery of the Supernatural*, 214.

103. Augustine, *City of God*, 1088 [XXII.30].

104. Catherine of Siena, *The Dialogue* (New York: Paulist, 1980), 91; cf. Marion, *In the Self's Place*, 188–89.

105. Karl Rahner connects the "actual concrete meaning of [one's] being" with God "revealing to him the actuality of eternity," in Rahner, "The Life of the Dead," 351.

106. See Rahner, "The Eternal Significance of the Humanity of Jesus," 40.

107. Augustine, *The Trinity*, 424 [XV.31]; cf. Coakley, *God, Sexuality, and the Self*, 143 and 312.

108. Ratzinger, *The God of Jesus Christ*, 98; cf. Rahner, "The Life of the Dead," 354–55. Ratzinger's consideration of the "inner openness of man" resonates

with Augustine's articulation of the communicative power given back to the soul of the redeemed sinner (see Augustine, *The Trinity*, 153–59 [IV.1.2–6] and 391–92 [XIV.17.23]; cf. Augustine, *City of God*, 511–12 [XIII.2] and 1075–76 [XXII.24]).

109. Balthasar, *Theo-Drama III*, 149–201; see also Ratzinger, *Introduction to Christianity*, 186–87; and Marion, *The Idol and Distance*, 175.

110. Marion captures this well when he writes that "to receive the gift amounts to receiving the giving act, for God gives nothing except the movement of the infinite kenosis of charity, that is, everything" (Marion, *The Idol and Distance*, 166); cf. Chauvet, *Symbol and Sacrament*, 509, 549; Karl Rahner, "The Theology of the Symbol," in *Theological Investigations*, trans. Cornelius Ernst et al., vol. 4 (Limerick, Ireland: Mary Immaculate College, 2000), 238–40; and Catherine of Siena, *The Dialogue*, 133–35.

111. See Balthasar, *Theo-Drama III*, 527; cf. Coakley, *God, Sexuality, and the Self*, 10.

112. Balthasar, *Theo-Drama III*, 247.

113. Ibid., 248. This point is the thesis of chapter 6 to follow.

114. Ibid., 249.

115. Romano Guardini's theological analysis of Jesus's High Priestly Prayer, which he calls "one of the holiest passages of the New Testament" (437), elucidates this central prayer of communion (see Romano Guardini, *The Lord*, trans. Elinor Briefs [Washington, D.C.: Regnery, 2013], 436–44).

116. The words that Catherine hears in prayer give voice to the inscrutable depth of meaning contained within the twin commandments of the Gospel, especially in relation to Matthew 25:14–46: "I loved you without being loved. Whatever love you have for me you owe me, so you love me not gratuitously but only out of duty, while I love you not out of duty but gratuitously. So you cannot give me the kind of love I ask of you. This is why I have put you among your neighbors: so that you can do for them what you cannot do for me—that is, love them without any concern for thanks and without looking for any profit yourself. And whatever you do for them I will consider done for me" (Catherine of Siena, *The Dialogue*, 121). Cf. Rahner, "Why and How Can We Venerate the Saints?" 20.

117. Augustine, *The Confessions*, 176 [IX.8].

118. Balthasar, *A Theological Anthropology*, 20.

119. See Ratzinger, *Dogma and Preaching*, 316–20; and Rahner, "The Theology of the Symbol," 244.

120. See Ratzinger, *Introduction to Christianity*, 336; cf. Balthasar, *A Theological Anthropology*, 28. The sacramental dimensions of this life in the Spirit structure chapter 5 of the present work.

121. See Coakley, *God, Sexuality, and the Self,* 6. For an Augustinian account of this weaning from the attachment to temporal goods and the strengthening of the will to cling to Christ, see Cavadini, "The Sweetness of the Word," 166–69.

122. Ratzinger, *Introduction to Christianity,* 358; cf. Rahner, "The Hermeneutics of Eschatological Assertions."

123. See Rahner, "The Eternal Significance of the Humanity of Jesus," 42–44.

124. Dante speaks to the mystery of this mutual inhering of charity among the communion of saints most notably toward the end of the third cantica of his *Commedia* (see Dante Alighieri, *Paradiso,* ed. and trans. Robin Kirkpatrick [New York: Penguin, 2006], 299 [31.1–3]). In chapter 6, I consider this mystery through a typological reading of Scripture beginning with the book of Exodus, which will ultimately focus our gaze on the significance of the tabernacle as God's dwelling place and, in the end, that of the saints.

125. This reading of the communion of saints emphasizes the themes "communion" and "fraternal and sororal charity" of which the *Dogmatic Constitution on the Church* speaks in order to better understand why and how the pilgrim Church remembers the blessed dead and turns in hope toward them, practices that the *Dogmatic Constitution* uplifts in the same section (Flannery, ed., "Lumen Gentium," §50).

126. For a substantive consideration of the way in which Dante's poetics energize theological possibilities, particularly as his poem serves as "a supplement to scripture," see Cyril O'Regan, "Theology, Art, and Beauty," in *The Many Faces of Beauty,* ed. Vittorio Hosle (Notre Dame, Ind.: University of Notre Dame Press, 2011), especially 448–49; cf. Rowan Williams, "Poetic and Religious Imagination," *Theology* 80, no. 675 (1977): 178–87.

127. Dante Alighieri, *Inferno,* ed. and trans. Robin Kirkpatrick (New York: Penguin, 2006), 15–19 [2.85–142]; see also Dante Alighieri, *Paradiso,* 317 [32.137–38].

128. Dante Alighieri, *Paradiso,* 321 [33.47], 327 [33.143–45].

129. The power of grace coincides with its humble yielding before the question of human freedom, as the end of Virgil's testimony to the origins of his commission indicates in *Inferno* 2.121–26. The thawing of Dante's own desire begins in the following verse, but the decisive moment occurs some dozen lines later when he suddenly declares, "Set off!" (*Or va,* line 139), making the choice to move in response to the "compassion" (*pietosa,* line 133) that brought a new hope to him. The suddenness of this decision in response to the influence of grace is reminiscent of the repetitions of *subito* in book VIII of Augustine's *Confessions,* where the turnings of the will in the stories of conversion preceding Augustine's own decisive moment remain, in the end, inexplicable occurrences. Furthermore, precisely because Dante testifies to the way in which he, as the

central pilgrim character of his poem, responds in increasing freedom to the call and influence of grace to the point of his completion in beatitude, the question of Virgil's own possibility of salvation—of turning with grace—is left open in the poem itself, beginning already here in the second canto. For Beatrice pledges to remember Virgil in praise to the Lord (lines 73–74), offering a new memory for one whose memory is otherwise locked outside the dynamics of mercy and praise. Whether he will or could accept this memory as his own is, by necessity, left unanswered (see Dante Alighieri, *Inferno*, 15–19 [II.70–142]).

130. Lewis, *The Great Divorce*, 99.

131. At the outset of the following chapter, we explore Dante's treatment of purgatory in connection to the transformation of memory by desire begun in Baptism and continued through the life in the Church. To do so, we will look especially at the presence of the *Paternoster* in the *Purgatorio*, as well as to the cleansing and renewal of memory in the rivers at the top of the mountain (see Dante Alighieri, *Purgatorio*, ed. and trans. Robin Kirkpatrick [New York: Penguin, 2006], 97 [11.1–23]).

132. Thérèse of Lisieux, *St. Thérèse of Lisieux: Her Last Conversations*, trans. John Clarke (Washington, D.C.: ICS, 1977), 102.

133. Flannery, ed., "Lumen Gentium," 76 [VII.50].

Chapter 5. Bodily Memory

1. Dante Alighieri, *Paradiso*, 321 [33.47]; see also 317 [32.137–38], 327 [33.143–45]; and Dante Alighieri, *Inferno*, 15–19 [2.85–142].

2. Thiel, *Icons of Hope*, especially 67 and 83.

3. Ibid., 67.

4. Ibid., 147 and 153.

5. Beyond Thiel, Elizabeth Johnson is notably more suspicious of hierarchical order as she critiques what she calls the patriarchal "patronage model" of the communion of saints, which leads her to espouse an egalitarian "companionship model." I return to Johnson's work later in the chapter (see Elizabeth Johnson, *Friends of God and Prophets: A Feminist Theological Reading of the Communion of Saints* [New York: Continuum, 1998]; and also Elizabeth Johnson, *Truly Our Sister: A Theology of Mary in the Communion of Saints* [New York: Continuum, 2003]).

6. This and all subsequent references to the *Purgatorio* draw on Dante Alighieri, *Purgatorio*, ed. and trans. Robin Kirkpatrick (New York: Penguin, 2006).

7. One of Thiel's significant proposals is that Christians erase from their eschatological imaginations the line between purgatory and heaven that keeps the

effects of sin from touching the heavenly saints (see Thiel, *Icons of Hope*, 172 and 181–82). The argument I am advancing allows for the heavenly saints to freely assume the burden of their penitential brothers and sisters as an act of charity that is rightly expressive of their blessed character but that does not impinge on their freedom from sin and all its effects. The freedom of the heavenly saints follows from (but is not identical to) the logic of divine transcendence in Patristic teaching. As I noted in chapter 3, this nuanced teaching distinguishes between involuntary influences from which God is absolutely free (divine immutability) and the freely chosen passivity that God willfully accepts out of love (divine mutability). On this point, I refer the reader again to Balthasar, *Theo-Drama V*, 216–33, 243–46; cf. Ward, "Kenosis," 43. I contend that God makes the heavenly saints sharers in God's own freedom from the influences that they would involuntarily suffer (such as the effects of sin) and thus enables them to freely "suffer" out of love for their neighbors in accordance with God's own way of loving.

8. In the following subsection I argue that the *Paternoster* does in fact appear in the *Paradiso*—precisely at its apical moment—in the form of the Virgin Mary's personal embodiment, as grace grants her the full union of word and deed in her unblemished integrity.

9. Henri de Lubac expresses this dynamic of growth in holiness in *Catholicism: Christ and the Common Destiny of Man*, trans. Lancelot Sheppard and Elizabeth Englund (San Francisco: Ignatius, 1988), 119. I return often to de Lubac's important text later in this chapter.

10. The Virgin Mary would obviously be above all and below none, save her Most Blessed Son.

11. Thiel rehearses these bases of concern most clearly in *Icons of Hope*, 147–53.

12. Ibid., 153.

13. Robin Kirkpatrick, "Introduction," in *Paradiso*, ed. Robin Kirkpatrick (New York: Penguin, 2006), xxxi.

14. For a penetrating analysis of the revolution in physical and indeed metaphysical thinking that Dante performs in this "ascent" to the Empyrean, see Christian Moevs, *The Metaphysics of Dante's Comedy* (New York: Oxford University Press, 2005), especially 15–36.

15. All parenthetical citations in this subsection come from Dante Alighieri, *Paradiso*, unless otherwise noted.

16. Cf. Paul's Claudel's "Cantique de Palmyre" as excerpted in de Lubac, *Catholicism*, 349.

17. See Cunningham, *The Meaning of Saints*, 32–56.

18. See Johnson, *Friends of God and Prophets*, 19–20, as well as 87–92, where she critiques what she calls a "hierarchy of importance"; cf. Rahner, "Why and How Can We Venerate the Saints?" 6–8.

19. See especially Johnson, *Friends of God and Prophets*, 163–80.

20. See ibid., 78–93.

21. Thiel, *Icons of Hope*, 154–55 and 174–76.

22. Ibid., 187.

23. Ibid., 146–47; Thiel, "For What May We Hope?" 537–41.

24. See Thiel, *Icons of Hope*, 165–68 and 180–82.

25. Ibid., 167.

26. Ibid., 166.

27. Ibid., 186.

28. Ibid., 54, 172, and 181–82. In a journal article in which Thiel consolidates his work on the doctrine of purgatory, he opines that the "loss of belief in purgatory" is related to the rise of a "noncompetitive understanding of Christian life" that has grown in prevalence in the post-conciliar period (see John Thiel, "Time, Judgment, and Competitive Spirituality: A Reading of the Development of the Doctrine of Purgatory," *Theological Studies* 69 [2008]: especially 782–85). Brian's Daley's work to elucidate the "hope of the Early Church" offers a basis for critiquing Thiel's proposal since the notion of purgatory that Thiel is dismissing seems to express the paradoxical concern for the gravest historical realism and the most serious eschatological hope that the Church fathers all emphasized (see Brian Daley, *The Hope of the Early Church: A Handbook of Patristic Eschatology* [Peabody, Mass.: Hendrickson, 2003], 217–21). Johann Baptist Metz goes even further in describing the Church itself as "a purgatory" in which the freedom of Jesus secures the memory of a future of freedom (see Johann Baptist Metz, *Faith in History and Society: Toward a Practical Fundamental Theology*, ed. and trans. J. Matthew Ashley [New York: Herder and Herder, 2007], 96).

29. Thiel acknowledges the resemblance between his picture of heaven and the more traditional view of purgatory (see Thiel, *Icons of Hope*, 54). Space prohibits me from engaging in a study of the doctrine of purgatory, though the point of contrast between the view I am advancing and that which Thiel describes highlights the importance of this doctrine in relation to the understanding of the communion of saints. Later in this chapter, the purgatorial dimensions of Christian life that begin in Baptism build upon the distinctions I have already made above, especially in relation to the Dantean illustration of the transformation of the will within a hierarchical order of mercy.

30. See Bradford Hinze, "Ecclesial Repentance and the Demands of Dialogue," *Theological Studies* 61 (2000): 207–38; cf. Thiel, *Icons of Hope*, 54, 195n50; and Thiel, "For What May We Hope?" 541.

31. Hinze, "Ecclesial Repentance," 225.

32. Ibid., 226.

33. Ibid., 227–28. For his part, de Lubac explicitly rejects monophysitism in ecclesiology in *Catholicism*, 75.

34. I argued for this notion of the double gratuity of grace in the previous chapter, primarily in accordance with de Lubac's modern retrieval of Augustinian theology.

35. Cf. Louis Bouyer, *The Church of God: Body of Christ and Temple of the Spirit*, trans. Charles Underhill Quinn (San Francisco: Ignatius, 2011), 576–90.

36. Augustine, *The Confessions*, 337 [XIII.28.43]; cf. Augustine, "On Genesis: A Refutation of the Manichees," in *On Genesis*, ed. John Rotelle, trans. Edmund Hill, vol. 13, The Works of Saint Augustine: A Translation for the 21st Century (Hyde Park, N.Y.: New City, 2013), 42–44 [I.3.5–4.7]; and Augustine, "Unfinished Literal Commentary on Genesis," in *On Genesis*, ed. John Rotelle, trans. Edmund Hill, vol. 13, The Works of Saint Augustine: A Translation for the 21st Century (Hyde Park, N.Y.: New City, 2013), 119–20 [4.11].

37. Augustine, *The Confessions*, 337 [XIII.31.46].

38. Ibid., 214 [X.17.26].

39. Augustine, *City of God*, 514 [XIII.4].

40. Ibid., 1090 [XXII.30].

41. Ibid., 535 [XIII.21].

42. See ibid., 573 [XIV.13].

43. Ibid., 502 [XII.22]; cf. 547 [XIV.1].

44. Ibid., 547 [XIV.1].

45. Ibid., 572 [XIV.13].

46. Ibid., 570 [XIV.12].

47. See again Augustine, *The Confessions*, 337 [XIII.31.46].

48. See again, among others, Rahner, "Theological Considerations Concerning the Moment of Death," 318.

49. See Augustine, *City of God*, 513–15 [XIII.4–6].

50. See Rahner, "The Theological Concept of Concupiscentia," 379; cf. Karl Rahner, "Concerning the Relationship Between Nature and Grace," in *Theological Investigations*, trans. Cornelius Ernst et al., vol. 1 (Limerick, Ireland: Mary Immaculate College, 2000), especially 304–15; and Karl Rahner, "Current Problems in Christology," in *Theological Investigations*, trans. Cornelius Ernst et al., vol. 1 (Limerick, Ireland: Mary Immaculate College, 2000), 183.

51. Rahner, "The Theological Concept of Concupiscentia," 380.

52. See ibid., 357.

53. Ibid., 372.

54. Ibid., 372–74; cf. Rahner, "The Sin of Adam," 260.

55. See again Rahner, "The Sin of Adam," 257–58.

56. Ibid., 260–61; cf. Rahner, "The Theological Concept of Concupiscentia," 378–79.

57. Rahner, "The Church of the Saints," 95.

58. See Karl Rahner, "The Sinful Church in the Decrees of Vatican II," in *Theological Investigations*, trans. Cornelius Ernst et al., vol. 6 (Limerick, Ireland: Mary Immaculate College, 2000), 270–94.

59. Rahner, "The Church of the Saints," 104.

60. Cf. Balthasar, *A Theological Anthropology*, 233.

61. Augustine, *The Confessions*, 337 [XIII.31.46].

62. The following parenthetical citations come from Dante Alighieri, *Purgatorio*, unless otherwise noted.

63. Dante Alighieri, *Inferno*, 3 [1.8].

64. Dante Alighieri, *Purgatorio*, 307 [32.103].

65. Ibid., 98 [11.15].

66. See ibid., 171 [18.115–16].

67. Ibid., 171 [18.134–35].

68. Augustine, *City of God*, 1089 [XXII.30]; cf. Balthasar, *A Theological Anthropology*, 30.

69. This interpretation of the Exodus narrative draws on the one that Joseph Ratzinger provides in *The Spirit of the Liturgy* (San Francisco: Ignatius, 2000), 15–23.

70. See Chauvet, *Symbol and Sacrament*, 237.

71. See Ratzinger, *The Spirit of the Liturgy*, 18–19.

72. See Bouyer, *The Church of God*, 194–204.

73. In his rich study of the typological dimensions of Scripture in relation to Christ and the liturgy, Jean Daniélou offers rich and abundant reflection on this theme. In one brief line on the typological fulfillment of the Feast of Tabernacles in the Christian liturgical year (which I deal with in greater detail in chapter 6), he states that "Commemorating the time of the crossing of the desert, between the Exodus from Egypt and the entrance into the Promised Land, [the Feast of Tabernacles] is a wonderful figure of the life of the Church between Baptism and heaven, which corresponds liturgically to the time after Pentecost" (see Jean Daniélou, *The Bible and the Liturgy* [Notre Dame, Ind.: University of Notre Dame Press, 2009], 344; cf. 35–53, 70–113, for further discussion of the types of Baptism).

74. See Flannery, ed., "Lumen Gentium," 73 [VII.48].

75. Balthasar, *A Theological Anthropology*, 35; cf. Augustine, *The Confessions*, 264–65 [XI.30].

76. Balthasar, *A Theological Anthropology*, 35.

77. Ibid., 335.

78. The structure of *Lumen gentium* stresses this order, beginning with "The Mystery of the Church" in chapter I, to "The People of God" in chapter II, all the way through to the uninterrupted "union of the wayfarers with the brothers and sisters who sleep in the peace of Christ" as expressed in chapter VII and the

trust in the Mother of God to "intercede before her Son in the communion of all the saints" for the consummation of history in the "peace and harmony [of] one people of God" in chapter VIII.

79. Benedict XII, *Benedictus Deus* (1336), http://www.papalencyclicals.net /Ben12/B12bdeus.html.

80. De Lubac, *Catholicism*, 123; cf. 39.

81. Again, this stands in profound agreement with Benedict XII, who states that faith and hope are no longer exercised in beatific life, leaving only love (charity) in the presence of God (see Benedict XII, *Benedictus Deus*); cf. Chauvet, *Symbol and Sacrament*, 264.

82. Dante Alighieri, *Purgatorio*, 267 [28.129].

83. Nathan Mitchell, "The Amen Corner: The Life of the Dead," *Worship* 66 (November 1992): 539–40.

84. Gary Anderson argues for an understanding of charity in the biblical tradition according to transhistorical economic terms in *Charity: The Place of the Poor in the Biblical Tradition* (New Haven, Conn.: Yale University Press, 2013).

85. Flannery, ed., "Lumen Gentium," 1 [I.1].

86. See Joseph Ratzinger, *Volk und Haus Gottes in Augustins Lehre von der Kirch* (Freiburg: Herder, 2011).

87. Joseph Ratzinger, "The Holy Spirit as Communion: Concerning the Relationship of Pneumatology and Spirituality in Augustine," trans. Peter Casarella, *Communio* 25 (Summer 1998): 324–37; cf. Ratzinger, *The God of Jesus Christ*, 103–13.

88. Ratzinger, "The Holy Spirit as Communion," 326.

89. Ibid.

90. Ibid., 327.

91. Augustine, *The Trinity*, 424 [XV.31].

92. Ibid.

93. Ibid., 424–25 [XV.18.32].

94. Ratzinger, "The Holy Spirit as Communion," 328–29.

95. Aiden Nichols probes Ratzinger's reading of Augustine's ecclesiology, particularly in relation to the Donatists in Aiden Nichols, *The Thought of Pope Benedict XVI: An Introduction to the Theology of Joseph Ratzinger* (New York: Burns & Oates, 2007), 18–29.

96. Benedict XVI elucidates the intrinsic connection between communion with God and communion with one's neighbors in relation to the communion of saints in *Sacramentum caritatis* (February 22, 2007), §76, http://www.vatican .va/holy_father/benedict_xvi/apost_exhortations/documents/hf_ben-xvi_exh _20070222_sacramentum-caritatis_en.html.

97. Ratzinger, "The Holy Spirit as Communion," 332. Ratzinger claims that Baptism itself means being opened up to the communication of love that is

God's *communio* (see 327 and 329), as elsewhere he envisions Christ's creating this space when he stretches out on the cross (see *God and the World: A Conversation with Peter Seewald*, trans. Henry Taylor [San Francisco: Ignatius, 2002], 218); cf. Augustine, *The Trinity*, 426–27 [XV.34]; and de Lubac, *Catholicism*, 25, 48–49, 52–53, 78–79, 82–88.

98. De Lubac, *Catholicism*, 222.

99. Ibid., 110–11; cf. 226.

100. See ibid., 230.

101. Augustine, *The Trinity*, 425 [XV.18.32].

102. Augustine treats Romans 8 in this manner especially in "Letter 194: Augustine to Sixtus," in *Letters 156–210*, vol. 3, The Works of Saint Augustine: A Translation for the 21st Century (Hyde Park, N.Y.: New City, 2004), 295–96 [4.16–17]. Cf. the way in which Balthasar speaks of the "role" of the Holy Spirit, specifically in regards to contemplation, in Hans Urs von Balthasar, *Prayer*, trans. Graham Harrison (San Francisco: Ignatius, 1986), 67–82.

103. De Lubac, *Catholicism*, 275.

104. Ibid., 16; cf. 81.

105. See, for example, Joseph Ratzinger, *Called to Communion: Understanding the Church Today*, 3rd ed. (San Francisco: Ignatius, 1996), 23; and de Lubac, *Catholicism*, 315, 333, and 343.

106. Benedict XVI, *Deus Caritas Est: God Is Love* (Boston: Pauline, 2006), §6; cf. Ratzinger, *God and the World*, 189; Ratzinger, *Introduction to Christianity*, 252–53; Benedict XVI, *Saved in Hope: Spe Salvi* (San Francisco: Ignatius, 2008), §38.

107. See Guardini, *The Lord*, 442–44.

108. See Bouyer, *The Church of God*, 271–72.

109. Benedict XVI, *Jesus of Nazareth I*, 141.

110. Joseph Ratzinger, *The Feast of Faith: Approaches to a Theology of the Liturgy* (San Francisco: Ignatius, 1986), 26–27. This point brings us back to the Christological affirmation at the center of Karl Rahner's theology of death and of hope, as I discussed in chapter 2 (see especially Rahner, "Ideas for a Theology of Death," 184).

111. Dante Alighieri, *Purgatorio*, 97 [11.7].

112. See again Balthasar, *Mysterium Paschale*, 34–35, which I treated in chapter 3.

113. See Ratzinger, *Called to Communion*, 75–103; Joseph Ratzinger, "Eucharist, Communion, and Solidarity" (2002), http://www.vatican.va/roman _curia/congregations/cfaith/documents/rc_con_cfaith_doc_20020602 _ratzinger-eucharistic-congress_en.html; cf. Peter Casarella, "Solidarity as the Fruit of Communio: Ecclesia in America, 'Post-Liberation Theology,' and the Earth," *Communio* 27 (2000): 98–123. For a view of the order of communion

and solidarity that is critical of Ratzinger's, especially as summarized by Casa-rella, see Joseph Capizzi, "Solidarity as a Basis for Conversion and Communion: A Response to Peter Casarella," *Communio* 27 (2000): 124–33.

114. Anderson, *Charity*, 4.

115. See Ratzinger, *Introduction to Christianity*, 331–33.

116. See Bouyer, *The Church of God*, 165.

117. See Ratzinger, *God and the World*, 218.

118. Benedict XVI, *Sacramentum caritatis*, §14; cf. John Paul II, *Ecclesia de Eucharistia* (2003), §1, vatican.va/holy_father/special_features/.../hf_jp-ii _enc_20030417_ecc lesia_eucharistia_en.html.

119. See Benedict XVI, *Sacramentum caritatis*, §30.

120. Marion, *God Without Being*, 164 and 169; cf. 177. With no less depth but with greater literary skill and humor, Flannery O'Connor uplifts the trans-formative substantiality of the Eucharistic host in "A Temple of the Holy Ghost," in *The Complete Stories* (New York: Farrar, Straus and Giroux, 1971), 236–48.

121. Marion, *The Idol and Distance*, 132; see also 118 and 129; cf. Louis-Marie Chauvet, "The Broken Bread as Theological Figure of Eucharistic Pres-ence," in *Sacramental Presence in a Postmodern Context*, ed. L. Boeve and L. Leijssen (Leuven: Leuven University Press, 2001), 260–61; and Kimberly Belcher, *Efficacious Engagement: Sacramental Participation in the Trinitarian Mys-tery* (Collegeville, Minn.: Liturgical, 2011), 32–46.

122. Marion, *God Without Being*, 174–78.

123. See Chauvet, *Symbol and Sacrament*, 5; and Louis-Marie Chauvet, *The Sacraments: The Word of God and the Mercy of the Body*, trans. Madeleine Beau-mont (Collegeville, Minn.: Liturgical, 2001), 111.

124. Marion, *God Without Being*, 140.

125. See Augustine, "Sermon 272," in *Essential Sermons*, trans. Edmund Hill and Boniface Ramsey, The Works of Saint Augustine: A Translation for the 21st Century (Hyde Park, N.Y.: New City, 2007), 317–18; cf. de Lubac, *Catholicism*, 88–101.

126. Benedict XVI, *Deus caritas est*, §14. The Augustinian influence is ap-parent here, especially with respect to Augustine's confession of dependence on God's gift: "On your exceedingly great mercy rests all my hope. Give what you command, and then command whatever you will" (*The Confessions*, 223 [X.29.40]).

127. I refer the reader back again to Catherine of Siena's insight into the pro-found connection between love of God and love of neighbor in *The Dialogue*, 121.

128. See de Lubac, *Catholicism*, 331–33 and 340–43.

129. See Ratzinger, *Eschatology*, 114–15.

130. Kelly, *Early Christian Creeds*, 389–90; cf. Wood, "Sanctam Ecclesiam Catholicam," 228; Marthaler, *The Creed*, 330.

131. Kelly, *Early Christian Creeds*, 394.

132. Ayo, *The Creed as Symbol*, 133.

133. See Cyprian Vagaggini, *Theological Dimensions of the Liturgy: A General Treatise on the Theology of the Liturgy*, trans. Leonard Doyle and W. A. Jurgens (Collegeville, Minn.: Liturgical, 1976), 336–43; as well as Sergius Bulgakov's treatment of the Deisis in *The Friend of the Bridegroom: On the Orthodox Veneration of the Forerunner*, trans. Boris Jakim (Grand Rapids, Mich.: Eerdmans, 2003), 141–45; cf. Neil Roy, "The Mother of God, the Forerunner, and the Saints of the Roman Canon: A Euchological Deesis," in *Issues in Eucharistic Praying in East and West: Essays in Liturgical and Theological Analysis*, ed. Maxwell Johnson (Collegeville, Minn.: Liturgical, 2010), 327–48.

134. In addition to the other works I cite below, I am indebted to Michael Driscoll and J. Michael Joncas for the clear and helpful elucidation of the Mass that they present in *The Order of Mass: A Roman Missal Study Edition and Workbook* (Collegeville, Minn.: Liturgical, 2011), especially 127–54. When I quote the words of the Mass in this section, the words are taken from the Roman Missal as Driscoll and Joncas reproduce it.

135. Roy expounds on the significance of the structure and content of these liturgical actions in "The Mother of God," 336–44; cf. Lawrence Cunningham, "The Roman Canon and Catholicity: A Meditation," *Church*, Spring 2006, 5–10.

136. In chapter 1, I claimed that the communion of saints is at once a Christological and pneumatological reality. In the Roman Canon, the truth of this claim is most clearly elucidated as proper to the Eucharistic liturgy. Dante's vision of the communion of saints in the Empyrean is apropos to this liturgical arrangement (see again Dante Alighieri, *Paradiso*, 295 [30.100–126].

137. Austin Flannery, ed., "Sacrosanctum Concilium: Constitution on the Sacred Liturgy," in *Vatican Council II: Constitutions, Decrees, Declarations*, rev. ed. (Northport, N.Y.: Costello, 1996), 121 [I.I.8]; cf. Romano Guardini, *The Spirit of the Liturgy*, trans. Ada Lane (New York: Herder and Herder, 1998), 36–42.

138. Cf. de Lubac's discussion of the unity of the "three elements" of the Eucharist in *Catholicism*, 96–101.

139. Cf. Catherine of Siena, *The Dialogue*, 142.

140. Cf. Balthasar's discussion of Christ's "effective representative action" that is communicated from head to body in the Eucharist in *Theo-Drama III*, 242–43.

141. See Roy, "The Mother of God," 335–36. Roy draws on the Russian Orthodox theologian Sergius Bulgakov, who offers a profound meditation on the theological meaning of the Deisis icon that, according to his interpretation, illumines the communicative order of mercy to which I have been attentive in my treatment of the Roman Canon (see Bulgakov, *The Friend of the Bridegroom*, especially 143–44).

142. Balthasar thus speaks of the communicants receiving Communion for those who do not receive in *Life Out of Death: Meditations on the Paschal Mystery*, trans. Maria Stockl (San Francisco: Ignatius, 2012), 67; cf. *Catholicism*, 233, where de Lubac makes the same point.

143. Irenaeus of Lyons, *Against Heresies*, ed. Alexander Roberts, James Donaldson, and Arthur Cleveland Coxe (South Bend, Ind.: Ex Fontibus, 2012), 570 [V.7.2].

144. Ibid.

145. A comprehensive treatment of the dogma of Mary's bodily Assumption exceeds the scope of the present work. For a recent study that treats the three scriptural pillars of the Assumption (i.e., the role of typological reasoning, the Church's authority as interpreter of Scripture, and the fittingness of the Assumption within the divine plan for salvation), see Matthew Levering, *Mary's Bodily Assumption* (Notre Dame, Ind.: University of Notre Dame Press, 2015). Levering offers careful and thorough notes in his study and provides a robust bibliography that would be of interest to those desiring to study the dogma of the Assumption further, in both Catholic and ecumenical settings.

146. Flannery, ed., "Lumen Gentium," 82–83 [VIII.56].

147. Levering, *Mary's Bodily Assumption*, 42.

148. See Pius XII, *Munificentissimus Deus* (1950), §14, http://w2.vatican.va /content/pius-xii/en/apost_constitutions/documents/hf_p-xii_apc_19501101 _munificentissimus-deus.html.

149. Flannery, ed., "Lumen Gentium," 84 [VIII.59].

150. Levering draws out this point in line with the theological treatment of Mary's Assumption that both Balthasar and Rahner undertake. See Levering, *Mary's Bodily Assumption*, 60; Hans Urs von Balthasar, *The Threefold Garland: The World's Salvation in Mary's Prayer* (San Francisco: Ignatius, 1982), 128; Karl Rahner, "The Interpretation of the Dogma of the Assumption," in *Theological Investigations*, trans. Cornelius Ernst et al., vol. 1 (Limerick, Ireland: Mary Immaculate College, 2000), 220.

Chapter 6. Work of Love

1. Quoted in John J. O'Keefe and R. R. Reno, *Sanctified Vision: An Introduction to Early Christian Interpretation of the Bible* (Baltimore: Johns Hopkins University Press, 2005), 130; cf. Augustine, *Teaching Christianity: De Doctrina Christiana*, 110 [I.10.10].

2. See Augustine, *The Confessions*, 3 [I.1].

3. Ratzinger, *The God of Jesus Christ*, 52.

4. See, for example, O'Keefe and Reno, *Sanctified Vision*, especially 73–78.

5. D. Moody Smith draws out the significance of the tabernacle in his exegesis of John 1:14: "Because the Word is from this point on incarnate (enfleshed), the term itself now disappears, and we read of the Son, or of Jesus Christ. That the Word lived among us is a very suggestive statement. The NRSV has 'lived' where the RSV had 'dwelt' (v. 14). 'Dwelt' may be preferable because the Greek verb (*skenoo*) used here means to take up residence as in a tent. The noun form (*skene*) means tent or tabernacle. It is the word used in Scripture of the tabernacle or tent of meeting where the Lord's presence dwelt in the wilderness (Exod 27:21; Lev 1:1; Num 1:1) and the people encountered him. 'The Lord summoned Moses and spoke to him from the tent of meeting . . .' (Lev 1:1). The very word suggests a subtle but important theme of the prologue and the Gospel, namely, that Jesus will become the place where the people will meet God, displacing the tent and its successor, the Jerusalem temple (cf. 2:19–21; 4:20–24). Like the temple and the tent, Jesus was a visible presence: We have seen his glory" (D. Moody Smith, *John*, Abingdon New Testament Commentaries [Nashville: Abingdon, 1999], 58–59).

6. In his commentary on the Gospel of John, Origen writes, "We must note in addition that the Old Testament is not gospel since it does not make known 'him who is to come,' but proclaims him in advance. On the other hand, all the New Testament is gospel, not only because it declares alike with the beginning of the Gospel, 'Behold the Lamb of God who takes away the sin of the world' (Jn 1:29), but also because it contains various ascriptions of praise and teaching of him on account of whom the gospel is gospel" (Origen, *Commentary on the Gospel According to John, Books 1–10*, trans. Ronald E. Heine, Fathers of the Church Patristic Series [Washington, D.C.: Catholic University of America Press, 2001], 35–36).

7. Smith, *John*, 59.

8. Augustine, *The Confessions*, 140 [VII.19.25].

9. Ibid., 132 [VII.9.13–14].

10. Simon Lee, *Jesus' Transfiguration and the Believers' Transformation: A Study of the Transfiguration and Its Development in Early Christian Writings* (Tübingen: Mohr Siebeck, 2009), 23. See also Daniélou, *The Bible and the Liturgy*, 339–43. For an especially robust treatment of the Transfiguration that touches on the elements noted here, see Harald Riesenfeld, *Jésus Transfiguré*, Acta Seminarii Neotestamentici Upsaliensis XVI (Copenhagen: E. Munksgaard, 1947), 243–306.

11. Daniélou, *The Bible and the Liturgy*, 333–47; cf. Riesenfeld, *Jésus Transfiguré*, 189, 277; and Jean Daniélou, *From Shadows to Reality: Studies in the Biblical Typology of the Fathers* (London: Burns and Oates, 1960), 223.

12. As Daniélou explains, "The manifestation of the glory of Jesus appears to Peter to be the sign that the times of the Messiah have arrived" (Daniélou, *The Bible and the Liturgy*, 340). In the book of Revelation, the dwelling of the

blessed in heaven recurs with some frequency, for example, in 7:15; 12:12; 13:6; and 21:3.

13. Throughout the Old Testament, the cloud is commonly associated with the Lord's presence (see 1 Kings 8:10; 2 Chron. 5:13; Isa. 6:4; Ezek. 44:4) and in the book of Revelation the *smoke from the glory of God and from his power* fills the temple completely (5:8, RSV).

14. Knowing Jesus for who he is only occurs in the Resurrection, which I strove to argue at the outset of chapter 4 with the extended treatment of the narratives of the Resurrection appearances.

15. For a word about the world as the site of God's revelation and conversion through the coming of Jesus in relation to John's prologue, which thus helps to further relate the Transfiguration narrative and the Exodus narrative to the movement of the Incarnation, see Smith, *John*, 56.

16. The Preface for the Mass of the Feast of the Transfiguration of the Lord (August 6) is worth pondering here: "For he revealed his glory in the presence of chosen witnesses and filled with the greatest splendor that bodily form which he shares with all humanity, that the scandal of the Cross might be removed from the hearts of his disciples and that he might show how in the Body of the whole Church is to be fulfilled what so wonderfully shone forth first in its Head" (Daughters of Saint Paul, eds., *Saint Paul Daily Missal* [Boston: Pauline, 2012], 909).

17. For instance, John Henry Newman reads Moses as a type of Christ according to three characteristics: he delivers the people from Egypt to Canaan as Christ delivers from the power of the devil to the glory of God, he reveals the will of God with whom he speaks as Christ shares intimacy with the Father and makes his will manifest, and he is an intercessor for the people who offers himself as the bearer of their burdens as Christ is the mediator who takes on the sin of the world. See John Henry Newman, "Moses the Type of Christ," in *Parochial and Plain Sermons* (San Francisco: Ignatius, 1997), 1488–95. The association of the transformation of Moses as prefiguring the dynamism of the saints and their communion is mostly an extension of this typological reading that exceeds the bounds of Newman's sermon. Daniélou observes the unparalleled importance of the Exodus for Christian typology: "But during the age of the prophets, the past events of the history of Israel, and of the Exodus in particular, were recalled only to nourish the hope of the people in the future events in which the power of Yahweh would manifest itself in a still greater way in favor of His Own: the events of the Exodus became the figures of eschatological realities. Here is the origin of typology" (Daniélou, *The Bible and the Liturgy*, 334). For more on reading across the narrative of a biblical text, see Robert Alter, *The Art of Biblical Narrative* (New York: Basic, 2011).

18. See Miguel Romero, "The Call to Mercy: Veritatis Splendor and the Preferential Option for the Poor," *Nova et Vetera* 11, no. 4 (2013): 1205–27.

19. God's knowledge of this human suffering is not simply cognitive, but rather the text indicates "a divine choice to enter into and experience Israel's suffering" (see Walter Brueggemann, Bruce C. Birch, Terence E. Fretheim, and David L. Petersen, *A Theological Introduction to the Old Testament* [Nashville: Abingdon, 2005], 106–7).

20. Origen concludes his homily on the birth of Moses with a charge to his audience to allow their wonder at Moses to grow without limit and he prays that the Lord will reveal his own glory to those who gaze on Moses: "Let us have Moses large and strong. Let us think nothing small, nothing lowly about him, but let him be totally magnificent, totally distinguished, totally elegant. For whatever is spiritual, whatever of elevated understanding is great in every respect. And let us pray to our Lord Jesus Christ that he himself might reveal and show us in what manner Moses is great and elevated. For he himself 'reveals' it to whom he wishes 'by the Holy Spirit'" (Origen, *Homilies on Genesis and Exodus*, trans. Ronald E. Heine [Washington, D.C.: Catholic University of America Press, 2002], 247). My claim here is that, especially in light of Stephen's speech in Acts, Moses's "greatness," "magnificence," "elegance," or, simply, "beauty" is revealed according to his likeness unto God, first in the resemblance of his disposition and action on perceiving suffering in 2:11–12, and then throughout Exodus in the manner of his growth into conformity with the logic and desire of God. Seeing Moses "in the Spirit" means seeing him according to God's own charitable activity in the world.

21. As Robert Alter notes, this designation of Moses "as God" is enabled because *'elohim* has the primary meaning of "god," inclusive of angels and divine messengers. In light of this meaning, the claim made here is somewhat mollified, guarding against the interpretation of Moses becoming anything like a divine being himself (see Robert Alter, *The Five Books of Moses: A Translation with Commentary* [New York: W. W. Norton, 2008], 312; cf. 345). All the same, in the reading I am providing, the movement of Moses from the beginning to the end of the book of Exodus shows him becoming ever more conformed to the image of God, and so I place special emphasis on this designation. When this designation is repeated in 7:1 for Moses, who will be as God to Pharaoh, an extra dramatic element is added because Pharaoh considers himself divine.

22. The prophet Elijah will repeat Moses's error when he flees from the people in his lament of abandonment and the apparent failure of his own mission (see 1 Kings 19:10, 14). Whereas Moses blames God on behalf of the people, Elijah blames the people before God—in each case, the prophet questions the bond of the covenant and, in different ways, the strength of God's fidelity. For

more on the connection between Moses and Elijah on this point, see Levering, *Mary's Bodily Assumption*, 116–19; cf. Peter Leithart, *1 & 2 Kings* (Grand Rapids, Mich.: Brazos, 2006), 141–42; and Jerome Walsh, *1 Kings* (Collegeville, Minn.: Liturgical, 1996), 271–72, 274, 277.

23. For a masterful theological commentary on Pharaoh's hardness of heart and the blindness of the Egyptians in relation to the issue of free will, see Gregory of Nyssa, *Life of Moses*, trans. Abraham Malherbe and Everett Ferguson (New York: Paulist, 1978), 70–74 [II.73–88].

24. Gregory of Nyssa discerns two events occurring in this one moment: "By spoken word [Moses] encouraged the Israelites and exhorted them not to abandon high hopes, but inwardly, in his thoughts, he pleaded with God on behalf of those who cowered in fear and he was directed by counsel from above how to escape the danger. God himself, the history says, gave ear to his voiceless cry" (ibid., 37–38 [I.29]). On the basis of the reading of Exodus that I continue to develop below, we might say here that Gregory detects in what Scripture does not say explicitly about this moment what becomes apparent with Moses through the rest of the text—that is, that Moses is configured to and by the plea for God's mercy on behalf of the people.

25. Matthew Levering's comments on Thomas Aquinas's treatment of divine mercy and our almsgiving is illuminating in relation to my point here, especially if we recall the work I initiated at the end of chapter 4 and completed in chapter 5 on the gift of charity and the person of the Holy Spirit: "Formed by God's gift in Christ and the Spirit, believers must be a community of gift. Indeed, when Aquinas identifies the Person of the Holy Spirit by the name 'Gift,' he explains that 'love has the nature of a first gift, through which all free gifts are given. So since the Holy Spirit proceeds as love . . . he proceeds as the first gift' [quoting from the *Summa Theologica*, I, q. 38, a. 2]. When we give material or spiritual alms to others in need, we manifest the eschatological indwelling of the Holy Spirit, by whom we are gifted" (Matthew Levering, *Jesus and the Demise of Death: Resurrection, Afterlife, and the Fate of the Christian* [Waco, Tex.: Baylor University Press, 2012], 80).

26. John Durham captures the significance of this requirement in the following comment: "The call for materials is prefaced by the instruction that the materials be given first as an offering, that is, as an act of worship, and second, as a joyous expression to be made only by those 'compelled' by their own desire to do so. Just how excessively successful this call was is shown by the sequel narrative, which dwells repetitively on the abundance of materials given (35:20–29; 36:2–7; cf. 38:21–31; 39:32–43)" (John Durham, *Exodus*, World Biblical Commentary, vol. 3 [Waco, Tex.: Thomas Nelson, 1987], 354). We will focus on this "sequel narrative" in due course. For commentary on the tabernacle as the

consummate institution of God dwelling with and among the people, taking upon himself the contours of their life, see Terence Fretheim, *Exodus* (Louisville, Ky.: John Knox, 1991), 275–76.

27. In this dynamic, Moses bears a resemblance to Dante's penitents who offer their prayers for those behind them as if it were for themselves (see again *Purgatorio* 11 and my treatment of this text in chapter 5, where I made the further claim that the saints in *Paradiso* were engaged in this activity perpetually).

28. In line with what I argued in chapter 3—that sin is the break in communication with God and thus sin is the only death—Moses prefigures Christ in seeking to take on the sin of the people, their break in communication with God, upon himself. Though this is a burden he cannot bear—and God will not allow him to bear—we see in him a glimpse of the salvific will that is made incarnate in Christ. About Moses's offer of self as atonement for the disobedience of the people, Durham points to the Christic allusion buried in this exchange: "No one save Yahweh himself can undertake to do what Moses here wants to do, and even he cannot accomplish it for those unwilling to open themselves" (Durham, *Exodus*, 432). Cf. Gregory of Nyssa, *Life of Moses*, 121–22 [II.259–63].

29. See Gregory of Nyssa, *Life of Moses*, 119 [II.251].

30. J. Gerald Janzen notes the significance of the Israelites' willingness to construct the tabernacle according to God's instructions, while also noting the importance of the commandment to observe the Sabbath as highlighting that the tabernacle is a miniature cosmos in which all is ordered as God would have it. This last point echoes the order of the first creation narrative. See J. Gerald Janzen, *Exodus* (Louisville, Ky.: Westminster John Knox, 1997), 269–70. For more on this point, see Fretheim, *Exodus*, 313–16.

31. Gregory of Nyssa's succinct comment on the birth and beauty of Moses pertains here: "Yet in his outward grace he anticipated the whole contribution which he would make in time. Already appearing beautiful in swaddling clothes, he caused his parents to draw back from having such a child destroyed by death" (Gregory of Nyssa, *Life of Moses*, 33 [I.16]). Toward the end of his work, Gregory completes his spiritual interpretation of Moses with the following: "For he who has truly come to be in the image of God and who has in no way turned aside from the divine character bears in himself its distinguishing marks and shows in all things his conformity to the archetype; he beautifies his own soul with what is incorruptible, unchangeable, and shares in no evil at all" (ibid., 136 [II.318]). For a meditation on the power of blessing, see Romano Guardini, *Sacred Signs*, trans. Grace Branham (London: Aeterna, 2015), 27–29.

32. Asking the key question about the meaning of this unmade tabernacle that Moses sees and then Israel replicates, Gregory of Nyssa declares, "This tabernacle would be Christ who is the power and the wisdom of God (1 Cor 1:24),

who in his own nature was not made with hands, yet capable of being made when it became necessary for this tabernacle to be erected among us. Thus, the same tabernacle is in a way both unfashioned and fashioned, uncreated in pre-existence but created in having received this material composition" (Gregory of Nyssa, *Life of Moses*, 98 [II.174]).

33. O'Keefe and Reno, *Sanctified Vision*, 82.

34. O'Keefe and Reno introduce the term "postfigure" in ibid., 81–82.

35. See Thérèse of Lisieux, *St. Thérèse of Lisieux*, 102.

36. Even as he largely praises the holiness of Thérèse, Hans Urs von Balthasar argues that she does not completely follow the logic of revelation in her existence, but goes a step too far in sometimes rendering the import of revelation through her own certainty in God's love for her and her own mission. She is not fully transparent in this sense, the way in which the Blessed Mother alone is. Her mission almost becomes "self-willed," but in the end she is saved through the handing over of her suffering to the priority of love, according to Balthasar (see Hans Urs von Balthasar, *Two Sisters in the Spirit: Therese of Lisieux and Elizabeth of the Trinity*, trans. Dennis D. Martin, Donald Nicholas, and Anne Englund Nash [San Francisco: Ignatius, 1998], especially 312–21). This critique is important to observe since both in Balthasar and in what follows here in this work, Thérèse will be featured as a model of holiness. Even as this occurs, one should always be on guard against taking the example too far. Christopher O'Donnell rebuts Balthasar's critique, although he mostly approves of the rest of Balthasar's treatment of the saint (see Christopher O'Donnell, *Love in the Heart of the Church: The Mission of Thérèse of Lisieux* [Dublin: Veritas, 1997], especially 107).

37. Ida Friederike Görres articulates this irony in her *The Hidden Face: A Study of St. Thérèse of Lisieux* (San Francisco: Ignatius, 2003).

38. Newman's sermon on the acquisition of a taste for heaven pertains here. See Newman, "Holiness Necessary for Future Blessedness," 3–11.

39. Thérèse of Lisieux, *Story of a Soul*, trans. John Clarke (Washington, D.C.: ICS, 1996), 75. On her conviction and "training" in the love of God the Father, Balthasar states that "On the whole, it is the mystery of total abandonment to God, without self-preoccupation, to God by whom one knows oneself to be loved infinitely, as the child is loved by his father. It is evident that such an ideal of pure and confident self-renunciation is possible only for a Christian, in the mystery of the eternal Son of God become a human child" (Hans Urs von Balthasar, "The Timeliness of Lisieux," in *Carmelite Studies: Spiritual Direction* [Washington, D.C.: ICS, 1980], 114).

40. John Paul II, *Divini amoris scientia* (1997), §10, vatican.va/holy_father /john_paul_ii/apost_letters/documents/hf_jp--ii_apl_19101997_divini --amoris_en.html.

41. Thérèse of Lisieux, *Story of a Soul*, 139–40.

42. For Thérèse, suffering was typically associated with separations, and there were plenty throughout her life, all of which she felt acutely: from her mother in infancy due to illness, from her wet nurse, from her mother at death, from her sisters who preceded her into the convent, from her father when she entered the convent, from her beloved sister Celine when she entered the convent, and from her father when he was committed to an asylum for mental illness, followed by his death.

43. Thérèse of Lisieux, *Story of a Soul*, 74 (emphasis in original text). As Balthasar observes, "Everything Thérèse achieves at the supernatural level [and here he has in mind her family leading to her religious vocation] is rooted in something she has experienced at the natural level. Nothing moved her more, perhaps, than the experience of being loved by her father and mother; consequently her picture of God is colored by a child's love" (Balthasar, *Two Sisters in the Spirit*, 125).

44. Thérèse of Lisieux, *Story of a Soul*, 38. For more on the essential connection between almsgiving and the Eucharist, see again Anderson, *Charity*.

45. Thérèse of Lisieux, *Story of a Soul*, 98–99. All quotes in the preceding paragraph come from these pages, and all emphases are in the original text.

46. Balthasar, "The Timeliness of Lisieux," 105.

47. Thérèse of Lisieux, *Story of a Soul*, 99.

48. Ibid.

49. Ibid., 100.

50. Ibid., 147.

51. Reflecting back on that day and the years that followed, Thérèse writes: "My desires were at last accomplished; my soul experienced a PEACE so sweet, so deep, it would be impossible to express it. . . . With what deep joy I repeated those words: 'I am here forever and ever!'" (ibid., 148).

52. Ibid., 151–52; cf. Thérèse of Lisieux, *St. Thérèse of Lisieux*, 11–12. Relaying the testimony of one of her sister Carmelites at her beatification, O'Donnell writes that "During her life in Carmel, the Servant of God passed by unnoticed in the community. Only four or five of the nuns, including myself, got close enough to her to realize the perfection hidden under the humility and simplicity of her exterior. For most of the nuns she was a very regular religious, always above reproach" (O'Donnell, *Love in the Heart of the Church*, 16).

53. See Balthasar, *Two Sisters in the Spirit*, 224; and Dorothy Day, *Thérèse: A Life of Thérèse of Lisieux* (Notre Dame, Ind.: Fides, 1960), 166. As Balthasar states plainly on the same page, "love seeks likeness."

54. Consider, for example, the words of her cousin Marie Guérin (Sister Marie of the Eucharist): "I thank God for permitting me to know this little saint,

for here in the community she is loved and appreciated as such. . . . Hers is not an extraordinary sanctity; there is no love of extraordinary penances, no, only love for God. People in the world can imitate her sanctity, for she has tried only to do everything through love and to accept all little contradictions, all little sacrifices that come at each moment as coming from God's hands. She saw God in everything, and she carried out all her actions as perfectly as possible. Daily duty came before everything else; as for pleasure, she knew how to sanctify it even while enjoying it, offering it up to God" (Thérèse of Lisieux, *St. Thérèse of Lisieux*, 251).

55. See Kieran Kavanaugh's "Introduction" to Teresa's work, where he identifies Fr. Diego de Yepes as this early biographer (Kieran Kavanaugh, "Introduction," in Teresa of Avila, *The Interior Castle*, trans. Kieran Kavanaugh and Otilio Rodriguez [New York: Paulist, 1979], 20).

56. Ibid., 35 [I.1.1]; cf. 164 [VI.10.3]; and Teresa of Avila, *The Way of Perfection*, ed. E. Allison Peers (Mineola, N.Y.: Dover, 2012), 188–90 [chapter 28].

57. Teresa of Avila, *The Interior Castle*, 173 [VII.1.3].

58. Ibid., 163 [VI.9.18].

59. Simone Weil, *Awaiting God: A New Translation of "Attente de Dieu and Lettre a un Religieux,"* trans. Bradley Jersak (Maywood, Conn.: Fresh Wind, 2013), 79.

60. Teresa of Avila, *The Interior Castle*, 184 [VII.3.6]; see also 190 [VII.4.8].

61. Sarah Coakley, "Deepening Practices: Perspectives from Ascetical and Mystical Theology," in *Practicing Theology: Belief and Practices in Christian Life*, ed. Miroslav Volf and Dorothy Bass (Grand Rapids, Mich.: Eerdmans, 2011), 91.

62. Teresa of Avila, *The Interior Castle*, 193 [VII.4.14].

63. See again Marion's essay on this very dynamic in Augustine ("Resting, Moving, Loving," 24–42).

64. Teresa of Avila, *The Interior Castle*, 194 [VII.4.15]. Consider also what Teresa hears the Lord saying to her in the fifth dwelling place: "No, my great love and the desire I have that souls be saved are incomparably more important than these sufferings; and the very greatest sorrows that I have suffered and do suffer, after being in the world, are not enough to be considered anything at all in comparison with this love and desire to save souls" (96 [V.2.13]).

65. Thérèse of Lisieux, *Story of a Soul*, 158. Karl Rahner speaks to the genius of the saint as one who contemplates the Sacred Heart of Jesus in the following way: "The theological and religious meaning of this contemplative making-present is rather this: the contemplator clearly grasps those historical events (which as such are in the past) which on the one hand have made the Lord what he now is, and without which he would not be in this concrete being here and now ('he who is pierced,' 'the Lamb that was slain,' 'he who has learnt obedience by suffering,' and so on, purely affirmations of the present) and in which alone

on the other hand that 'law' can be read off which as the entelechy implanted in us by the grace of Christ and of his life should permeate our life and to which we must freely open ourselves" (Karl Rahner, "Some Theses for a Theology of Devotion to the Sacred Heart," in *Theological Investigations*, trans. Cornelius Ernst et al., vol. 3 [Limerick, Ireland: Mary Immaculate College, 2000], 347–48); cf. Karl Rahner, "'Behold This Heart!': Preliminaries to a Theology of Devotion to the Sacred Heart," in *Theological Investigations*, trans. Cornelius Ernst et al., vol. 3 (Limerick, Ireland: Mary Immaculate College, 2000), 321–30.

66. Teresa of Calcutta, *Come Be My Light: The Private Writings of the "Saint of Calcutta,"* ed. Brian Kolodiejchuk (New York: Doubleday, 2007), 232.

67. Mother Teresa repeatedly referred to the condition, the abandonment, and the plight of the poor of Calcutta in terms of their "dark holes." See, for example, ibid., 42–43, 66, 104–21, 168–69.

68. This map was drawn line by line over years of practice, beginning with the Sunday apostolate Teresa chose when still a Sister of Loretto to visit the poor of Calcutta's slums on Sundays (see ibid., 27).

69. Ibid., 41.

70. Ibid., 230.

71. Gazing beyond the horizon of her own earthly existence, Teresa of Calcutta contemplates the implications of the "vow within a vow" that she made to Jesus: in vowing to "refuse Jesus no sacrifice," she offers herself in union with his mission (ibid., see especially 28–38).

72. When she was leaving the community of Loretto to become a missionary to the poorest of the poor and thus found her new order, Mother Teresa wrote, "The first step towards the slums is over. It cost a very good deal, but I am grateful to God for giving the grace to do it and also for showing me how very weak I am" (ibid., 124).

73. Dorothy Day, *The Long Loneliness* (San Francisco: Harper & Row, 1952), 286.

74. Day, *Thérèse*, vii.

75. Ibid. Elsewhere, Day connects this story with wanting her child to "have a way of life and instruction," which led her to "belonging" to the Church (see Day, *The Long Loneliness*, 140–41; cf. 11).

76. While commenting on the profundity of Thérèse's grasp of the union of love of God and of neighbor, Balthasar claims that "She provides us with the image of first-class Christian humanism" (Balthasar, "The Timeliness of Lisieux," 112).

77. Day, *Thérèse*, 31.

78. Ibid.; cf. Day, *The Long Loneliness*, 170, 280; and Dorothy Day, *By Little and By Little: The Selected Writings of Dorothy Day*, ed. Robert Ellsberg (New York: Alfred A. Knopf, 1984), 43, 98, 126.

79. Day, *Thérèse*, 43; cf. Thérèse of Lisieux, *Story of a Soul*, 33; and Thérèse of Lisieux, *The Letters of St. Thérèse of Lisieux, Vol. I: 1877–1890*, trans. John Clarke (Washington, D.C.: ICS, 1982), 117–18.

80. Day, *Thérèse*, 44.

81. Balthasar, *Two Sisters in the Spirit*, 124.

82. For more on the Martin family, see Stephane-Joseph Piat, *The Story of a Family: The Home of St. Thérèse of Lisieux*, trans. A Benedictine of Stanbrook Abbey (Rockford, Ill.: Tan, 1994).

83. Day, *Thérèse*, 30.

84. Ibid., 145.

85. See especially Dorothy's essays on the Works of Mercy in Day, *By Little and By Little*, 91–97.

86. Day, *Thérèse*, 76. To appreciate the extent to which Thérèse's Little Way influenced Dorothy, one might consider, for example, lines such as these: "We all wish for recognition of one kind or another. But it is mass action people think of these days. They lose sight of the sacrament of the present moment—of the little way" (Day, *By Little and By Little*, 104).

87. Day, *The Long Loneliness*, 204–5.

88. Ibid., 214.

89. Day, *By Little and By Little*, 91.

90. Ibid., 110.

91. Ibid., 114–19.

92. This story is widely circulated, but at least two sources that present it are Robert Louis Wilken, *The Spirit of Early Christian Thought: Seeking the Face of God* (New Haven, Conn.: Yale University Press, 2005), 224–26; and Leonard Foley and Pat McCloskey, eds., *Saint of the Day: Lives, Lessons and Feasts* (Cincinnati, Ohio: St. Anthony Messenger, 2009), 228–29.

93. The rich man ("Dives") did not act on suffering perceived and thus, in the end, forfeited both the vision and the will for mercy: he had no taste for it, to return to Newman's understanding of the training for heavenly bliss.

94. For an overview of the debate over the "intermediate state" in twentieth-century Catholic theology, see Levering, *Mary's Bodily Assumption*, 50–80; cf. Levering, *Jesus and the Demise of Death*, 15–26. For Karl Rahner's position, see Rahner, "The Intermediate State," 114–24; and Rahner, "The Interpretation of the Dogma of the Assumption," 215–27. For more on Ratzinger's view in response to the question of the "immortality of the soul," see his extensive treatment in Ratzinger, *Eschatology*, 104–61.

95. Ratzinger, *Eschatology*, 184.

96. Ratzinger turns to a homily from Origen to underscore his point: "What does it mean when [Jesus] says, 'I will not drink [from the fruit of this vine until I drink it with you in the Kingdom of my Father]'? My Saviour grieves even

now about my sins. My Saviour cannot rejoice as long as I remain in perversion. Why cannot he do this? Because he himself is 'an intercessor for our sins with the Father'. . . . How can he, who is an intercessor for my sins, drink the 'wine of joy,' when I grieve him with my sins? . . . For the apostles too have not yet received their joy: they likewise are waiting for me to participate in their joy. So it is that the saints who depart from here do not immediately receive the full reward of their merits, but wait for us, even if we delay, even if we remain sluggish. They cannot know perfect joy as long as they grieve over our transgressions and weep for our sins. . . . Do you see, then? Abraham is still waiting to attain perfection. Isaac and Jacob and all the prophets are waiting for us in order to attain the perfect blessedness together with us. This is the reason why judgment is kept a secret, being postponed until the Last Day. It is 'one body' which is waiting for justification, 'one body' which rises for judgment. . . . You will have joy when you depart from this life if you are a saint. But your joy will be complete only when no member of your body is lacking to you. For you too will wait, just as you are awaited" (ibid., 185–86).

97. Day, *By Little and By Little*, 110.

98. Charles Péguy, *Le porche du mystère de la deuxième vertu* (Paris: Gallimard, 1986).

99. Of course, Dorothy Day's cause has been introduced; however, explicating the meaning of the canonization process exceeds the scope of this study. For further reading, the most widely read recent study on the topic is Kenneth L. Woodward, *Making Saints: How the Catholic Church Determines Who Becomes a Saint, Who Doesn't, and Why* (New York: Touchstone, 1996). Woodward provides a helpful bibliography in his study.

100. Guardini's words are instructive here: "The requirements of the liturgy can be summed up in one word—humility: humility by renunciation; that is to say, by the abdication of self-rule and self-sufficiency, and humility by positive action; that is to say, by the acceptance of the spiritual principles which the liturgy offers and which far transcend the little world of individual spiritual existence" (Guardini, *The Spirit of the Liturgy*, 16).

101. Daughters of Saint Paul, eds., *Saint Paul Daily Missal*, 2344.

102. Ibid., 2349.

103. Ibid., 2559.

104. Guardini, *Sacred Signs*, 34.

105. Romano Guardini, *Meditations before Mass*, trans. Elinor Briefs (Notre Dame, Ind.: Ave Maria, 2014), 95.

106. Daughters of Saint Paul, eds., *Saint Paul Daily Missal*, 2566.

107. Balthasar contemplates this mystery in relation to the Marian prayer of the Rosary when he writes the following: "Christian prayer can attain to God only along the path that God himself has trod; otherwise it stumbles out of the

world and into the void, falling prey to the temptation of taking this void to be God or of taking God to be nothingness itself. God is not a worldly object, but neither is he a supraworldly thing to be aimed at and conquered, after making adequate technical preparations, by a kind of spiritual trip to the moon. God is infinite freedom, which opens up to us only on its own initiative. He not only addresses his Word to us, but makes it live among us. Thus, the Word that comes from God is also the Word that returns to him" (Balthasar, *The Threefold Garland*, 19).

108. See again Flannery, ed., "Lumen Gentium," 1 [I.1].

109. Francis, *Evangelii gaudium* (2013), §123.

110. Ibid., §125.

111. Ibid., §282.

112. Thérèse of Lisieux, *Story of a Soul*, 197.

113. Austen Ivereigh, *The Great Reformer: Francis and the Making of a Radical Pope* (New York: Henry Holt, 2014), 338–39.

114. Ibid., 339–40; cf. 338, 360.

115. Ibid., 310.

116. Augustine, *The Confessions*, 190 [IX.11.27].

117. Ibid., 195 [IX.13.34].

118. Ibid., 176 [IX.8].

119. Ibid., 174 [IX.6].

120. Ibid., 180 [IX.6.14].

Conclusion

1. Ratzinger, *The God of Jesus Christ*, 33.

2. De Lubac's summary of the Church's unfailing belief in the corporate nature of salvation is especially pertinent here: "Christ the Redeemer does not offer salvation merely to each one; he effects it, he is himself the salvation of the whole, and for each one salvation consists in a personal ratification of his origi-nal 'belonging' to Christ, so that he be not cast out, cut off from this Whole" (de Lubac, *Catholicism*, 39).

SELECTED BIBLIOGRAPHY

Adams, Nicholas. "Eschatology Sacred and Profane: The Effects of Philosophy on Theology in Pannenberg, Rahner, and Moltmann." *International Journal of Systematic Theology* 2, no. 3 (2000): 283–306.

Agamden, Giorgio. *Remnants of Auschwitz: The Witness and the Archive.* Translated by Daniel Heller-Roazen. New York: Zone, 2002.

Alison, James. *The Joy of Being Wrong: Original Sin Through Easter Eyes.* New York: Herder and Herder, 1998.

———. *Raising Abel: The Recovery of the Eschatological Imagination.* New York: Herder and Herder, 1996.

Alter, Robert. *The Art of Biblical Narrative.* New York: Basic, 2011.

———. *The Five Books of Moses: A Translation with Commentary.* New York: W. W. Norton, 2008.

Amore, Agostino. "La canonizzazione vescovile." *Antonianum* (April–September 1977): 231–66.

———. "Culto e canonizzazione dei santi nell' antichita cristiana." *Antonianum* (January–March 1977): 38–80.

Anatolios, Khaled. "Quest, Questions, and Christ in Augustine's 'Confessions.'" *Logos: A Journal of Catholic Thought and Culture* 3, no. 2 (2000): 47–76.

Anderson, Gary. *Charity: The Place of the Poor in the Biblical Tradition.* New Haven, Conn.: Yale University Press, 2013.

———. *The Genesis of Perfection: Adam and Eve in Jewish and Christian Imagination.* Louisville, Ky.: Westminster John Knox, 2002.

———. *Sin: A History.* New Haven, Conn.: Yale University Press, 2009.

Aquinas, Thomas. "Appendix A: Summa Theologiae 1.45.5." In *Aquinas on Creation,* translated by Steven Baldner and William Carroll, 110–14. Toronto: Pontifical Institute of Medieval Studies, 1997.

———. *Of God and His Creatures: An Annotated Translation of "The Summa Contra Gentiles" of Saint Thomas Aquinas.* Translated by Joseph Rickaby. Whitefish, Mont.: Kessinger, 2010.

———. *Summa Theologica*. Complete English Edition. Westminster, Md.: Christian Classics, 1981.

———. "Writings on the 'Sentences' of Peter Lombard 2.1.1." In *Aquinas on Creation*, translated by Steven Baldner and William Carroll, 63–109. Toronto: Pontifical Institute of Medieval Studies, 1997.

Ariès, Philippe. *The Hour of Our Death: The Classic History of Western Attitudes Toward Death over the Last One Thousand Years*. Translated by Helen Weaver. 2nd ed. New York: Vintage, 2008.

———. *Western Attitudes toward Death: From the Middle Ages to the Present*. Translated by Patricia Ranum. Baltimore: Johns Hopkins University Press, 1975.

Astell, Ann. "St. Catherine of Siena, Charitable Practice, and the Debt of Charity." University of Notre Dame. Unpublished, 2013.

Augustine. *City of God*. Translated by Henry Bettenson. New York: Penguin, 2003.

———. *The Confessions*. Translated by Maria Boulding. New York: Vintage, 1998.

———. "Letter 194: Augustine to Sixtus." In *Letters 156–210*, 3:287–308. The Works of Saint Augustine: A Translation for the 21st Century. Hyde Park, N.Y.: New City, 2004.

———. "On Genesis: A Refutation of the Manichees." In *On Genesis*, edited by John Rotelle, translated by Edmund Hill, 13:25–104. The Works of Saint Augustine: A Translation for the 21st Century. Hyde Park, N.Y.: New City, 2013.

———. "Sermon 272." In *Essential Sermons*, translated by Edmund Hill and Boniface Ramsey, 317–18. The Works of Saint Augustine: A Translation for the 21st Century. Hyde Park, N.Y.: New City, 2007.

———. *Teaching Christianity: De Doctrina Christiana*. Translated by Edmund Hill. Hyde Park, N.Y.: New City, 1996.

———. *The Trinity*. Edited by John Rotelle. Translated by Edmund Hill. Hyde Park, N.Y.: New City, 2012.

———. "Unfinished Literal Commentary on Genesis." In *On Genesis*, edited by John Rotelle, translated by Edmund Hill, 13:105–54. The Works of Saint Augustine: A Translation for the 21st Century. Hyde Park, N.Y.: New City, 2013.

Ayo, Nicholas. *The Creed as Symbol*. Notre Dame, Ind.: University of Notre Dame Press, 1990.

Babcock, William. "Caritas and Signification in De Doctrina Christiana 1–3." In *Augustine's De Doctrina Christiana: A Classic of Western Culture*, edited by Duane Arnold and Pamela Bright, 145–63. Notre Dame, Ind.: University of Notre Dame Press, 1995.

Badcock, Francis John. *The History of the Creeds*. New York: Macmillan, 1938.

Balthasar, Hans Urs von. *Credo: Meditations on the Apostles' Creed*. Translated by David Kipp. San Francisco: Ignatius, 2005.

———. *Dare We Hope "That All Men Be Saved"?; With, a Short Discourse on Hell*. Translated by David Kipp and Lothar Krauth. San Francisco: Ignatius, 1988.

———. *Elucidations*. Translated by John Riches. San Francisco: Ignatius, 1998.

———. *Explorations in Theology, Volume 1: The Word Made Flesh*. Translated by A. V. Littledale and Alexander Dru. San Francisco: Ignatius, 1989.

———. *The Glory of the Lord: A Theological Aesthetics, Volume I: Seeing the Form*. Edited by John Kenneth Riches. Translated by Erasmo Leiva-Merikakis. San Francisco: Ignatius, 2009.

———. *The Glory of the Lord: A Theological Aesthetics, Volume V: The Realm of Metaphysics in the Modern Age*. Edited by John Riches. Translated by Erasmo Leiva-Merikakis. San Francisco: Ignatius, 1991.

———. *The Glory of the Lord: A Theological Aesthetics, Volume VII: Theology: The New Covenant*. Edited by Joseph Fessio. Translated by Brian McNeil. San Francisco: Ignatius, 1990.

———. *Life Out of Death: Meditations on the Paschal Mystery*. Translated by Maria Stockl. San Francisco: Ignatius, 2012.

———. *Love Alone Is Credible*. Translated by D. C. Schindler. San Francisco: Ignatius, 2005.

———. *Mysterium Paschale: The Mystery of Easter*. Translated by Aidan Nichols. San Francisco: Ignatius, 2000.

———. *New Elucidations*. Translated by Mary Theresilde Skerry. San Francisco: Ignatius, 1986.

———. *Prayer*. Translated by Graham Harrison. San Francisco: Ignatius, 1986.

———. *Theo-Drama: Theological Dramatic Theory, Volume II: The Dramatis Personae: Man in God*. Translated by Graham Harrison. San Francisco: Ignatius, 1990.

———. *Theo-Drama: Theological Dramatic Theory, Volume III: The Dramatis Personae: The Person in Christ*. Translated by Graham Harrison. San Francisco: Ignatius, 1993.

———. *Theo-Drama: Theological Dramatic Theory, Volume IV: The Action*. Translated by Graham Harrison. San Francisco: Ignatius, 1994.

———. *Theo-Drama: Theological Dramatic Theory, Volume V: The Last Act*. Translated by Graham Harrison. San Francisco: Ignatius, 1998.

———. *Theo-Logic: Theological Logical Theory, Volume III: The Spirit of Truth*. Translated by Graham Harrison. San Francisco: Ignatius, 2005.

———. *A Theological Anthropology*. Eugene, Ore.: Wipf & Stock, 2010.

———. "Theologie und Spiritualitat." *Gregorianum* 50 (1969): 571–87.

———. *The Theology of Henri de Lubac: An Overview.* Translated by Joseph Fessio and Michael Waldstein. San Francisco: Ignatius, 1991.

———. *A Theology of History.* San Francisco: Ignatius, 1994.

———. *The Threefold Garland: The World's Salvation in Mary's Prayer.* San Francisco: Ignatius, 1982.

———. "The Timeliness of Lisieux." In *Carmelite Studies: Spiritual Direction.* Washington, D.C.: ICS, 1980.

———. *Two Sisters in the Spirit: Therese of Lisieux and Elizabeth of the Trinity.* Translated by Dennis D. Martin, Donald Nicholas, and Anne Englund Nash. San Francisco: Ignatius, 1998.

Balthasar, Hans Urs von, and Joseph Ratzinger. *Mary: The Church at the Source.* Translated by Aiden Walker. San Francisco: Communio, 1997.

Bauckman, Richard. "Eschatology in 'The Coming of God.'" In *God Will Be All in All: The Eschatology of Jürgen Moltmann,* edited by Richard Bauckman, 1–34. Edinburgh: First Fortress, 2001.

———. "Time and Eternity." In *God Will Be All in All: The Eschatology of Jürgen Moltmann,* edited by Richard Bauckman, 155–93. Edinburgh: First Fortress, 2001.

Beaton, Rhodora. "The Sacramentality of the Word: Contributions of Karl Rahner and Louis-Marie Chauvet to a Roman Catholic Theology of the Word." Ph.D. diss., University of Notre Dame, 2009.

Becker, Ernest. *The Denial of Death.* New York: Free Press, 1975.

Belcher, Kimberly. *Efficacious Engagement: Sacramental Participation in the Trinitarian Mystery.* Collegeville, Minn.: Liturgical, 2011.

———. "The Feast of Peace: The Eucharist as a Sacrifice and a Meal in Benedict XVI's Theology." In *Explorations in the Theology of Benedict XVI,* edited by John Cavadini, 254–75. Notre Dame, Ind.: University of Notre Dame Press, 2013.

Benedict XII. *Benedictus Deus* (1336). http://www.papalencyclicals.net/Ben12/B12bdeus.html.

Benedict XVI. *Deus Caritas Est: God Is Love.* Boston: Pauline, 2006.

———. *Jesus of Nazareth, Part I: From the Baptism in the Jordan to the Transfiguration.* New York: Doubleday, 2007.

———. *Jesus of Nazareth, Part II: Holy Week: From the Entrance into Jerusalem to the Resurrection.* San Francisco: Ignatius, 2011.

———. *Sacramentum caritatis* (February 22, 2007). http://www.vatican.va/holy_father/benedict_xvi/apost_exhortations/documents/hf_ben-xvi_exh_20070222_sacramentum-caritatis_en.html.

———. *Saved in Hope: Spe Salvi.* San Francisco: Ignatius, 2008.

Benoit, Pierre. "Resurrection: At the End of Time or Immediately after Death?" *Concilium* 60 (1970): 103–14.

Bernard of Clairvaux. "Sermons on the 'Song of Songs.'" In *Bernard of Clairvaux: Selected Works*, translated by G. R. Evans. New York: Paulist, 1987.

Bonhoeffer, Dietrich. *The Communion of Saints: A Dogmatic Inquiry into the Sociology of the Church*. Translated by Ronald Smith. New York: Harper & Row, 1963.

Bouyer, Louis. *The Church of God: Body of Christ and Temple of the Spirit*. Translated by Charles Underhill Quinn. San Francisco: Ignatius, 2011.

Braine, David. "The Debate Between Henri de Lubac and His Critics." *Nova et Vetera* 6, no. 3 (2008): 543–90.

Brueggemann, Walter, Bruce C. Birch, Terence E. Fretheim, and David L. Petersen. *A Theological Introduction to the Old Testament*. Nashville: Abingdon, 2005.

Bulgakov, Sergius. *The Friend of the Bridegroom: On the Orthodox Veneration of the Forerunner*. Translated by Boris Jakim. Grand Rapids, Mich.: Eerdmans, 2003.

Capizzi, Joseph. "Solidarity as a Basis for Conversion and Communion: A Response to Peter Casarella." *Communio* 27 (2000): 124–33.

Cary, Phillip. *Augustine's Invention of the Inner Self: The Legacy of a Christian Platonist*. Oxford: Oxford University Press, 2000.

Casarella, Peter. "Solidarity as the Fruit of Communio: Ecclesia in America, 'Post-Liberation Theology,' and the Earth." *Communio* 27 (2000): 98–123.

Catherine of Siena. *The Dialogue*. New York: Paulist, 1980.

Cavadini, John. "Book Two: Augustine's Book of Shadows." In *A Reader's Companion to Augustine's "Confessions,"* edited by Kim Paffenroth and Robert Kennedy, 25–34. Louisville, Ky.: Westminster John Knox, 2003.

———. "The Darkest Enigma: Reconsidering the Self in Augustine's Thought." *Augustinian Studies* 38, no. 1 (2007): 119–32.

———. "Review of Phillip Cary's 'Augustine's Invention of the Inner Self: The Legacy of a Christian Platonist.'" *Modern Theology* 18 (2002): 425–28.

———. "The Sweetness of the Word: Salvation and Rhetoric in Augustine's 'De Doctrina Christiana.'" In *Augustine's De Doctrina Christiana: A Classic of Western Culture*, edited by Duane Arnold and Pamela Bright, 164–81. Notre Dame, Ind.: University of Notre Dame Press, 1995.

Chantraine, Georges. "The Supernatural: Discernment of Catholic Thought According to Henri de Lubac." In *Surnatural: A Controversy at the Heart of Twentieth-Century Thomistic Thought*, edited by Serge-Thomas Bonino, translated by Robert Williams and Matthew Levering, 21–40. Ave Maria, Fla.: Sapientia Press of Ave Maria University, 2009.

Chauvet, Louis-Marie. "The Broken Bread as Theological Figure of Eucharistic Presence." In *Sacramental Presence in a Postmodern Context*, edited by L. Boeve and L. Leijssen, 236–64. Leuven: Leuven University Press, 2001.

———. *The Sacraments: The Word of God and the Mercy of the Body.* Translated by Madeleine Beaumont. Collegeville, Minn.: Liturgical, 2001.

———. *Symbol and Sacrament: A Sacramental Reinterpretation of the Christian Experience.* Translated by Patrick Madigan and Madeleine Beaumont. Collegeville, Minn.: Liturgical, 1995.

Childs, Brevard S. *The Book of Exodus: A Critical, Theological Commentary.* New ed. Philadelphia: Westminster, 1974.

Choron, Jacques. *Death and Western Thought.* New York: Collier, 1963.

Coakley, Sarah. "Deepening Practices: Perspectives from Ascetical and Mystical Theology." In *Practicing Theology: Belief and Practices in Christian Life,* edited by Miroslav Volf and Dorothy Bass, 78–93. Grand Rapids, Mich.: Eerdmans, 2011.

———. *God, Sexuality, and the Self: An Essay "On the Trinity."* Cambridge: Cambridge University Press, 2013.

Corkery, James. "The Communion of Saints." *The Way* 36, no. 4 (1996): 285–93.

Cunningham, Lawrence. *The Meaning of Saints.* San Francisco: Harper & Row, 1980.

———. "The Roman Canon and Catholicity: A Meditation." *Church,* Spring 2006, 5–10.

———."Saints and Martyrs: Some Contemporary Considerations." *Theological Studies,* no. 60 (n.d.): 529–37.

Dahlstrom, Daniel. "Truth and Temptation: Confessions and Existential Analysis." In *A Companion to Heidegger's "Phenomenology of Religious Life,"* edited by Sean McGrath and Andrzej Wiercinski, 263–84. New York: Rodopi, 2010.

Daley, Brian E. *The Hope of the Early Church: A Handbook of Patristic Eschatology.* Peabody, Mass.: Hendrickson, 2003.

Daniélou, Jean. *The Bible and the Liturgy.* Notre Dame, Ind.: University of Notre Dame Press, 2009.

———. *From Shadows to Reality: Studies in the Biblical Typology of the Fathers.* London: Burns and Oates, 1960.

Dante Alighieri. *Inferno.* Edited and translated by Robin Kirkpatrick. New York: Penguin, 2006.

———. *Paradiso.* Edited and translated by Robin Kirkpatrick. New York: Penguin, 2006.

———. *Purgatorio.* Edited and translated by Robin Kirkpatrick. New York: Penguin, 2006.

Daughters of Saint Paul, eds. *Saint Paul Daily Missal.* Boston: Pauline, 2012.

Day, Dorothy. *By Little and By Little: The Selected Writings of Dorothy Day.* Edited by Robert Ellsberg. New York: Alfred A. Knopf, 1984.

————. *The Long Loneliness*. San Francisco: Harper & Row, 1952.

————. *Thérèse: A Life of Thérèse of Lisieux*. Notre Dame, Ind.: Fides, 1960.

De Lubac, Henri. *Augustinianism and Modern Theology*. Translated by Lancelot Sheppard. New York: Herder and Herder, 2000.

————. *Brief Catechesis on Nature and Grace*. Translated by Richard Arnandez. San Francisco: Ignatius, 1984.

————. *Catholicism: Christ and the Common Destiny of Man*. Translated by Lancelot Sheppard and Elizabeth Englund. San Francisco: Ignatius, 1988.

————. *The Drama of Atheist Humanism*. Translated by Mark Sebanc. San Francisco: Ignatius, 1995.

————. *The Mystery of the Supernatural*. Translated by Rosemary Sheed. New York: Herder and Herder, 1998.

————. *Surnatural: Etudes historiques*. Paris: Aubier, 1946.

Derrida, Jacques. *The Gift of Death & Literature in Secret*. Translated by David Wills. 2nd ed. Chicago: University of Chicago Press, 2007.

Doyle, Dennis. *Communion Ecclesiology: Vision and Versions*. New York: Orbis, 2000.

Driscoll, Michael, and J. Michael Joncas. *The Order of Mass: A Roman Missal Study Edition and Workbook*. Collegeville, Minn.: Liturgical, 2011.

Duffy, Stephen. *The Graced Horizon: Nature and Grace in Modern Catholic Thought*. Collegeville, Minn.: Liturgical, 1992.

Durham, John. *Exodus*. World Biblical Commentary, vol. 3. Waco, Tex.: Thomas Nelson, 1987.

Eire, Carlos. *A Very Brief History of Eternity*. Princeton, N.J.: Princeton University Press, 2010.

Eliot, T. S. *Four Quartets*. New York: Harcourt, 1971.

Englander, Alex. "Kant's Aesthetic Theology: Revelation as Symbolisation in the Critical Philosophy." *Neue Zeitschrift für Systematische Theologie und Religionsphilosophie* 53, no. 3 (2011): 303–17.

Enns, Phil. "Reason and Revelation: Kant and the Problem of Authority." *International Journal for Philosophy of Religion* 62, no. 2 (2007): 103–14.

Esposito, Constantino. "Memory and Temptation: Heidegger Reads Book X of Augustine's 'Confessions.'" In *A Companion to Heidegger's "Phenomenology of Religious Life,"* edited by Sean McGrath and Andrzej Wiercinski. New York: Rodopi, 2010.

Fiddes, Paul. *The Promised End: Eschatology in Theology and Literature*. Oxford: Blackwell, 2000.

Figura, Michael. "Concupiscence and Desire from the Point of View of Theological Anthropology." *Communio*, no. 27 (Spring 2000): 3–13.

Flannery, Austin, ed. "Lumen Gentium: Dogmatic Constitution on the Church." In *Vatican Council II: Constitutions, Decrees, Declarations*, 1–96. Revised translation. Northport, N.Y.: Costello, 1996.

―――. "Sacrosanctum Concilium: Constitution on the Sacred Liturgy." In *Vatican Council II: Constitutions, Decrees, Declarations*, 117–63. Revised translation. Northport, N.Y.: Costello, 1996.

Foley, Leonard, and Pat McCloskey, eds. *Saint of the Day: Lives, Lessons and Feasts*. Cincinnati, Ohio: St. Anthony Messenger, 2009.

Francis. *Evangelii gaudium: The Joy of the Gospel*, 2013.

Frei, Hans. *The Identity of Jesus Christ: The Hermeneutical Bases of Dogmatic Theology*. Philadelphia: Fortress, 1975.

Fretheim, Terence. *Exodus*. Louisville, Ky.: John Knox, 1991.

Fritsch, Matthias. "Cura et Casus: Heidegger and Augustine on the Care of the Self." In *The Influence of Augustine on Heidegger: The Emergence of an Augustinian Phenomenology*, edited by Craig de Paulo, 89–114. Lewiston, N.Y.: Edwin Mellen, 2006.

Fritz, Peter. *Karl Rahner's Theological Aesthetics*. Washington, D.C.: Catholic University of America Press, 2014.

―――. "Sublime Apprehension: A Catholic, Rahnerian Construction." Ph.D. diss., Notre Dame, 2010.

Frohlich, Mary. "Desolation and Doctrine in Thérèse of Lisieux." *Theological Studies*, no. 61 (2000): 261–79.

Frye, Northrop. *The Great Code: The Bible and Literature*. San Diego: Harcourt, 1982.

Gorer, Geoffrey. *Death, Grief, and Mourning*. New York: Arno, 1977.

―――. "The Pornography of Death." In *Death, Grief, and Mourning*, 192–99. New York: Arno, 1977.

Görres, Ida Friederike. *The Hidden Face: A Study of St. Thérèse of Lisieux*. San Francisco: Ignatius, 2003.

Gregory of Nyssa. *Life of Moses*. Translated by Abraham Malherbe and Everett Ferguson. New York: Paulist, 1978.

Guardini, Romano. *The End of the Modern World*. Translated by Elinor Briefs. Wilmington, Del.: ISI, 1998.

―――. *The Last Things: Concerning Death, Purification after Death, Resurrection, Judgment, and Eternity*. Translated by Charlotte E. Forsyth and Grace B. Branham. Notre Dame, Ind.: University of Notre Dame Press, 1965.

―――. *The Lord*. Translated by Elinor Briefs. Washington, D.C.: Regnery, 2013.

―――. *Meditations before Mass*. Translated by Elinor Briefs. Notre Dame, Ind.: Ave Maria, 2014.

————. *Rilke's Duino Elegies: An Interpretation*. Translated by K. G. Knight. London: Darwen Finlayson, 1961.

————. *Sacred Signs*. Translated by Grace Branham. London: Aeterna, 2015.

————. *The Spirit of the Liturgy*. Translated by Ada Lane. New York: Herder and Herder, 1998.

Hahnenberg, Edward. "The Mystical Body of Christ and Communion Ecclesiology: Historical Parallels." *Irish Theological Quarterly* 70 (2005): 3–30.

Hawkins, Peter. "Dante and the Bible." In *The Cambridge Companion to Dante*, edited by Rachel Jacoff, 125–40. 2nd ed. Cambridge: Cambridge University Press, 2007.

Heidegger, Martin. *Being and Time*. New York: Harper Perennial Modern Classics, 2008.

————. "Nietzsche, Volume I: The Will to Power as Art." In *Nietzsche: Volume I: The Will to Power as Art and Volume II: The Eternal Recurrence of the Same*, translated by David Farrell Krell. New York: HarperOne, 1991.

————. "Nietzsche, Volume II: The Eternal Recurrence of the Same." In *Nietzsche: Volume I: The Will to Power as Art and Volume II: The Eternal Recurrence of the Same*, translated by David Farrell Krell. New York: HarperOne, 1991.

————. "The Origin of the Work of Art." In *Poetry, Language, Thought*, translated by Albert Hofstadter. New York: Harper Perennial Modern Classics, 2001.

————. *The Phenomenology of Religious Life*. Translated by Matthias Fritsch and Jennifer Anna Gosetti-Ferencei. Bloomington: Indiana University Press, 2010.

————. "What Are Poets For?" In *Poetry, Language, Thought*, translated by Albert Hofstadter. New York: Harper Perennial Modern Classics, 2001.

Henrix, Hans Hermann. "Von der Nachahmung Gottes: Heilighkeit und Heiligsein im Biblischen und Judischen Denken." *Erbe und Auftrag* 65 (1989): 177–87.

Hinze, Bradford. "Ecclesial Repentance and the Demands of Dialogue." *Theological Studies* 61 (2000): 207–38.

Hofstadter, Albert. "Introduction." In *Poetry, Language, Thought*. New York: Harper Perennial Modern Classics, 2001.

Hoover, Rose. "The Communion of Saints: Lest the Journey Be Too Long." *The Way* 30 (1990): 216–30.

Hunt, Anne. *The Trinity and the Paschal Mystery: A Development in Recent Catholic Theology*. Collegeville, Minn.: Liturgical, 1997.

Irenaeus of Lyons. *Against Heresies*. Edited by Alexander Roberts, James Donaldson, and Arthur Cleveland Coxe. South Bend, Ind.: Ex Fontibus, 2012.

Isaac, Jules. *The Teaching of Contempt: Christian Roots of Anti-Semitism*. Translated by Helen Weaver. New York: Holt, Rinehart and Winston, 1964.

Ivereigh, Austen. *The Great Reformer: Francis and the Making of a Radical Pope*. New York: Henry Holt, 2014.

Janzen, J. Gerald. *Exodus*. Louisville, Ky.: Westminster John Knox, 1997.

John Paul II. *Divini amoris scientia* (1997). vatican.va/holy_father/john_paul _ii/apost_letters/documents/hf_jp--ii_apl_19101997_divini--amoris _en.html.

―――. *Ecclesia de Eucharistia* (2003). vatican.va/holy_father/special_features /.../hf_jp-ii_enc_20030417_ecc lesia_eucharistia_en.html.

Johnson, Elizabeth. *Friends of God and Prophets: A Feminist Theological Reading of the Communion of Saints*. New York: Continuum, 1998.

―――. *Truly Our Sister: A Theology of Mary in the Communion of Saints*. New York: Continuum, 2003.

Kant, Immanuel. *The Conflict of the Faculties*. Translated by Mary Gregor. New York: Abaris, 1979.

―――. "The End of All Things." In *On History*, edited by Lewis White Beck, translated by Robert E. Anchor and Emil L. Fackenheim. Indianapolis: Bobbs-Merrill, 1963.

―――. *Religion within the Boundaries of Mere Reason: And Other Writings*. Translated by Allen Wood and George Di Giovanni. Cambridge: Cambridge University Press, 1999.

Kastenbaum, Robert. *The Psychology of Death*. 3rd ed. New York: Springer, 2000.

Kelly, J. N. D. *Early Christian Creeds*. New York: Longman, 1972.

Kirkpatrick, Robin. "Introduction." In *Paradiso*. New York: Penguin, 2006.

Kisiel, Theodore. *The Genesis of Heidegger's "Being & Time."* Berkeley: University of California Press, 1993.

Koenig, Elizabeth. "Keeping Company with Jesus and the Saints." *Theology Today* 56 (1999): 18–28.

Komonchak, Joseph. "Theology and Culture at Mid-Century: The Example of Henri de Lubac." *Theological Studies* 51 (1992): 579–602.

Krieg, Robert. "Romano Guardini's Theology of the Human Person." *Theological Studies* 59 (1998): 457–74.

Kruse, Heinz. "Gemeinschaft der Heiligen: Herkunft und Bedeutung des Glaubensartikels." *Vigiliae Christianae* 47, no. 3 (1993): 246–59.

Lafontaine, Rene. "'Arrives a Jesus, ils le trouverent mort' (Jo. Xix, 39): Hans Urs von Balthasar, theologien du samedi saint." *Revue Thomiste* 86 (1986): 635–43.

Lamirande, Emilien. "The History of a Formula." In *The Communion of Saints*, translated by A. Manson, 15–38. New York: Hawthorn, 1963.

Latourelle, Rene. "La saintete signe de la revelation." *Gregorianum* 46, no. 1 (1965): 36–65.

Lee, Simon. *Jesus' Transfiguration and the Believers' Transformation: A Study of the Transfiguration and Its Development in Early Christian Writings.* Tübingen: Mohr Siebeck, 2009.

Leithart, Peter. *1 & 2 Kings.* Grand Rapids, Mich.: Brazos , 2006.

Levenson, Jon. *Resurrection and the Restoration of Israel: The Ultimate Victory of the God of Life.* New Haven, Conn.: Yale University Press, 2006.

Levering, Matthew. *Jesus and the Demise of Death: Resurrection, Afterlife, and the Fate of the Christian.* Waco, Tex.: Baylor University Press, 2012.

———. *Mary's Bodily Assumption.* Notre Dame, Ind.: University of Notre Dame Press, 2015.

Levi, Primo. *The Drowned and the Saved.* Translated by Raymond Rosenthal. New York: Vintage, 1998.

———. *If This Is a Man.* Translated by Stuart Woolf. London: Abacus, 1987.

———. *The Periodic Table.* Translated by Raymond Rosenthal. New York: Everyman's Library, 1996.

Lewis, C. S. *The Great Divorce.* San Francisco: HarperOne, 2000.

Long, Thomas, and Thomas Lynch. *The Good Funeral: Death, Grief, and the Community of Care.* Louisville, Ky.: Westminster John Knox, 2013.

Lynch, Thomas. *The Undertaking: Life Studies from the Dismal Trade.* New York: W. W. Norton, 2009.

Marina, Jacqueline. "Kant on Grace: A Reply to His Critics." *Religious Studies* 33, no. 4 (1997): 379–400.

Marion, Jean-Luc. *God Without Being: Hors-Texte.* Translated by Thomas A. Carlson. Chicago: University of Chicago Press, 1995.

———. *The Idol and Distance: Five Studies.* Translated by Thomas A. Carlson. 2nd ed. New York: Fordham University Press, 2001.

———. *In the Self's Place: The Approach of Saint Augustine.* Translated by Jeffrey Kosky. Stanford, Calif.: Stanford University Press, 2012.

———. "Resting, Moving, Loving: The Access to the Self According to Saint Augustine." *Journal of Religion* 91, no. 1 (2011): 24–42.

———. "Sketch of a Phenomenological Concept of Sacrifice." In *The Reason of the Gift.* Charlottesville: University Press of Virginia, 2011.

Maritain, Jacques. *Reflections on America.* New York: Gordian, 1975.

Marthaler, Berard. *The Creed: The Apostolic Faith in Contemporary Theology.* 3rd rev. ed. New London, Conn.: Twenty-Third, 2007.

Martin, Jennifer Newsome. *Hans Urs von Balthasar and the Critical Appropriation of Russian Religious Thought.* Notre Dame, Ind.: University of Notre Dame Press, 2015.

————."Hans Urs von Balthasar and the Press of Speculative Russian Religious Philosophy." Ph.D. diss., University of Notre Dame, 2012.

McGrath, Sean. "Alternative Confessions, Conflicting Faiths: A Review of 'The Influence of Augustine on Heidegger.'" *American Catholic Philosophical Quarterly* 82, no. 2 (2008): 317–35.

————. "The Young Heidegger's Problematic Reading of Augustine's Ontological Restlessness." *Journal for Cultural and Religious Theory* 4, no. 1 (2002).

McIntosh, Mark. *Christology from Within: Spirituality and the Incarnation in Hans Urs von Balthasar.* Notre Dame, Ind.: University of Notre Dame Press, 2000.

Metz, Johann Baptist. *Faith in History and Society: Toward a Practical Fundamental Theology.* Edited and translated by J. Matthew Ashley. New York: Herder and Herder, 2007.

Michalson, Gordon. "Kant, the Bible, and the Recovery from Radical Evil." In *Kant's Anatomy of Evil,* edited by Sharon Anderson-Gold and Pablo Muchnik, 57–73. Cambridge: Cambridge University Press, 2010.

Milbank, John. *The Suspended Middle: Henri de Lubac and the Debate Concerning the Supernatural.* Grand Rapids, Mich.: Eerdmans, 2005.

Mitchell, Nathan. "The Amen Corner: The Life of the Dead." *Worship* 66 (November 1992): 536–44.

————. "Rituality and the Retrieval of Sacrament as 'Language Event.'" In *Sacraments: Revelation of the Humanity of God: Engaging the Fundamental Theology of Louis-Marie Chauvet,* edited by Philippe Bordeyne and Bruce Morrill. Collegeville, Minn.: Liturgical, 2008.

Mitford, Jessica. *The American Way of Death.* New York: Simon and Schuster, 1963.

————. *The American Way of Death Revisited.* New York: Alfred A. Knopf, 1998.

Moevs, Christian. *The Metaphysics of Dante's Comedy.* New York: Oxford University Press, 2005.

Moltmann, Jürgen. *The Coming of God: Christian Eschatology.* Translated by Margaret Kohl. Minneapolis: Fortress, 2004.

————. "To Believe with All Your Senses." In *The Catholic Theological Society of America: Proceedings of the Sixtieth Annual Convention,* edited by Richard Sparks, 1–12. Berkeley, Calif.: Newman Hall, 2005.

Moltmann, Jürgen, and Elisabeth Moltmann-Wendel. "Love, Death, Eternal Life: Theology of Hope—the Personal Side." In *Love: The Foundation of Hope: The Theology of Jürgen Moltmann and Elisabeth Moltmann-Wendel,* edited by Frederic Burnham, Charles S. McCoy, and Douglas M. Meeks. San Francisco: Harper & Row, 1988.

Murphy, Francesca. "Papal Ecclesiology." In *Explorations in the Theology of Benedict XVI,* edited by John Cavadini, 215–35. Notre Dame, Ind.: University of Notre Dame Press, 2013.

Navasky, Miri, and Karen O'Connor. "The Undertaking." *Frontline*. PBS, 2008.

Newman, John Henry. "Holiness Necessary for Future Blessedness." In *Selected Sermons, Prayers, and Devotions*, 3–11. New York: Vintage, 1999.

———. "Moses the Type of Christ." In *Parochial and Plain Sermons*, 1488–95. San Francisco: Ignatius, 1997.

———. "The Orthodoxy of the Body of the Faithful During the Supremacy of Arianism." In *The Arians of the Fourth Century*, 445–68. Eugene, Ore.: Wipf & Stock, 1996.

Nichols, Aiden. *The Thought of Pope Benedict XVI: An Introduction to the Theology of Joseph Ratzinger*. New York: Burns & Oates, 2007.

Nietzsche, Friedrich. "The Anti-Christ." In *The Nietzsche Reader*, edited by Keith Ansell Pearson and Duncan Large. Oxford: Blackwell, 2006.

———. "The Gay Science." In *The Nietzsche Reader*, edited by Keith Ansell Pearson and Duncan Large. Oxford: Blackwell, 2006.

———. "Genealogy of Morality." In *The Nietzsche Reader*, edited by Keith Ansell-Pearson and Duncan Large. Oxford: Blackwell, 2006.

———. "Human, All Too Human." In *The Nietzsche Reader*, edited by Keith Ansell-Pearson and Duncan Large. Oxford: Blackwell, 2006.

———. "Thus Spoke Zarathustra." In *The Nietzsche Reader*, edited by Keith Ansell Pearson and Duncan Large. Oxford: Blackwell, 2006.

———. "Twilight of the Idols." In *The Nietzsche Reader*, edited by Keith Ansell-Pearson and Duncan Large. Oxford: Blackwell, 2006.

Nussberger, Danielle. "Saint as Theological Wellspring: Hans Urs von Balthasar's Hermeneutic of the Saint in a Christological and Trinitarian Key." Ph.D. diss., University of Notre Dame, 2007.

Oakes, Edward, and Alyssa Pitstick. "Balthasar, Hell, and Heresy: An Exchange." *First Things: A Monthly Journal of Religion and Public Life* 168 (2006): 25–32.

———. "More on Balthasar, Hell, and Heresy." *First Things: A Monthly Journal of Religion and Public Life* 169 (2006): 16–18.

O'Connor, Flannery. "A Temple of the Holy Ghost." In *The Complete Stories*, 236–48. New York: Farrar, Straus and Giroux, 1971.

O'Donnell, Christopher. *Love in the Heart of the Church: The Mission of Thérèse of Lisieux*. Dublin: Veritas, 1997.

O'Keefe, John J., and R. R. Reno. *Sanctified Vision: An Introduction to Early Christian Interpretation of the Bible*. Baltimore: Johns Hopkins University Press, 2005.

O'Neill, Onora. "Kant on Reason and Religion." Paper presented at the Tanner Lecture on Human Values, Harvard University, 2006.

O'Regan, Cyril. "Augustine and Heidegger: Desire." In *Martin Heidegger's Interpretations of Saint Augustine: Sein und Zeit und Ewigkeit,* edited by Ben Vedder, 211–34. Lewiston, N.Y.: Edwin Mellen, 2005.

———. "Balthasar: Between Tubingen and Postmodernity." *Modern Theology* 14 (1998): 325–53.

———. "Benedict the Augustinian." In *Explorations in the Theology of Benedict XVI,* edited by John Cavadini, 21–62. Notre Dame, Ind.: University of Notre Dame Press, 2013.

———. "The Mystery of Iniquity: Augustine and Heidegger." In *Martin Heidegger's Interpretations of Saint Augustine: Sein und Zeit und Ewigkeit,* edited by Frederick Van Fleteren, 383–440. Lewiston, N.Y.: Edwin Mellen, 2005.

———. "Theology, Art, and Beauty." In *The Many Faces of Beauty,* edited by Vittorio Hosle. Notre Dame, Ind.: University of Notre Dame Press, 2011.

———. "Von Balthasar and Thick Retrieval: Post-Chalcedonian Symphonic Theology." *Gregorianum* 77 (1996): 227–60.

Origen. *Commentary on the Gospel According to John, Books 1–10.* Translated by Ronald E. Heine. Fathers of the Church Patristic Series. Washington, D.C.: Catholic University of America Press, 2001.

———. *Homilies on Genesis and Exodus.* Translated by Ronald E. Heine. Washington, D.C.: Catholic University of America Press, 2002.

Otten, Willemien. "Jean-Luc Marion: 'Au lieu soi. L'approche de Saint Augustin.'" *Continental Philosophy Review* 42 (2010): 597–602.

Péguy, Charles. *Le porche du mystère de la deuxième vertu.* Paris: Gallimard, 1986.

Pelikan, Jaroslav. *Credo: Historical and Theological Guide to Creeds and Confessions of Faith in the Christian Tradition.* New Haven, Conn.: Yale University Press, 2005.

———. *The Shape of Death: Life, Death, and Immortality in the Early Fathers.* New York: Abingdon, 1961.

Pelikan, Jaroslav, and Valerie Hotchkiss, eds. *Creeds and Confessions of Faith in the Christian Tradition.* Vol. I, *Early, Eastern, and Medieval.* New Haven, Conn.: Yale University Press, 2003.

Perkins, Pheme. *The Resurrection: New Testament Witness and Contemporary Reflection.* New York: Doubleday, 1984.

Phan, Peter. *Eternity in Time: A Study of Karl Rahner's Eschatology.* London: Associated University Press, 1988.

Piat, Stephane-Joseph. *The Story of a Family: The Home of St. Thérèse of Lisieux.* Translated by a Benedictine of Stanbrook Abbey. Rockford, Ill.: Tan, 1994.

Pitstick, Alyssa. *Light in the Darkness: Hans Urs von Balthasar and the Catholic Doctrine of Christ's Descent into Hell.* Grand Rapids, Mich.: Eerdmans, 2007.

Pius XII. *Munificentissimus Deus* (1950). http://w2.vatican.va/content/pius-xii/en/apost_constitutions/documents/hf_p-xii_apc_19501101_munificentissimus-deus.html.

Plekon, Michael. *Hidden Holiness.* Notre Dame, Ind.: University of Notre Dame Press, 2009.

———. *Saints as They Really Are: Voices of Holiness in Our Times.* Notre Dame, Ind.: University of Notre Dame Press, 2012.

Rahner, Karl. "All Saints." In *Theological Investigations*, translated by Cornelius Ernst et al., 8:24–29. Limerick, Ireland: Mary Immaculate College, 2000.

———. "'Behold This Heart!': Preliminaries to a Theology of Devotion to the Sacred Heart." In *Theological Investigations*, translated by Cornelius Ernst et al., 3:321–30. Limerick, Ireland: Mary Immaculate College, 2000.

———. "Being Open to God as Ever Greater." In *Theological Investigations*, translated by Cornelius Ernst et al., 7:25–46. Limerick, Ireland: Mary Immaculate College, 2000.

———. "The Body in the Order of Salvation." In *Theological Investigations*, translated by Cornelius Ernst et al., 17:71–89. Limerick, Ireland: Mary Immaculate College, 2000.

———. "The Church of the Saints." In *Theological Investigations*, translated by Cornelius Ernst et al., 3:91–104. Limerick, Ireland: Mary Immaculate College, 2000.

———. "The Comfort of Time." In *Theological Investigations*, translated by Cornelius Ernst et al., 3:141–57. Limerick, Ireland: Mary Immaculate College, 2000.

———. "The Concept of Mystery in Catholic Theology." In *Theological Investigations*, translated by Cornelius Ernst et al., 4:36–73. Limerick, Ireland: Mary Immaculate College, 2000.

———. "Concerning the Relationship Between Nature and Grace." In *Theological Investigations*, translated by Cornelius Ernst et al., 1:297–317. Limerick, Ireland: Mary Immaculate College, 2000.

———. "Current Problems in Christology." In *Theological Investigations*, translated by Cornelius Ernst et al., 1:149–213. Limerick, Ireland: Mary Immaculate College, 2000.

———. "The Dignity and Freedom of Man." In *Theological Investigations*, translated by Cornelius Ernst et al., 2:235–63. Limerick, Ireland: Mary Immaculate College, 2000.

———. "The Eternal Significance of the Humanity of Jesus for Our Relationship with God." In *Theological Investigations*, translated by Cornelius Ernst et al., 3:35–46. Limerick, Ireland: Mary Immaculate College, 2000.

———. "Experiencing Easter." In *Theological Investigations*, translated by Cornelius Ernst et al., 7:159–68. Limerick, Ireland: Mary Immaculate College, 2000.

———. *Foundations of Christian Faith: An Introduction to the Idea of Christianity.* New York: Crossroad, 1994.

———. "Guilt-Responsibility-Punishment within the View of Catholic Theology." In *Theological Investigations*, translated by Cornelius Ernst et al., 6:197–217. Limerick, Ireland: Mary Immaculate College, 2000.

———. *Hearer of the Word: Laying the Foundation for a Philosophy of Religion.* Translated by Joseph Donceel. New York: Continuum, 1994.

———. "The Hermeneutics of Eschatological Assertions." In *Theological Investigations*, translated by Cornelius Ernst et al., 4:323–46. Limerick, Ireland: Mary Immaculate College, 2000.

———. "Ideas for a Theology of Death." In *Theological Investigations*, translated by Cornelius Ernst et al., 13:169–86. Limerick, Ireland: Mary Immaculate College, 2000.

———. "The Ignatian Mysticism of Joy in the World." In *Theological Investigations*, translated by Cornelius Ernst et al., 3:277–93. Limerick, Ireland: Mary Immaculate College, 2000.

———. "The Intermediate State." In *Theological Investigations*, translated by Cornelius Ernst et al., 17:114–24. Limerick, Ireland: Mary Immaculate College, 2000.

———. "The Interpretation of the Dogma of the Assumption." In *Theological Investigations*, translated by Cornelius Ernst et al., 1:215–27. Limerick, Ireland: Mary Immaculate College, 2000.

———. "The Life of the Dead." In *Theological Investigations*, translated by Cornelius Ernst et al., 4:347–54. Limerick, Ireland: Mary Immaculate College, 2000.

———. *On the Theology of Death.* Translated by C. H. Henkey. 2nd ed. New York: Herder and Herder, 1967.

———. "The Resurrection of the Body." In *Theological Investigations*, translated by Cornelius Ernst et al., 2:203–16. Limerick, Ireland: Mary Immaculate College, 2000.

———. "The Sin of Adam." In *Theological Investigations*, translated by Cornelius Ernst et al., 11:247–62. Limerick, Ireland: Mary Immaculate College, 2000.

———. "The Sinful Church in the Decrees of Vatican II." In *Theological Investigations*, translated by Cornelius Ernst et al., 6:270–94. Limerick, Ireland: Mary Immaculate College, 2000.

———. "Some Theses for a Theology of Devotion to the Sacred Heart." In *Theological Investigations*, translated by Cornelius Ernst et al., 3:331–52. Limerick, Ireland: Mary Immaculate College, 2000.

———. *Spirit in the World*. Translated by William Dych. New York: Continuum, 1994.

———. "The Theological Concept of Concupiscentia." In *Theological Investigations*, translated by Cornelius Ernst et al., 1:347–82. Limerick, Ireland: Mary Immaculate College, 2000.

———. "Theological Considerations Concerning the Moment of Death." In *Theological Investigations*, translated by Cornelius Ernst et al., 2:309–21. Limerick, Ireland: Mary Immaculate College, 2000.

———. "Theology of Freedom." In *Theological Investigations*, translated by Cornelius Ernst et al., 6:178–96. Limerick, Ireland: Mary Immaculate College, 2000.

———. "The Theology of the Symbol." In *Theological Investigations*, translated by Cornelius Ernst et al., 4:221–52. Limerick, Ireland: Mary Immaculate College, 2000.

———. "Theos in the New Testament." In *Theological Investigations*, translated by Cornelius Ernst et al., 1:79–148. Limerick, Ireland: Mary Immaculate College, 2000.

———. "Why and How Can We Venerate the Saints?" In *Theological Investigations*, translated by Cornelius Ernst et al., 8:3–23. Limerick, Ireland: Mary Immaculate College, 2000.

Ratzinger, Joseph. *Called to Communion: Understanding the Church Today*. 3rd ed. San Francisco: Ignatius, 1996.

———. *Dogma and Preaching: Applying Christian Doctrine to Daily Life*. Edited by Michael Miller. Translated by Michael Miller and Matthew O'Connell. San Francisco: Ignatius, 2011.

———. *Eschatology: Death and Eternal Life*. Edited by Aidan Nichols. Translated by Michael Waldstein. 2nd ed. Washington, D.C.: Catholic University of America Press, 2007.

———. "Eucharist, Communion, and Solidarity" (2002). http://www.vatican.va/roman_curia/congregations/cfaith/documents/rc_con_cfaith_doc_20020602_ratzinger-eucharistic-congress_en.html.

———. *The Feast of Faith: Approaches to a Theology of the Liturgy*. San Francisco: Ignatius, 1986.

————. *The God of Jesus Christ: Meditations on the Triune God.* Translated by Brian McNeil. San Francisco: Ignatius, 2008.

————. "The Holy Spirit as Communion: Concerning the Relationship of Pneumatology and Spirituality in Augustine." Translated by Peter Casarella. *Communio* 25 (Summer 1998): 324–37.

————. *Introduction to Christianity.* 2nd ed. San Francisco: Ignatius, 2004.

————. *The Spirit of the Liturgy.* San Francisco: Ignatius, 2000.

————. *Volk und Haus Gottes in Augustins Lehre von der Kirch.* Freiburg: Herder, 2011.

Ratzinger, Joseph, and Peter Seewald. *God and the World: A Conversation with Peter Seewald.* Translated by Henry Taylor. San Francisco: Ignatius, 2002.

Riesenfeld, Harald. *Jésus Transfiguré.* Acta Seminarii Neotestamentici Upsaliensis XVI. Copenhagen: E. Munksgaard, 1947.

Rilke, Rainer Maria. *Duino Elegies & The Sonnets to Orpheus.* Translated by Stephen Mitchell. New York: Vintage, 2009.

————. *Letters of Rainer Maria Rilke, 1892–1910.* Translated by Jane Bannard Greene and M. D. Herter Norton. New York: W. W. Norton, 1969.

————. *Letters of Rainer Maria Rilke, 1910–1926.* Translated by Jane Bannard Greene and M. D. Herter Norton. New York: W. W. Norton, 1969.

Robinette, Brian. "The Difference Nothing Makes: 'Creatio Ex Nihilo.'" *Theological Studies,* no. 72 (2011): 525–57.

————. *Grammars of Resurrection: A Christian Theology of Presence and Absence.* New York: Herder and Herder, 2009.

Romero, Miguel. "The Call to Mercy: Veritatis Splendor and the Preferential Option for the Poor." *Nova et Vetera* 11, no. 4 (2013): 1205–27.

Roy, Neil. "The Mother of God, the Forerunner, and the Saints of the Roman Canon: A Euchological Deesis." In *Issues in Eucharistic Praying in East and West: Essays in Liturgical and Theological Analysis,* edited by Maxwell Johnson, 327–48. Collegeville, Minn.: Liturgical, 2010.

Samuel, Lawrence. *Death, American Style: A Cultural History of Dying in America.* New York: Rowman & Littlefield, 2013.

Sara, Juan. "Descensus ad Infernos, Dawn of Hope: Aspects of the Theology of Holy Saturday in the Trilogy of Hans Urs von Balthasar." *Communio* 32 (2005): 541–72.

Saward, John. *The Mysteries of March: Hans Urs von Balthasar on the Incarnation and Easter.* Washington, D.C.: Catholic University of America Press, 1990.

Schlabach, Gerald. "Augustine's Hermeneutic of Humility: An Alternative to Moral Imperialism and Moral Relativism." *Journal of Religious Ethics* 22, no. 2 (1994): 299–330.

Six, Jean-Francois. *Light of the Night: The Last Eighteen Months in the Life of Thérèse of Lisieux.* Notre Dame, Ind.: University of Notre Dame Press, 1998.

Smith, D. Moody. *John.* Abingdon New Testament Commentaries. Nashville: Abingdon, 1999.

Teresa of Avila. *The Interior Castle.* Translated by Kieran Kavanaugh and Otilio Rodriguez. New York: Paulist, 1979.

———. *The Way of Perfection.* Edited by E. Allison Peers. Mineola, N.Y.: Dover, 2012.

Teresa of Calcutta. *Come Be My Light: The Private Writings of the "Saint of Calcutta."* Edited by Brian Kolodiejchuk. New York: Doubleday, 2007.

———. *A Simple Path.* Edited by Lucinda Vardey. New York: Ballantine, 1995.

Thérèse of Lisieux. *The Letters of St. Thérèse of Lisieux, Vol. I: 1877–1890.* Translated by John Clarke. Washington, D.C.: ICS, 1982.

———. *The Letters of St. Thérèse of Lisieux, Vol. II: 1890–1897.* Translated by John Clarke. Washington, D.C.: ICS, 1982.

———. *Story of a Soul.* Translated by John Clarke. Washington, D.C.: ICS, 1996.

———. *St. Thérèse of Lisieux: Her Last Conversations.* Translated by John Clarke. Washington, D.C.: ICS, 1977.

Thiel, John. "For What May We Hope? Thoughts on the Eschatological Imagination." *Theological Studies* 67 (2006): 517–41.

———. *Icons of Hope: The "Last Things" in Catholic Imagination.* Notre Dame, Ind.: University of Notre Dame Press, 2013.

———. *Senses of Tradition: Continuity and Development in Catholic Faith.* New York: Oxford University Press, 2000.

———. "Time, Judgment, and Competitive Spirituality: A Reading of the Development of the Doctrine of Purgatory." *Theological Studies* 69 (2008): 741–85.

Thomson, Iain. "Can I Die?: Derrida on Heidegger on Death." *Philosophy Today* 43, no. 1 (1999): 29–42.

Turner, Denys. *Faith Seeking.* London: SCM, 2012.

Vagaggini, Cyprian. *Theological Dimensions of the Liturgy: A General Treatise on the Theology of the Liturgy.* Translated by Leonard Doyle and W. A. Jurgens. Collegeville, Minn.: Liturgical, 1976.

Walsh, Jerome. *1 Kings.* Collegeville, Minn.: Liturgical, 1996.

Ward, Graham. "Kenosis: Death, Discourse, and Resurrection." In *Balthasar at the End of Modernity.* Edinburgh: T & T Clark, 1999.

Ware, Timothy Kallistos. "The Communion of Saints." In *The Orthodox Ethos,* edited by A. J. Philippou. Oxford: Holywell, 1964.

Weigel, Gustave. "The Historical Background of the Encyclical 'Humani Generis.'" *Theological Studies* 12 (1951): 208–30.

Weil, Simone. *Awaiting God: A New Translation of "Attente de Dieu and lettre a un Religieux."* Translated by Bradley Jersak. Maywood, Conn.: Fresh Wind, 2013.

Wilken, Robert Louis. *The Spirit of Early Christian Thought: Seeking the Face of God.* New Haven, Conn.: Yale University Press, 2005.

Williams, Rowan. *On Christian Theology.* Oxford: Blackwell, 2000.

————. "Poetic and Religious Imagination." *Theology* 80, no. 675 (1977): 178–87.

————. *Resurrection: Interpreting the Easter Gospel.* New York: Pilgrim, 1984.

Wood, Susan. "Sanctam Ecclesiam Catholicam, Sanctorum Communionem." In *Exploring and Proclaiming the Apostles' Creed,* edited by Roger Van Harn. Grand Rapids, Mich.: Eerdmans, 2004.

Woodward, Kenneth L. *Making Saints: How The Catholic Church Determines Who Becomes a Saint, Who Doesn't, And Why.* New York: Touchstone, 1996.

Wright, N. T. *The Resurrection of the Son of God.* Christian Origins and the Question of God: vol. 3. Minneapolis: Fortress, 2003.

————. *Surprised by Hope: Rethinking Heaven, the Resurrection, and the Mission of the Church.* New York: HarperOne, 2008.

Wyschogrod, Edith. *Spirit in Ashes: Hegel, Heidegger, and Man-Made Mass Death.* New Haven, Conn.: Yale University Press, 1985.

INDEX

Leonard J. DeLorenzo is director of Notre Dame Vision in the McGrath Institute for Church Life and associate professional specialist in the Department of Theology at the University of Notre Dame.

CPSIA information can be obtained
at www.ICGtesting.com
Printed in the USA
LVOW01*1256080217

523392LV00006B/9/P